Transatlantic Divide
Comparing American and European Society

Transatlantic Divide

Comparing American and European Society

Edited by

Alberto Martinelli

OXFORD

UNIVERSITY PRESS

OXFORD
UNIVERSITY PRESS

Great Clarendon Street, Oxford OX2 6DP

Oxford University Press is a department of the University of Oxford.
It furthers the University's objective of excellence in research, scholarship,
and education by publishing worldwide in

Oxford New York

Auckland Cape Town Dar es Salaam Hong Kong Karachi
Kuala Lumpur Madrid Melbourne Mexico City Nairobi
New Delhi Shanghai Taipei Toronto

With offices in

Argentina Austria Brazil Chile Czech Republic France Greece
Guatemala Hungary Italy Japan Poland Portugal Singapore
South Korea Switzerland Thailand Turkey Ukraine Vietnam

Oxford is a registered trade mark of Oxford University Press
in the UK and in certain other countries

Published in the United States
by Oxford University Press Inc., New York

British Library Cataloguing in Publication Data
Data available

Library of Congress Cataloging in Publication Data
Data available

Typeset by SPI Publisher Services, Pondicherry, India
Printed in Great Britain
on acid-free paper by
Biddles Ltd., King's Lynn, Norfolk

ISBN 978–0–19–920452–6 (hbk.)
ISBN 978–0–19–920453–3 (pbk.)

10 9 8 7 6 5 4 3 2 1

☐ PREFACE

This volume is not a collection of essays, but the coherent work of an international research group, the *Comparative Charting of Social Change Group (CCSC)* which was formed twenty years ago by Henri Mendras and Theodore Caplow. Throughout the activities of this group, we have formed a kind of scientific 'invisible college' and we have developed a habit of scientific dialogue and intellectual exchange. We have been meeting regularly a couple of times a year in order to discuss the products of our scientific research and to plan common projects. The first years were dedicated to writing a series of country monographs on the social transformations of contemporary societies according to an agreed upon common framework of analysis; the countries studied include the United States, Canada, France, Germany, Italy, Spain, Russia, Greece, Bulgaria. The CCSC Group has also published comparative volumes on specific topics such as inequalities and the transformations of the state.

The remote origins of *Transatlantic Divide* are to be found in my lifelong interest in the study of American society—my PhD dissertation at the University of California, Berkeley examined the American system of higher education and its relationship with American society and polity—and also in my equally long running interest in the processes of economic, political, and cultural integration in Europe, which has produced a number of essays on questions like the nature of European identity and the role of interest groups in European policy-making. I am committed to the realization of the project of a united Europe, I consider that to be the most important political goal of my generation, and I am acutely conscious of the value of the strong ties which exist between the peoples and the polities on either side of the Atlantic.

The nearer origins of this project can be traced to the CCSC Group meeting in Bad Homburg in 2001, where I advanced for the first time the proposal to produce a country study of the European Union in comparative perspective, based on the assumption that the EU could be analysed as a single country, considering the various member countries as regions of a single social system. The proposal was modified in later meetings in Nice, Madrid, Trento, Paris, Sofia, Delmenhorst and Athens: the comparative perspective became a more specific and focused comparative analysis of the two unions, the well established American union and the European union still in the making. The assumption was that the two unions are similar enough to make the comparison meaningful and different enough to make the comparison interesting. American society and European society can, in fact, be considered as two variants of Western modernity and the United States is clearly the biggest comparator for the European Union.

Some friends and colleagues have gone through the final draft of some chapters of the book, lAlessandro Cavalli, Marco Giuliani, David Moss, Marco Sioli, but also the members of the CCSC Group who have not taken part in the volume, and have provided valuable comments suggestions on the outline of the project and in the discussion of the drafts of various chapters. Thanks, therefore, are due to: Laura Alipranti, Dimitris Charalambis, Louis Chauvel, Nikolai Genov, Wolgang Glatzer, Andromaque Hadjiyannis, Louis Hicks, Simon Langlois, Yannick Lemel, Heinz Herbert Noll, Lance Roberts, and Suzanne von Below.

A first version of Chapter 5 on politics and institutional architectures was presented in February 2005 in Madrid at the Fundacion del Pino Conference on "Europa/Estados Unidos: Comparacion y Relaciones" entre "Europa y America cuatrocientos anos despues del Quijote", organised by Salustiano Del Campo, in a stimulating session with Karl Otto Hondrich, Julian Santamaria, and Philippe Schmitter. It was also discussed in a department seminar in the Faculty of Political and Social Sciences of the University of Milan where it received interesting comments from my friends and colleagues. A first draft of the concluding chapter on the American and the European models of society was discussed in Delmenhorst at the March 2005 Hanse Wissenschaftskolleg Workshop on "Europe and North America-Societies in Contrast" organized by Wolfgang Glatzer.

I am grateful to all contributors to the volume for their intelligent and fruitful cooperation in the realization of the project, with a special thank you to Laurence Duboys Fresney for her generous help with the draft and in drawing-up the statistical appendix.

A very special thought goes to the memory of Henri Mendras and Karl Otto Hondrich, great scholars and precious friends, who are no longer with us. I am sure I reflect the sentiment of all contributors in dedicating this book to them.

☐ CONTENTS

☐ LIST OF FIGURES

⬚ LIST OF GRAPHS

☐ LIST OF TABLES

☐ ABBREVIATIONS

CASMIN	Comparative Analysis of Social Mobility in Industrial Nations
CCSC	Comparative Charting of Social Change
CFSP	Common Foreign and Security Policy
ECJ	European Court of Justice
ECSC	European Coal and Steel Community
EDD	Europe of Democracies and Diversities
EEC	European Economic Community
ELDR	Group of the European Liberal, Democrat and Reform Party
EMS	European Monetary System
EP	European Parliament
EPP	European People's Party
ESM	European Social Model
EU	European Union
EURATOM	European Atomic Energy Commission
GDI	Gender-related Development Index
GDP	Gross Domestic Product
GEM	Gender Empowerment Measure
GNP	Gross National Product
LIS	Luxembourg Income Study
OMC	Open Method of Co-ordination
PES	Group of the Party of the European Socialists
TMR	Total Mobility Rates
UEN	Union of Europe of the Nations Group
UK	United Kingdom
UN	United Nations
WASP	White, Anglo-Saxon, Protestant
WTO	World Trade Organization
WVS	World Value Survey

1 The European Union and the United States as two variants of Western modernity

Alberto Martinelli

1.1. Aim of the volume

The first aim of the volume is *describing, interpreting, and analyzing key selected features of European society and American society and major social trends in the United States and in the European Union (EU) in the past fifty years* (since the 1957 Treaty of Rome), looking for convergences and divergences. The United States of America and the European Union are the two strongest economic powers in the contemporary world, roughly equivalent in terms of gross national product (GNP), market size, and scientific potential, but asymmetrical in terms of political influence and military might. The United States and the EU can be seen as successful examples both of economic development and of political and cultural modernization. But they have followed different paths to reach such a position. They can be considered as two variants of Western modernity.

The systematic description of trends for the United States and the EU taken as whole societies, and the interpretation of similarities and differences and of major changes over time would be already a significant scientific work since they would fill a void in today's social science literature. In fact, there are several studies comparing the United States with one or more European countries, but *there is no comparative study of the United States with the European Union taken as a single society.* The importance of the comparison is self-evident, for discussing such questions as American exceptionalism, the existence of a European society in the making, the cross-fertilization between American culture and European culture, and the respective roles of the United States and the EU in global governance.

The approach is new insofar as it assumes the countries of the EU as increasingly forming a single society and as a single political unit with gradually converging trends and common features, and considers the differences among member countries as regional differences within the European society.

The underlying hypotheses are that the structural arrangements, cultural values, and individual behaviors and attitudes of the European societies and peoples have become more similar in recent years, and *that a European model of society is emerging, which is comparable for its importance to the American model of society*, and that the emerging European model of society can foster the growth of a European society. This emerging model is both influenced by, and contributes to, the process of European political integration through common institutions. In our interpretation of convergent trends of the EU member-states, we will try to distinguish between those which become more similar 'spontaneously' and those which are the outcome of the conscious efforts of European policies.

These hypotheses are related, but their relation is problematic and even controversial. Some scholars think that European societies are actually becoming less similar, since internal differences which cut across national boundaries are growing, and that we cannot identify a single type of European society. Others contest the comparability itself between a well-established and stable political union and a union in the making with shifting boundaries and changing institutions. Still others think that even if we can demonstrate that a European model of society is taking a more clearly defined shape, we cannot simply deduce that a European society exists. Offe argues that 'it is simply a non sequitur to deduce from the similarity of European societies the desiderability and/or probability of their eventually becoming "one" society'. And he goes further, affirming that it is exactly because European societies are so similar already that their fusion into a 'unitary' sociopolitical arrangement of a European society is unlikely to occur, as little is to be gained, as well as much to be lost, from such fusion.

We counterargue that an integrated economy, a shared cultural heritage, common institutional arrangements and public policies, and similar lifestyles contribute to the formation of a single society defined both as an interdependent structure and as a normative order. In light of these different views, the comparison itself and the related theoretical questions are of central importance in today's intellectual debate and public discourse.

One may wonder why study national societies at a time in history when global trends of interconnectedness are reducing the independence of countries and eroding the sovereignty of nation-states. The answer is that the existence of a world system as an interdependent whole does not imply that a world society has replaced different societies. Societies are increasingly interconnected, but the contemporary global world is still a system made up of national societies and nation-states. The nation-state is still the basic unit of political organization in the world polity, but it is no longer the only locus of political authority, and national sovereignty is being eroded by global flows of people, goods, information, and ideas. Globalization is marked by the fundamental contradiction between an open economy and partially closed cultures; it entails that societies cannot be studied as separate entities, since each part of the world is increasingly interdependent with many others, and global social reality consists of multiple interconnected local social realities. Yet globalization does not make the comparative study of national societies obsolete; on the contrary, better understanding is required of the internal dynamics and structures, the distinctive cultural codes, the specific mechanisms of integration, conflict and change of major societies in the contemporary world, and using for the purpose an explicitly comparative approach framed within the context of global interdependence.

National societies are very different in terms of economic and social resources, political power, and cultural influence. *One can hardly overestimate the importance of the United States, and the EU in the contemporary world.* They are the two strongest economies, the two largest markets, and the source of major scientific discoveries and technological innovations. The United States is the hegemonic global power and the EU is, at least potentially, a major global player too.

In the nineteenth century Europe was at the apogee of its power in the world. In the first half of the twentieth century, European nations fought a disastrous 'Thirty Years War'—which left exhausted winners and losers alike—and in the second half, the countries in the Western part of Europe tried to develop a new type of political union and a new type of society, redefining their role in the world community. In the course of the twentieth century the United States became the hegemonic power; in the first half the United States helped European democracies to defeat fascism (with the Soviet alliance) and after 1945 built the institutions of the new world order around the United Nations (UN) and fought a cold war for world hegemony with the USSR—the other superpower in a bipolar world. With the collapse of the Soviet Union, the United States remained the only global power and entered the twenty-first century as the key player in a new 'uni-multipolar' world. A further set of questions that this volume tries to answer are: which are the respective roles of the United States and the EU in the contemporary global world, what are their relations of competition and cooperation, and which model of society seems to be more reactive to the challenges of globalization.

1.2. **The comparative perspective**

The major feature of the volume is its comparative perspective. In order to evaluate the degree of convergence among European states and peoples, we should compare them with those of the United States of America—the oldest and foremost multiethnic democratic state in the world. In order to assess to what extent American society is exceptional and to what extent is just a variant of Western modernity we should compare it with the EU in the making, the most original experiment in institution-building of the past decades.

The comparative method is the method of social sciences par excellence. Our project is *a chapter in binary comparison* focusing on the two most successful variants of Western modernity, which share core values and structural arrangements, but are also significantly diverse in terms of institutions and cultural attitudes. In order to interpret such similarities and differences, we will have to analytically cut both the EU and the United States into many dimensions and make a series of binary comparisons based on empirical evidence, mostly social trends' data. The shared values and institutions of scientific innovation, market economy, and representative democracy have been institutionalized in different ways. We ask ourselves to what extent differences in many domains can be just differences of degree and to what extent one can instead speak of European 'uniqueness' and American 'exceptionalism'; in other words, to what extent the two societies appear at the global level as *Gestalten* and have different organizing principles, and to what extent their values, institutions, and behaviors fit into specific functional wholes.

There is no doubt about considering the United States as a single society in spite of the high degree of internal diversity. The questions we discuss are whether and to what extent one can speak of American 'exceptionalism' and the ways and the degree to which American society is changing, that is whether it is departing from its core culture and institutions. The conceptualization of the EU as a society is much more complex and controversial than for the United States. The question we discuss is whether a European society is in the making.

We intend to analyze the similarities and differences of the United States and the EU as models of society, and whether they are converging or diverging. We can rely on a rich literature on social changes in American society and EU member countries; but there are only few contributions attempting to consider the European society as a single social system, like those of Kaelble, Mendras, Crouch, and Rumford. Kaelble (1987) produces a history of European social integration stressing exchange relations, institutional arrangements, and the cultural attitudes of both elites and common citizens. Mendras (1997) works out an analytical scheme for the comparative study of social change stressing a few basic features. Both authors look for cultural and institutional characteristics which are peculiar to European societies, and for convergences and divergences among them. Crouch's (1999) *Social Changes in Western Europe* confines the question of the existence of a European society to the last chapter and is rather skeptical about it (in addition to this he includes Norway and Switzerland in his notion of 'Europe'). Rumford's book on the EU (2002) argues that if something like a European society exists, it is characterized by fragmentation and disunity.

Much more abundant are country monographs on the American social and political system, from Lipset's *The First New Nation* (1979) to Caplow's *The First Meausured Century* (2001), Fiorina, Petersen, and Johnson (2002), Huntington (2004), Gitlin (1995), and Reimers (2005), and on the EU member-states, among which are the country monographs of our *Comparative Charting of Social Change* (CCSC) group: Louis Dirn (1990), Del Campo (1993), Glatzer et al. (1992), Martinelli, Chiesi, and Stefanizzi (1999), Genov and Kzasteva (1999), Charalambis, Maratou-Alipranti, and Hadjiyanni (2004). There is also a substantial literature of comparative multicountry studies, among which I wish to stress the contributions of our CCSC group: *Convergence and Divergence* (Langlois et al. 1994) and *Leviathan Transformed* (Caplow 2001). This general literature can help in the selection of the relevant areas to be studied and of the relevant hypotheses to be tested. For example, *Convergence and Divergence* showed that most of the trends analyzed in France, Germany, Canada, and the United States are strongly

convergent but, because they occur in dissimilar cultural contexts, their consequences are quite diverse. And *Leviathan Transformed* showed that although the
basic goals stated in the written constitutions of liberal democracies (France,
Germany, Italy, Spain, Canada, and the United States) are about the same, state
policies aimed at achieving these goals can be quite different.

Statistical aggregate data and survey data, policy documents, and official statements will be prominent in our comparisons, but qualitative analysis will also
have a role, as well as 'personal experience' with both societies, cultures, and ways
of life (as it is found in our 'transatlantic group'). Sources for the EU include data
from Eurostat, the European Community Household Panel, the European Value
Survey, the Eurobarometer, OECD, and ILO studies on comparative welfare states.
Sources for the United States are the data gathered in *The First Measured Century*,
data from ISSP, and World Value Survey (WVS).

Comparisons are based on the assumptions that the EU can be interpreted as a
single federation of states and that it is possible to find a sufficient number of comparable trends coming from European institutions, and when they are not available it is possible to compute trends combining weighted data at country level.
Whenever possible, each trend is plotted to show change over time of three lines
in most cases: one for the United States, one labeled *EuPol*, for the EU member-
states each year (Belgium, France, Italy, Luxembourg, the Netherlands, and West
Germany joined in 1957; Denmark, Ireland, and United Kingdom (UK) entered in
1973; Greece in 1981; Spain and Portugal in 1986; Austria, Finland, and Sweden in
1995; and Cyprus, the Czech Republic, Estonia, Hungary, Latvia, Lithuania, Malta,
Poland, Slovakia, and Slovenia in 2005, Bulgaria and Romania in 2007), and one
labeled *Euro*, for the set of fifteen countries during the entire period.

1.3. **Methodological problems to be clarified**

The definition of the research questions, the formulation of hypotheses, and the
selection and interpretation of the data raise *a few methodological problems which
must be briefly clarified*.

A first set of problems concerns *the geographical boundaries* of the compared
units and the time span of our research. There is no problem for the United
States's boundaries; but for the EU we have to make a choice between two major
alternatives. The first is to reconstruct the history of the EU, comparing data which
specifically refers to the European Communities at different points in time, in the
fifty years since the 1957 Treaty of Rome to the present. The second is to consider
the EU as it is now (twenty-seven countries) and to compare data concerning
today's member countries since the end of World War II (when they were all
separate countries) to the present. The major advantage of the first alternative is to
stress the idea of the European Communities/EU as a specifically distinct societal
entity from the beginning and to trace its process of growth and enlargement (a
study on social change in nineteenth-century United States would not consider the

data on the Western states before their joining the Union). The major advantage of the second alternative is to appreciate the scope and intensity of social changes taking place in all the EU member-states—which now constitute the EU. But it runs into the serious difficulty of comparing data only partially available and reliable, mostly as far as the new ten members are concerned. We choose a pragmatic compromise between the two alternatives: whenever possible; we use data both for the member countries since the start of the EU and for the EU as a progressively enlarging entity.

As far as *the time span* of our research is concerned, fifty years is a convenient period which allows us to appreciate significant transformations, and the second half of the 1950s is a good starting point in terms of the international context in which the comparison takes place, since both economic (the long economic expansion of 'les trente glorieuses') and political relations (the bipolarism between the two superpowers) are structured and stabilized. The fifty-year time span is adopted whenever possible, often the time series used are shorter because data are not available.

A second related problem stems from the fact that within the United States and even more within the EU there are important regional differences, and the risk exists that with only one indicator for each of the two unions these differences do not appear. A solution to this problem is to add, whenever appropriate the coefficients of variations among the member states of the two unions. Another device is that of defining regional clusters of countries and states; for instance, a typology of welfare state models in Anglo-Saxon, Mediterranean, Central European, and Northern countries.

A third problem concerns *the type of data* to be taken into account. Again the problem concerns the European side. The alternative is whether to confine ourselves to the use of data which have been gathered for the EU as a whole, such as those of Eurobarometer and Households Panel—which are comparable and standardized, or to consider data gathered on a national basis from the statistical bureaus of different member countries as well—which are not perfectly comparable due to different time series, different definitions of relevant concepts, different indicators, and collecting techniques. Again we made a pragmatic choice, using data both from the EU and national sources.

A further problem concerning the geographical boundaries of the EU lies in the fact that this volume is published three years after the enlargement of the EU from fifteen to twenty-five member countries and one year after the EU at twenty-seven. The enlargement raises both substantial and methodological problems. In Chapter 10, I argue that the emerging European model of society is strong enough to incorporate and assimilate new social entities, most of which, although sharing common features with the fifteen existing ones, show significant differences due to a different historical experience in the 1945–90 period ('real socialism', communist ideology, planned economy, one party system, and Soviet hegemony in foreign affairs). The former communist countries of Central and Eastern Europe joining the EU are well advanced in the process of transition to market economy, political democracy, and 'Western' culture, and are becoming more and more similar to the fifteen EU members. Besides, the previous experience of Spain and Portugal shows that a nondemocratic past does not have lasting impact on social institutions and cultural attitudes.

But the enlargement creates methodological problems for this book. In the case of the recent new members, unreliable data prevent in many cases comparisons from the start of the EU, although we will make them whenever possible. In order to cope with this problem, however, we present a series of charts on major trends for twenty-five EU member-states in the Appendix.

A second set of problems concern *the number of trends and macro-trends* to be identified and, more generally, the dimensions of the two unions to be discussed. The analysis of trends will follow with a high degree of freedom the model adopted by the CCSC group in the country monographs. The selection of the aspects of American and European society which are analyzed in the various chapters of the book, and the interpretation of the macro-trends within them, are based on the criterion of highlighting the most significant similarities and differences, convergences and divergences between the United States and the EU. Each chapter describes and interprets major differences and similarities between the United States and the EU—assessing which are stable, diminishing, or growing—and, whenever possible, similar and different features, convergent and divergent trends among European countries and regions, as well as within the United States.

Having stated the major aims, research questions, and methodological problems of the book, I now discuss two key underlying hypotheses of the work: first, the hypothesis that the societal models of the EU and the United States are two variants of the same civilization (I shall define the key features of Western modernity and compare the European and the American variants). Second, the hypothesis that the member countries of the EU are increasingly forming a single society and a single polity with gradually converging trends and common institutions at the EU level (I shall discuss the main critical approaches that cast doubts over the existence, and indeed the very possibility, of a European society, and the main historical processes which account for the growing homogeneity of European societies).

1.4. **Two variants of Western modernity**

A first question of this work is what kind of society the United States and the EU constitute and a first answer is that they are two variants of the same civilization, or more specifically two variants of Western modernity. The question entails a preliminary conceptualization of what a society is.

A society is a de facto network of social relations with mutual expectations for which a *de jure* normative consensus—reflected in commonly accepted institutions—may be present to various extents. The members of a society are interrelated through more dense interaction and functional interdependency than the bonds that tie them to outsiders or members of other societies. Systemic interdependence, however, is a necessary but not sufficient condition for societal integration. A society must possess certain key normative and institutional features for this to come about. In terms of the history of ideas, the materialistic view that the social order requires shared interests, division of labor, and economic interdependence must be blended with the idealistic view that the social order requires shared beliefs. The internal cohesion of a society is guaranteed by enduring institutionalized rules which impose constraints on the individual pursuit of scarce resources (wealth, power, and prestige) and by a core group of shared values rooted in the historical tradition which define a collective identity and orient action. These rules are not self-executing through spontaneous sympathy or solidarity; on the contrary, their making and enforcement imply an apparatus of political rule and control. In democratic politics, rule is based on consensus and the rulers are freely chosen by the will of the ruled, who are granted inalienable rights and are protected by mechanisms binding the exercise of power.

In the historical experience of European modernity, the sovereign national state has been the institutional embodiment of political authority, an impersonal and sovereign political entity with supreme jurisdiction over a clearly delimited territory and a clearly defined population. It has claimed monopoly over coercive power and enjoyed legitimacy as a result of citizens' support. The nation-state has been the basic element in the structuring of modern society; for it is within its framework that the basic normative questions of the nonviolent regulation of conflict, social justice, and individual freedom have been addressed. The nation-state is both an organization and a community (real and imagined at the same time). It developed historically through the growth of a civil bureaucracy, an army, and a diplomatic corps, and through the formation of the nation as the 'imagined community' (Anderson 1991) resulting from the action of nationalist elites in the modernization process (Gellner 1983) and able to evoke primordial ethno-symbolic roots (Smith 1991).

Social integration and institutionalized control, however, do not depend on the nation-state alone; in other words, alongside institutions based on the authority principle, 'society-making' may come about in two other basic ways: through markets, which are primarily but not exclusively based on the exchange principle; and through communities, which are primarily but not exclusively based on the solidarity principle (Martinelli 2003). Both the United States and, to an even greater extent, the EU have not followed the path of nation-state building of the European countries. Various forms of market and community played a relevant role in forging the normative and the institutional foundations of these societies. And different values, or at least different interpretations of the same values, contributed—through the work of intellectuals and political leaders—to shape social relations and political institutions.

In terms of cultural heritage, the European identity is not significantly different from that of the United States. The main factor accounting for this similarity is that European culture and American culture are two variants of the same modern Western civilization. The identity of European society is, in fact, not easily distinguishable from that of the West, or of what I call 'Europe outside Europe', this being the part of the world that has assimilated the fundamental traits of the European spirit. American culture radicalizes some key features of modern values and institutions, such as an orientation to the future, confidence in scientific progress, the creative destruction of capitalism, the mastery of technique, the ceaseless quest for individual freedom, and self-gratification, while the European seems less enthusiastic, more heterogeneous, more critical and historically aware, and more concerned with the failures of the market, egotism and consumerism, and with the still unaccomplished goals of the modern project (Habermas 1985). In a recent essay (Martinelli 2005*b*), I discuss the core values and institutions of European identity, arguing that they apply to the 'Europe outside Europe' as well as (and above all) to the United States. I now briefly reiterate some of my arguments, adding the word 'Western' to the word 'European'.

I identify the value core of European and Western identity in the constant tension between rationalism and individualism/subjectivity as both opposing and complementary principles. Rationalism and individualism/subjectivity characterized European history from Greek philosophy and Roman law to the Judaean and Christian religious traditions, but they coalesced into a specific set of cultural values and institutional arrangements with the advent of modernity. They expressed the tension between individual liberty and social organization. As core cultural roots, they engendered the specific modern attitude which consists in the absence of limits. 'European identity is that of a civilisation that has constantly exceeded limits—internal and external—that has freed itself from the bonds, thus creating its own distinctive mark' (D'Andrea 2001: 134). The portrait of Ulysses in Dante's *Inferno* is an appropriate metaphor. The unlimitedness that defines modernity— and European identity as its place of origin—is primarily evident in the infinite quest for knowledge.

A similar view was expressed by Jaspers (1947) during the heated debate on the foundations for the reconstruction of Europe that followed the end of World War II. Jaspers identified the three factors constituting the essence of Europe as liberty, history, and science, three factors which do not know any limit. The first of them, the longing for freedom, is universal, but it has developed to its fullest extent in Europe. It has signified victory over despotism and a sense of justice transformed into concrete institutions; and it has fostered a constant state of restlessness and ferment among Europeans. Liberty has bred the second factor: the need to understand historical time and the active role of human beings within the polis. For Jaspers, in fact, true liberty is the quest for political freedom within the community, that is the development of the individual together with the social world around him. The third factor, science, is also related to liberty in that it is defined as the constant endeavor to get to the heart of everything that can be penetrated. It is knowledge and the love of knowledge that make human beings free, giving them not only the external freedom achieved through the knowledge of nature but also, and above all, internal freedom.

The quest for knowledge was common to various ancient civilizations, but it was with modernity that it received new impetus in Europe, when knowledge was freed from its subordination to a given religious truth or to a single political end.

The ceaseless quest for knowledge is the product of the critical mind which orig-inated in the Greek philosophical ethos and developed with the Enlightenment's constant critique of its historical era. The development of science is linked with the driving force of capitalism and the massive development of technology, both of which are related in their turn to belief in constant progress. European modernity was the age of 'Prometheus Unbound' [Shelley] which metaphorically expresses the absence of ethical and religious limits on the technical domination of nature. Capitalism is a mode of production based on technical instrumentality and on the maximization of economic rationality in order to compete successfully on the market.

European rationalism has manifested itself in a variety of different forms: from Romanesque architecture to Renaissance painting, from the philosophy of Descartes to the music of Bach, from the democratic man of the Enlightenment to the *homo œconomicus* of capitalism. It can be defined *lato sensu* as the capacity of the human mind to know, control, and transform nature (according to a conception of the world as an environment that can be molded to the purpose of fulfilling human needs and wants), and as the confidence of human beings that they can rationally pursue their own ends and, ultimately, be the masters of their own destinies.

With its confidence in the power of reason to control and transform nature, European rationalism has been the breeding ground for scientific and geograph-ical discoveries and technological and entrepreneurial innovations. Reason is related to perception of an absence of limits, to that particular 'restlessness' of the European people portrayed in such paradigmatic figures of European literature as Dante's *Ulysses* to Goethe's *Faust*, and as exemplified in many events of European history: from transoceanic voyages to colonial adventures, to the 'spirit of the frontier' distinctive of the American variant of European culture.

At the same time, reason has been conceived as a system of shared rules which make social coexistence possible. Kant did not write an apology for reason, but an inquiry into its limits. The rational mind is strong only if it is aware of its own limits, does not claim to know the truth, and opens the way to an endless search. In this sense, reason is by definition antitotalitarian and directly related to individual freedom.

Rationalism is closely linked, complementary with, and opposed to the other core cultural traits of European/Western identity consisting in individualism and subjectivity. Individualism has found many different expressions in the time and space of Europe: evangelical personalism, the individualism of free citizens in the late medieval independent republics, the individual economic actor in the market, the individual rights of the free citizen in modern liberal democracies, and the reflexive subjectivity of contemporary Europeans. Like rationalism, indi-vidualism developed within the cultural heritage of European history, but it only fully emerged with the advent of modernity. Individualism is at the root of the principles of liberty and equality affirmed by *Ius naturalismus* (which holds that all human beings are equal insofar as they are endowed with reason), and by English political thought and French and German philosophy of the Enlightenment;

principles which were recognized in the prerogatives of the English Parliament after the Glorious Revolution of 1688–9 and solemnly proclaimed in the American Constitution of 1776 and in the *Declaration des Droits de l'Homme et du Citoyen* of 1789.

These principles affirm the inviolable rights of the individual to life, freedom, and the full accomplishment of his or her potential. Liberty expresses itself both as negative freedom (i.e. as the protection of human rights against the abuses of power) and as positive freedom (i.e. as the citizen's right to participate in the formation of the common will). Equality was initially defined as the equality of the rights and duties of citizenship and the equality of citizens before the law. But it soon thereafter became the equality of opportunities and life chances as well, and thus opened the way for the conceptions of progressive liberalism, social democracy, and welfare policies which became integral parts of Europe's political culture in the twentieth century. Being European means striving to realize principles of both equality and freedom; indeed, the struggle to strike a balance between equality and freedom is a leitmotiv of the history of European political thought (Cerutti and Rudolph 2001*b*).

Individualism and subjectivity are not identical, of course. There is a tendency for the former term to be used by scholars who prefer positive (societal) accounts of modernity—where the individualistic understanding of the self is set alongside the growth of scientific consciousness, the development of a secular outlook, the doctrine of progress, and the contractual understanding of society as the essential features of modernity. The latter term is preferred by the proponents of the alternative (cultural) view of modernity which is critical of middle-class pragmatic calculation, the soulless pursuit of money, and the lack of moral passion, being on the contrary concerned with care for the self, spontaneous expression, and authentic experience. Political and economic individualism and aesthetic and moral subjectivity are in fact dimensions of the same principle; and this principle is dialectically related to the principle of rationality. They are not the roots of two alternative types of modernity (the supportive and the critical, the societal and the cultural) but rather the elements of the same cultural and institutional syndrome (Martinelli 2005*a*). The world of the capitalist entrepreneur is a world of incessant change and deadening routine which provides the proper context for the aesthetics of the self as well. Imagination and reason are not enemies; rather, they are allies in the work of both the scientist and the artist. Both seek to explore and experience everything without being subject to limits.

The dialectical relationship between the principle of rationality (with its institutional forms as market-driven industrial economies, bureaucratically administered states, and functionally organized metropolitan cities) and the principle of subjectivity/individualism is also manifest in the double matrix of change and routine in which the modern self lives. 'Each of those unforgettable figures of modernity—Marx's "revolutionary", Baudelaire's "dandy", Nietzsche's "superman", Weber's "social scientist", Simmel's "stranger", Musil's "man without qualities", and Benjamin's "flaneur"—is caught and carried in the intoxicating rush of an epochal change and yet finds itself fixed and formulated by a disciplinary system of social roles and functions' (Gaonkar 2001: 3). The list (to which I would add Schumpeter's 'entrepreneur') is strictly European, which is further proof that the culture of modernity is closely linked with the European identity (including therein the peoples of the 'Europe outside Europe'), although today it is no longer confined to the West.

Rationalism, individualism/subjectivity, the ceaseless quest for knowledge, innovation and discovery, the constitution of the self as an autonomous subject, the rejection of limits, the principles of liberty, and equality of rights and opportunities represent the core elements of a European identity nurtured in European historical heritage—primarily in the legacy of Christianity and Greek–Roman antiquity but then fully developed in the civilization of modernity which first arose in Western Europe and then expanded to other parts of Europe, to the Americas and throughout the world. This gave rise to continuously changing cultural and institutional patterns constituting different responses to the challenges and possibilities inherent in the core characteristics of the distinct civilizational premises of modernity (Eisenstadt 2001; Martinelli 2005a).

In the civilization of modernity, the values, attitudes, and interpretations of the world—which coalesced into a distinct cultural program—combined with a set of new institutional formations (these too European-born and disseminated first to America and then throughout the world) to assume a variety of forms: the capitalist market and firm, the nation-state and the democratic polity, the university, and the research community. These elements I now briefly discuss individually.

First, European/Western science and technology, by which is meant a particular approach to the knowledge of physical and human reality able to transform nature in order to satisfy human wants. The depth of Indian and Chinese religion and philosophy, the richness of Muslim scientific and religious thought, the advanced astronomical knowledge of Mesopotamia and pre-Colombian America are only some examples evidencing the fact that Western knowledge is not exceptional at all. What is distinctive, though, is its more marked capacity to unite abstract theory and empirical research and, even more importantly, to link scientific discovery, invention, and technological innovation under the constant pressure of either war or commercial competition. Also specific to European/Western culture is its greater ability to design institutions particularly suited to the formation and diffusion of knowledge: the Italian and French medieval universities, the seventeenth-century British scientific academies, the nineteenth-century German research universities, and the great American research laboratories of the present day. European modernity was not simply a package of technological and organizational developments; it was intimately bound up with a political revolution, and with an equally important transformation in the nature of scholarly and scientific practices and institutions (Wittrock 2000). Europe has invented and perfected an understanding of science which has become a global example and role model. The main characteristics of this understanding of science as it has developed since the Renaissance are, as Rudolph argues, the recognition of mathematics as the measure of exactness in science, the unity of freedom of scientific inquiry and scientific criticism, and the dependence of empirical knowledge on conceptual reflection (Cerutti and Rudolph 2001*b*: 8).

Second, market-driven industrial capitalism. The governing principle of capitalism is a constant search for the rational maximization of individual utility in order to compete successfully on the market. The efficient combination of the production factors in the industrial firm and the exchange of goods and services in a self-regulating market slowly expanding throughout the world have been the two basic institutions of capitalist development. The Industrial Revolution of the eighteenth century (a most powerful process of innovation, capital accumulation, and market expansion) came about because of agricultural surpluses and long-distance trade surpluses and the availability of iron and coal. But it was first and foremost generated by a specific linkage with the scientific and technological revolutions of modernity. Trades and markets flourished in the early empires, and in many non-European parts of the world as well, but the particular combination of the Industrial Revolution with a self-regulating market was a European specificity which gave capitalist growth unprecedented strength and dynamism.

The specific link between those two institutions—technology and capitalism—has been much criticized, first of all in the Marxist tradition. According to Marcuse (1964), the major social and cultural implications of capital concentration, technological change, and the growth of private and public bureaucracies are: (*a*) the triumph of 'instrumental reason', that is, the overriding concern with efficiency, which reduces choice to the selection of the most appropriate means to achieve predefined ends, which themselves are not questioned; (*b*) the 'depoliticization' of public life, that is, the eradication of political questions both because of the dominance of instrumental reason and because of the impact of the mass media, which, responding to the concerns of the advertising industry and to the need to encourage mass consumption, destroy the cultural traditions of subordinate classes, and create a kind of 'false consciousness' of conformity in consumption; and (*c*) the repressive integration of society, that is, the achievement of mass acquiescence by the power of large bureaucracies, instrumental reasoning, and the quest for affluence and consumerism on the part of the masses; people pay for their material comfort and security with powerless and 'repressive desublimation'.

The third basic component of the European heritage—the nation-state—is more controversially related to the values of rationalism and individualism than are scientific curiosity, the technical domination of nature, or the capitalist market and industry. The nation-state is the institutional embodiment of political authority in modern society, an impersonal and sovereign political entity with supreme jurisdiction over a clearly delimited territory and population which claims monopoly over coercive power, and enjoys legitimacy as a result of its citizens' support. It is a particular institution resulting from the encounter between a sovereign, autonomous, centralized political organization, on the one hand, and a community (real and imagined at the same time) founded on ties of blood, language, shared tradition, and collective memory, on the other. In the late Middle Ages, Europe (at least in its Western part) came increasingly to be made up of societies of peasants, lords recognizing the authority of a king, city merchants, and artisans, all of whom were united by a commonality of blood, language, and religious belief (Mendras 1997).

The nation-state characterized by the unity of a people, a territory, and a distinctive culture slowly took shape in opposition to the multiethnic empires and the supranational church, and it developed historically through the growth of a civil bureaucracy, an army, and a diplomacy, and through the formation of a nation as the 'imagined community' (Anderson 1991) resulting from the action of nationalist elites in the modernization process (Gellner 1983) and able to evoke primordial ethno-symbolic roots (Smith 1991). The nation-state is a typically European construction which has been exported to the other parts of the world. Its relation with the culture of individualism and rationalism is ambivalent and complex. One of the two components, the nation, has long been rooted in primordial ties; it has appealed to the emotions, and it has emphasized collective goals. The other component, the state, is a rationally organized construct which has evolved through the development of law and an efficient bureaucracy. Today, the nation-state is subject to the twofold pressure applied by the growing global interconnectedness of social relations from above and by the reaffirmation of regional and local identities and claims of autonomy from below. But it is still the basic political organization and the key actor in international relations, as well as a more or less successful export by European culture to every part of the world, judging from the growing number of independent states.

The growth of the nation-state also implied a process of centralization and the breaking of the many regional/local and social/cultural autonomies of premodern societies. But the risks of state centralization for individual freedom were kept under control by the development of the institutions of representative democracy, that is a political system made up of elected officials representing the interests and opinions of citizens in a context characterized by the rule of law, based on the consensus of citizens, and developed in order to protect their basic rights.

Representative democracy is a fourth element of European/Western identity. The Greek polis, the Roman republic, and the free cities of medieval Italy, Germany, and Flanders were all antecedents of this European specificity. The various forms of parliaments, majority rule in government and the protection of minority rights, free and periodical elections, the separation of powers, the free press are all institutional innovations which were born and developed in the culture of Europe and then developed in the United States (the 'first new nation' constructed by European immigrants) in the course of the three major democratic revolutions: the English, the French, and the American.

The 'list' of distinctive elements of the European identity would not be complete without an appraisal of the role of Christianity at both the cultural and institutional levels. The Christian religion is a transcendent monotheism that postulates the direct relation of every creature with its Creator. It has fostered great collective movements and given birth to one of the oldest and most durable institutions of human history, the Roman Catholic Church. The two aspects, the subjective one—which originated in the individualism of the message of the Gospel and has periodically reemerged in mysticism and asceticism—and the collective/institutional aspect—manifest in the church's hierarchical organization, in liturgical rites and ceremonies—have been often dialectically opposed, as witnessed by the centuries-long conflicts between Rome and Byzantium, the campaigns to stamp out heretical movements, and the religious wars of the Reformation.

The relation of the Christian religion with individualism/subjectivity and with rationalism is ambivalent. On one hand, Christianity together with Roman law has contributed to the development of European/Western individualism. And, as Weber argued, the great rational prophecies of the Old Testament, the rational life plan of the religious orders, and the theory of predestination all contributed to the growth of the rational mind (1920). On the other hand, the Christian religion has had from the outset a strong communitarian element—which was apparent in several ways, for instance the early Christian communities, the transformation of hermits into the religious orders from Saint Benedict's onwards, and in the mediation between the believer and God provided by religious rites and the clergy. This communitarian spirit has acted as a complement and antidote to the subjective dimension of faith and vice versa.

Christianity has deeply influenced European and American institutions and mentality, sometimes as their source of inspiration, sometimes as their adversary: our highest values and associated norms (such as human dignity and its inviolability, the rights of the person, individual conscience, and responsibility) cannot be extrapolated from—and have developed their specific form through—Jewish–Christian theology and religion. The distinction between temporal and sacred power achieved through centuries-long struggle is a well-grounded principle of modern democracy. On the other hand, the notion of the absence of limits and the belief in man as the master of his own destiny—these being distinctive aspects of the modern mind have encountered strong opposition in the 'antimodernist' stance of the Catholic Church. Although Christianity was not born in Europe, but rather in the East, its borders came increasingly to coincide with those of Europe until, from the fifteenth century onwards, it spread from Europe to the rest of the world by colonial expansion. Through evangelization of the barbaric peoples of the north and the east, and the centuries-long confrontation with Arab and Turkish Islam, Christianity has tended to coincide with European identity. This holds despite the fact that, as Adriaanse (2001) points out, the religious factor in the cultural identity of Europe has not been a simple undifferentiated unity. Religions other than Christianity, primarily Islam, have played an important role, and there has been great religious diversity within Christianity itself with its numerous heretical movements, the schism between Orthodox Constantinople and Catholic Rome, and the Protestant Reformation.

The institutions typical of Western modernity have characterized Europe and America in different ways. Some of them have found favorable terrain for further development in the United States: contemporary American research universities receive greater financing and achieve more significant scientific results than their European counterparts; research-based innovation and technology transfer from universities to firms is greater and easier in the United States than Europe; the US economy records higher rates of growth than the European economy; and market capitalism is more fully institutionalized in the United States than in the EU, as is argued in Chapter 2. Other institutions, like political democracy, assumed different forms at the outset but are now more similar than in the past, as is argued in Chapter 5 with regard to the model of the compound republic. Still other institutions, like religion, assumed different forms from the beginning, in particular in the relationship with the state, and continue to play a significantly different role on the two sides of the Atlantic, as is discussed in Chapter 8.

1.5. Criticisms and qualifications about Western civilization

These core cultural and institutional elements have contributed to the definition of the identity of both Europe and the United States. However, they do not form a coherent system: they have in fact conflicted with each other, as in the cases of market and democracy, religious beliefs and scientific research, nationalism and peace. Nor have they produced solely desirable effects or positive outcomes. A few qualifications are needed in order to counter objections and to prevent misunderstandings.

First, some critics maintain that it is impossible to single out substantive values or concrete cultural contents that would unambiguously characterize European and American culture. True, the core values and institutions of European identity are not necessarily unambiguous; even less are they unambiguously 'positive'. As Jaspers (1947) remarks, for every position Europe has also developed the exact opposite. European history has been constantly marked by deep cleavages, violent conflicts, idiosyncratic controversies, and numerous errors and crimes. The values of rationalism and individualism and the institutions of the market and the nation-state have given rise to many contradictions, violations, and deformations—as witness the profound contradictions between capital and wage labor, economic growth and environmental conservation, colonial and neocolonial exploitation and the quest for freedom, not to speak of wars, mass murders, and genocide. Indeed, polar opposites characterize almost every core element of European culture: the Christian faith of universal love has inspired some of the most intolerant doctrines and bloodiest religious wars in the heart of twentieth-century Europe, democracy collapsed into devastating totalitarianism; the free market constantly reproduces monopoly and oligopoly; the quest for political independence has degenerated into aggressive nationalism. In other words, there is no value that Europe has promoted without at the same time promoting its opposite: faith/reason, tolerance/religious warfare, democracy/totalitarianism, etc. But this is not a convincing objection: we certainly do not cease to regard ancient Athens as the cradle of democracy because it also experienced tyranny, the opposite of democracy.

Related to the previous point is the criticism that we cannot consider values and institutions with harmful effects, which have produced violent conflicts, suffering, and crimes, as elements constitutive of a European identity. This criticism could be accepted if no learning from past errors had taken place. But the salient feature of contemporary European identity is precisely that history has been subject to reflexive reassertion through a process of historical learning. The religious wars of the sixteenth and seventeenth centuries, and the national wars of the twentieth, were culturally rooted in contradictory values shared by the vast majority of Europeans. But they have been latterly perceived as lessons of the past from which unity can be forged—if it is true that European integration was born of the desire to put an end to the centuries-long European civil wars. And the new European identity is the product of learning from painful past errors and crimes. As Therborn argues, 'The conception of history that underlies the efforts to establish an ever closer union of the peoples of Europe is not couched in terms of some "manifest destiny" of Europe, or in terms of Europeans as a chosen people ... rather, it is the view of history's disciples and not of its masters'. Europe 'is a process of historical learning and a focus of institutionalisation ... This construction has its cultural prerequisites, but the cultural underpinning of the new European set of normative institutions is not a deep and ancient culture of Europeans, rather it is a collection of Western European lessons from recent European modernity: nationalism and any other "ism" is dangerous and must be regulated' (Therborn 1995: 73, 85). I agree; but I would not confine the process of historical learning to lessons from recent European modernity, rather I would extend it to the whole of European history (an example of this attitude is John Paul II's asking pardon for crimes committed by the Catholic Church and his reiterated demands for religious peace and ecumenical dialogue). In this respect, I agree with Cacciari (1994) that, rather than being a celebration of European culture and identity, the EU can be seen as 'a silent maturation of the coming of Europe into the serene evening of its stormy history'.

Nor are the core values and institutions of American identity either necessarily unambiguous or unambiguously 'positive', but they are so to a lesser extent than in Europe. American democracy has never been seriously threatened by totalitarian movements; American society has not been plagued by religious wars. American patriotism is of a blend different from many European nationalisms. And yet the slavery of the African-Americans and the de facto ethnic cleansing of the Native Americans were dramatic violations of democratic culture. The United States has not been a colonial power in the strict sense of the word, but it has exercised various forms of neocolonial rule. And, mostly during the cold war, US foreign policy has not shown abroad the same respect for liberal values and democratic institutions that American governments show at home.

The United States seems today less willing and able to learn from the past than the EU. Most American leaders, and a good part of the American people, seem persuaded of American exceptionalism, of their 'manifest destiny' as the redemptive nation, of their mission to export freedom and democracy to the whole world (as Bush Jr reiterated in the speech inaugurating his second presidential term), and convinced of the superiority of the American way of life. National pride can be an asset for a people. Pericles' famous funeral speech, attributed to Thucydides, proclaims that Athens' system of government 'does not copy the institutions of our neighbors. It is more the case of our being a model to others, than of our imitating anyone else'. But in the contemporary world, so politically complex and culturally heterogeneous, seeking to impose one's own societal model is a risky undertaking, since it is widely perceived as arrogance and it raises more opposition than support.

The third criticism focuses on the actual salience of the values and institutions which I have identified for the contemporary EU and United States. No doubt some of them are not as influential as in the past, but what is needed in order to define them as core elements is that they have been relevant to the making of European identity. The case of Christianity is paradigmatic. There is much evidence in contemporary Europe of the continuing importance and influence of religion: a sizable percentage of Europeans affirm that they belong to one of the Christian churches and sects; despite the constitutional separation of state and church, church institutions and leaders wield considerable influence in the political and cultural lives of the EU member countries; there are close links between Christianity and nonreligious ethics; the great achievements of European culture in architecture, fine art, music, literature, and also philosophy and science would be inconceivable without the presence, benevolent or critical, of religious doctrine and authority. Nevertheless, there is some truth to Adriaanse's argument that 'in the cultural identity of Europe the religious factor is predominantly a matter of memory. Religion is what Europe has been' (2001: 31–2). But even if this were the case, we should not forget that in any definition of identity, individual or collective, what one has been is very much part of what one is and will be.

Here again there is a clear difference between the United States and most EU member states. As it is argued in Chapters 7 and 8, individual faith is more widespread and religion is becoming politically more important in the former. European secularism went together with anticlericalism because it had to fight against a monolithic church and fostered—together with the utilitarian distortion of classical liberalism—a materialistic culture and the subordination of moral considerations to economic ones, and more recently skepticism about beliefs, permissiveness of lifestyles, maximization of wants and claims, and multiculturalism. American secularism, by contrast, was built on Christian moral institutions and fostered a widespread moral consensus which only in recent decades has been challenged, opening a cleavage between the defenders of individual rights and the believers in God and the family, as is argued in Chapter 5.

Fourth, some critics maintain that the core elements of Western identity are no longer exclusive because they have been successfully 'exported' and assimilated in other parts of the world. The fact that the civilization of modernity was born in Europe and spread first to America and then throughout the world induces them to believe that in spreading worldwide, Europe has lost its specific character. In other words, because European identity is being intrinsically de-territorialized, it can no longer define the specificity of a single part of the world. According to D'Andrea, 'the Europeanization of the world is also the end of Europe as an entity in itself' (2001: 141). Opposite to D'Andrea's is Huntington's view which claims that the identification of Western civilization with modern civilization is totally false (1997: 69), since the central characteristics of the West, those which distinguish it from other civilizations, antedate the modernization of the West.

Both views miss the point, although for different reasons. The view represented by Huntington neglects the fact that the cultural roots distinctive of Europe since antiquity crystallized into a specific set of cultural and institutional forms with the advent of Western modernity, fostering bold institutional innovations through a process of historical learning (science and technology, market-led industrial capitalism, representative democracy, and nation-state citizenship). The European and American identities are closely related to the culture of modernity, that is to a particular conception of the modern age as an epoch oriented toward the future, conceived as being novel, and as better than the present and the past (Martinelli 2005).

The view represented by D'Andrea fails to consider the fact that global modernization has Western roots, and more specifically that European origins do not entail that countries approaching and undergoing the process of modernity can not develop their own cultural codes and institutions. In other words, it fails to consider that the contemporary world is a world of multiple modernities (Eisenstad 2001; Wittrock 2000; Martinelli 2005), especially in its non-Western parts. Any transition to modernity requires a process of creative adaptation, and it does not imply the inexorable establishment of a certain type of mental outlook (scientific rationalism, pragmatic instrumentalism, and secularism). Traditional culture and modern technology to some extent coexisted in twentieth-century Japan, and the market economy goes together with a political authoritarian state in contemporary China. Science, technology, and capitalism are the dimensions of Western culture most widespread in the world because they are largely indifferent to ends and able to outperform any other rival instrument. Other aspects of Western culture, such as modern individualism, civil rights, the critical mind, democratic representation, and the rule of law, have proved much more difficult to export because of the resistance raised in many parts of the world against the superseding of holistic or traditional views of the individual–society relationship.

Within the context of multiple modernities, those of Europe and the United States are by far the most similar, so that it is more appropriate to regard them as two variants of the same civilization. There are, moreover, specific reasons for them now to grow more similar than they have been in the past, which I discuss in Chapter 10. On the other hand, there are also factors pushing toward a greater diversity between American society and the EU society, which I also discuss in Chapter 10.

1.6. Critics of the existence of a European society in the making

A second main hypothesis of the book lies in the fact of considering the countries of the EU as increasingly forming a single society and a single political entity with gradually converging trends and common features. This hypothesis—which contributes to the novelty of the book—must be justified, first, through a critical rebuttal of the approaches which deny the existence of, and indeed the very possibility, of a distinct European society and, second, through an appraisal of the main factors accounting for the growing homogeneity of European societies.

Several social scientists are skeptical not only about whether a European society exists but also whether it could ever be possible. They are convinced that the necessary normative and institutional features are not in place at the EU level, and that it is therefore not possible to speak of a European 'society'. In a similar vein, the supporters of the intergovernmental approach argue that the EU is nothing more than a confederation of sovereign nation-states and that decision-making is still predominantly conducted on the basis of agreements among them.

These commentators all maintain that European integration is purely—or largely—economic and financial in character, with little corresponding activity at the other levels of the societal whole. But they differ in terms of the level on which they focus. Keeping our definition of a society in mind, we can distinguish skeptics into five categories according to which requirements they consider most lacking in the present state of Europe: mass consensus, homogeneous territory, democratic institutions, national/cultural identity, and statehood.

The first group of critics focuses on the class composition of European society, and argues that the elitist, socially circumscribed character of the EU leaves the majority of the European people at the margins. They maintain that, although Europe has strengthened its market linkages, it is far from attaining the level of a coherent social system, largely because European networks of social interaction exist mainly to serve the specialized sector interests of mostly elites and upper social classes rather than those of the masses (Mann 1998). It is easy to counterargue that political communities have often been the product of active elites promoting a project which has subsequently proved able to achieve larger consensus through its own success. European society has problems of social cohesion, status inequality, and democratic participation which are no greater than those of other well-established societies, the United States included. Sufficient for a society to form is the convergence of a critical mass of interests and value preferences on a project which appears to meet basic challenges and to grasp relevant opportunities.

The creation of the European communities in the 1950s and the acceleration of European integration in the past twenty years were originally pursued by long-sighted elites, but were then more and more accepted by the general public. Society formation and nation-building have generally been the output of modernizing elites, the outcome of the alliance among specific economic and political groups. What is needed is that the project upheld by a minority wins a larger consensus by persuading people that it corresponds to the basic interests and beliefs of the many. Both the start of the process of European integration and its acceleration at a given time can be explained in terms of this scheme. European unification was grounded on the decision to put an end to the European civil wars and on the perception of common economic interests; and it was the product of enlightened elites. The acceleration of the project in the 1980s, following the 'Eurosclerosis' of the 1970s, can be interpreted as the outcome of the alliance between two groups of actors—transnational corporations and states—which responded to the urgent pressure 'to rearrange the political economy at a time when the cornerstone of a societal model (Keynesianism) and interstate coordination run into crisis and when the relative decline of the hegemon (the United States) and emerging new competitors (Japan) jeopardize the stability of the world political economy' (Bornschier 2000: XIII).

There is however more than an element of truth in this type of critique. The process of unification, in fact, slows down or even comes to a stop—as it happens now—whenever social cleavages among those who can gain (the younger, better educated, and active in the competitive sectors of the economy) and those who can lose (like older workers with obsolete skills, working in sectors suffering from competition) from further integration become too deep, and ideological differences about the model of society to be developed (for instance about what kind of mix between market competitiveness and social cohesion should be pursued) become too acute.

A second line of criticism claims that Europe is not a single society, but rather a system of highly differentiated historical regions, a sum of heterogeneous cultural areas. It is true, the division of Europe into different, autonomous entities is the combined effect of different types of factors or processes: (*a*) religious factors (the Great Schism of 1054 AD between Orthodox and Catholics, the religious wars between Catholics and Protestants in the sixteenth-century Reformation and in the seventeenth-century Religious wars); (*b*) economic factors (the different timing and sequence of the modernization of European countries which gave rise to different roles—core, periphery, semi-periphery—in the international division of labor); and (*c*) political factors (the failure of the universalistic projects of popes and emperors, the rise of independent nation-states). Throughout these great transformations, however, the core elements of Europe's cultural unity did not disappear. Present regional differences are often no greater than those within other great countries, primarily the United States, and, most important, the European project is an attempt to take advantage of differences and achieve unity through diversity.

A parallel line of critique—which points out to the great socioeconomic differences within the EU—can also be countered by arguing that in the past the EU has been rather successful in reducing differences among member countries with different starting points—such as France and Spain, or the UK and Ireland—and that differences within the member countries—such as the north and south of Italy, the west and east of Germany—are sometimes not smaller than those among countries. The chapters on the economy, the family, and cities all provide evidence on converging trends in the EU member countries.

A third group of skeptics focus on the democratic deficit of the EU and the lack of a genuine democratic European polity. These critics stress, first, the lack of essential elements of parliamentary democracy, such as parliament's legislative dominance and control over European decision-making (Bogdanor 1989; Lodge 1991) and, second, the lack of such basic prerequisites for democracy as truly European parties and mass media, and an active European public sphere (Grundmann 1999). The question of the democratic deficit is discussed in Chapter 5 and I very shortly anticipate the argument here to counter this criticism. European democracy is certainly imperfect, limited, and unaccomplished, but it is a democracy in the making: first, because the present institutional design of the EU does not correspond to the model of parliamentary democracy, but rather to the model of pluralist compound democracy. Second, because the member-states with embedded democratic traditions exert a strong influence on the political processes at the union level (Laffan 1999). The principles of liberty, democratic competition, respect for human rights, the rule of law and the related institutions have been projected upwards onto the European level, and they have been solemnly affirmed at Nice and enshrined in the Treaty for the adoption of a European Constitution. Moreover, the EU has successfully 'exported' democracy not by force but by 'peaceful aggression' to countries with a nondemocratic past— like Spain, Portugal and more recently the former communist countries of Eastern Europe. In order to join the EU, a country must meet *rigorous* liberal democratic requirements.

The last two criticisms emphasize that the essential features of the nation-state are lacking as regards both national identity and statehood. A fourth criticism contends that what is most lacking is a common identity and a shared common culture. For instance, Delanty writes that 'Europe does not have a shared cultural community which could be the basis of a common cultural identity. There is no common language nor ethnic commonalities on which a European identity could be built' (2000: 84). And Offe argues that the prospects for uniting a European society, that is the supranational equivalent and extension of national societies, are exceedingly discouraging. People belonging to a society typically communicate in one (or a small number) of idiom(s), and they presuppose their mutual familiarity with aesthetic and other forms of symbolic expression, ranging from styles and pieces of music to religious and national holidays. None of these features is present—nor could they be created in a foreseeable future—at the European level. 'Patterns of religious affiliation and national cultures differ and are mutually perceived as constituting significant differences of collective identity, not minor diversities within a cultural heritage that Europeans basically have in common' (Offe 2002: 5, 13).

The question of the European identity is a complicated one for at least two reasons. First, because Europe identifies itself with Western cultural modernity.

As Giner points out, the early European colonization of a large part of the world now reflects back on Europe itself, with the result that it is hard to separate what is typically European from what is typically American; a question that this book seeks to clarify. Second, because the most distinctive feature of Europe is its cultural diversity and we know that common identities are usually formed on the basis of an us/them distinction and through the creation of real or imagined adversaries. European peoples have made no exception: the European identity has been idealized as the highest stage of human civilization and constructed through time in opposition to various types of barbarians (oi barbaroi) by fashioning 'distorted mirrors' of the identities of others (Fontana 1994). And the risk exists in today's multicultural world that a European identity will be only negative, constructed only in opposition to others. But, as I argue in Chapter 10, the challenge of the European project is to achieve unity through diversity, to combine pride for its own values and institutions and respect for other beliefs and ways of life.

A variant of this critique focuses on the risk of the enlargement of the EU. Even supposing that a shared common culture exists in the EU as it is now, further enlargement beyond a certain point will make the formation of a single society and a real political union very difficult or altogether impossible. These critics contend that any further enlargement to new members slows down and even threatens the process of unification. Mendras (1997) argued that the enlargement of the EU to Eastern Europe raised serious questions about the maintenance of a common European identity. Numerous intellectual and politicians maintain that the future joining of Turkey threatens to stop the process entirely, because too much cultural and religious diversity cannot be tolerated within a single union. This critique is usually counterargued by pointing out that the enlargement is an inherent component of the making of the EU, an integral part of the specific style of the EU in international relations and that the European project can develop with varying geometry, with member countries proceeding at different speeds: a core inner circle of countries which experience more advanced forms of integration and tighter bonds, an intermediate circle, and an outer circle of countries at first included into the single economic space and later, also because of that, can proceed toward greater political and social integration.

The fifth criticism maintains that there is no European society because there can be no European nation-state. For scholars like Offe, society-building can only take place through state-initiated nation-building. 'Nation states "make" societies and build a demos by imposing on some pre-existing patchwork of heterogeneous regional cultures and political units (such as kingdoms and principalities) clearly defined borders, as well as, within those borders, a relatively homogeneous military, fiscal, educational, economic, religious and judicial regime and institutional order' (2002: 5). But 'Europe is not a state, and hence not a society. The building of European statehood and, by implications, the emergence of a "European society" is not a goal that societies within Europe could credibly and plausibly pursue in the name of some notion of "liberation" (as opposed to market liberalization which, however, does not presuppose a common statehood)' (2002: 8). 'The core problem of European integration and political unity is not so much the extent of ethnic, historical, cultural, linguistic, and economic diversities and cleavages, in spite of the vast discrepancies in the size of member states and their level of economic development, but the total absence of an appeal of liberation in the service of which unity must be pursued. "Europe" does—perhaps—yield a surplus value in terms of prosperity, but no such surplus value in terms of liberty' (2002: 7). European integration presents clear benefits of global competitive advantage, economies of scale, and more effective use of pooled resources; but these results can be obtained within the framework of intergovernmental cooperation; they do not require a supranational society.

Offe grants that there indeed exists a type of European society, in the sense that the national societies of Europe share, to a lesser or greater extent, numerous affinities and similarities. Some of their common features—welfare systems for example, as argued in Chapter 6—are most clearly visible in regional clusters of national societies and their historical experience and cultural and religious profiles (the countries of the Mediterranean, Central Europe, and Scandinavia; the Anglo-Saxon, Orthodox, and German-speaking countries, etc.). But there are a number of features that are shared by virtually all of them—market economies and liberal democratic polities—as well as the fact that they are all enabled and constrained by membership of the EU. But 'it is simply a non sequitur to deduce from the similarity of European societies the desirability and/or probability of their eventually become "one" society' (2002: 9).

In at least partial opposition to these accounts, I maintain that a European society is in the making. My critique of the Euroskeptics, however, does not make me join the group of those 'Euro-enthusiasts' like Rifkin (2004), who speaks of the new European dream and portrays the EU as 'the new house upon the hill' or Leonard (2005) who defines the EU as the power which 'will run the 21st century'. They not only affirm the absolute novelty of the European project (and here I agree), but consider it already accomplished (and here I disagree). Again, in at least partial opposition to these accounts, I maintain that a European society is in the making, but far from being accomplished, and that it requires courage, vision, and enthusiasm both on the part of its citizens and its leaders to succeed.

This hypothesis of a European society and political union in the making will be tested in the various chapters of this volume through a systematic appraisal of the similarities and singularities among the national societies of the EU countries in key selected areas. The argument is developed in Chapter 10 in two ways: first, on the basis of the findings of various chapters I will summarize the growing affinities within the EU. The growing similarity of European societies does not necessarily imply, as Offe argues, the desirability and/or probability of their even-tually becoming 'one' society, but it certainly helps. The relative homogeneity of European societies appears more clearly when contrasted with American society. Although it is a much more complicated undertaking to distinguish the EU from the United States than from China or India, Brazil or Nigeria, since the EU and the United States share many affinities, we argue in this volume that their differences are large enough for them to be considered two specific variants of the same Western civilization.

Second, I argue that an institutional cement (the specific EU form of governance) and a normative consensus (European common cultural roots and the
European project) both exist to a large extent in the EU. They can be considered
the organizing principles of an emerging European society that is different from
American society. In order to respond to Offe's contention that the emergence of
'one' society does not follow from the similarity of European societies and that
the EU cannot be a society because it has never been a state, I argue that the
EU is attempting to build a new type of society without following the historical
model of European nation-states; and that this societal model is more capable
of coping with the challenges of contemporary globalization. Here, I anticipate a
brief discussion of the main historical processes which account for the growing
homogeneity of European societies.

1.7. Main historical processes which account for the growing homogeneity of European societies

A major hypothesis of this book is that the societies of EU member-states are
growing increasingly similar. Their economies have become integrated into a
single market; their political regimes have consolidated a common democratic
tradition after the defeat of authoritarian and totalitarian states; ideological cleavages and traditional class conflicts have diminished; welfare institutions have
increased social cohesion, although specificities remain with regard to the different
modes of conflict institutionalization and dispersion; and a common mass culture,
common styles of life, and consumption patterns have further reduced differences
among countries. This growing similarity does not necessarily entail the emergence of 'one' society, but it helps normative consensus and the acceptance of
common institutions.

The main factors responsible for this growing homogeneity among European
societies can be grouped into three broad categories. The first type of interpretation focuses on the political dimension of recent European history, and specifically
on the end of ideological divisions and political rivalries among European nation-
states which threatened to dismantle Europe altogether. Aggressive nationalism,
economic protectionism, and above all the division during the inter-world war
period between democratic countries, on the one hand, and authoritarian and
totalitarian regimes on the other, played a crucial role in differentiating European
societies. But then? The collapse of Nazi Germany at the end of World War II
made full acceptance possible of not only market economy and democratic politics
but also of Western culture, thereby putting an end to the '*Sonderweg*'—that
is, the distinctive German path toward and through modernization. The more
recent collapse of the USSR terminated another *Sonderweg* toward and through
modernity and laid the basis for enlargement of the European model of society to
the East, although the process has only just started and is still controversial. The
borders of the EU have already moved further eastwards with enlargement to a

further ten countries, eight of which were former members of the Soviet bloc. The EU can be interpreted as the fulfillment of the project to put an end to centuries of European 'civil wars'.

The second type of interpretation focuses on the socioeconomic dimension, and specifically on the long-term processes of industrialization and modernization. In spite of the different timing and sequences of these processes in the various member countries (exemplified by the distinction between first-comers and late-comers), growing dependence on the international market and the development of information and communication technologies have played a major role in the social integration of EU countries, and they have diminished the specificities and peculiarities due to geographical and cultural isolation. In the early phases of modernization, differences among developing countries may become stronger, but as the process proceeds the similarities increase because of growing economic integration and social imitation. This kind of interpretation stresses long-term socioeconomic change.

The third kind of interpretation also emphasizes a socioeconomic dimension, but does so in the short term: it identifies a basic homogenizing factor in the high and rapid economic growth achieved in the 'Trente glorieuses' and which contributed greatly to growing homogeneity among institutional arrangements, cultural attitudes, and lifestyles; in particular, it had a lasting impact on the structure of employment, and on welfare and education policies. It should be stressed that the lower growth rates, greater uncertainty, and more conflict relations of the 1970s did not prompt a resumption of the protectionist economic policies and nationalist ideologies of the past in the Western European states.

A fourth interpretation focuses on the homogenizing impact of contemporary globalization (global market, global finance, global technologies, and global media), which reduces the differences among countries and more so among countries which share similar economic and political institutions.

Finally, European social integration is seen as resulting more from deliberate EU policies than from 'spontaneous' social changes in the various EU countries. The formation of a European common economic space for the exchange of people, capital, goods, and services, the creation of the European currency, and the strengthening of EU institutions have intensified the effects of technological change, industrialization, and modernization on growing social homogeneity. The integrating influence of EU institutions—the European Council, Commission and Parliament, the High Court of Justice, the European Central Bank, and the common currency—can be hardly underplayed.

In the previous sections of this introduction I argued that European peoples have a common history and may have a common fate as well. The following chapters show that they increasingly share similar societal characteristics. But are a common past and widespread social similarities sufficient to construct one society and a single political union? A society is defined in terms not only of structural interdependence but also of common institutions and values. Common institutions are slowly emerging in Europe, but what about a common normative order? Can we argue that a common European identity exists? And if it existed for the original member countries, and even for the EU 15, will it continue to exist after further enlargements? The chapters of this volume provide various tests of these hypotheses. In the conclusion I outline the distinctive features of the European model of society and the basic aims of the European project, to combine competitiveness and social cohesion, 'national interest and peacemaking in the world, to achieve unity through diversity'.

As Holderlin's gaze, in his novel *Hyperion*, ranges from the great lands of Asia toward the West, toward Europe, it first meets the sea rich of islands, the archipelago—the beloved islands both divided and interconnected by the sea (Cacciari 1997: 16). Among the islands springs Athens—the original polis— 'where for the first time the voice of the people thundered in the agora'. The archipelago can be seen as a metaphor of Europe: a cluster of peoples who are different and united at the same time, who compete and clash but are also com-pelled to cooperate, discuss and live together. For centuries Europe was plagued by divisions, wars, and despotic rule; now the ambitious project of building a united, democratic, prosperous, and peaceful European society is under way. We will assess the feasibility of this project through a systematic comparison with its biggest comparator, the American Union.

1.8. **Structure of the book**

This volume is not a collection of chapters but a coherent work by a research group (the CCSC group) that has developed a habit of scientific dialogue and intellectual cooperation through the years. It is articulated in ten chapters.

In this introductory chapter I have defined the main aims, research questions, and methodological problems of the work and discussed two key underlying hypotheses: (*a*) the hypothesis that the societal models of the EU and the United States are two variants of the same civilization and (*b*) the hypothesis that the member countries of the EU are increasingly forming a single society and a single polity with gradually converging trends and common institutions at the EU level.

Chapter 2 looks at the economic sphere; Antonio Chiesi systematically com-pares economic trends with different indicators in the United States and the EU at variable geometry, with specific reference to market size, economic sectors, work, public expenditure and welfare, household well-being, and consumption.

In Chapter 3, Paul Kingston and Laura Holian discuss how and to what extent the American society and the European society are unequal both in terms of inequality of results (conditions) and inequality of opportunity, whether class divisions exist and what is the place of women in the stratification system.

In Chapter 4, Theodore Caplow and Salustiano Del Campo show how mod-ernization and the gradual progress of equality transformed family life in both the EU and the United States in the past fifty years and argue that, while similar trends were recorded in the EU and the United States, they started and ended at different levels and their consequences were never identical.

In Chapter 5, I analyze the institutional architectures and the main features of both the American and the European political systems, focusing on their essential similarities and basic differences, and discussing the quality of democracy on the two sides of the Atlantic and the major challenges confronting it.

In Chapter 6, Gérard Cornilleau focuses on the analysis of welfare in the two unions, the different institutional arrangements—and more specifically the greater role of the state in Europe—and the variety of welfare systems within the EU.

In Chapter 7, Michel Forsé and Maxime Parodi analyze cultural values and attitudes and focus specifically on individualism and the progress of reason, arguing that Europeans and Americans are both individualistic and rational in a specific reasonable way.

In Chapter 8, Mathias Bös and Kai Hebel focus on religion, the area where differences both between the EU and the United States and within the EU are more striking, comparing religious belief and religious practice, as well as the relations between churches and state on both sides of the Atlantic.

In Chapter 9, Patrick Le Galès and Mathieu Zagrodzki focus on cities, arguing that the similarities between American and European cities are more apparent than real: the EU and the United States resemble each other in their levels of urbanization, but they differ in the form of their cities, in the relationships between the centers and the peripheries, and in the quality of urban life, because of such differentiating factors as the existence of a medieval urban heritage and the continuity of a historical urban identity, and the experience of regulatory policies of urban development and of city planning in most European cities.

Finally, in Chapter 10 the main arguments are brought together with a critical discussion of the basic questions of the work; first, salient similarities and differences and trends of convergence and divergence in selected aspects of the two societies are analyzed in light of the findings of the various chapters; then, the organizing principles of American society are outlined, discussing how and to what extent its basic values and institutions are changing; then, I discuss whether a European society is in the making and what shape is taking the European project of building unity through diversity; and, finally, I focus on the implications of globalization for the two societies and on the cooperative/competitive role of the United States and the EU in global governance.

2 The economic sphere

Antonio M. Chiesi[1]

The European capitalist economies have always been considered very different due to their origins in different times, their different pace of development, and their different position in the international division of labor. Nevertheless, the long process of economic unification has brought increasing integration to a common market, while different models that have sometimes been presented as alternative have inspired differentiated welfare regimes and degrees of state intervention in the economy.

The economy of the United States is also very differentiated across the fifty states, but unlike Europe, it is characterized by the same institutions and the same market–state mix.

It is well known that the process of European integration was undertaken mainly for political reasons after World War II (Gilbert 2003) in order to avoid future conflicts. Wars had recurrently stained the ground of the continent with blood since the Middle Ages and brought millions of casualties in the wars of the twentieth century. The fathers of the EU have been aware since the very beginning that integration in the political sphere was a very difficult task due to the centrality of nation-states and national identities. For this reason, economic integration was pursued earlier than political integration and was conceived as a way to ease the latter. On the contrary, the independence of the United States was pursued both for economic and political reasons at the same time at the end of the eighteenth century. A national identity could take place in spite of the fact that the country was mainly formed by immigrants coming from different countries, mainly European, with different languages and traditions.

While the United States could enjoy earlier a common, although diversified economy, the most important steps of European economic integration took place only in the past decades of the twentieth century. They were the Treaty of Paris, which established the European Coal and Steel Community (ECSC) in 1951, the Treaty of Rome, which set up the European Economic Community (EEC), and the European Atomic Energy Commission (EURATOM) in 1957. Customs duties between the six founder countries were completely removed in 1968 and common policies—notably on trade and agriculture—were also set up during the 1960s. The success of this initiative brought Denmark, Ireland, and the UK to join the Communities in 1973. In that period, the Communities took on new tasks and introduced new social, regional, and environmental policies. To implement

[1] I am indebted to Federico Podestà, Department of Sociology and Social Research, University of Trento, who has collected the data and computed most of the time series.

regional policy, the European Regional Development Fund (ERDF) was set up in 1975 in order to foster the reduction of economic inequality at regional level.

In the early 1970s, the need to bring national economies into line with one another brought about the idea of a monetary union. At about the same time, however, the United States decided to suspend the dollar's convertibility into gold. This ushered in a period of great instability on the world's money markets, made worse by the oil crises of 1973 and 1979. The introduction of the European Monetary System (EMS) in 1979 helped stabilize exchange rates and encouraged the Community member-states to implement policies that allowed them to maintain their coordination and discipline their economies.

When Greece joined the Communities in 1981, followed by Spain and Portugal in 1986, it became more urgent to introduce 'structural' programs such as the first Integrated Mediterranean Programs (IMP), aimed at reducing the economic development gap between the twelve member-states.

Meanwhile the EU was beginning to play a more unified role in the international economy, signing a series of conventions on aid and trade with the countries of Africa, the Caribbean, and the Pacific (the 'ACP' countries). In this perspective, the Lomé conventions were signed between 1975 and 1989 that led to the Cotonou Agreement in 2000.

The worldwide economic recession in the early 1980s brought additional difficulties to this policy, but in 1985 the European Commission, under Delors' presidency, published a 'White Paper' setting out a timetable for completing the European single market by January 1, 1993. The Communities adopted this goal with the Single European Act, which came into force in 1987.

The fall of the Berlin Wall in 1989 brought new economic perspectives along with the dramatic political change of the collapse of the Soviet Union. This led to the reunification of Germany on October 3, 1990 and the coming of democracy to the countries of Central and Eastern Europe. These changes fostered a negotiation between the member-states that led to a new treaty that was adopted by the European Council at Maastricht in December 1991. The 'Treaty on European Union' came into force on November 1, 1993. The EEC was renamed simply 'the European Community' (EC). Moreover, by adding areas of intergovernmental cooperation to the existing Community system, the treaty created the EU. It also timetabled the formation of a monetary union by 1999, besides new political goals of European citizenship, new common policies—including a common foreign and security policy (CFSP)—and arrangements for internal security.

Austria, Finland, and Sweden joined the EU in 1995, so that the Union had fifteen member-states and on January 1, 2002, euro notes and coins came into circulation in twelve EU countries (the 'Euro area'). The euro is now a major world currency.

With the beginning of the new century it appeared that the original reasons for European unification had turned to new opportunities related to the need to face globalization (Castells 1998). During the Lisbon meeting in 2000, the European Council adopted a more comprehensive strategy for modernizing the EU's economy in order to face competition on the world market with other major players such as the United States and the emerging industrialized countries. The aim has been to open up all sectors of the economy to competition, encouraging innovation and business investment, and modernizing Europe's education systems to meet the needs of the information society. On the other side, unemployment and the rising cost of pensions are both putting pressure on the member-states' economies, and this makes reform all the more necessary.

Accession negotiations with other twelve candidate countries were launched in Luxembourg in 1997. The Union was on the way to its biggest enlargement ever. The EU received membership applications from the former Soviet bloc countries (Bulgaria, the Czech Republic, Hungary, Poland, Romania, and Slovakia), the three Baltic states that had once been part of the Soviet Union (Estonia, Latvia, and Lithuania), one of the republics of the former Yugoslavia (Slovenia), and two Mediterranean countries (Cyprus and Malta). For ten of the candidate countries, negotiations were completed in Copenhagen at the end of 2002. As a result, the EU had twenty-five member-states in 2004.

This process has raised a number of questions about the nature of the European economy, the variety of its capitalisms (Soskice 1989; Albert 1991; Esping-Andersen 1999) and its capacity to face global competition and to grant increasing and widespread welfare for its citizens. Unlike the United States, which has a long-standing national identity, the EU is not a supranational state intended to replace existing states, but it is more than other international organizations. Its member-states have set up common institutions to which they delegate some of their sovereignty so that decisions on specific matters of joint interest can be made democratically at a European level. These institutions are mainly economic, because European integration has historically worked better in the sphere of economic interests rather than political ones.

In the first years of the new century, the European economy has faced serious difficulties in confronting the global competition of the emerging Asian economies. A poorer economic performance, the difficulties of controlling state expenditures, in keeping the Maastricht requirements, and in reforming unbearable welfare regimes in most countries have led again to a phase of Euroskepticism that became evident with the rejection of the European Constitution in the French referendum of May 2005.

At the same time the American economy, although affected by a huge deficit both of the federal government and the balance of trade, has shown a better performance and its rate of development is twice the European average in the new millennium. This diverging performance has fed the long-standing debate about models of capitalism.

In this chapter I want to show and discuss a systematic comparison between the trends collected by Caplow, Hicks, and Wattenberg (2001) on a century of social transformation of American society, and those that can be gathered about the EU. The aim is to contribute to a deeper understanding of the specificities of both systems. This perspective is based on two assumptions: (*a*) it is possible to find a sufficient number of comparable trends coming from European institutions, and when they are not available it is possible to compute trends combining weighted data at country level; (*b*) it is possible to interpret the EU as a single federation of states with an increasing identity, as it was for the formation of the United States during the nineteenth century.

In the following pages, economic trends are plotted with different indicators, concerning a variety of topics. Trends are clustered around the following economic dimensions: market size, sectors of the economy, work, public expenditure and welfare, household well-being, and consumption. Each trend is plotted to show change over time of three lines in most cases: solid line for the United States; dash line, labeled EuPol, for the set of states that were members of the EU in that year (Belgium, France, Italy, Luxembourg, the Netherlands, and West Germany joined in 1957; Denmark, Ireland, and the UK entered in 1973; Greece in 1981; Spain and Portugal in 1986; and Austria, Finland, and Sweden in 1995); and dotted line, labeled EU15, for the set of fifteen countries during the entire period.

2.1. **The creation of wealth**

The EU increased its population at a faster pace than the United States, but this increase is mainly due to progressive enlargement. On the contrary, the demographic increase of the population in the fifteen member-states since the 1960s has been lower than in the United States, especially after the mid-1970s. As a result of the accession of new members from Eastern Europe, at the end of 2004 the internal market of the EU had increased to 4,549 million people, against 2,914 million in the United States.

In modern economies the formation of value added, as a measure of well-being, is usually measured through the variation of gross domestic product (GDP). Its size and increase is interpreted as a proxy of the strength of the economy at large. To get a sound comparison, we plotted both the index number for the United States and the EU15 states (1995 = 100). Figure 2.1 compares only changes over time of the two economies, not the levels of GDP, and shows three different periods. During the 1960s, until the mid-1970s, the performance of the fifteen European countries has been better in terms of increase of GDP. After the first oil shock the performance of the US economy has been moderately better, while the divergence has been increasing in favor of the United States since the beginning of the 1990s, when the GDP increase has been twice that of the EU.

Different scholars have commented on this increasing divergence in performance as the capacity of the United States to react in a more flexible way to the new challenges of globalization, in terms of both innovation and productivity, thanks to different institutional mechanisms that are based on the centrality of a competitive market. A more regulated economy through state coordination in the EU (Soskice 1993) has been considered responsible for a poorer performance. Although the European national economies are affected by a variety of institutions and by a different state–market mix (De Joung 1995), the prevalence of what has

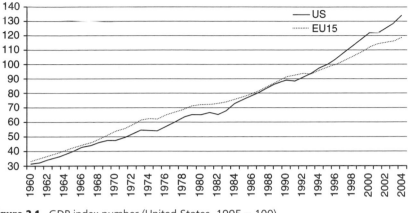

Figure 2.1. GDP index number (United States, 1995 = 100)

Sources: OECD, *Statistical Compendium*, and <http://www.oecd.org>

been called the 'Rhine model' (Albert 1991) to depict most Continental national economies has limited their reaction to the emerging global competition both in terms of flexibility and innovation.

In spite of these different dynamics, if we compare the United States with the fifteen countries of the EU over the entire period, the original moderate differences of GDP at constant prices have not changed dramatically. In 1960, the proportion was 1 to 1.13 in favor of Europe, while in 2000 the proportion had changed to 1 to 0.91 in favor of the United States. While the fifteen European countries had worsened their performance since the first oil shock, compared with the United States (Maddison 1995; Valli 1999), the increase in the overall GDP of the EU has been eased by recurrent phases of enlargement, until the entrance of the last ten countries in 2004. The total GDP increase has gone together with a relative decline of per capita income.

While GDP is a measure of the absolute strength of an economy, GDP per capita is a measure of economic well-being based on the average income at individual level. In 1960, each American could enjoy an income 56 percent higher than their European counterpart. In 1982, the gap was reduced to 31 percent, but since then the United States' better performance has allowed an increase in the gap until 49 percent in 2000. This is more evidence in favor of some interpretations that stress the higher capacity of the 'Rhine model' in managing economic and social problems during the Fordist period, while the 'noncoordinated market' model has shown a better performance during the post-Fordist period (Soskice 1993; Crouch and Streeck 1997).

Figure 2.2 shows the degree of openness of the two economies with the rest of the world, in terms of import and export, as a percentage of GDP. In the long run, both economies have become more integrated in the world economy, but for the EU15, this integration has been faster in the 1960s and 1970s, while for the United States the increasing trend is more constant over the entire period. Moreover,

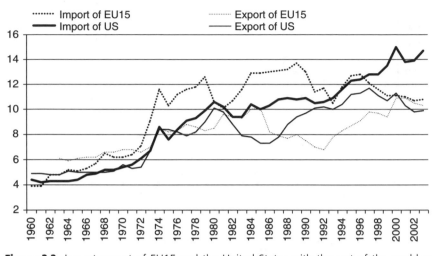

Figure 2.2. Import–export of EU15 and the United States with the rest of the world as percentage of GDP at market prices

Sources: OECD, *Statistical Compendium*, and <http://www.oecd.org>

during the first twenty years imports and exports of the European Community had been relatively higher than those of the United States. The increasing prices of raw materials, following the first oil shock of the mid-1970s, contributed to higher imports and to a consequent problem of foreign trade balance for European countries. This became a structural problem and contributed in turn to stop a further increase of the rate of foreign exchange over the European GDP. On the contrary, the US economy kept up evidencing a continuous increase of import and a more cyclical course of export. Unlike Europe, in the 1990s the United States shows a different pattern with an increasing trade balance deficit of the United States.

These different economic performances have been obtained from different structures of the economy. In the following section, we compare some features of the two economic structures, the labor markets, the role of the state in the economy, and the economic behavior of households.

2.2. The distribution of employment across sectors

Since the 1960s, the share of employment in agriculture on total employment has been decreasing in both the EU and the United States as a typical trend of modernization. The pace of the decrease has also been declining in both cases. Although this trend has been steeper in Europe because of its higher starting point, the share of employment in agriculture remains larger in the United States. The dash line (EuPol) shows a downward step in 1974 due to the inclusion of the UK in the EU and an increase in 1981 and 1986 respectively when Greece, and then Spain and Portugal joined the Union.

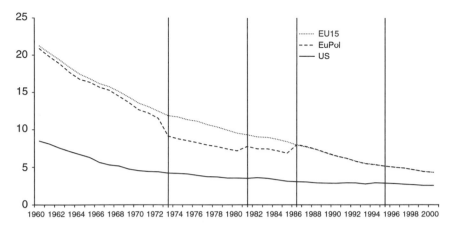

Figure 2.3. Employment in agriculture (1960–2000): as percentage of total employment

Source: Adapted from OECD, *Labor Force Statistics*

The trend in the United States has been almost flat since the mid-1980s, while in the EU the decrease is still at work at the end of the century (Figure 2.3).

The share of employment in industry has been decreasing in the long run in both cases, but in the United States the decline has been more constant over the period since the mid-1960s, while in the EU there has been a modest increase until 1970. A persistent feature of the European economy has been its higher level of industrial employment, always at least five points above that of the United States. The highest difference was reached during the first half of the 1970s. After that period the decline increased to some extent from the inclusion of Greece, Portugal, and Spain whose industrial employment has always been lower than the European average. At the end of the century, almost one employee out of three is still employed in industry in the EU, while less than one in four in the United States. The persisting centrality of industry in Europe makes this economy more vulnerable to the increasing competition of the emerging Asian industrial powers (Figure 2.4).

The share of employment in the service sector is mirror-like to the former, but its trend is more constant in both cases. The American economy has always been more tertiary, although the gap with the EU has been decreasing. At the beginning of the 1960s, the United States already had an economy mainly based on the service sector, while the EU was almost 20 percent points behind. At the beginning of the new century, almost three employed out of four are in this sector in the United States, while the proportion is two out of three in the EU, but the gap reduced to 10 percent points. Again Figure 2.5 shows that the entrance of the UK sped up the trend in the EU and vice versa when Spain and Portugal joined the Community in 1986.

Due to the importance of state intervention in the economy, as an institutional factor that can affect the specificities of different types of capitalism, we have

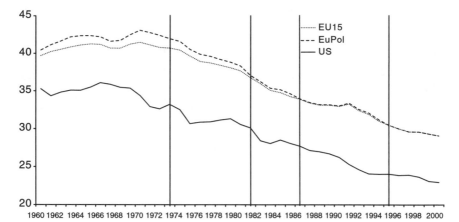

Figure 2.4. Employment in industry (1960–2000): as percentage of total employment

Source: Adapted from OECD, *Labor Force Statistics*

gathered data on government employment, both at central and local administration level. Figure 2.6 shows that during the 1960s and the first part of the 1970s, the share of government employment on total employees had been similar in both economies and followed a similar increase. The entrance of the UK, Denmark, and Ireland in the mid-1970s brought a sharp increase in the share of civil service employment in the EU. Since then a diverging trend is evident: while in the United States the employees in Public Administration (highest level 18% in 1976) begin to diminish their share at a rather constant pace, they keep increasing until the mid-1980s in the European countries (highest level

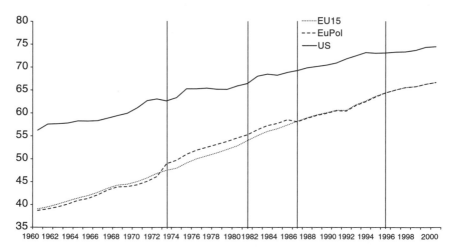

Figure 2.5. Employment in the service sector (1960–2000): as percentage of total employment ·

Source: Adapted from OECD, *Labor Force Statistics*

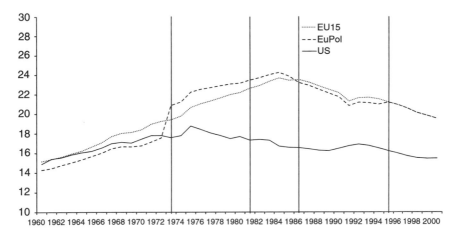

Figure 2.6. Employment in government (1960–2000): as percentage of total employees

Source: Adapted from OECD, *Labor Force Statistics*

24% in 1985). Since then, although diminishing at a faster rate than in the United States, European Public Administration employment has always kept above 19 percent.

Figure 2.7 gives evidence of the share of armed forces over total employment. In spite of the very different impact of the European armed forces in the world equilibrium, the number of personnel as a simple sum of the different national armies is surprisingly similar to that of the United States. The only period of difference is that of the Vietnam War, when the American Army accounted for around 4 percent of the employed workforce. Apart from that, during the following quarter of the century the size of the armed forces has been not only similar in the two societies but also diminishing, together with the tendency to replace

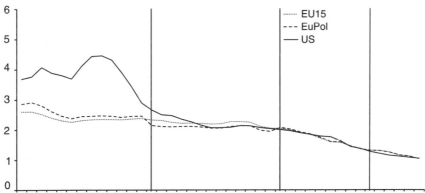

Figure 2.7. Armed Forces (1960–2000): as percentage of total employment

Source: Adapted from OECD, *Labor Force Statistics*

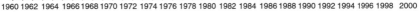

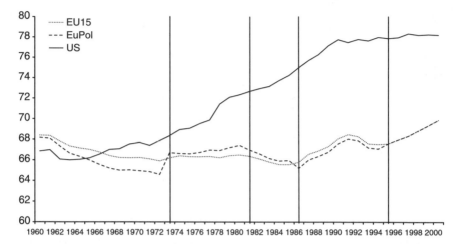

Figure 2.8. Participation rate—total (1960–2000): total labor force as percentage of the population aged 15–64

Source: Adapted from OECD, *Labor Force Statistics*

compulsory national service with professional soldiers. As a result, at the beginning of the new century the share of the armed forces on total employment has declined to 1 percent in both cases.

2.3. **Work and labor market**

The functioning of the labor market has been considered one of the most important institutional characteristics in the debate about the different models of capitalism (Esping-Andersen 1999). As is shown in Figure 2.8, during the past forty years the United States and the EU have experienced a diverging trend in the participation rate, that is the percentage of total labor force on the population aged 15–64 years. While in the United States there has been a constant increase from around 65 percent to almost 80 percent, and this increase has been steeper during the 1980s, the EU rate has always stayed below 70 percent with the lowest level around 65 percent in the mid-1980s. It is worthwhile to stress the fact that the inclusion of the UK in 1973 has brought an increase in the overall rate. This is evidence of the fact that, as far as this feature is concerned, the structure of the British labor market has constantly been more similar to that of the United States rather than Continental Europe. Before the entrance of the UK, until the beginning of the 1970s, the activity rate had been declining in the EU. The decline of the participation rate in 1986 is due to the inclusion of Spain and Portugal. Since the second half of the 1980s, the rate of EU has been moderately increasing.

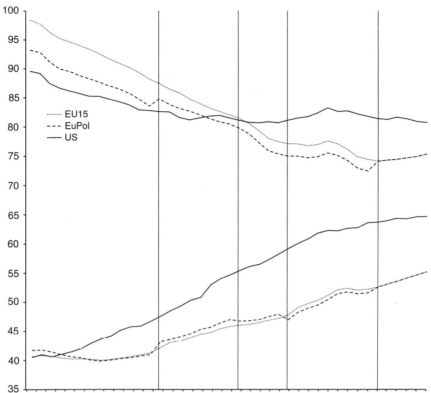

Figure 2.9. Participation rate (male above, female below): total labor force as percentage of the population aged 15–64

Source: Adapted from OECD, *Labor Force Statistics*

The overall picture is the result of diverging changes that affected male and female participation (Figure 2.9). While male participation rate has been decreasing in both economic systems due to early retirement and longer education, the female one has been increasing due to long-term changes to women's roles both in the household and in the labor market. These trends are roughly similar to both systems, but present different paces and intensities. The decrease in the male participation rate has been steeper in Europe until the mid-1990s, falling from 98 percent in 1960 to 80 percent in 1996. These high values are due to the fact that the denominator of the rate counts only people from 16 to 65 years, while in the numerator employed people of any age are taken into account. The rate has inverted its direction during the last years of the century. In the United States the decline has been lower, with a period of moderate increase during the 1980s. As a result of long-term trends, the male participation rate that has been higher in the EU until the beginning of the 1980s, became lower in the following period.

The increase in female participation has taken place since the very beginning of the series in the United States and has also been steeper, while the rate has stayed constant during the 1960s in Europe. Only during the second half of the 1990s, does the difference between the two economies begin to diminish modestly due to a decreasing pace in the United States, where the female participation rate approached the male one. Nonetheless, the difference of the two female rates is still above ten points at the end of the century.

Figure 2.9 also shows that in both systems there has been a convergence of male and female rates as evidence of long-term diminishing gender differences both in the United States and the EU. This convergence has been quicker in Europe.

A rough measure of well-being can be given by the average relation between income and working time: the higher both income and free time, the higher the well-being. (We use average per capita income of employees at PPP expressed in US dollars, according to OECD, *National Accounts: Volume 1. Main Aggregates*, various years.) Although time series data are not available, we report data collected by Lee and Przeworski (1992) which refer to the relation between income and free time in different countries between the end of the 1970s and the beginning of the 1980s, and estimate free time as the difference between 3,000 conventional hours and the actual average number of hours worked in a year in a given country. Data depict a relatively homogeneous situation within Europe in comparison with the United States and Japan (Figure 2.10).

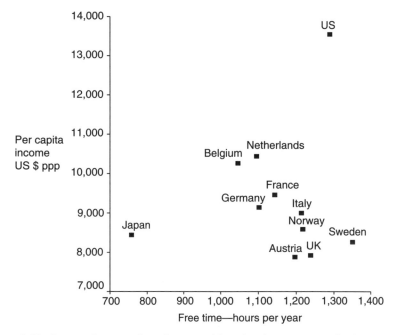

Figure 2.10. Average income of employees and free time in some countries (1976–85)

Source: Lee and Przeworski (1992)

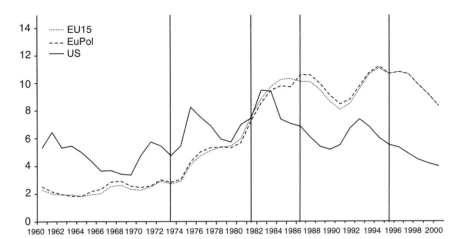

Figure 2.11. Unemployment rate—total (1960–2000): as percentage of the labor force

Source: Adapted from OECD, *Statistical Compendium*

The figure shows that in the European countries income levels are more similar to Japan and the availability of free time is more similar to the United States. Moreover, in that period the United States showed high average levels of income and free time while Japan was lower in both dimensions.

An important indicator of economic performance that has direct and profound social implications is unemployment. Figure 2.11 shows again that as a whole the European economy performs better than the American one during the first part of the time series, while since the beginning of the 1980s the US rate of unemployment has always been lower.

Unemployment rates for the United States show the highest level in the years of the second oil shock. Moreover, the trend is affected by a cyclical course. All in all the level at the beginning of the series is similar to that at the end, after forty years.

In the EU, on the contrary, the rate has dramatically increased from a level well below the American one at the beginning of the 1960s to the highest level during the second half of the 1990s. As a result, the official unemployment rate quadrupled during the entire period. Another specificity of the EU trend is the absence of a cyclical trend, especially in the first period but also in the second one, when the EU performance has been worst. This means more specifically that since the 1970s increasing unemployment, which could not be absorbed during the following recovery, has followed the economic slowdowns. This is very visible during the cycle at the end of the 1970s, but also in the two subsequent cycles of the following decades. In the literature, this trend has been interpreted as an evidence of the rigidity of the Continental labor market. Europe kept a low rate until the first oil shock; at the beginning of the 1980s the advantage with the United States was lost, and since the end of the 1980s the trend of the two cases has been more correlated, but still unfavorable for the EU. The second part of the 1990s also evidences a decline in unemployment for both economies.

The comparison of male and female unemployment rates shows that the difference between the two economies is mainly due to the female component, because of a greater difficulty for women to enter and to stay in the EU labor market. This gender disadvantage, which is dramatically high in some European countries, has been interpreted as a consequence of the segmented structure of some national labor markets (Rubery, Smith, and Fagan 1999) and of specific welfare regimes (Esping-Andersen 1990). In the United States, the male and female curves show similar shape and level over the entire period. More specifically, the female unemployment rate is moderately higher until the end of the 1970s and becomes lower during the following twenty years. At the beginning of the new century, the two rates are substantially similar. In the EU, not only has the female unemployment rate been constantly higher than the male one, but the female disadvantage also grew over time, especially during the decade following the first oil shock. Again, we have a diverging trend in those characteristics that are more related to the welfare state regimes and the functioning of the labor market.

Another important difference lies in the role played by self-employment in the two systems. The increasing role of self-employment as a specific feature of post-Fordist economies has been recently stressed (OECD 2000). Since the end of the nineteenth century, scale economies have contributed to the diffusion of large corporations, to increase the size of big business, and to the expenses of small business and self-employment, especially in the United States (Chandler 1990). In the most advanced economies, this trend continued until the mid-1970s, bringing a decline in self-employment especially in agriculture. Some authors state that since the beginning of the 1980s this historical decline has stopped due to the different functional needs of post-Fordist economies and the increase of service economy (Piore and Sabel 1984; Light and Rosenstein 1995; Crouch, 2001).

Available data show on the contrary that the share of self-employment on total employment has been consistently declining in both economies, but the European percentage has always been higher, about two times that of the United States. The average value results from very different situations in the European member countries, as is evident from the difference between the dotted and dashed lines of Figure 2.12. The European rate of self-employed declined in 1973 due to the entrance of the UK, but was again pushed up by the inclusion of Greece in 1981 and Spain and Portugal in 1986.

To enrich the picture of the labor market, we have used data on union membership for both economies (Ebbinghaus and Visser 2000 and OECD). Figure 2.13 shows that at the beginning of the 1960s the two rates were rather similar, with a moderate diverging tendency during the decade. During the 1970s the divergence has widened, showing quicker trends of decline in the United States and of increase in Europe, where the considerable increase in 1973 is due to the entrance of the UK into the Union. The highest rate was reached in Europe at the end of the 1970s. Some authors have interpreted this increase, together with an increasing

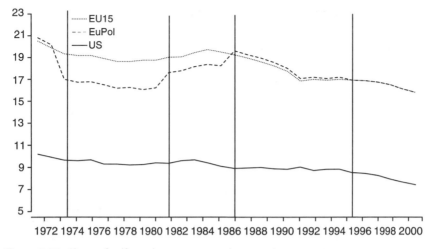

Figure 2.12. Share of self-employment on total occupation

Source: Adapted from OECD

role of the state (see Figure 2.6), as evidence of the diffusion of neocorporatist regimes in many European countries (Lehmbruch and Schmitter 1979) and as a response to the problem of stagflation that affected most European countries after the first oil shock of the mid-1970s (Cameron 1984; Bruno and Sachs 1985). As a combined result, the highest difference between the two systems was reached during the mid-1980s, when the membership rate was less than 19 percent in the United States and almost 35 percent in the fifteen European countries. During the following years both trends have been declining, but Europe has constantly kept a difference of at least fifteen points more than the United States.

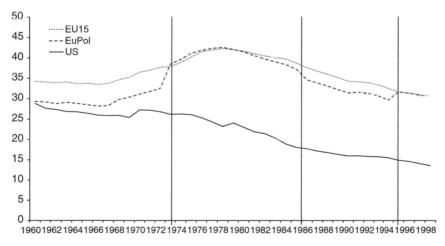

Figure 2.13. Union members (1960–98): as percentage of total employees

Source: Ebbinghaus and Visser (2000)

2.4. **The role of the state in the economy**

So far we have discussed evidence about the structure of the economy and the labor market, but we could not avoid considering the state as an important actor that affects the economic performance of the two systems.

The role of the state in the economy has been seen as one of the main features that distinguishes the two models of capitalism proposed by the literature (Soskice 1989; Esping-Andersen 1999). The market-driven model, represented by the United States, implies a lower rate of taxation as well as public expenses. This model has been followed by Great Britain during the past two decades of the century. Nevertheless, in spite of a notable heterogeneity among the European national economies in state involvement, the weight of Germany, Italy, and France in the overall picture contributes to depict a situation in which the role of nation-states is heavier in Europe than in the United States, in terms of taxation and public expense.

Figure 2.14 gives the trend of total taxation revenues for the two economies. We use the figures from the OECD database that take into account not only central government incomes but also local government. In order to get the overall picture for the EU, the different taxation systems at country level have been weighted according to the national GDP. While in the United States the overall taxation burden has been rather stable except for the second half of the 1960s and a moderate increase during the past twenty years of the century, European society shows not only a higher level but also a constant increase over the entire period. At the end of the century, the European average taxation burden is around 42 percent of GDP, while in the United States it is less than 30 percent.

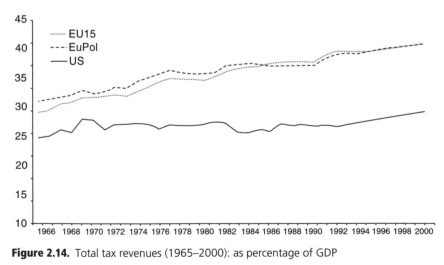

Figure 2.14. Total tax revenues (1965–2000): as percentage of GDP

Sources: OECD, Financial and Fiscal Affairs Database, *Statistical Compendium* 2002

Also the composition of taxation has been different. In the European case taxes on goods and services and social security contributions have had a higher share on total revenues in the public sector, while taxation on property, profits, and capital gain plays a larger role in the United States.

The economic theory suggests a correlation between higher taxation on work and goods on one side and higher unemployment and lower household consumption on the other. In the United States lower taxation on work brings higher-employment levels, while less taxation on goods and services brings lower saving rates by households. This is consistent with the figures commented on in the following paragraph.

In both systems, the burden of taxation as a percentage of GDP has increased rather constantly over the period, but the pace of this trend has been different. While in the EU the total tax revenues have increased from around 30 percent in the mid-1960s to 40 percent at the end of the century, in the United States it has shifted from 25 percent to only 28 percent. Important differences are also visible in the composition of taxation. While the burden of taxation on property, capital gains, and income is similar in the two systems, the difference is at the level of goods and services (indirect taxation) which is more than double in Europe. The same is true at the level of social security contributions and taxes on payroll and workforce, which is double in Europe. The difference in the composition of taxation between the EU and the United States has remained substantially stable over the period, with the only exception being social security contributions which increased more in the United States until the beginning of the 1990s and then diminished. A decrease in social security contributions is also visible only during the last years of the century in the EU.

Expensive social security contributions in Europe correspond to higher transfers to workers and their families, as Figure 2.15 shows. In the EU, social security transfers grew from 10 percent of GDP in 1960 to 17 percent in the mid-1980s for the fifteen members; then the trend was lateral. In the United States, the increase has been higher, starting from 5 percent in 1960 up to 12 percent in the 1990s. In both systems, social security transfers have clearly shown an anti-cyclical course since the 1970s. They increased by more than two points of GDP during the mid-1970s as a consequence of the economic slowdown following the first oil shock. A similar trend is also visible at the beginning of the 1990s, after the first Iraq war.

Figure 2.16 shows a clear difference between most EU members and the United States in the combined effects of market mechanisms of earning distribution and state redistribution through taxation and transfers. Data have been taken from Iversen and Soskice (2005) who has computed an index of poverty reduction as the percentage of poverty rate (percentage of families with income below 50% of the median) from before to after taxes and transfers. The inequality ratio is computed between the earnings of a worker in the top decile of the earnings distribution and the earnings of a worker with a median income.

While the United States is plotted apart in the area of high inequality and low poverty reduction through income redistribution, the European countries are plotted in a rather homogeneous area of less inequality and higher redistribution.

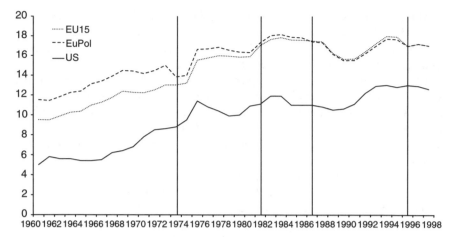

Figure 2.15. Social security transfers (1960–98): as percentage of GDP

Source: Adaptation and integration from Armingeon, Beyeler, and Denegale (2002)

They form two clusters consisting of Northern Europe on one side, and Italy, Germany, the UK, and France on the other. These countries are put in a line of increasing inequality and intermediate redistribution efficacy. Specifically the UK, which is considered as an example of the market-driven model, takes a position which is closer to the other European countries and far from that of the United States.

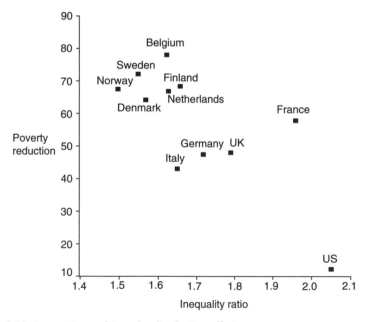

Figure 2.16. Income inequality and redistribution effects

Source: Adaptation form Iversen and Soskice (2005) on Luxembourg Income Study and OECD

Although the EU does not have a unified welfare system and each state has developed different social policies, according to their traditions and different government orientations, converging evidences reported in this chapter show a clear difference between the two systems. The US welfare model has been called residual or liberal welfare (Esping-Andersen 1990), while the EU as an average shows a model based on a greater centrality of state intervention and social expenditure.

The American welfare system is based on a political commitment to minimize state intervention, to individualize risks, and to promote market solutions, both in private insurance schemes and in the supply of social services. Its residualism resides in the fact that to address market failures in the field of social risks, only the most serious are selected and faced by state intervention, while minor or more general risks are confronted through a self-reliant attitude in the market.

In spite of important differences across countries, postwar Europe has devised welfare regimes based on the concept of solidarity, influenced by the Catholic doctrine, and on the concept of equal rights, influenced by socialist regimes. Even in a country like Britain, where a liberal welfare regime has been introduced since the reforms of the conservative governments at the beginning of the 1980s, the presence of a previous tradition and of a rooted unionism gave a specificity in the application of the liberal model. Also the familistic version of welfare (Esping-Andersen 1999), which is more typical of southern European countries, gives a more central role to the state expenditure in supplying transfers to households.

This is why social security transfers as a percentage of GDP have always been higher in the EU than in the United States. Nevertheless, Figure 2.15 shows also that this percentage has been increasing in both systems and that the difference between them has been decreasing in the longer term.

A look inside the composition of social security transfers shows that benefit expenditure for pensions has been most of the total in the United States and only about a half in the EU, but also the trends have been different. The proportion has been steadier in Europe and affected by a substantial decrease in the United States. This decrease has been in favor of other kinds of expenses, namely those for sickness and maternity that grew from a few percentage points to about 30 percent in the mid-1980s and then declined.

Also benefit expenditures on unemployment have been significantly different. In the United States, the proportion has been decreasing, having reached its apex of more than 27 percent at the beginning of the 1960s. In the EU, it has always been proportionally lower and grew progressively after the first oil shock in the mid-1970s, until its highest level of almost 10 percent in the 1980s.

2.5. **Household consumption and savings**

This section is devoted to the comparison of the economic behavior of households and their changes over the last forty years of the century. Figure 2.17 shows a U-shaped consumption rate, computed as a percentage of households' disposable

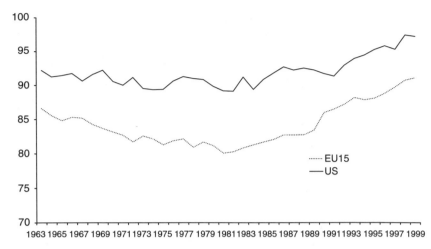

Figure 2.17. Consumption rate (1963–2000): household consumption as percentage of household disposable income

Source: OECD, *Statistical Compendium* 2003

income. In both economies the consumption rate decreased moderately during the 1960s and 1970s in favor of an increasing saving rate.

In the last twenty years of the century both trends inverted their course and the saving rate declined sharply. European households halved their rate of saving from almost 20 percent to less than 10 percent, while in the United States the decline was even more dramatic: from the highest level of around 10 percent in 1983, it dropped to 3 percent in 2000. Although the European rate is the average of very different situations at country level, a higher saving propensity seems to be a feature of these economies, compared with the United States.

A lower saving rate of American households is coherent with the data concerning the diffusion of home ownership. Home ownership has always been more widespread in the United States and rather stable at around 65 percent of households during the entire forty-year period. Only in the first years of the new century has the home ownership rate increased to 68 percent, taking advantage of unusual favorable interest rates (US Census Bureau, www.census.gov), while in the European countries it has been constantly increasing, from 40 percent as an average in 1960 to 67 percent at the beginning of the 1990s. The only moderate decline was due to the inclusion of East Germany into the EU. Therefore this original difference across the Atlantic has diminished over time.

To compare the standard of living, we have also collected some comparable figures on the diffusion of durable goods such as television sets and vehicles. The following figures give their density over 1,000 people.

As far as the diffusion of television sets is concerned (Figure 2.18), the two trends have been increasing during the period, but both the level and the pace have been higher in the United States. At the end of the century in the United States, households could enjoy eight television sets for every ten people, while

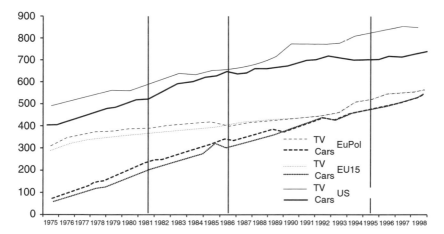

Figure 2.18. Diffusion of television sets and motor vehicles: index number over 1,000 people

Source: World Bank, *Development Indicators*, 2000

in the EU the rate was a bit more than one out of two. The picture shows that the entrance of Spain and Portugal has produced a decrease in the overall rate in the EU. The situation is partially different for motor vehicles. While the trend in the United States reached an apex at the beginning of the 1990s, in Europe it has been constantly increasing, so that the difference between the two economies has diminished.

No other durable good has a higher density in the United States due to a higher income per capita and a higher consumption rate. As is shown in Table 2.1— which is not complete for Europe, due to the lack of some national economies— Europeans seem more fond of mobile phones, while in the United States this device is not so fashionable. On the contrary, the household diffusion of personal computers with Internet access—which is very uneven across Europe, following a North–South divide—is again higher in the United States compared with the EU average.

2.6. **An increasing homogeneity of European Union members into an integrated economy?**

So far we have mainly compared a couple of trends over time assuming that not only the United States but also the EU are distinctive and consistent economic systems. As discussed in other chapters, the idea that the EU is in a progressive, process of unification into a single society, not only a persisting collection of separated countries, is a hypothesis that has to be backed up by empirical evidence.

This section wants to add integration and an insight to the data. The aim is to concentrate the analysis on the distributions around the average values

Table 2.1. Diffusion rate of internet and mobile phones in households in 2002

Country	Internet rate	Mobile rate
Sweden	63	82
Denmark	56	72
Netherlands	53	75
Finland	51	83
Germany	47	67
UK	46	80
Austria	41	63
Italy	36	91
France	28	62
Spain	25	78
Portugal	25	
United States (2001)	50	49

Sources: IDATE taken from CREDOC 2004 and US Census Bureau (www.census.gov)

of the most important trends in order to show the degree of homogeneity within the EU countries and to compare it with that within the American states. This exercise permits to analyze a set of hypotheses concerning the progressive homogeneity of the European countries as a result of the unification process in terms of economic integration and political and cultural convergence.

The two sets of cases are not easily comparable because of their different size. Nevertheless, we try to give more insight into the question is it possible to interpret the EU as a single federation of states with an increasing identity and homogeneity, in spite of its progressive enlargement, as it was for the formation of the United States during the nineteenth century? The following idea is tested across a secondary analysis of our indicators: the United States is a nation and therefore is supposed to be rather homogeneous in terms of economy, culture, policies, and lifestyle, while the EU is nothing more than a system of unified states, as Flora (2000) states in reference to its history before unification.

In line with the research tradition of the CCSC Group, we think that this issue can be correctly addressed only with a comparative perspective, that is confronting a set of indicators. We start from the concept of homogeneity and treat it as a trend in itself. For different indicators that have been presented as an average value in the previous sections, we have computed the yearly coefficient of variation in order to ascertain if there is convergence or divergence over time, both within European countries and within American states.

The study is limited to some trends, because of the partial availability of time series about all the units of analysis. Therefore, the results can give only some suggestions of internal convergence or divergence and by no means can be generalized to other dimensions of the two societies. Moreover, the results of this exercise can give some evidence of an increasing or decreasing homogeneity within each economic system, but cannot be compared across the two systems because of their different sizes. While for the United States we consider

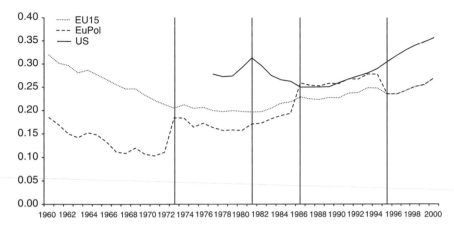

Figure 2.19. GDP per capita (1960–2000): coefficient of variation

all the fifty-one states, the analysis of the EU is limited to the fifteen states that formed the Union until May 2004. There is no doubt that the enlargement has produced an increase in internal economic diversity that in many ways represents a challenge for the economic integration of the Union. Our hypothesis is that the entrance of uneven economies activates mechanisms and policies aimed at reducing divergent features like unemployment and GDP per capita in the long run.

The coefficient of variation of some indicators is plotted and compared as a percentage of the average. The higher the line, the more heterogeneous the unities are, and vice versa. As in the previous sections, each plot shows three lines: a solid line for the United States, a dash line, labeled EuPol, for the EU member-states, and dotted line, labeled EU15, for the set of fifteen countries during the entire period.

Figure 2.19 shows the trend of the coefficient of variation in income per capita at constant prices. Although the series for the United States is not complete for the entire period, data show that: (*a*) there has been an increasing homogeneity during the 1960s and the 1970s within the European countries, (*b*) increasing heterogeneity characterized both the United States and the EU in the following period. These trends are coherent with the idea that post-Fordist economies are more unequal due to the effects of globalization (Wade 2001).

Moreover, the comparison between the lines of EU15 and EuPol gives evidence of the fact that the new countries joining the EU have increased the internal variance, but not in the case of the entrance of Austria, Finland, and Sweden in 1995. The increase in inequality was particularly high with the entrance of the UK, Denmark, and Ireland in 1973, but the coefficient of variation diminished slightly in the following years. All in all, the coefficient has been constantly higher between the American states than the European ones.

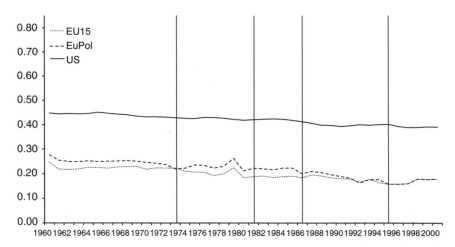

Figure 2.20. Manufacturing employment (1960–2000): coefficient of variation

Another interesting issue concerns the transformation of the economic structure. In Figure 2.20, we use the percentage of employment in the manufacturing
sector over total employment (excluding employment in agriculture). This indicator, originally computed from Kenworthy (1999), takes into account the transformation of the economies at country or state level toward a more industrial structure of employment in Europe during the 1960s and the 1970s. At
the same time, this indicator can grasp the postindustrial trend that affected
the American states and the European countries after the first oil shock of the
mid-1970s.

The coefficient of variation can therefore be interpreted as a measure of the heterogeneity in the sequence of economic transformation. Leaving apart the fact that
in this case the European society also shows lower values of the coefficient—about
half that of the United States—both societies show an increasing homogeneity
across the period. In fact, the difference in the share of manufacturing employment has been decreasing in all the European countries as well as the American
states.

Figure 2.21 is related to the analysis of the heterogeneity in the welfare
regimes and shows the differences in taxation burdens across American states
and European countries. To make the comparison more correct, in the case of the
United States transfers from the federal government also are taken into account.
Figure 2.21 shows that the entrance of the European countries in the Union has
fostered a reduction in the differences between tax burdens across countries, as
shown by the convergence between the dotted (EU15) and the dash lines (political
Europe). On the other side, since the second half of the 1970s, the differences
within the United States have been increasing.

From the analysis we can also state that the EU is less homogeneous
with regard to a series of indicators concerning labor markets. This is
true for unemployment levels, although the coefficient of variation has

Figure 2.21. Total tax revenue as % of GDP (1965–99): coefficient of variation

decreased over time, especially during the 1970s since when it has remained rather steady (Figure 2.22). Although the series for the United States begins only in the mid-1970s, the picture shows clearly that the differences in unemployment rates have always been less than a half of those within the EU.

For example, for the year 2000 the European coefficient of variation is the result of differences in unemployment that range from 1.9 percent in Luxembourg to 13.9 percent in Spain, while for the United States the differences range from 6.7 in Alaska to 2.2 in Virginia and Connecticut.

In spite of a smaller number of cases in the European group of countries, also the differences in the participation rate are higher in Europe than in the

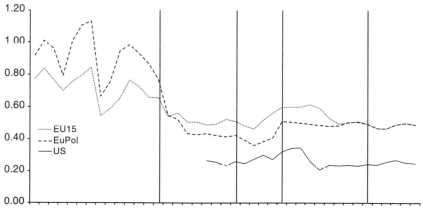

Figure 2.22. Unemployment rate (1960–2000): coefficient of variation

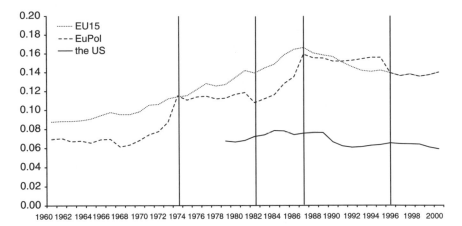

Figure 2.23. Employment rate (1960–2000): coefficient of variation

United States, where the coefficient of variation is also more stable over time. Within Europe the entire period has been characterized by increasing differences during the 1960s and the 1970s. The entrance of Great Britain into the EU has brought a jump in heterogeneity due to its higher activity rate compared with the European average. During the 1980s and part of the 1990s the differences have been decreasing, while the beginning of the new century has brought the index to again invert its direction. In 1960, the highest participation rate was in Sweden and the lowest in the Netherlands, while in 2000 Luxembourg shows the highest level with 60.82 percent and Italy the lowest with 41.48 percent, followed by Greece and Belgium. In the United States, the highest and lowest rates were respectively those of Nevada (51.99) and of West Virginia in 1978, while Minnesota (57.95) and Kansas (46.19) took the two extremes in 2000.

The analysis of the coefficient of variation for employment rates draws similar considerations. The EU has always been more heterogeneous than the United States and the heterogeneity was growing until the entrance of Spain and Portugal in 1986. From then on the differences between countries have diminished, but have always kept above the US level. The entrance of Austria, Finland, and Sweden in 1995 has helped diminish the differences (Figure 2.23).

2.7. The challenge of globalization to capitalist diversity within the EU and between the EU and the United States

The trends analyzed in the previous sections over a period of forty years show that both the United States and EU economies are far from being close to the two models of capitalism that have been proposed to interpret their differences.

While this empirical result is not surprising in the case of the EU, because of the long-standing cohabitation of different types of capitalism within its member-states, even in the case of the United States it cannot be taken for granted.

In the US economy, we have seen that the role of the state is still central and in the long run has been increasing in terms of taxation, expenditure, and even social security transfers. We have pointed out that social security transfers have been diminishing as a percentage of GDP in both systems only in the last years of the century. In the long term, the only indicator of diminishing state intervention in the United States is the number of civil servants which has been decreasing since the mid-1970s. As an average, the EU countries followed this trend only a decade later. As a consequence, we can say that even the US economy does not match the pure market-driven model.

The picture of the EU comes out as an average of dissimilarities that have been depicted as the 'Rhine model'—inspired by the German case, the north European welfare system, the Scandinavian countries, the Mediterranean or familistic variant of the welfare state, which fits the southern countries of catholic tradition, but also the market-driven model of the UK. However, for the following reasons the role of the state in the EU economy appears more central: the fact that all three Continental models of welfare state in different ways imply more public expenditure and taxation than in the 'market-driven' model; the relative weight of the German economy within the EU, especially after unification; the fact that although a program of privatizations and liberalization of the economy was launched in the UK in 1979—before the introduction of a similar model in the United States—the remnants of the previous system have exerted their effects for a long period in the time series of some indicators.

Beyond the differences between the two systems that can be interpreted in terms of the two consistent models of capitalism, trends show constant differences in the structure of the productive system, in the functioning of the labor market, and in consumption patterns of households. The US economy has been consistently more centered on services than the EU one, but the service sector has gained progressive importance in both systems. A more regulated labor market in the EU and a stronger presence of trade unions have brought lower participation rates, for both males and females, and a constant higher proportion of self-employed, but the performance in terms of unemployment has not always been in favor of the United States. Data show that the EU had lower unemployment rates during the Fordist period, while a better performance in the United States has been typical of the post-Fordist phase. Households in the United States have always shown lower propensity to save, in spite of a less widespread public welfare system, and have been more prone to the consumption of durable goods.

The process of globalization is often considered as a condition that can affect national economies and induce them to respond to common opportunities and risks. As long as they face the same kind of challenges coming from increasingly unified markets of capital, goods, and labor force—it has been hypothesized by Lindert and Williamson (2003)—nation-states should be more and more subject to similar policy choices and convergent trends. On the other side, increasing global competition could also deepen the divide between winners and losers (Wade 2001).

The evidence collected in Section 2.6 shows persisting but diminishing differences within the EU countries, although the effectiveness of EU policies aimed at reducing the economic development gap between member-states has been continually challenged by the progressive integration of new country members. Recently with the entrance of Eastern European countries, the internal heterogeneity has increased again in terms of per capita GDP, unemployment, and average productivity of national economies. This heterogeneity, together with the differentiated capacity to face the challenges of global competition in different EU countries, has favored the renewal of euroskepticism that can in turn slow down the process of social and political integration. Some indicators also show higher interstate inequality in the United States than in the EU.

The Luxembourg income study shows that personal income inequality in the 1990s has been considerably higher within the United States than within the EU, while the redistribution effects have been considerably lower. This has contributed to keep the two models of capitalism well differentiated in spite of globalization. On the contrary, a set of common trends (diminishing importance of employment in industry, decreasing proportion of self employment, decreasing propensity to save, decreasing union membership, and increasing female participation in the labor market) seem more related to the process of progressive modernization rather than globalization (Martinelli 2005).

3 Inequality

Paul W. Kingston and Laura M. Holian

Matters of inequality go to the very heart of the argument for American exceptionalism. In much American public lore and some scholarly arguments America is above all the land of equality. Tocqueville, early on, famously noted the spirit of equality that permeated American life. Since then, stories of rags to riches have been commonly invoked, emblematic of the belief that in America social origins have little impact on economic achievements—and that the impact of individual talent and hard work is decisive. Even if the disparities between the successful and unsuccessful can be stark, this is often viewed as the price to be paid for having a dynamic system that generates great aggregate wealth and wide opportunities for individual success. This egalitarianism presumably flowed from America's origins as the 'first new nation', unshackled by the weight of a feudal past with rigid hierarchies and social distinctions (Lipset 1979a).

The counterpoint here is 'Europe', an often-amorphous reference that at most includes selective attention to a few of the larger European nations, and certainly predates the formation of the EU. The case for American exceptionalism rests on the presumption that European societies have been structured by class and that, in contrast, American society has always been relatively classless, despite its evident inequalities in material conditions (e.g. Hartz 1964).

The main counterargument is that the 'logic of industrialism' generates uniformity in social arrangements in all advanced societies, particularly their stratification systems. Presumably, a relentless pressure to rationalize the productive process leads to similar basic patterns in the division of labor and to a common commitment to rewarding people for their productive talents, not their background (e.g. Treiman 1970). In this view the common trajectory, on both sides of the Atlantic, is toward a more open society. Recently, however, some analysts have argued that an emerging 'European model' has become more egalitarian than the United States, part of a larger shift to postindustrial/postmaterialist values and institutions (e.g. Rifkin 2004).

Yet, for all the public resonance of these competing views, comparative stratification research makes clear that there is not a single, overriding difference: an inegalitarian Europe vs. an egalitarian United States—or the reverse. Indeed, in important respects the United States is exceptional in its distinctly strong *inequality*, and in other respects it is difficult to distinguish Europe and the United States. We must separate cultural myths and political hopes from empirical fact—and, moreover, recognize that many facts are relevant.

Conceptually, inequality has multiple dimensions. Therefore, when we want to analyze whether the United States and Europe have distinctive stratification systems (and whether European nations are alike), we must first ask: Inequalities of what? That question has numerous good answers, each related to significant and distinct features of society—for instance, how equally is the total 'economic pie' divided up, and how equally are chances of success distributed? Our comparison would be incomplete and misleading if we focused on just one dimension of inequality. As we will detail, depending on the dimension considered, American stratification is both distinctly different from the European pattern and remarkably similar to it. And, by the same token, the member nations of Europe more or less share a common pattern depending on the analytical focus.

To organize this discussion, we make a preliminary distinction between *equality of results* (conditions) and *equality of opportunity*. This is a common analytical distinction that can be briefly explained. When we talk about equality of results, we are simply referring to the dispersion of living conditions—that is, the extent to which people (or households/families) get different-sized slices of the economic pie. In this light, it does not matter why the slices are bigger or smaller than others; the focus is just on the brute fact of the distributional outcomes. It is essentially a static concern, usually measured as an annual outcome, though measures of dispersion over longer periods, even lifetimes, are possible. This is the concern of Section 3.1.

When we talk about equality of opportunity, we refer to chances of getting ahead or falling behind. In this perspective, we can consider intergenerational mobility—for example, the chances that the offspring of rich families will become rich themselves vs. the chances that the offspring of poor families will become rich. The underlying notion is that equality of opportunity means that all individuals' chances of attaining desirable social positions are independent of their social origins. At the most basic level this is a matter of detailing the advantages of privileged origins, but the analysis can be elaborated to include differential chances of acquiring status-enhancing training and credentials—and to detail the advantages of family origins that accrue among equally well-qualified people. With this elaboration the analysis gets at why inequality exists. This dimension of inequality is the focus of Section 3.2.

At the outset we should emphasize that neither dimension of inequality is inherently more important than the other, though analysts on the left often give greater attention to inequality of condition while analysts on the right tend to emphasize opportunities for mobility. In our view each has important social consequences, crucially marking the fundamental nature of a society. Moreover, they do not necessarily go hand in hand. It is possible that a society distributes very unequal pieces of the economic pie while creating equal chances for everyone to get a big piece, as some celebrators of the American Dream suggest. However, as we will see, Americans cannot take solace in notably greater equality of opportunity as compensation for greater inequality of results. Yet it is also true that the greater equality of condition in Europe does not routinely translate into greater equality of opportunity. Furthermore, as we discuss in Section 3.3, the existence of inequalities per se does not necessarily indicate the existence of ongoing *class* divisions.

In Section 3.4, we consider the place of women in the stratification system. In important respects, it is misleading to talk about *the* stratification system as some genderless phenomenon. If there is any one fact established by comparative stratification research, it is that occupational distributions are gendered—and that women are thereby disfavored in the distribution of economic rewards. This concern is especially pertinent for our comparative analysis of change because in both Europe and the United States the economic role of women has changed so dramatically since 1960.

As our brief introduction suggests, we take a broad but still limited look at European and American stratification systems. We emphasize the concrete matters of money and jobs. No apologies for that—so much of collective and individual life pivots on material conditions. Yet we should note that we exclude such important dimensions of stratification as *social equality*, the manner in which people interact (Tocqueville's focus). We also ignore the distribution of prestige and honor. These dimensions relate to the subjective experiences of inequalities, all socially significant but also difficult to capture in comparative indicators.

Even with our focus on material conditions, we should caution that our analysis is necessarily less than complete. We compare the United States to the fifteen EU nations that were members before the recent expansion. 'Europe' is thus the population-adjusted average for these fifteen countries on such matters as the GINI index. This restriction seems sensible because of (*a*) the greater availability of comparable data for these countries than the full set in the current European Union, and (*b*) the greater comparability of this 'Europe' and the United States in terms of overall level of economic development. However, even with this restriction, for some matters we will have to rely on limited trend analysis or even one-time studies. On other matters we will have to consider 'Europe' in light of an even more limited roster of nations. Nevertheless, while it is appropriate for us to be cautious in interpreting the available data, we are also convinced that important features of the European and American stratification systems can be meaningfully compared.

3.1. **Slices of the pie**

In terms of equality of results, Europe and the United States now differ sharply. The differences are so stark that it is appropriate to talk of two distinct social models, but as we will detail, that has not always been the case.

Standard measures of income dispersion make this point clear. While statisticians rightly note that all such measures emphasize some parts of the distribution over others, the most commonly used measure is the GINI index, which ranges from 0 (perfect equality) to 1. As Table 3.1 indicates, the GINI (multiplied here by 100) for the United States in 2000 was 40. At this time, the population-weighted average for the fifteen EU countries was 34. Within Europe, the most egalitarian

Table 3.1. GINI coefficients for Europe and the United States, 1960–2000

Country	Year closest to 1960	GINI coefficient 1960	Year closest to 1970	GINI coefficient 1970	Year closest to 1980	GINI coefficient 1980	Year closest to 1990	GINI coefficient 1990	Year closest to 2000	GINI coefficient 2000
Austria	—	—	1970	29.30	1981	31.40	1991	26.30	1997	30.35
Belgium	—	—	1969	36.37	1979	28.25	1988	25.70	1997	26.92
Denmark	1961	38.00	1968	43.86	1980	41.27	1990	32.81	1995	36.00
Finland	1962	46.00	1971	31.00	1980	30.86	1990	25.50	2000	26.89
France	1962	50.00	1970	41.40	1979	40.30	1990	46.10	1995	32.70
Germany	1960	49.00	1970	39.20	1980	36.60	1990	26.00	1997	32.88
Greece	1960	41.08	1970	45.32	1981	33.29	1988	37.67	1993	32.70
Ireland	—	—	1973	38.69	1980	35.65	1987	34.60	1996	35.62
Italy	1967	40.00	1970	38.00	1980	34.29	1991	32.90	2000	35.87
Luxembourg	—	—	—	—	1985	26.77	1991	26.79	2000	30.24
The Netherlands	1962	44.35	1973	34.43	1981	28.30	1990	32.20	1999	30.77
Portugal	—	—	1973	40.58	1980	33.05	1990	32.00	1995	35.60
Spain	1965	38.93	1973	37.11	1980	34.52	1990	32.43	1994	35.00
Sweden	1960	54.30	1970	38.72	1980	32.44	1990	27.15	2000	27.32
UK	1960	40.00	1970	25.50	1980	25.30	1990	33.70	1999	37.06
EU[a]	1960s	44.45	1970s	36.60	1980s	33.80	1990s	33.05	2000	33.81
United States	1960	38.65	1970	36.40	1980	36.50	1990	39.60	2000	40.19
EU c.v.[b]	—	0.09		0.07		0.07		0.07		0.07
United States c.v.	—	—		0.07		0.05		0.06		0.06

[a]population adjusted.
[b]c.v. for the 50 states.

Source: UNU/WIDER World Income Inequality Database, version 2.0 beta, December 3, 2004. <http://www.wider.unu.edu/wiid/wiid.htm>

nations are Sweden, Belgium, and Finland. On the other extreme within Europe, the UK is the least egalitarian.

Note that in 2000 *every* single European nation was more egalitarian than the United States. In fact, every European nation was more equalitarian than every state within the United States. In short, the distinctiveness of Europe and the United States is established by the differences in average GINI coefficients *and* the complete absence of any overlap in the range of scores.

Yet, to establish whether there is a common European pattern, we should also consider the range within Europe. As we suggested, European nations are hardly alike: the range has been about 10, somewhat greater than the difference between the EU and US averages in recent years. The coefficient of variation for Europe is 0.07. By comparison, the range in the United States across the states is the same, and the coefficient of variation is also similar, 0.06. Here is a simple translation of these statistics: the European states are not notably more divergent in their inequality than are the American states.

While discussion of GINI coefficients is routine among analysts of inequality, they do not convey an intuitive sense of the actual distribution of income. Table 3.2 makes this matter more concrete by indicating the share of the pie that goes to each quintile (and the top 10th) in the income distribution. Thus we see that in the United States the bottom fifth of households takes home 5 percent of all income, while the top fifth takes home 46 percent of the total. As a simple matter of division (see last column), this means that the top fifth gets 9.4 times more income than the lowest fifth. In contrast, the European average is 7.3 percent for the lowest fifth and 40.3 percent for the top fifth—a ratio of 5.5, 58.5 percent of the American ratio. All these numerical divisions indicate that in relative terms the gap between the top and bottom is much larger in the United States than Europe, just as the GINI coefficients also indicated. Furthermore, in recent years in no European nation did the bottom quintile take home as little of the economic pie as their American counterparts, nor did the top quintile in any European nation take home as much of the pie as equally favored Americans.

Let us emphasize, however, that Europe was not always so distinctly egalitarian compared to the United States (see Table 3.1 again). From 1960 to 1970, both Europe and the United States became more egalitarian, so that by 1970 they had almost identical levels of inequality. From that date the general trend in Europe was toward greater equality. By contrast, in the United States a slight decrease in inequality through the 1960s and 1970s was followed by a notable increase in inequality. At the turn of the century, the difference between the United States and Europe had never been greater than in the postwar years.

At the end of this period, however, Europe was not distinctly more 'unified' in its level of inequality than previously. The coefficient of variation stayed constant in these decades. Furthermore, the coefficient of variation for the United States was essentially static throughout these years, lower than the European coefficient.

The fact that this fundamental difference in equality emerged over a relatively short period is remarkable. It suggests that the current European and US

Table 3.2. Income share in Europe and the United States

Country	Survey year	Share of income or consumption poorest 20%	Share of income or consumption poorest 10%	Share of income or consumption richest 20%	Share of income or consumption richest 10%	Ratio of richest 20% to poorest 20%	Ratio of richest 10% to poorest 10%
Austria	1997	8.1	3.1	38.5	23.5	4.7	7.6
Belgium	1996	8.3	2.9	37.3	22.6	4.5	7.8
Denmark	1997	8.3	2.6	35.8	21.3	4.3	8.1
Finland	2000	9.6	4.0	36.7	22.6	3.8	5.6
France	1995	7.2	2.8	40.2	25.1	5.6	9.1
Germany	2000	8.5	3.2	36.9	22.1	4.3	6.9
Greece	1998	7.1	2.9	43.6	28.5	6.2	10.0
Ireland	1996	7.1	2.8	43.3	27.6	6.1	9.7
Italy	2000	6.5	2.3	42.0	26.8	6.5	11.6
Luxembourg	2000	8.4	3.5	38.9	23.8	4.6	6.8
The Netherlands	1994	7.3	2.8	40.1	25.1	5.5	9.0
Portugal	1997	5.8	2.0	45.9	29.8	8.0	15.0
Spain	1990	7.5	2.8	40.3	25.2	5.4	9.0
Sweden	2000	9.1	3.6	36.6	22.2	4.0	6.2
UK	1999	6.1	2.1	44.0	28.5	7.2	13.8
EU (population-adjusted)	1990s	7.3	2.7	40.3	25.2	5.6	9.7
United States	2000	5.4	1.9	45.8	29.9	8.4	15.9

Source: Human Development Report 2004. <http://hdr.undp.org/statistics/data>

'models' are not reflections of long-standing divergent cultural orientations, but instead reflect relatively recent different social choices and patterns of political mobilization.

3.1.1. THE IMPOVERISHED

The greater inequality in America largely reflects the dismal conditions of its least fortunate members—poverty in the midst of general affluence. Yet until recently it has been difficult to accurately assess poverty in Europe and the United States, simply because comparable data were not available. That task is further complicated by the fact that poverty can be considered in different lights—in absolute and relative terms.

In brief, with an absolute definition analysts consider the number of people below some fixed cutoff point in actual income. This cutoff point is supposedly the dividing line between living poorly and living adequately. The official poverty line in the United States is an example of this approach: with adjustments for family size and location, it is calculated as three times the cost of an 'emergency temporary low budget diet'. By most accounts those who are below this cutoff point have difficult lives. So, with adjustments for inflation, trend lines in an absolute rate like the US calculation indicate changes in the proportion of people who have comparably difficult lives.

On the other hand, data collection agencies in Europe favor a relative approach, measuring the numbers who live substantially less well than the typical citizen in a particular society—often those whose income is less than half the median income. It is often portrayed as an indicator of social exclusion: presumably, individuals cannot really 'belong' to a society if their material comforts fall substantially below the typical level in the society. In a relative perspective, the poverty rate is essentially a measure of dispersion within a particular society. So defined, the 'poor' in one society may live better or worse in absolute terms than the 'poor' in another society—and, accordingly, 'poverty' can be reduced only if inequalities of condition are reduced. Any change in the rate of relative poverty, then, reflects a change in the distribution of income.

So what definition of poverty should we use? There is no right answer. We opt to present both relative and absolute rates because each is revealing—either of the numbers who cannot have typical lives in their own society or the numbers who endure objectively difficult lives. As we will see, high absolute and high relative rates tend to go hand in hand, but they are not necessarily linked. As a parenthetical remark, we note that the European focus on relative measures reflects a larger cultural concern for equality of results. By comparison, the much less prominent attention to relative measures in official US statistics seems to reflect a lesser cultural concern for the dispersion of income.

For the comparison of relative rates, the convention is to compute the number of people who fall below half the median income within a country. Although

Table 3.3. Recent relative poverty rates in Europe and the United States

Country	Year	Percent of population below 40% of median income	Percent of population below 50% of median income	Percent of population below 60% of median income
Austria	1997	4.40	8.00	14.20
Belgium	1997	3.30	8.00	14.40
Denmark	1997	5.70	9.20	17.10
Finland	2000	2.10	5.40	12.40
France	1994	3.40	8.00	14.10
Germany	2000	4.90	8.30	13.10
Greece	—	—	—	—
Ireland	1996	4.00	12.30	21.80
Italy	2000	7.30	12.70	19.90
Luxembourg	2000	1.40	6.00	12.50
The Netherlands	1999	4.60	7.30	12.70
Portugal	—	—	—	—
Spain	1990	5.20	10.10	17.30
Sweden	2000	3.80	6.50	12.30
UK	1999	5.80	12.50	21.30
EU (population adjusted)		5.54	10.65	17.84
United States	2000	10.80	17.00	23.80
EU c.v.		0.08	0.08	0.08

Source: Luxembourg Income Study

commonly used, this cutoff is somewhat arbitrary. Why not 60 percent, as the European Statistical Office has recently recommended? Or why not 40 percent (roughly the relation of the US absolute poverty cutoff to median income in that country)? Obviously the precise size of the 'poor population' can be easily reduced or increased by definitional fiat. But within the normal range of definitions, the relative rank of the United States and all the European countries stays pretty stable. See Table 3.3 that includes three relative definitions of poverty.

As one more preliminary point, we should note that measurement of income is not a clear-cut exercise—What is to be included? The issue is complicated by the difficulty of accounting for many welfare state benefits as well as the impacts of taxation. Analysts from the Luxembourg Income Study (LIS), the state-of-the-art in comparative poverty research, have focused on 'disposable cash and noncash income (that is, money income minus direct income and payroll taxes, and including all cash and near-cash transfers, such as food stamps and cash housing allowances, and refundable tax credits, such as the Earned Income Tax Credit)'. This seems to be a suitably broad definition that allows for cross-national comparisons.

If relative poverty is an indicator of social exclusion, then we can say that a substantially larger proportion of Americans are excluded from their own social mainstream than their European counterparts. At the turn of the century, the income of about 17 percent of Americans fell below half the country's median; the comparable European rate 10.6 percent. Within Europe only Italy (12.7%) and the UK (12.5%) begin to match the American rate. At the other extreme within Europe, only 5.4 percent of the citizens of Finland are poor by this standard.

Using the higher standard of 60 percent of the median, almost a quarter of Americans in 2000 were poor/socially excluded. The European average was lower, 17.8 percent. By this standard, Ireland and the UK just slightly trailed the US rate, while Finland and Sweden had much lower rates.

Using the lower yardstick of 40 percent of the median, American distinctiveness is even more apparent. (Recall that in recent years the official absolute poverty line in the United States—an indicator of objective stress—is about 40% of the median income.) By this standard, 10.8 percent of Americans are removed from the social mainstream; but only 5.5 percent of Europeans are so excluded. Within Europe, again only the rate in Italy began to approach the American rate, and in Luxembourg and Finland the extent of this extreme poverty is minor.

What about changes in relative poverty? The LIS offers a limited perspective on this matter, essentially changes from rates in the late 1970s/early 1980s to the late 1990s (eleven EU countries). Using the 40 percent of median measure, the rate slightly increased in both the United States and Europe. Italy was the outlier, with an almost 5 percent increase. Otherwise the range within Europe was small; four others had slightly higher rates of poverty and six nations had slight decreases.

3.1.2. ABSOLUTE POVERTY

An absolute perspective on poverty also confirms the distinctive plight of the less fortunate in America. Compared to Europeans, a greater proportion of Americans live badly, not just less well than the 'average person' in their own society. Until recently such a statement would have been impossible to make because it is so difficult to 'translate' income figures into a common currency. However, the LIS has used PPP exchange rates (developed by the OECD) to express household incomes in seven EU countries in terms of American dollars, and then calculated the proportions of the population that fell below the official American poverty line. So, in effect, this analysis allows us to answer the question, what proportion of Europeans would be poor if they lived in America? (If anything, this analysis understates the difference between Europe and the United States: it does not account for in-kind benefits, which tend to be relatively high in Europe and thereby inflates European poverty rates.)

In 1994, 13.6 percent of Americans were officially poor. (The rate varies with the business cycle; in the 1990s the rate averaged 12.3%, and has declined slightly in this century.) By comparison, 10 percent of Europeans (seven countries) were poor by American standards. This is so despite the fact that the United States is substantially richer (GDP per capita) than six of these countries. Only Luxembourg is richer.

Only one of the seven European countries in this comparison has a higher absolute rate of poverty than the United States—the UK (15.7%). At the other extreme Luxembourg has virtually abolished absolute poverty; less than 1 percent of its population suffers this fate. Thus the European range in absolute poverty rates is quite large, though the two countries at the extremes (the UK and Luxembourg) may be seen as outliers. The range from France (9.9%) to Finland (4.8%) is much more modest—about 5 percent. For point of comparison, in 2000 the range within the American states was 12 percent (17.6% in Mississippi vs. 5.6% in New Hampshire).

Because there are only seven EU countries in this analysis, we cannot specify the extent to which the pre-expansion EU and the United States differ in the incidence of absolute poverty—or that 'Europe' shares a common pattern. However, this limited comparison strongly points to a decisive average difference between the two societies and a level of internal similarity in Europe that roughly matches that among the American states.

3.2. **The inheritance of privilege**

As suggested earlier, at least in the popular imagination, the case for American exceptionalism has significantly rested on the presumption that opportunities to get ahead are relatively unaffected by family origins. Even if the rich and poor are separated by great differences in material comforts, the American commitment to equality is supposedly expressed in relatively equal chances to become a 'winner'— or 'loser'. As a basic test of this proposition, analysts have long turned to considering the connection between 'class' origins and destinations, usually meaning the association between a father's and son's (sometimes daughter's) occupational status.

Early analyzes (Lipset and Zetterberg 1959) indicated that American intergenerational mobility was hardly exceptional, that there was a basic similarity across industrial nations. Yet these conclusions were open to doubt because they were based on data of very uncertain comparability and generally involved crude categorizations of occupational status, usually flows across the blue-collar–white-collar divide. Only in the late 1980s, through the prodigious efforts of the Comparative Analysis of Social Mobility in Industrial Nations (CASMIN) project, were suitable data available—matrices of fathers' and sons' occupational status, measured similarly across countries, with a categorization scheme that reflected fundamental occupational distinctions in complex industrial societies. Here we draw on the invaluable efforts of CASMIN researchers who first studied the 'mobility regimes' of the 1970s (Erikson and Goldthorpe 1993); and those who replicated the early studies in the 1990s (Breen and Luijkx 2001; Breen 2004), thus allowing for some analysis of change. In drawing on the results of the CASMIN project, we cite state-of-the-art research, but it means that we will not be able to consider the experiences of all fifteen pre-expansion EU nations. In 2000, Germany, France, Italy, Ireland, Great Britain, and Sweden accounted for 72 percent of the total population in the fifteen pre-expansion EU countries. We should also note that the original CASMIN data only had information on three EU countries and not the United States, and the later comparisons also lacked information about US women. We therefore necessarily concentrate on male class mobility.

The CASMIN researchers have categorized class in terms of the seven categories—service class (professionals, managers, and administrators), routine nonmanual workers, petty bourgeoisie, farmers, skilled workers, nonskilled workers, and agricultural laborers. While there are competing demarcations of the class structure, the Goldthorpe schema has become the most commonly used and seems to represent significant divisions in the occupational hierarchy.

Using this schema, the class structures of the United States and Europe were broadly alike in the mid-1970s. In both societies, there was a roughly even split between white-collar and blue-collar farmwork, divisions commonly considered the fault line between the middle and working classes. However, the United States was on the 'postindustrial side' of this pattern: a relatively high proportion of workers in the Service and Routine Nonmanual classes. In this regard, then, the United States was not distinctive; it matched the pattern in a few other European nations, even if it slightly differed from the overall European pattern. Since then, the change in the European class structure has been relatively modest, though it has become increasingly like the US structure. The common pattern in Europe and the United States is a declining blue-collar working class and fewer farmers.

In neither Europe nor the United States do class origins represent class destiny. The CASMIN researchers calculated what they called total mobility rates (TMR)—the proportion of men who ended up in a 'class' *different from* their fathers' class. In the 1970s, for America, this intergenerational mobility rate was 70 percent; in Europe the rate was 66 percent. In the 1980s, the respective rates were 70 and 67 percent, and in the 1990s they were 69 and 67 percent. In short, Europe and the United States were essentially similar throughout this period. The important point here is that in both societies a large majority of men end up in a different class from their class of origin. Class mobility is the common experience for Americans and Europeans. Moreover, given the common shift in occupational structures toward more white-collar employment, upward mobility was much more common than downward mobility in both societies, roughly to the same degree.

The TMR reveals the gross pattern of intergenerational mobility, though detailed inspection of 'flows' from particular origins to destinations also does not indicate much in the way of American distinctiveness. If the United States does depart from the European pattern, it is generally in the direction of greater openness—for example, the sons of manual workers appear to have a somewhat higher chance of rising to the service class in the United States than Europe. For the most part, the American patterns fall within the European range. Looking at all these outflows, we are inclined to agree with Erikson and Goldthorpe's pithy summary (1993: 331), '...it would not be difficult for the US and Australia to be taken as just two more European nations'. That is what they wrote about the mobility in the 1970s; we believe that is still an apt description of the situation two decades later.

The same conclusion holds if we consider rates of *intra-generational* mobility—that is, the chances of moving up or down the occupational hierarchy in the course of one's own career. For example, in the United States the chances of starting out in a blue-collar position and subsequently having a service class position (20%) are not distinctly great, just at the high end of the European range. Nor do Americans who start out as blue-collar workers have distinctly great chances of coming to own their own business; indeed, a number of the European nations have higher rates.

In this discussion, we have focused on what are called absolute rates—the simple probabilities of being mobile or stable in the class structure. Yet, as stratification analysts have long recognized, much of the observed mobility is in effect forced by changes in the occupational structure—that is, people from the lower classes have to be 'recruited' to fill the increasing number of positions at the higher levels of the occupational structure. This structural mobility—not some greater democratization of the stratification system—accounts for most of the high rates of class mobility in advanced Western societies.

At issue are the *relative rates* of mobility (*social fluidity*)—that is, the amount of mobility that cannot be attributed to structural change, thus reflecting the openness of the system. The related research is technically complex (fearsomely so) and does not lend itself to a simple statistical summary. The scholarly debate centers on the magnitude of differences. It is generally agreed that there are cross-national differences in a statistically significant sense, but whether these differences represent socially meaningful differences or a fundamental similarity is open to debate.

For our discussion, though, here are the relevant points. In the 1970s, the United States did not appear to be distinctly open, though its fluidity was on the high side of the European range, roughly comparable to Sweden and more open than France, Germany, and Great Britain. Two decades later the United States was still on the fluid end of the European range, as was Sweden. While fluidity in the United States remained essentially stable, it appears to have generally increased in Europe (for both men and women), though a couple of European countries did not become more open. Thus, America and Europe seem to have converged, even as the distinctiveness of the mobility regimes in individual European nations remains evident (Breen and Luijkx 2001; Breen 2004). In sum, to turn Erikson and Goldthorpe's expression to the matter of social fluidity, we might say that the United States again appears like another European nation.

3.3. **Class structuration?**

In considering the stratification systems of Europe and the United States, we must also consider whether they are *class societies*. It is crucial to recognize that the inequality per se does not imply the existence of classes in any meaningful sociological sense. That might seem like a strange claim when our own discussion has invoked groups like 'rich families' and 'poor families', a discrepancy that seemingly suggests a class system. However, particular points on the income distribution do not designate real classes in any sociologically meaningful way. For all the conceptual jousting about the meaning of class, all class theories make a distinctive claim that goes beyond asserting the reality of differences in material conditions. The basic claim is this: *the stratification system most fundamentally consists of a small set of distinct groups—classes—defined and ordered by their economic position* (Kingston 2000). Thus, when analysts invoke terms like 'the working class' or 'the middle class', they are implying that a large group with broadly comparable occupational positions has similar life experiences—and that these experiences are distinctly different from the experiences of those in other classes. Class theorists have argued that classes are marked by distinct differences in such matters as mobility chances, political views, cultural outlooks, and consumption patterns. In a nutshell, a class society is a stratification system fundamentally divided by relatively few *categorical* distinctions instead of finely gradated, *continuous* differences of rank. Although inequality is necessary for the existence of classes, a class society is not the necessary outcome of inequality. In much common lore, distinct classes are more pronounced in Europe than in the United States, but that belief is based more on limited comparisons and selected anecdotes than systematic analysis.

This complex issue cannot be resolved by referring to a few well-measured indicators, nor can comparative researchers even begin a systematic discussion by citing comparable data from all European nations and the United States. Even a limited effort involving just the United States, Canada, France, and Germany was hampered by the difficulties of acquiring comparable data—and deciding what factors are most decisive in determining the class *structuration* of a society (Giddens 1973; Kingston et al. 2002).

Even so, the common high rates of social mobility in both Europe and the United States would seem to undermine the existence of sharp class boundaries. (Recall that the 'class destinations' of about two-thirds of all Americans and Europeans differ from their 'class origins'.) Any class effects on individual consciousness and activity would seem more likely if people are stable in the class system, thus receiving a consistent class-rooted 'social message'. Yet with so many people experiencing multiple class positions in their lives, these societies seem to lack fertile grounds for the growth of distinct class cultures that decisively shape individual lives. Mobility would seem to be the solvent of class structure.

We cannot directly test this conjecture here, however. We would like to know, for example, whether presumed class divisions (e.g. working class vs. middle class) demarcate relatively distinct cultural orientations or social networks in the two societies. Unfortunately, we lack the data to examine such subtle matters in the necessary detail.

The best we can do here is to suggest that there may be *some* greater class structuration in Europe than the United States, even if the signs of distinct classes are relatively muted in both societies. For example, it seems reasonable to say that class distinctions are more significant if the 'members' of particular classes are united by common political sentiments. In the United States class is a very weak predictor of voting choice and political ideology. In European nations, there is some greater tendency for the working class to lean left and the middle class(es) to lean right, though European countries differ in the strength of this connection, and although debated this connection seems to have generally declined (De Graaf, Niewbeerta, and Heath 1995; Evans 1999; Nieuwbeerta 2001).

Similarly, comparing the United States to just France and Germany, there appears to be some greater class structuration in the two European nations, especially in Germany, in terms of class consciousness (Do people feel a sense of 'belonging' to a particular class?) and cultural matters (Kingston et al. 2002). At the same time, there is no evidence of clear-cut visible class barriers in everyday life. One could not say that particular behaviors or attitudes represented 'middle class culture' or 'working-class culture' because cultural practices commonly cross class lines. Rather, class location is *correlated* with a wide range of attitudes, and these correlations are moderately substantial in some cases.

Now, of course, the French and German patterns may not reflect Europe as a whole. Any attempt to generalize here is suspect. But they represent two cases (with large populations) that might be presumed to point to any gross US–European difference in class structuration. Germany is one of the least 'open' European societies in terms of intergenerational mobility, and France is frequently thought to be marked by pronounced differences in class cultures (Bourdieu 1984). If these two countries can at least suggest any European pattern, it is one of at most modest class structuration. The contrast is therefore not one between an 'open' New World and a 'class-ridden' Old World. We speculate that further research will reveal minor differences of degrees, not significant differences of kind.

3.4. **Gender stratification**

As for stratification in general, gender stratification is a multidimensional concept. It involves such concrete matters as the size of paychecks and the division of household labor, as well as more subjective matters like the respect accorded different occupations and the connotations of language. No single measure can purport to capture *the* pattern of gender stratification in a society, nor are good comparable measures of all relevant dimensions available.

With the great general increase in female labor force participation since 1960 in both Europe and the United States, the inequalities between men and women have commanded increasing public attention. Progress is surely visible on some fronts, but on other fronts progress has been modest and halting. The selection of indicators clearly affects any assessment and is understandably contentious for that reason.

To address this complexity, we simply propose to concentrate on two indices developed by the UN that reflect the judgment of international researchers about what is important and reasonably reliably measured: (*a*) the Gender-related Development Index (GDI) that taps sex differences in longevity, knowledge/education, and earned income; and (*b*) the Gender Empowerment Measure (GEM) that taps earned income, shares of high-level positions, and parliamentary representation (see Table 3.4).

Table 3.4. Recent measures of gender equality in Europe and the United States

Country	GEM 2003	Estimated ratio of female to male earned income	Female professional/ technical workers as % of total	% female seats in parliament	GDI 2002
Austria	0.782	0.50	48	30.6	0.924
Belgium	0.695	0.44	50	24.9	0.938
Denmark	0.825	0.71	51	38.0	0.931
Finland	0.801	0.70	57	36.5	0.933
France	—	—	—	—	0.929
Germany	0.776	0.57	50	31.4	0.921
Greece	0.519	0.45	47	8.7	0.894
Ireland	0.683	0.40	49	14.2	0.929
Italy	0.561	0.45	44	10.3	0.914
Luxembourg	—	—	—	—	0.926
The Netherlands	0.794	0.53	48	33.3	0.938
Portugal	0.647	0.53	50	19.1	0.894
Spain	0.709	0.44	45	26.6	0.916
Sweden	0.831	0.68	49	45.3	0.946
UK	0.675	0.60	43	17.1	0.934
EU (population adjusted)	0.697	0.53	47	23.4	0.923
United States	0.760	0.62	54	14.0	0.936
EU c.v.	0.083	0.08	0.08	0.09	—

Source: 2003 Human Development Report <http://www.undp.org/hdr2003/indicator/indic_207_1.html>

On both of these composite measures, the EU15 countries and the United States rank highly (in the top twenty-five of all countries in the world), but the differences between them are modest. For the GDI, the US score (0.760) is slightly higher than the EU average (0.697), but Sweden, the Netherlands, and Belgium exceed the US score.

For the GEM, the US score again exceeds the EU average. However, eight of the EU countries have higher scores than the United States. In light of these composite indices, then, the differences in gender stratification are more matters of slight degree, not distinct differences in kind.

Yet looking at the separate components of the GEM indicates some distinctiveness: the United States is higher on measures of economic empowerment and lower in political empowerment. The US ratio of female to male earned income is 0.62 compared to the EU average of 0.54. This seems to be a fairly significant difference, but it is misleading to talk of a 'European pattern'. The EU range is substantial: three countries have ratios that exceeded the United States, while in five countries the ratio is less than 0.50.

Similarly, the US ratio of professional and technical workers (54%) exceeds the EU average (48.5%), but that average reflects considerable variance. The UK stands at the low end (43%) while Finland (57%) exceeds the US rate. In effect, in terms of both pay and occupational standing, the United States appears as a relatively 'progressive' European nation.

On the other hand, at least by one measure of political power, European women perform better than their American counterparts. The EU average female proportion in parliament is 26 percent; the US figure is only 14 percent. Even so, the EU average reflects very different political cultures among its member nations—9 percent in Greece, 45 percent in Sweden.

3.5. **Conclusion**

As should be evident from this brief review of empirical data, it is impossible to make any overall assessment of whether *the* American stratification system is distinctly different from *the* European stratification system—or whether it makes sense to speak of the European pattern. It is absolutely essential to consider multiple dimensions of inequality, thereby recognizing the important differences and similarities of the societies.

On the matter of inequality of results (how the economic pie gets divided), there is a new, pronounced difference, so much so that it is fair to say there is a European model and an American model. While income inequalities certainly persist in both societies, Europe is now notably more egalitarian than the United States in this respect. Despite some recent retrenchment in welfare state provisions and lesser restraints on market forces in Europe (and generally throughout the developed world), the European commitment to equality of results distinguishes it from the United States. Trend lines do not suggest that this difference will disappear in some general convergence with the American pattern.

This difference is also sharply evident in poverty rates—and, indeed, the much worse condition of the US poor accounts for much of the overall difference in equality. We should emphasize that the American poor fare worse whether poverty is measured in absolute or relative terms. More Americans than Europeans live badly in objective terms *and* live outside the economic mainstream that prevails in their society. Social exclusion is more tolerated in the United States than Europe.

Yet, as different as the European and American models may be, we should also highlight that Europe is not all alike. As other observers have noted (e.g. Esping-Andersen 1990), there are multiple 'Europes', and this is so for the overall division of the economic pie. However, variation within the 'states' of Europe is about the same as variation within the American states, making it plausible to speak of a European pattern that incorporates ongoing internal differences.

On the matter of inequality of opportunity, however, it is inaccurate to refer to distinct models. According to the best evidence available for a restricted number of nations, the sheer absolute rate of intergenerational mobility in Europe and the United States is now very similar. A few decades ago, the US rates seemed to slightly exceed the European rate, but this difference did not suggest different 'models' had existed and then had disappeared. Rather, what is crucial to recognize is that throughout this period Europe and the United States shared a generally high level of mobility. Although the intergenerational 'flows' from particular origins to particular destinations may differ between the United States and individual European countries, that fact does not gainsay the fundamental similarity in overall mobility rates. An image of class-ridden societies, reproducing themselves from generation to generation, does not fit either society.

In light of recent research on social fluidity (the extent to which access to class positions is equally distributed), there is also little indication of significant differences between the two societies. In recent decades, the United States has just appeared to be on the more 'open' end of the European range—and if anything, European nations have recently tended to more closely approximate the US pattern. Despite this general trend, significant differences within Europe persist and some countries have not become more open.

As scholars versed in the debates about mobility will recognize, this pattern of results does not fit readily with what had been until recently conventional wisdom. Lipset and Zetterberg (1959) had initially posited a fundamental similarity in absolute rates across developed countries. This claim seemed to have been decisively contradicted by subsequent, more sophisticated work. Lipset and Zetterberg were generally held to be wrong—and probably were for the time they wrote about and for the 1960s and 1970s. However, the recent results reported here indicate a fundamental similarity in total mobility, a challenge to the anti-LZ consensus, as Breen (2004) argued.

On the other hand, many researchers had posited a fundamental similarity in social fluidity (despite differences in absolute mobility)—the so-called FJH thesis (Featherman, Jones, and Hauser 1975). Subsequent research has found statistically significant differences across societies, but whether you think the thesis is supported or contradicted hinges on how you judge the magnitude of differences.

Researchers associated with the CASMIN project have tended to emphasize the differences that represent departures from a 'core' pattern and the lack of any general trend in openness. Recent results, however, suggest the continuation of differences across countries but a general (though not universal) increase in the openness of European societies.

Do class divisions demarcate social life in Europe and the United States so that 'members' of particular classes have distinct senses of social identity, cultural outlooks, patterns of interaction, and political dispositions? We cannot deliver here a systematic verdict on this complex matter. However, we are inclined to doubt that sharply distinct class cultures exist in either society primarily because economic mobility (inter- and intra-generational) is so common in both societies. Is it likely that class location pervasively and significantly shapes the contours of individual lives if so many people 'belong' to multiple classes in their own life? At the same time, there may be some modest 'class structuration' in some dimensions of European social and political life—more so than the United States where it appears low in all domains. Whether that is actually the case cannot be settled without further research incorporating the full roster of European countries and a large range of comparable data.

While we have focused on 'class' distinctions, we also argue that inequalities between women and men must be central to any overall assessment of stratification. The brevity of our attention does not signal that it is a secondary concern. Clearly gender represents an axial division in both societies, but on this score there is little indication of distinct European and US models. On some matters (e.g. the ratio of female to male earnings), the United States appears somewhat more egalitarian; on other matters (e.g. representation in parliament), the Europeans are more egalitarian. Overall, widely used summary indices of women's status point to modest differences between the US and European averages. However, with considerable variation around the European average, the United States appears to be on the 'progressive' side of the European range—hardly a distinct vanguard for the empowerment of women.

So, considered together, what do our findings suggest about the central question of this book—is there a coherent European society that is distinctly different from American society? With a multidimensional perspective on inequality, the answer is both yes and no. Yes, if we consider the distribution of the economic pie: Europe is more egalitarian. No, if we consider the distribution of opportunity or the position of women: the United States generally tends to be on the egalitarian side of the European range, a modest difference of degree not kind. As for class structuration, we lack enough evidence to render a clear judgment, though class boundaries may be somewhat more visible in Europe than in the United States where they are weak. This complex pattern suggests neither an overarching trend toward convergence nor any overriding cultural distinction between the United States and Europe.

4 Family

Theodore Caplow and Salustiano Del Campo

Three master trends—modernization, the gradual progress of equality, individuation—exerted a strong influence on both EU and US families between 1960 and 2000.

The direct effects of modernization include the steady decline of the infant mortality rate (deaths of infants in the first year of life), dramatic declines in fertility, corresponding decreases in average household size, and a vast improvement in the material equipment of family households.

The gradual progress of equality greatly reduced the long-standing differences between men and women in sexual opportunity, access to the labor market, occupational careers, control of property, freedom to divorce, and relationships with children.

In both the EU and the US, the families of 1960 functioned within a legal and customary framework wherein the mutual obligations of husbands and wives, the authority of parents over children, the obligations of kinship, the disadvantages of extramarital births, the rules of inheritance and adoption, and the prevailing sexual taboos were mostly of long standing, and perceived as part of the natural order. But in the ensuing four decades, on both sides of the Atlantic, that framework was changed beyond recognition.

It goes without saying that the direct effects of the three master trends interacted with each other and with other happenings so that the causal sequences are not easily untangled. The decline of fertility and of household size seems to have been both cause and effect of the entry of married women into the labor force which, in turn, seems to have been both cause and effect of the feminist movement and of the rise in divorce. The introduction of oral contraception in the 1960s and the legalization of abortion in the US and in most of the EU states accounted for declining fertility but did not account for the great increase of extramarital births that followed.

While similar trends were recorded in the EU and the US, they started and ended at different levels and their consequences were never identical. The decline of fertility in the US was arrested and partly reversed in the 1980s, while in the EU fertility continued downward to levels unknown to history. On the other hand, the improvement of infant mortality was far more impressive in the EU. Starting from a 1960 rate, three times higher than that of the US, the EU rate is now significantly lower.

Americans indulge in marriage, divorce, and remarriage far more freely than Europeans. The postponement of marriage and the increasing popularity of divorce in both systems have only served to widen the gap. The abandonment of sexual taboos is visible everywhere but takes different forms from country to country.

The best way to view these interconnections is to examine the major family trends one at a time, starting with the decline of fertility and moving on to the increase of divorce and remarriage, the entry of married women with small children into the labor force, the abandonment of restrictions on consensual unions and extramarital births, the legalization of abortion and cohabitation, the trend toward later marriage or no marriage since 1960, and the cumulative impact of all these trends on living people.

4.1. Demographic arithmetic

Between 1960 and 2002, the population of the fifteen member states of the EU grew by 21 percent, to 380 million, while the population of the US grew much faster, by 59 percent, to 287 million. Forty years from now, according to the median projections, the two populations would be about equal, at approximately 380 million (Statistical Abstract of the United States 2002, tables 2 and 3; Eurostat Yearbook 2003: 81). The figures refer to the fifteen states that belong to the EU in 2003. In effect, with the enlargement at twenty-seven states in 2007 the EU population will rise to almost 500 millions.

The projections assume that the US population will grow because of continued immigration and the high fertility of the Hispanic minority, while the EU will barely sustain its present numbers as continued immigration from Eastern Europe, North Africa, and the Middle East is offset by the low fertility of native-born women.

Both populations are huge but they shrink in a global perspective. The EU and the US together, although still holding the lion's share of the world's economic and cultural capital, now have barely 11 percent of the world's inhabitants, down from 35 percent early in the past century.

The natural growth or decline of a population is measured by the total fertility rate; roughly equivalent to the number of grown children the average woman contributes to the next generation. More specifically, the total fertility rate is the number of births that 1,000 women would have in their lifetime, if at each year of age they experienced the birth rate occurring in the specified year. It is divided here by 1,000 for easier comprehension (Statistical Abstract of the United States 2002, note to table 71).

Under the prevailing conditions (low rates of juvenile mortality) in the EU and the United States, a total fertility rate of 2.11 in a closed population with no migration would achieve full replacement from one generation to the next. Figure 4.1 shows the trend of the total fertility rate in the EU and the United States since 1960.

The EU trend began at 2.50 in 1960, which was comfortably above the replacement level, but declined steadily thereafter, reaching the abysmally low level of

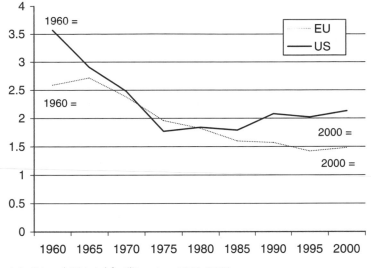

Figure 4.1. EU and US total fertility rates, 1960–2000

1.42 in 1995. It still remains in that neighborhood, presaging dramatic changes in the ethnic composition of most of the EU member-states as indigenous citizens are replaced by immigrants and their offspring. Although the total EU population is still slowly growing, that growth is entirely attributable to immigration.

The demographic collapse is unequally distributed. Germany, Greece, Spain, Italy, and Austria display fertility rates in the range between 1.24 and 1.29, far below anything ever experienced since the dawn of their respective histories. Belgium, Denmark, Luxembourg, the Netherlands, Portugal, Finland, Sweden, and the UK show higher but still alarming rates between 1.41 and 1.74. Only France and Ireland are close to the replacement level (Eurostat Yearbook 2003: 89).

Even lower rates occur among the twelve new member countries of the EU; the Czech Republic holds the record with a total fertility rate of 1.14 (Eurostat Yearbook 2003: 33).

If these trends persist, the young people of the EU a generation on are more likely to be Muslim or Orthodox than Protestant or Catholic, and more Muslim than Orthodox. The immigration pressure created by a deficit of births within rich nations is very strong.

By contrast, some of the world's poorest countries, Rwanda and the Dominican Republic for example, have total fertility rates above eight, thereby doubling their populations every fifteen years. This contrast will haunt the twenty-first century. The mismatch between the distribution of wealth and the distribution of people gets sharper by the day.

Mendras (1997) identified three distinct patterns of fertility in the EU countries. In the north, the high rates of divorce and extramarital births, and the large number of single-person households signal the virtual disappearance of the conventional nuclear family. In the south, the nuclear family has proved more resistant. Adult children (or more commonly the lone adult child) remain in the family until they marry, even when they marry late. Grandmothers are often included in the household and women still rule the domestic arena. The central countries seem to be in transition toward the Scandinavian model; their statistics all point in that direction.

The total fertility rate in the United States shows a different pattern. From a high point in 1960, in the last phase of the baby boom, it fell well below the replacement level by 1975 but then, unlike the European rate, it began to rise again, reaching the replacement level by 1990 and holding there ever since. As of 2000, the total fertility rates of non-Hispanic whites, blacks, Asians and Pacific Islanders, and American Indians were all clustered around the replacement level (Statistical Abstract of the United States 2002, table 72), but Hispanics were far above it and their numbers were daily augmented by legal and illegal immigrants flooding into the country from Mexico and other parts of Central and South America. Spanish is a second official language in the western and southwestern states and in New York, Washington, Atlanta, and Miami. The restriction of Hispanic immigration, although favored by public opinion, became unthinkable as the newcomers gathered voting strength and learned to use it. In January 2004, the Bush administration announced a plan that would offer a degree of amnesty to millions of illegal immigrants and, in effect, permit unlimited future immigration from Latin America. The existing situation, together with the projected measures, guarantees an ethnic transformation in the US on the same scale as the ongoing ethnic transformation of the EU, although with different components. Diversity is further enhanced in the US by substantial immigration from Asia, the Caribbean islands, and Africa. Non-Hispanic whites are now a minority in each of the ten largest US cities, where they were the overwhelming majority as recently as 1960.

American states show a somewhat wider range of fertility rates than EU member-states. The rate in Utah is twice the rate in Vermont while the rate in France is only 70 percent higher than the rate in Italy (Statistical Abstract of the United States 2002, table 70).

One effect of low fertility is an increase in the elderly population. The proportion of the EU population aged 65 and older rose from 11 percent in 1960 to 16 percent in 2000; the corresponding increase for the United States was from 9 percent in 1960 to 12 percent in 2000 (Statistical Abstract of the United States 1979, table 29; Statistical Abstract of the United States 2002, table 11; Eurostat Yearbook 2003: 98).

The median age of both populations is now over 35, in sharp contrast to developing countries with median ages in the teens. The EU is somewhat healthier than the United States, as measured by life expectancy at various ages, but both populations are the healthiest ever known (Statistical Abstract of the United States 2002, table 92; Eurostat Yearbook 2003: 96). An extraordinary increase in centenarians has taken place since 1980. Women in both populations live, on average, about six years longer than men.

The decline of fertility appears to be a normal consequence of modernization and is adequately explained by the declining value of children's labor, the rising status of women, the mechanization and simplification of housework, the increasing cost of child-raising, and the availability of means for the voluntary control of conception. But it is not easy to explain why the norm of the two-child family still prevails in France and the United States, while the one-child family has become normal in Italy, Spain, and Greece. Since women in the one-child countries are less educated and less often employed than women in the two-child countries, and the church is more influential in the one-child countries, the commonsense explanations fail.

The difference between the United States, where fertility has hovered slightly above the replacement level since 1980 and such countries as Germany, Italy, and Spain, where fertility has plunged far below the replacement level in the same interval of time, is equally puzzling. Throughout the world, the most powerful depressants of fertility are higher education for women and the labor market participation of married women. Yet the US has relatively more women with university educations and more married women in the labor force than the EU, but higher fertility nevertheless.

The most likely explanation is that marriage, for obscure cultural reasons, has been and remains more popular in the US than in the EU. Only one in twenty-five white Americans arrives at age 65 without ever having been married (Statistical Abstract of the United States 2002, table 48) and that is probably close to the irreducible minimum. Some of the unmarried have physical or mental handicaps that preclude marriage; others are confirmed homosexuals. Middle-aged bachelors and spinsters of heterosexual inclination are astonishingly rare in the United States but fairly common in the EU.

4.2. **Marriage and divorce**

Trends in marriage can be measured in several ways—by the number of marriages per thousand persons per year (Figure 4.2), by the number of marriages per thousand adults, by the number of marriages per thousand unmarried women, by the percent of married persons in a population at a given time or by the percent of households headed by a married couple. These methods give slightly different results but they all show more marriages in the US than in the EU.

Figure 4.2 compares the crude marriage rates of the EU and the US from 1960 to 2000. Both trends turned down sharply around 1975 but the decline was steeper in the EU.

Before the 1960s, the institution of marriage was still maintained by enormous social and economic pressures. It was the only way for men and women to have long-term sexual relationships without danger or stigma. It was the only legitimate

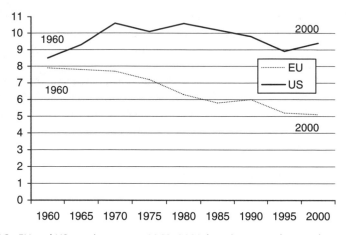

Figure 4.2. EU and US marriage rates, 1960–2000 (marriages per thousand people)

setting in which to bear children and the only prudent way to provide for their care. For most women and children, it offered the only reliable means of support. For men and women and alike, it provided the only convenient channel for the management and transfer of property. Not only were men and women coerced into marriage by these circumstances, they were coerced to remain there by punitive divorce laws.

In both the EU and the US, the mean age of first marriage for women declined during the baby boom, then rose by several years to the present level of about 27 for women, although there are striking variations in the EU between the three Nordic countries, where the average new bride is 30, and, for example, Portugal, where she is only 25. In the US, the age of women at first marriage has been rising from year to year and now approaches the European level. Grooms are about two years older in every case.

There is no clear pattern of differential marriage rates among the member-states of the EU, where Germany had the highest marriage rate (6.6) and Sweden the lowest (4.0) in 2001. The Swedish marriage system has long been distinctive in that many betrothed couples choose to delay marriage until the birth of a child or indefinitely, but that has not been the custom in Belgium (4.1) or Austria (4.2) with rates nearly as low. Among the American states, where Nevada had the highest marriage rate (75.5) and Connecticut the lowest (5.6), the pattern is easier to decipher (Eurostat Yearbook 2003: 87; Statistical Abstract of the United States 2002, table 111).

Cross-border marriages are far more frequent in the US, where states like Nevada, Arkansas, and Hawaii offer instant wedding facilities for couples from states with more restrictive requirements. Nevada might be said to specialize in serial monogamy, offering both quick divorce and quick remarriage to transient couples.

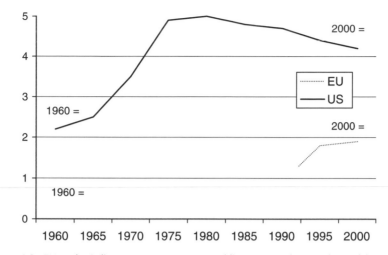

Figure 4.3. EU and US divorce rates, 1960–2000 (divorces per thousand people)

Divorce rates, like marriage rates, can be measured in several different ways, but for our purposes the crude rate will do nicely. Figure 4.3 shows the EU and US trends from 1960 to 2000.

In 1960, an American couple could only get a divorce by proving that one spouse was at fault, and the other innocent. If both were known to be at fault, divorce was denied. Different states had different rules about the kinds and degrees of fault that were necessary, but in all cases the laws were intentionally restrictive. In 1966, New York State rewrote its divorce law. It was one of the oldest in the nation, having been written by Alexander Hamilton, himself an acknowledged adulterer. It was also one of the most rigid, allowing divorce only on proof of adultery. The new law allowed divorce by mutual consent after an agreed-upon separation of two years. Though no one recognized it at the time, this was the first no-fault divorce law. California enacted an explicit no-fault divorce law in 1969, and within a few years all fifty states adopted some form of no-fault divorce. During those years, the crude divorce rate approximately doubled to 4.9 per thousand inhabitants, near which it has remained ever since.

Divorce has been, and remains, far less frequent in the EU, which did not begin to calculate a union-wide rate until 1990; it reached 1.9 in 2001, about a third of the US rate. The 2001 range was from Ireland, which still banned divorce entirely, and Greece, with the extremely low rate of 0.9, to Belgium, whose rate of 2.9 was comparable to the less divorce-prone US states.

Greece has been relatively unaffected by the recent fragilisation of marriage in Europe. Consensual unions are still rare and divorces are still disreputable. Remarkably, women's labor force participation does not seem to encourage divorce in Greece, as it does in other European countries (Symeonidou, Working paper. Athens: National Center for Social Research). In Belgium, by contrast, the number of divorces exceeded the number of marriages for the first time in 2001. Nearly all divorces are by mutual consent, and many of them are followed by remarriage so that about a third of all Belgian marriages are remarriages for one or both of the parties. Furthermore, divorce remains frequent throughout the marital cycle; many couples separate after twenty years or more (Vanhove and Matthijs 2002).

Using survey data from 1989 to 1997, Anderson (2002) calculated life tables of marriages for nine of the EU member-states and the US. Sweden, unsurprisingly, has the lowest rates of marital survival in Western Europe; only 72 percent of still-living Swedish couples remain together after fifteen years; marital survival is a little better in France and Germany, very much better in Italy and Spain, where 92 percent are still together after fifteen years, and much worse in the United States, where only 58 percent of still-living married couples are together fifteen years after the wedding.

Combining marital and consensual unions we get much lower survival rates after fifteen years—only 39 percent—in the United States and 46 percent in Sweden, for example. A study of European marital and consensual unions by Darleen and Liefbroer (2002) introduces another element into the equation; it shows much lower survival for the unions of women born in 1963–7 than for the unions of women who were born five or ten years earlier.

4.3. **The disestablishment of monogamy**

According to Mendras (2002), describing the aftermath of May 1968 in France:

Youthful pre-marital sexual relations spread with uncanny speed, first in the middle classes, then among the elites, so that the most proper grandmother had to tolerate the grand-daughter living with a boyfriend. Then came the young workers of the factories and the farms. Finally, the widowed and the divorced gave up remarrying. If one no longer divorced in order to remarry, the revolution was complete. Cohabitation was legitimate; eventually the homosexuals demanded legitimacy for their unions, Single-parent families became normal too....In twenty years, the absolute monogamy instituted by Christ and forcefully reiterated by Saint Paul, who did not even want widowers to remarry, the cornerstone of western Christian civilization crumbled under the influence of a few youthful demonstrators—a moral revolution of millennial scale whose ultimate consequences for our system of relationships and for the development of children have yet to be measured.

In the US, the revolution may have started a little earlier with the Supreme Court's decision in the 1965 case of *Griswold* v. *Connecticut*, which struck down a state law banning contraceptives by discovering in the Constitution a hitherto unknown right to privacy. Until that time, American law attempted to enforce monogamy by a variety of ingenious provisions. The cohabitation of unmarried couples was repressed by laws against false registration in hotels and lodging houses, by a federal statute (the Mann Act) that severely punished the interstate transportation of a female for 'immoral purposes', and by ordinances that made it impossible for unmarried couples to buy a house or rent an apartment. Hotelkeepers and landlords often went beyond the law in refusing to accommodate such couples. In residential institutions, men and women were kept out of each other's rooms by locked gates and armed guards. Sexually active adolescents were defined as juvenile delinquents and sometimes imprisoned. Adolescent girls who became pregnant were automatically expelled from school and placed in institutions which kept them out of public sight and gave their babies out for adoption. Adolescent boys were often convicted of statutory rape for consorting with girls of their own age. Those laws are still on the books but seldom enforced, although in 2003, an 18-year-old boy in Georgia was sentenced to prison for the statutory rape of a girl just under 16. The explanation for the unusual action appeared to be that the boy was black and the girl white (*Washington Post*, January 25, 2004).

Adultery was a criminal offense in theory and sometimes in practice but was more effectively punished in civil actions for separation, support, divorce, or custody where the spouse accused of adultery was treated very harshly. Custom and regulations required the exclusion of an identified homosexual from any responsible position.

As the structure of official regulation was dismantled, the private regulators had no choice but to follow suit. College deans abandoned the *in loco parentis* role that made them responsible for students' chastity. Dormitories became coed and moderately tolerant of sex. Hotelkeepers lost interest in the marital status of their guests. Banks encouraged homosexual couples to take out mortgage loans. One of the most important changes was a shift in the policies of social agencies so that unmarried mothers became fully entitled to welfare payments and other forms of family assistance.

As the restrictions were removed, cohabitation became entirely respectable in the United States. At most American weddings today, it is taken for granted, unless otherwise specified, that the bride and groom have already begun to live together and the same may be said in most of the EU countries.

On both sides of the ocean, the exact connection between the increase of cohabitation and the increase of extramarital births is unknown since we cannot tell what proportion of extramarital births occur in ongoing consensual unions or result from already broken consensual unions or from casual encounters. But the connection is certainly strong. Figure 4.4 shows the astonishing rise of extramarital births in the EU and the United States since 1960.

For both the EU and the United States, the trend of extramarital births starts at 5 percent in 1960—only one out of twenty pregnant women was so bold as to offend the moral standards of the time. But the figures mask important internal differences.

In 1960, Belgium, Spain, Greece, Ireland, Italy, and the Netherlands had negligible numbers—1 or 2 percent—of what were then called illegitimate births. France, Luxembourg, and Finland had a few more—3–6 percent. Denmark, Germany, Portugal, and Norway were a little higher, but still under 10 percent. Austria and

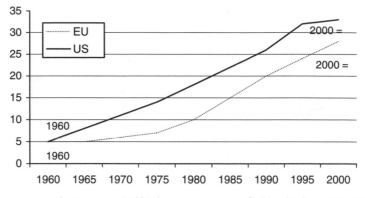

Figure 4.4. EU and US extramarital births as percentage of all live births, 1960–2000

Sweden exceeded 10 percent (Eurostat Yearbook 2003: 90). The case of Austria is explained by an old regulation that required rural couples to get an official certificate before marrying; those of Sweden and Iceland by the local practice of postponing marriage until the birth of the first child. The few women who bore children out of wedlock in the other countries typically belonged to the most disadvantaged minorities.

The US figure for 1960 conceals the sharp contrast between the 2 percent of white births that were called illegitimate and the 23 percent of black births so classified (Becu 1999). The difference was even sharper than it appears since a considerable number of the white infants but very few of the black infants were eventually legitimated by the marriage of their natural parents. No one could have predicted the subsequent increase of extramarital births in the white population from 2 percent in 1960 to 33 percent recently (Statistical Abstract of the United States 2002, table 75).

On both sides of the ocean, the great majority of 1960 babies were born to married couples. That began to change in the 1970s and changed a great deal more in the 1980s and 1990s. By 2000, more than one in four births in the EU and among white Americans were extramarital. But the figure was 45 percent in Denmark, 56 percent in Sweden, and 70 percent for black Americans. Moreover, while the extramarital births of 1960 were presumed to be unwanted, the extramarital births of 2000 were largely voluntary, given the availability of reliable contraception and legal abortion.

One result was the creation of great numbers of families consisting of a single parent and children under 18. By 1999, more than 11 million EU citizens lived in households of this type (Eurostat Yearbook 2003: 131). In the great majority of these households, the single parent was a woman, and most of them were poor. The corresponding figure for the US in 2000 was over 21 million (Statistical Abstract of the United States 2002, table 57) and they, on average, were even poorer.

There are several intersecting trends here that need to be disentangled: the increase of nonmarital births, the increase of single-parent families, the increase of consensual unions, the postponement of marriage, the creation of single-parent families by divorce as well as by nonmarital births, the creation of complex families by remarriage and adoption, and the effect of all these novelties on the adults and children involved.

Concurrent with the increase of single-parent and complex families since 1960, there has been a huge increase in the number of one-person households: more than 40 million in the EU today and almost 30 million in the US (Statistical Abstract of the United States 2002, table 60; Eurostat Yearbook 2003: 131) not counting additional millions of persons who live with nonrelatives.

4.4. **The control of conception**

Although contraception was in wide use in the EU countries and the United States before 1950, as can be seen from the sharp drop in birth rates during the Depression of the 1930s, the methods then in use had high rates of failure so that coitus generally involved some risk of pregnancy. Voluntary abortion was illegal everywhere in the EU and the US. Illegal abortions were expensive, dangerous, and disreputable. Voluntary sterilization was almost unknown. The pregnancy of an unmarried woman or the unwanted pregnancy of a married woman often ended in tragedy. All of this changed with the introduction in the 1960s of oral contraceptives that were highly reliable. The methods of contraception available before the 1960s had failure rates of 5–10 percent *per month*; the failure rate of oral contraceptives, properly used, was near zero. Surgical sterilization became generally available at about the same time. By 1970, legal abortion was available in most EU countries and in eighteen US states, and abortion tourism was thriving.

A woman's decisions about whether and when to become pregnant were now, for the first time in human experience, quite separate from her decisions about whether and with whom to have sex. So a fundamental change in the relation between the sexes was bound to have far-reaching consequences. As soon as women could freely choose how many children to have, they chose to have fewer.

The legalization of abortion in the EU occurred piecemeal and against considerable religious and medical opposition. It was far advanced by 2002 when eleven of the EU member-states permitted abortion on request during the first trimester of pregnancy, although with various impediments such as waiting periods, counseling requirements, high fees, and insufficient facilities. Swiss legislators did not legalize abortion on request until 2003 and then by a very narrow margin. Ireland, the UK, Spain, and Portugal deny abortion on request but allow it under stipulated conditions, which are rigorous in Ireland and generally ignored in Spain. Mefepristone, the 'morning after' abortion pill, is currently available in eleven EU countries and banned in the other four. But nothing in the European struggle over abortion compares in fury and political significance with the ongoing abortion controversy in the US (Adams 1997).

No national consensus about abortion had developed when early in 1973, the US Supreme Court in the case of *Roe* v. *Wade* undertook to settle the issue out of hand by enacting that (*a*) states might not regulate abortions during the first twelve weeks of pregnancy except to require that they be performed by a licensed physician; (*b*) that the states' only interest in regulating abortions during the second twelve weeks of pregnancy was to protect maternal health; and (*c*) that in the last twelve weeks of pregnancy, states might choose to prohibit abortion except in life-threatening situations. Where in the constitution the Supreme Court discovered these detailed provisions remains a mystery. The immediate effect of the Court's foray into legislation without the benefit of a popular mandate was to activate an antiabortion movement that has been a potent factor in US politics ever since (Hunter 1994).

The ratio of abortions to live births is about 1:3 in the US (Statistical Abstract of the United States 2002, table 88). We have no overall ratio for the EU but estimates of legal abortion rates from 1975 to 1996 are available for ten of the fifteen member states (Henshaw, Singh, and Haas 1999), whence it appears that abortion is much more widely practiced in the EU than in the United States. For Denmark, the UK, and Sweden abortions significantly outnumbered live births in 1996; for France, the numbers were about equal, and for Belgium, the Netherlands, Italy, and Spain births outnumbered abortions but not nearly as much as in the United States. Nowhere in the EU do we see the extraordinary rates observed in some socialist and ex-socialist countries where abortions outnumber live births by as much as six to one.

The principal effect of abortion is to reduce the incidence of extramarital births because few abortion patients are married. Even fewer are educated or affluent. Some are very young. Ignorance, carelessness, and contraceptive failure account for most abortions in the EU and the US; elsewhere in the world, abortion is a substitute for unavailable or unaffordable contraceptives (Kitting 2000).

4.5. **Sexual transactions**

From remote antiquity to around 1960, sexual transactions were governed by certain conditions that appeared to be part of the natural order. Maternity was self-evident. Paternity was hypothetical. A Spanish hidalgo of the seventeenth century would present his son at court with the formula, 'his mother is virtuous and I believe him to be mine'. In all the lineages that involved the transmission of property and reputation—peasants, merchants, and aristocrats—nubile women were dangerous assets, only partially secured by the tokens of virginity displayed at weddings, by careful chaperonage, by nonstop pregnancy and breast feeding, and by a heavy domestic workload. In the United States in 1800, there were 278 births for every thousand women aged 15–44. On the conservative assumption that a fourth of this group were single or widowed, the figure tells us that every year more than a third of all eligible wives gave birth. A natural division of labor entrusted women with childcare, meal preparation, washing and cleaning, and men with the outside work that supported the household.

The details varied by social class but the pattern remained the same. For affluent women, household chores were replaced by the supervision of servants; for affluent men, physical labor was replaced by the management of property or the duties of office, and though a good deal of sexual freedom crept into these more comfortable circles, upper-class women were still generally confined to the private sphere.

Male chastity had no independent social value and men were encouraged to seek out sexual partners before marriage and to some extent, afterward. But since coitus ordinarily involved some risk of pregnancy, premarital and extramarital encounters were hazardous for both sexes, unless the woman were a prostitute or certifiably barren. The man might be confronted with an unwanted responsibility or by angry male relatives. The woman risked social demotion and the ugly choice between a dangerous abortion (or infanticide) and an unwanted child. No wonder Marguerite went mad when Faust deserted her, and no wonder he deserted her.

The choice of a marriage partner was critical for both parties. The man assumed lifelong responsibilities and accepted a permanent loss of sexual freedom and personal autonomy. For the women, that choice implied lifelong dependence and a career of childbearing. For both, the choice of a marriage partner was intrinsically dramatic since it meant the abandonment of other and possibly more promising marital candidates—some real, some hypothetical. That critical choice was the central theme of Elizabethan comedies, Victorian novels, and early Hollywood films precisely because it resonated so strongly with the prospective choices of the unmarried people in the audience and the retrospective choices of those already married.

In principle and often in practice, the marriage transaction brought compensating gains to both parties. The man gained status, an assured sexual outlet, and the prospect of heirs. The woman gained status, a permanent right to support, an assured sexual outlet (not always viewed as a gain), and the company and affection of children. Both acquired new relatives and found their existing kin ties strengthened.

The expectation that marriage would be indissoluble ('till death do us part') arose under preindustrial conditions in which the economic resources of the average husband at any but the highest social level were barely sufficient to support himself, his wife, and their numerous children in the style appropriate to their station. Moreover, among all but the poorest families, marriage entailed an intermingling of property not easily reversed. The expectation of permanence persisted in the industrial era as long as most families were wholly supported by a male breadwinner. It began to disappear when that was no longer true.

Once again, it is difficult to disentangle cause and effect. As chemical innovations made conception voluntary and mechanical inventions greatly reduced the hours required to maintain a family household, the labor pool in the United States and in the EU was greatly enlarged by an influx of married women—no longer fully occupied by childcare and housework. Was it cause or effect that at about the same time the standard of living for the average family rose so high that the wages or salary of a sole breadwinner no longer sufficed? And was it cause or effect that a huge social movement appeared at about the same time to reject traditional gender roles and to claim full participation in the public sphere for women?

Sexual transactions took on a different character. Unmarried women claimed the same freedom as men to pleasure themselves with multiple lovers or to seek out casual sexual encounters. Virginity, once so desperately prized, became mildly disreputable. Men and women entered consensual unions on equal terms and without long-term obligations. Single women routinely decided to bear children without recognized fathers. Married women commonly limited themselves to one child, or to none. Homosexual couples demanded legal recognition of their unions.

Marriage, still widely practiced in the US and in most of the EU countries, now embodies a much simpler transaction, whose principal term is mutual sexual exclusivity. Husband and wife have nearly equal support obligations and husbands may in principle if not often in practice be drafted for childcare and housework. The family now has two heads rather than one. Either can initiate a divorce and either may be called on for child support. Wives are no longer required to take their husbands' names, and children may be named after father, mother, or both.

The distinction between the public and private spheres is disappearing along with the associated gender roles of breadwinner and homemaker. On the one hand, the public sphere is no longer reserved for men. On the other hand, the private sphere is no longer exempt from administrative oversight.

Meanwhile, the obligations of husbands to wives, and indeed of men to women, have been much reduced. This appears in trivial ways, in precedence through doors and moderation of language, but the important effects are transactional. Husbands no longer have an unqualified responsibility to support their wives during marriage; to the extent that spouses pool their resources, husbands and wives have reciprocal claims on each other's incomes, but the pooling is itself elective. The change appears most clearly after divorce. Until quite recently, the husband's support obligations survived the dissolution of the marriage and alimony was customarily awarded for life or until the wife remarried. Alimony today, if awarded at all, is for a limited term and American women are sometimes ordered to pay alimony to ex-husbands, which until quite recently, would have been unthinkable. Aside from marriage, any sexual relationship between a man and a woman used to create legal and moral responsibilities for the man, most obvious if the woman became pregnant. They were part of a traditional scenario in which the man in such a case was presumed to have seduced a reluctant woman and therefore to be liable for any damage she suffered in reputation or body. That presumption has entirely vanished.

It is fair to say that the sexual norms of West Europeans and their descendants have changed more since 1960 than in the previous 2000 years. In practice, most married couples in the EU and the United States continue to enact many of the traditional gender roles, but neither the law nor social pressure compels them to do so.

The parent–child relationship has changed also. The paternal role has been greatly abbreviated by law and custom. In part, this reflects the rise of the female-headed family. But the changes within families composed of married couples and their children have been equally striking. In two-parent families, the father is no longer regarded, even pro forma and conventionally, as the final disciplinarian. The corporal punishment that he formerly reserved for serious child misde-meanors is now morally suspect and can be legally actionable. New ideas about children's rights and new concerns about child abuse have given the sophisticated television-raised child the information he or she needs to resist any show of paternal authority he, or especially she, considers excessive and to invoke outside sanctions against a male parent whose actions are sexually suspect.

The reduction of maternal authority is less evident, if only because mothers are seen as cobelligerents in the revolt against patriarchy. Opposition to paternal authority seems to be particularly marked in families formed by remarriage in which the husband is stepfather to some or all of the children. But since parental authority is more often than not exercised jointly in functioning two-parent fam-ilies, the undermining of the father means that parents acting together have less authority than they had before, are less able to influence their children's choice of friends or schools or vocations, and less able to demand loyalty to family or sect or principles. Concurrently, the expansion of governmental retirement systems has virtually removed the obligation of adult children to share income with elderly parents, while the escalation of child-raising costs at every stage from playpen to university has greatly increased the fiscal obligations of parents to children.

4.6. **Working women**

In recent years, the employment of women has gained on the employment of men, the employment of married women has gained on the employment of single women, and the employment of married women with children has gained on the employment of married women without children. In the EU, 54 percent of women between aged 15 and 64 were employed in 2000. Men of the same age were only ten percentage points higher.

Married women living with their husbands are now more likely to work outside the home if they have children than if they have none and the same is true of single, divorced, separated, and widowed women.

In earlier times, the employment of married women in the US was confined to underprivileged families. In their 1924–5 study of Middletown, the Lynds found that more than half of the wives of factory workers entered the labor force intermittently when their husbands were out of work or incapacitated. The Lynds were unable to find any business class wives who took paid employment (Lynd and Lynd 1929).

The business class wives of that era stayed home for the duration of their married lives. But even in the working class the employment of married women with children under 6 was negligible in that era. Today, two-thirds of married women with children under 6 hold outside jobs, as well as three quarters of married women with older children at home—higher than the average rate for men (Statistical Abstract of the United States 2000, table 654).

The motive most often mentioned is economic pressure. The growth of family real income virtually ceased in the United States around 1970, while living standards continued to rise and the cost of housing, health care, automobiles, and college educations rose faster than the general rate of inflation. The earnings of one middle-income breadwinner were no longer sufficient to provide a family with a middle-class standard of living. But this does not explain why the employment of married women with young children had already risen substantially by 1970 and other factors must be invoked. The simplification of housework, which began half a century earlier with the electric washing machine and the vacuum cleaner, continued with such innovations as wash-and-wear clothing, precooked frozen meals, and microwave ovens. Concurrently, the doctrines of feminism called on women to shake off their dependence on men and compete with them on equal terms. The domestic role was denigrated and married women came to see employment more as an opportunity for self-fulfillment than as a burden. The new viewpoint was widely accepted by married men too; it decreased their obligations without much affecting their comfort, since working wives continued, for the most part, to be responsible for housekeeping and childcare.

Studies of the division of family labor both in the US and in the EU showed that it changed only marginally when wives entered the labor force, except, of course, for an enormous increase in external childcare, both in the homes of relatives and friends and in group care centers, a vast increase in preprimary schooling, and a marked decline in the average duration of parenting as families became smaller. Other factors were the enlargement of the service sector and the gradual disappearance of dirty and strenuous work in industry—trends that increased the proportion of jobs for which women were well qualified, and the earlier retirement of male workers, which also enlarged job opportunities for women.

This shift in the role of married women was arguably the most far-reaching social change to affect the US and most of the EU countries in the later decades of the twentieth century.

4.7. **Countervailing tendencies**

The great recent changes in family structure that we have just reviewed suggest that we ought to look for correspondingly important changes in family attitudes and values, but they turn out to be rather elusive. One reason is that the traditional attitudes and values are both persistent and flexible. Contemporary Americans and Europeans continue to disapprove of divorce in general while accepting and even welcoming the divorces of their relatives and friends. Parents favor adolescent chastity but discover as little as they possibly can about the sexual activities of their adolescent children. Unmarried mothers, whose own mothers were unmarried, express as much attachment to the ideal of a happy marriage as married professional women.

The fragilisation of marriage is real but there are two countervailing tendencies: (a) the extraordinary value placed on marriage by people who reject most of its traditional obligations; and (b) the emotional and social importance of the parentele or extended family.

Although few penalties are now attached to unmarried cohabitation, most of the cohabiting couples who stay together eventually marry. Although divorce signifies the failure of a marriage, a great many divorced persons choose to marry again. The removal of the legal and economic constraints on which the institution of marriage seemed to depend has left intact many elements of its cultural pattern.

Does this mean that the traditional family is not crumbling away? The evidence is contradictory. On the one hand, the number of nonmarital births and of consensual unions continues to increase, while the experience of the African-American population shows that the exclusion of men from the nuclear family is not unthinkable, and the Swedish experience shows that the elimination of marriage in favor of consensual relationships without long-term obligation is feasible also.

But the emotional values of marriage have proved remarkably tenacious. Although people marry late and their marriage vows to cherish each other 'until death do them part' are merely contingent, their weddings are more elaborate, costly, and ceremonious than ever before. The US 'wedding industry' channels billions of dollars into gowns, flowers, rings, invitations, services, receptions, banquets, orchestras, and honeymoon travel—all planned with professional consultants. And in Rome or Paris on any spring weekend, there is no break in the parade of gorgeously costumed and coiffed brides arriving in hired limousines with their attendants to be photographed in front of iconic monuments.

Nor is this mere outward show. In a 1990 survey, four out five EU respondents rejected the view that marriage is an outdated institution, close to nine out of ten agreed that children need a home with both a mother and a father to grow up happily (Ashcroft and Timms 1992).

As the nuclear family weakens, another form of the family moves to the foreground—what French sociologists call the parentele. The word has long existed in both French and English to denote a set of kindred, but its recent use to denote a set of relatives who maintain a network of close interaction is still relatively unfamiliar. Indeed, the thing itself has attracted less scholarly attention than any social phenomenon of comparable importance. The neglect has been so persistent that we have no way of telling how today's parenteles compare with those of former generations.

In American and British literature it is sometimes miscalled the 'extended family'. But that is a designation that takes in all recognized kin. The parentele, as now defined, consists only of the relatives and near-relatives with whom a given subject maintains close and continuous contact. For the typical EU or US resident, the parentele includes undivorced parents, some step-parents, nearly all children and grandchildren, siblings living nearby and some distant ones, and a few individuals selected from the roster of aunts, uncles, nieces, nephews, and cousins. It often includes a few persons not connected by blood or marriage— friends, lovers, servants, even neighbors, but it is always grounded on kinship. When a West European or American speaks of 'my family', it is usually possible to tell by the context whether she means her nuclear family or her parentele. A statement like 'We always spend Christmas with my family', plainly refers to a parentele. 'My family was very poor when I was growing up', refers to a nuclear family. The members of an intact nuclear family may share the same parentele, but cohabiting adults and some married couples participate in separate parenteles linked by themselves. Nearly all one's remoter kin, especially in-laws, have parenteles somewhat different than one's own.

The great majority of Western Europeans and Americans settle close to their parents and find other relatives by blood or marriage in the same vicinity with whom they maintain continuous communication in person or by telephone, with whom they gather for weddings, funerals, christenings, birthdays, anniversaries, graduations, and holidays; with whom they exchange the appropriate gifts and tokens on these occasions; and from whom they receive emotional support routinely and material support when needed. They live their personal histories with the parentele as audience and supporting cast. Nothing new, of course; about the nineteenth century, Michelle Perrot writes. 'For workers, migrations and changes of residence were never accidental. Considerations of kinship and occupation determined where people went' (Perrot 1999).

About three-quarters of adult children in Western Europe, according to Mendras, live within 20 km of their parents and most of them see their parents at least once a week. These proportions are even higher in Italy where unmarried adults are likely to remain in the same house as their parents; somewhat lower but still over half in France and Britain. In the US, where while only about half of adults with living parents are settled in the same vicinity, more than 95 percent of them see or speak to their parents at Christmas (Caplow 1982; Mendras 1997).

The few recent, empirical studies of parenteles suggest that they are often heterogeneous with respect to occupational status and income, since membership is open to appropriately related persons without much screening. Of course, the more affluent the participants, the greater the area within which close contact can be maintained.

When a nuclear family is broken by divorce or bereavement, it is usually the parentele that picks up the pieces, binds the wounds, and decides collectively what new arrangements must be made. That this key social institution should have escaped scholarly notice until quite recently almost defies belief. One reason for the neglect may be the myth of the isolated nuclear family that long prevailed in the sociological literature as an offshoot of the Gemeinschaft–Gesellschaft model, which denied the possibility of social solidarity in modern, urban settings. Another explanation might be found in the career pattern of academic scholars who are seldom able to find teaching or research positions located close to their relatives, and who therefore underestimate the importance of the parentele for the great majority who do settle close to their relatives.

Although we have no way of reconstructing the long-term trend of parentele activity, it is reasonable to propose that the fragilization of the nuclear family has shifted functions to the parentele and strengthened it.

One trend that has visibly changed the composition, if not the size, of the typical parentele in recent decades is the development of what Mendras has identified as the Third Age—the life situation of healthy, retired people, with the energy and means to engage in activities of their own choosing. In former times, as he points out, only civil servants enjoyed a well-paid retirement. Most workers persisted until death or disability. But the combination of greater life expectancy, nearly universal pensions and retirement at younger and younger ages has created a new stage of the life cycle, marked by active leisure and relative affluence. The typical parentele has been extended by a generation, sometimes by two. The age-old problem of dependent elders has nearly disappeared, and it is now more often the elders who provide material and emotional support for their descendants than the other way around.

But if kinship continues to be the cement that holds these two societies together at the micro level, its meaning has changed profoundly in recent decades. The individual is no longer visualized as part of a biological organization stretching from the past into the future. He is not bound to serve the family; the family exists to serve him, and it can be discarded at will.

Some of the trends that have shaken this primal institution have run their course. The pace of women's entry into the labor force has necessarily slackened where most women already hold paid employment. The shift of gender roles has not much further to go. Elective childbearing is firmly established in the EU and the US, although not yet in the rest of the world. But the trend toward later marriage—or no marriage—is still running, together with the steady increase of extramarital births, and no one can say how far the decline of fertility in the EU will go.

This last point reminds us that, despite the massive convergences between our two societies, there are some ineradicable differences. The peasants of Western Europe developed a great variety of family patterns linked to different modes of cultivation, mate selection, and inheritance, which commonly varied not only between nations but even between adjoining valleys, and the influence of these customary practices is still traceable among their urban descendants today. There is much less regional variation in the US and relatively less variation by ethnicity and social class, so that family trends in the EU are clearly more difficult to understand.

5 Politics and institutional architectures

Alberto Martinelli

There are several studies comparing the political system of the United States with one or more nation-states of Europe which show significant differences both between the countries on the two sides of the Atlantic and great interstate diversity within Europe. These include different types of electoral systems (majority vs. proportional), different rates of voting behavior and political participation, different forms of organized interests representation and pressure politics, different party systems and different party ideologies and organizational structures, different institutional architectures in the form of the state (centralized vs. federal) and in the mechanisms of democratic accountability (parliamentary, semi-presidential, and presidential), differences in policymaking and policy implementation, differences in the structure and function of the judiciary, and differences in the role of the media.

Rare, however, are comparisons between the political systems of the United States and the EU. Such comparison is difficult for several reasons. First, the timing and sequence of the historical processes of the two unions are quite different: the United States is more than two centuries old, while the formation of the EU started less than 60 years ago and is still in progress. Second, the territorial boundaries of the United States have long been consolidated, while those of the EU are still enlarging. Third, the United States polity is the most powerful nation-state in the contemporary world, whereas the European polity cannot be considered as simply an enlarged version of the nation state; it is rather a multidimensional, quasi-federal polity characterized by supranational governance. Forth, both the EU and the United States are ethnically heterogeneous, multicultural polities, but whereas the internal diversity of the United States is due to successive waves of ethnic migrations into the country, that of the EU primarily results from the different genetic codes of the various nations constituting the EU member-states, and only secondarily from immigration. However, the comparison is both justified and worthwhile because it makes more sense to compare equivalents, and the comparison fosters intellectual debate on such key issues as the quality of modern democracy and the roles which both the United States and the EU can perform in contemporary global politics.

The differences between the United States and most of the European states are striking despite the fact they are all variants of poliarchic democracy. However, if one shifts the comparison to the level of the two unions, they appear more alike than is generally believed. The model of democratic decision-making at the EU supranational level is more similar to the US 'pluralist' model of Madison's 'compound republic'—with its fragmented governmental structure and pervasive societal interest groups—than it is to the 'parliamentary' model existing in various forms in most EU member-states.

In order to argue this thesis, I shall first analyze the main features of both the American and the European political systems. I shall then identify their essential similarities and basic differences; finally, I shall focus on parties and elections, interest groups, and political culture, also accounting for the type and degree of internal differentiation of the two unions.

5.1. **The main features of the American polity**

The United States is a federal democracy with both a vertical and a horizontal separation of powers. According to Madison's notion of the 'compound republic', freedom is protected through a constitutional structure where each part can keep the other within its own constitutional limits through a system of checks and balances. There is a basic distinction between the division of powers and the separation of powers (Olstrom 1987). Power is divided in every democracy, in the sense that the legislative, the executive, and the judiciary are functionally differentiated, but only in some democracies are the legislative and the executive branches institutionally separated as well—in the sense that they are reciprocally independent in terms of electoral legitimization—and are therefore forced to cooperate.

The notion of a 'compound republic' implies both a vertical and a horizontal separation of powers. The vertical separation of powers between the federal center and the states is guaranteed by the principle of double representation in Congress: territorial, whereby the states have equal representation in the Senate; and individual, whereby representatives are elected in proportion to the population in the House. The basic tenet of federalism is applied in the sense that the powers attributed to the federal center are carefully defined and circumscribed, the justifying principle being that they can be better performed at that level of government, while all other powers are left to the member-states. Indeed, since the Civil War, the national government has grown steadily more powerful in relation to the states. Congress and the judiciary have expanded the federal role in many areas formerly reserved to the states, such as crime control, education, health care, environmental protection, and product safety. And yet, as the recent debate on gay and lesbian marriages has shown, conflicts of competence among local authorities, states, and the federal government still exist.

The horizontal separation of powers implies that the executive bodies, the legislatures, and the judiciaries enjoy equivalent and independent legitimization and that the function of government, both at the federal and at the state level, is shared by several institutions. The president does not depend on the Congress's confidence. Laws must be approved separately by the Senate and the House and then signed into law by the president. The president can veto (or threaten to veto) a law, thus influencing the legislative process, and when she or he does so, Congress can vote on the law again but with a two-thirds majority in both chambers (an event which has seldom occurred in American political history). The president enjoys extensive powers in policymaking and in appointing the members of his or her administration, judges of the Supreme Court, and diplomats abroad, but she or he is subject to the Senate's advice and consent and to Congress's approval of the budget, which gives the president the means with which to implement his or her policy. With his or her veto power the president takes part in the legislative process; with its power of advice and consent the Congress takes part in the executive process. The president and the Congress are induced to cooperate because each has powers which are necessary for the functioning of the other. And the Supreme Court regulates conflicts which may arise among institutions and between institutions and the citizens. Minority rights are strong, since the constitution requires qualified majorities to ratify a treaty and to close off debate, and very seldom has either party held such a majority. Mindful of Hirschmann's analysis of the complementary role played by passions and interests in politics, we can agree with Bell that the American political system is a two-tiered structure: the presidency is a plebiscitarian referendum, in which the person, not the party, is the object of identification and evaluation, the focus of mass sentiments and passions, while the Congress is elected by a responsiveness to group interests (Bell 1988: 25).

According to some critics (Lowi 1979), the two-tiered structure is no longer balanced: power has shifted from the legislative branch to the executive as a consequence of central government's increasing role as a major provider of benefits to individuals, groups, and organizations since the New Deal, and—we can add—as a result of the United States's hegemonic role in global politics. And yet Congress still wields real power, and uses it vis-à-vis the president especially in periods of divided government.

The performance of American political institutions is in fact increasingly affected by divided government, this being the situation which occurs when the two major parties divide control of the executive and legislative branches. Unified control by one party over both the presidency and Congress has dramatically declined in recent decades: in the past thirty-nine years since 1968 there have been only ten years (1977–80, 1993–4, 2003–6) of unified control. Contrary to the widely held opinion—well-argued by Mayhew (1991)—that divided government is not dramatically different from periods of united party control, I maintain that it leads to several important consequences which were particularly evident in the 1990s.

First, divided government fosters greater interinstitutional conflict—as exemplified, on the one hand, by the growing use of congressional hearings to challenge the legitimacy of presidential decisions and, on the other, by the use of federal agencies to bring the behavior of congress members under scrutiny. Second, there is a growing vote polarization between the two parties in Congress; the percentage of cases, in both the Senate and the House of Representatives, in which the majority of one party has voted against the majority of the other grew from less than 30 percent in 1972 to over 80 percent in 1996, diminishing once again to 45 percent in 2002 (Congressional Weekly Report, various years). Third, the role of the Speaker of the House has been strengthened: Newt Gingrich in 1994 resembled the premier of a shadow government with a program alternative to that of President Clinton (a program that was clearly set out in *The Contract with America* and adopted by the vast majority of the elected Republican congressmen). Finally, confusion in decision-making has grown, with the consequence that it is increasingly difficult to identify the decision-makers to be held accountable and responsible for given political decisions. Divided government does not result in political stalemate, but it certainly makes it more difficult for the president to implement his or her decisions—as exemplified by Clinton's inability to overcome the resistance raised by powerful pressure groups, such as the American Medical Association and major insurance companies, against his health care reform—and it makes the president highly adept at symbolic politics but largely incapable of policy effectiveness (Lowi 1979); a president who increasingly resorts to rhetorical appeals to the people (Fabbrini 2005).

The American political system is indeed a compound democracy as originally defined by Madison, where sovereignty is fragmented among different institutions—the president and the federal government, the two houses of Congress, and state governments—which compete for power and control over each other in the exercise of power. Between the early decades of the nineteenth century and the 1930s, the primacy of Congress was replaced by the primacy of the president, and the federal government gained power at the expense of the states owing to the major structural changes taking place in the American economy and the increasingly hegemonic role of the United States, but the complex system of institutional checks and balances substantially held firm. In recent decades, although Congress has been unable to reestablish its primacy in policymaking, it has challenged the presidency on both domestic and foreign policy. In periods of divided government, this has given rise—also because of the weak aggregative power of parties—to permanent conflict between the two institutions. And this in its turn has increased the political influence of the judiciary in the regulation of that conflict (and its growing politicization), as manifested by the Supreme Court's decision to uphold the contested results of the 2000 presidential election. The presidency is increasingly personalized, but American democracy has not become plebiscitarian, for no power can claim to be above the constitution. The robust constitutional basis of the US political system also prevents its abuse by a majority. But this is at the price of intense institutional conflict between the president and Congress, the difficult assessment of political accountability, and the strong influence exerted by powerful pressure groups on policymaking.

5.2. **The main features of the European polity**

The politico-institutional nature of the EU is more complex and less neatly defined, and it is in constant flux. Understanding it requires particular attention to be paid to such questions as: What sort of polity does the EU represent? What are the main features of the pan-European structures of governance? At what levels and through what agencies does the EU government operate? And what role is played by the politics of multiple identities?

Three main approaches to these matters are usually adopted in the literature on the institutional nature of the EU: (*a*) the intergovernmental approach, which argues that EU decision-making is still predominantly conducted on the basis of agreements reached between sovereign member-states; (*b*) the supranationalist approach, which argues that the EU is a supranational state; and (*c*) the multidimensional governance approach, which views the EU as a tiered polity characterized by multilevel and multiagency governance with new levels of political authority which have emerged in addition to, and alongside, those already in existence.

These approaches reproduce to some extent both the old controversy between neofunctionalists and neorealists and attempts to combine the two perspectives. The central idea behind the neofunctionalist approach is that of 'functional' and 'political' spillovers, these being spontaneous and incremental processes resulting from the internal logic of integration. Functional spillover occurs when states decide to integrate certain economic sectors, forcing them to incorporate further sectors because of economic interdependence. Political spillover is the result of a new political reality arising from the shift of political decision-making from the national to the supranational level. As decisions are now taken at the supranational level, powerful interest groups shift their lobbying to that level in order to influence the decision-making process, and they pressurize their national governments into shifting ever more political functions to the supranational level. Neorealists, and world system theorists, on the other hand, maintain that national governments are still the truly significant actors in the integration process and that they enter into agreements in accordance with the national interest (George 1991; Bornschier 2000: 27–8).

On the one hand, the supranationalist approach fits better with what the 1992 Maastricht Treaty defines as the EU's 'first pillar' of economic integration. This pillar consists of the communities, which are often thought to be a single Community but are, in fact, three: the EEC, by far the most important of them, which was established by the 1957 Treaty of Rome; the ECSC established by the 1951 Treaty of Paris; and EURATOM, established in the April 24, 1957 Treaty of Rome. The EU subsequently developed through the 1986 Luxembourg Single European Act, the 1997 Amsterdam European Community Treaty, and the 1992 decision to form the European monetary union. On the other hand, the intergovernmental cooperation approach applies better to the second pillar, which consists of 'common foreign and security policy', and to the third pillar comprising 'police and judicial cooperation in criminal matters' (previously called 'justice and home affairs').

It is, however, the third approach that, I submit, yields the best characterization of the European polity. In fact, the EU is not a simple international organization with limited and clear objectives, no autonomous institutions, and unanimous votes on all matters. Nor is it a superstate, a kind of enlarged copy of the nation-states of its member countries. The EU functions like a state, that is a sovereign polity endowed with the autonomy and legitimacy necessary to impose its decisions on a defined population and territory, but it lacks what Max Weber distinguished as the most significant features of the sovereignty of a modern state: monopoly over legitimized violence, fiscal authority, and effective law enforcement institutions. The EU also suffers from a 'democratic deficit', and it lacks the major features of a parliamentary democracy in which the European Council, the Council of Ministers, and the European Central Bank are not accountable to the European Parliament (EP). And yet Community law is superior to the law of member-states, and the EU performs several functions which are typical of nation-states, such as regulating markets and money, implementing public policies, delivering public goods and services, holding elections, administering a budget, and acting as a single player in international organizations.

The EU is a peculiar type of polity, an original form of organization of political power, which shares some important features with nation-states but lacks many others, and which is constantly evolving toward an unsettled future (see figure 1, from Hix 1999: 6). It is, however, less peculiar than one might think, for two main reasons. First, because it can be viewed—like the American polity—as a variant of the 'compound republic', although the analogy with the United States should not be pushed too far, and it is not likely that the EU will evolve in the direction of the American union, given that the strength of its constituent nations is greater, and that the EU will continue to develop its own specific institutional architecture. Second, because the EU is, and will become, less peculiar in the future insofar as it represents a model for similar supranational unions in other regions of the world and has proved consistent with the new context of globalization and the needs of democratic global governance (Martinelli 2004). In the age of globalization, in fact, it is no longer possible to conceive the nation-state—and the party politics associated with its rule—as the only locus of political power and governmental action. It is instead necessary to examine the state within the wider field of the various forms of governance. The process of European integration is a form of political organization which is both a product of globalization and a constituent element of global governance. It is so not only in the sense that it stems from the desire of European nations to unite in order to be an active participant in globalization rather than a passive recipient thereof (Beck 2000), because global competitiveness requires larger and stronger political players (Commission White Paper 1993), but also in the sense that it is consistent with the requirements of global governance in the information age and with the idea that the state is better conceived as just one element in the decentralized array of government and authority with which the EU seeks to regulate and harmonize the European economic space. According to Castells (1998), globalization has transformed European integration from a series of defensive projects into a network state.

In the intentions of its intellectual parents, European integration would extend beyond the nation-states of the member countries and finally replace them, although it must necessarily be created under the control of nation-states. The resistance of nation-states to any attempt to move into a federal direction has, however, always been strong; and the stronger it has been, the larger the amounts of sovereignty that have been functionally shifted to the supranational level. But the nationalists have been converted to acceptance of the European project by globalization. After the slowing down of European integration in the 1970s, the process once again accelerated in the 1980s and 1990s, because it became clear that a supranational union is the best way to enable nation-states to adapt to the new challenges of globalization and play a role in global competition without losing too many of their national prerogatives. No single EU member country, however economically powerful or politically ambitious, can seriously contemplate acting as a global player, whereas the EU has the potential to do so. Ironically, the European integration intended to supersede the nation-state may guarantee its survival in a more complex world (Badie 1995).

The EU does not substitute for the nation-states of member countries, since these have been simultaneously strengthened and weakened by European integration. To a certain extent, the EU can be seen as an instance of 'consensual democracy' (Lijphart 1999), insofar as the different sociocultural components of European society are recomposed at the political level by democratic elites open to cooperation and agreement. Another prominent feature is multilevel governance.

Rather than replacing the nation-state, the European Union has developed a system of governance that relies on action taken at a whole series of levels (local, regional, national, supranational) by a variety of state and non-state actors who exist in an integrated hierarchy of decision making (Rumford 2002: 50).

Multilevel governance rather than government, regulation rather than rule, are more appropriate connotations of the European institutions and policies, as argued in the works of Stone and Sandholz (1998) and Majone (1996).

According to Stone and Sandholz, the EU is changing from an interstate bargaining system into a multidimensional, quasi-federal polity characterized by supranational governance. Growing integration does not necessarily stem from intergovernmental bargaining; it may even come about without the conscious leadership of EU institutions, which explains why the process—as measured in terms of exchanges across borders and the amount of communitarian legislation—continued even during the 'Eurosclerosis' period of the 1970s and early 1980s. The nongovernmental actors of European transnational civil society that engage in intra-EU exchanges (economic trade and investment, social, political, and cultural relations) directly or indirectly influence policymaking processes and outcomes at the European level because they generalize demand for European-level rules (standardization) and policies and for the institutionalization of supranational policy domains. Integration consequently does not proceed uniformly, and is necessarily more complete in certain sectors and policy areas than others.

Majone argues that the EU is essentially a 'regulatory state', something other than a supranational state or the result of interstate agreements, which works by encouraging the development of a panoply of independent or quasi-independent regulatory agencies designed to correct market failures (monopolies, environmental pollution, and industrial crises), and by creating a space across which regulatory innovation can be disseminated and within which the regulatory systems of member-states can be harmonized. The EU activity has not replaced national activity, but it has 'actually created new regulatory responsibilities on an unprecedented scale'. The decline of the Keynesian welfarist state has brought, not deregulation, but intense regulatory reform. Although in need of updating and reformulation since the creation of the euro and the European Central Bank in charge of monetary policy, Majone's key thesis that the EU regulates, rather than rules, is still valid.

Governance rather than government, regulation rather than rule, also take the form of various kinds of informal coordination—such as peer reviews, benchmarking, and policy learning—all of which are characteristic features of the EU. A typical example of European policymaking is the open method of coordination (OMC). The OMC was announced as a new instrument of governance at the Lisbon EU socioeconomic summit in March 2000. Drawing on experience with the coordination of employment policies over the preceding decade, OMC has been broadly applied to a great range of policy fields as part of the Lisbon strategy aimed at turning the EU into 'the most competitive and dynamic knowledge-based economy in the world capable of sustainable economic growth with more and better jobs and social cohesion by 2010'. The OMC can generally be defined as a process based on participation and transparency as general principles and on guidelines and timetables, indicators and benchmarking, regional and national targets and measures, periodic monitoring, evaluation, peer review and feedback as key steps (Zeitlin and Pochet 2005). The OMC has been praised as a 'third way' for EU social policy between regulatory competition and harmonization, an alternative to both intergovernmentalism and supranationalism and as a new way for enhancing democratic participation and accountability within the EU by opening up the policymaking process to inputs from NGOs, social partners, and local/regional actors (Rodrigues 2002). On the other hand, it has been criticized as a potential threat to the 'Community method' of European integration through binding legislation and social dialogue agreements—an unnecessary 'soft law' option even in domains where the EU already possesses legislative powers (Goetschy 2003) and mostly as an exercise in symbolic politics where national governments repackage existing policies to demonstrate their apparent compliance with EU objectives (Radaelli 2003). Whatever evaluation can be made, OMC is an attempt to respond to the challenges of globalization, and to the need of enhancing EU competitiveness without abandoning traditional concern with employment and social cohesion. This implies a more active strategy in a wide group of policy areas, such as research/innovation, information society, enterprise promotion, structural economic reform, and education and training, besides the more traditional social policy areas of employment, social inclusion and pension, health and long-term care. The main reason for the slow implementation of the ambitious Lisbon strategy and OMC is that European integration has hitherto been mostly a 'negative integration', as Scharpf (1996) points out, where consensus has often been easily reached because the abolition of obstacles against the free circulation of people, capital, goods, and services has been a positive sum game. Competition in the global market, however, requires more positive integration as well, with greater coordination and further regulation, with the risk of arousing strong reactions by national governments and by key actors of the civil society.

Another key question of European democracy is that it has been an 'output democracy' legitimized by the success of the decisions taken rather than by the quality of democratic decision-making. Given these basic features, functional spillover and path dependency in the behavior of European elites are key factors in an explanation of why and how integration has proceeded in spite of many obstacles. A basic question is whether the achievement of further political integration does not require something more, and specifically a shared European identity as strong as the various national identities, and the closer involvement of European citizens in the European democracy.

The European polity is a mixed institutional system, one that is both federal and confederate. The EU does not have a formally clear separation of powers, but its logic of functioning actually upholds this principle (Figure 5.1).

Although the Commission is predominantly an executive body and the Union Council a legislative body, there is no clear distinction between the executive and the legislative functions. The Council is an extraordinarily powerful second chamber whose task is to discuss and approve laws, but it is made up of representatives of national governments with executive powers in their own countries. Moreover, the Council's meetings are as secret as are the meetings of executive bodies (the minutes of meetings are secret, although how the various nation-states have voted is now made public).

The Commission performs traditionally executive tasks—for instance, controlling the implementation by national governments of the Council's decisions—but it also has the power to initiate legislation, in the sense that the Council can decide only on matters defined and instructed by the Commission. The European Parliament has been the weakest institution to date, but it is now strengthening its role. The main change introduced by the Maastricht and the Amsterdam treaties was the co-decision procedure, which gave the EP—already influential on agenda setting (Tsebelis 1994)—absolute veto power in some areas of legislation. Previously, after approval of the Single European Act, Parliament had participated in the legislative process only on the basis of the cooperation principle, by virtue of the creation of a conciliation committee, and through the possibility of a third reading. The Amsterdam Treaty further enhanced the equal statuses of the Parliament and the Council in conciliation, and the powers of the former were enlarged by the provision that the Commission's president, who is nominated by the Council, must obtain the approval of the Parliament as well. Although the Parliament is institutionally less powerful than national parliaments, in the thirty

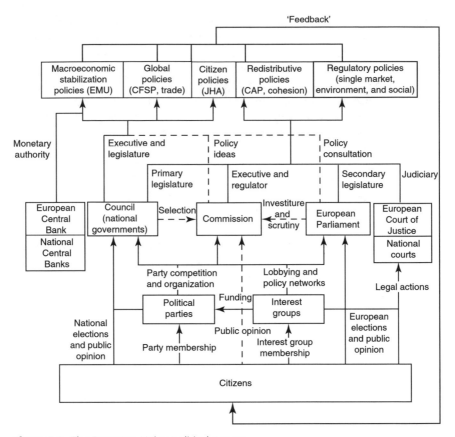

Figure 5.1. The European Union political system

years since the first significant increase in its powers (the 1970 Budget Act), it has been transformed from a consultative assembly into a true legislative body (Kreppel 2002: 89).

The legislative process is rather complex in the EU (Figure 5.2). The Commission starts the process, initiating a proposal and sending it to the Parliament; the Parliament gives its opinion and may suggest amendments; the Council discusses the proposal on the basis of the procedure (consultation, cooperation, co-decision, etc.) required by the nature of the policy suggested and may adopt the act after the first reading if there are no amendments; if amendments have been made, the proposal goes back to the Parliament, the Commission, and the Council for second readings. If opinions differ among the Council, the Commission, and the Parliament, the proposal is sent to a Conciliation Committee consisting of fifteen representatives each for the Parliament and the Council. If a joint text is successfully approved, within a maximum of eight weeks, the Parliament can approve it by a majority of votes cast, and the Council by a qualified majority (see figure 1, from Hix 1999: 86–7).

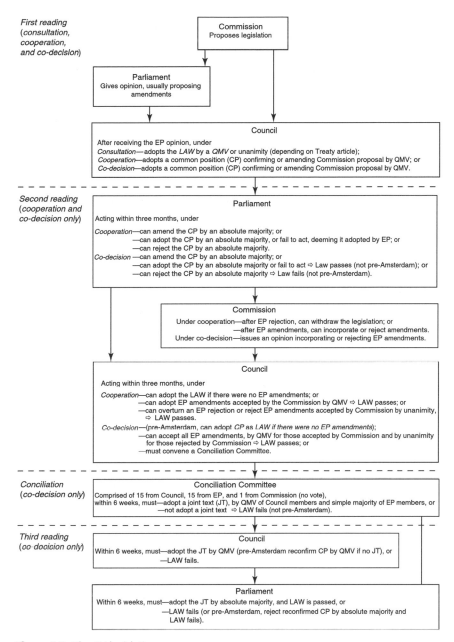

Figure 5.2. The EU legislative process

Although complex, this procedure is similar to that of the United States, where there is no decisional priority of either the president or Congress. In both cases, the passing of a new law requires diffused and reiterated negotiation aimed at consensus-building and which involves a plurality of institutional actors—working in both plenary sessions and in subcommittees—and allowing for extensive lobbying by interest groups.

The role of the judiciary is particularly important in building the political union. The Court of Justice has the key responsibility for reviewing whether the measures adopted by the member-states of the European Community and its institutions are in conformity with the basic constitutional charter. National sovereignty is no longer unlimited, because states must respect Union laws and implement their policies in accordance with it, lest violations be sanctioned by the Court of Justice. Access to the Court is not restricted to the member-states and the institutions of the Community. Legal proceedings may also be initiated by national courts of law, which can request a preliminary ruling concerning the interpretation or the validity of Community Acts. Community law is thus made much more stable by its decentralized enforcement, which is indirectly entrusted, beyond national governments, to a large number of national judges (Mancini 2000; Tesauro 2001).

The constitutional treaty (the exact formulation is 'Treaty to Adopt a Constitution for Europe'), which was approved in 2004 by the political leaders of the twenty five member-states and ratified by most EU member-state parliaments, was intended to consolidate the institutional architecture of the EU at the time of its enlargement to the east. The treaty, however, was rejected by referenda in France and the Netherlands—that is, two of the six founding member-states—for different reasons (fears that the European welfare model would be dismantled by a free-market-oriented EU in the French case, and worries about the consequences for human rights and national cultures and traditions of the EU enlargement in the Dutch case). As a result, the entire process is now in need of thorough reconsideration. The Union still functions, of course, since the existing treaties provide the necessary bases for cooperative action and supranational policymaking, but how to proceed and the form that integration will take are open questions. It is therefore worthwhile to assess the constitutional treaty briefly, although it is at present in abeyance, in order to evaluate the *status quaestionis* of European integration.

The constitutional treaty is a compromise between the supporters of two visions of the EU: the intergovernmental one which upholds the autonomy of the nation-states, and the federalist one which affirms the centrality of the EP and Commission. It is a compromise, however, which is strongly weighted in favor of the former approach. The national 'soul' has in fact prevailed, since states are still the source of sovereignty, and member-states have the right to withdraw from the Union. And yet the incipit to the constitution solemnly affirms that it 'is inspired by the will of the citizens and the states of Europe to build a common future'.

The constitution carries forward the process of political unification in various ways: first, it incorporates the charter of fundamental rights approved at the Conference of Nice: respect for human dignity and human rights (minorities' rights included), freedom, democracy, equality, rule of law, pluralism, nondiscrimination, tolerance, justice, solidarity, and gender parity. And it makes the pledge to uphold these values a necessary requirement for future membership.

Second, it rationalizes and simplifies the complex array of directives, norms, and procedures into a single legal framework. Third, it establishes a clearer division of competences between the Union and the member-states and it introduces a hierarchy of normative sources. Fourth, it extends the majority vote rule and introduces the possibility for the EC to extend, by unanimous vote, the range of policy decisions taken by majority. Fifth, it establishes a uniform legislative procedure which strengthens the EP's role, although it makes the process even more complex through the involvement of national parliaments. Sixth, it introduces the new figure of the foreign minister, unifying the two previously different roles of the commissioner for foreign relations and of the high representative for foreign policy.

On the other hand, however, the most important reforms have not been undertaken, owing to sharp disagreement among member-states. The two most significant unresolved questions are: (*a*) the dualism of authority between the Commission's president and the Council's president, which has been maintained and indeed reinforced by prolonging of the latter's mandate; and (*b*) the failure to introduce the majority principle in foreign and security policy decisions, which must still be taken by unanimous vote—thus rendering the EU impotent in this key area (as in several others).

A potential solution to this deadlock is official recognition of so-called 'reinforced cooperation' as was applied, for example, in the case of monetary union. Reinforced cooperation can take place whenever at least one-third of the member-states decide to pursue a project of further integration in areas of nonexclusive competence of the EU, and in CFSP, which cannot be achieved in a reasonable amount of time by the whole Union. Required for the purpose is a qualified majority of at least 55 percent of the representatives of the member countries in the European Council which account for at least 65 percent of the population. Authorization is granted by the European Council, which decides on the Commission's proposal after the Parliament's approval. Testifying to the importance of reinforced cooperation is the fact that the member countries involved can develop specific forms of coordination: as evidenced by the autonomy granted to the 'Eurogroup' formed by the countries belonging to the monetary union, which can nominate their own president for a thirty-month term. The increase in the policy areas where decisions can be taken by majority vote is, of course, a major step toward the construction of a European polity, but it also exacerbates the problem of the EU democratic deficit because it increases the cost of legitimacy: minorities can accept majority decisions only if there exist binding ties of reciprocal trust and common identity.

Although the rejection of the constitutional treaty by the French and Dutch referenda does not jeopardize the normal functioning of the EU, and could even foster reinforced cooperation, it has brought to the surface deep-seated disagreements about the EU institutional architecture and basic questions concerning European policy, such as reform of the European social model (ESM) and the availability of a CFSP. The EU will continue to evolve toward an unsettled future.

5.3. Similarities and differences between the US and EU polities

Outlined thus far have been the specific institutional architectures of the United States and the EU, and it has been suggested that they share a 'uniqueness' which is less unique than one might think. The United States and the EU can be seen as different variants of the 'compound republic', the pluralist model of democracy which differs from the parliamentary model (Coultrap 1999; Fabbrini 2002). From this brief outline, we may now draw up a list of basic similarities and differences.

The similarities can be summarized in light of the vertical and horizontal separation of democratic powers and the process of democratic representation and policymaking, as follows:

(*a*) democratically legitimate authority has different bases in the two legislative bodies, one representing the subsystems (the fifty US states and the twenty-seven EU member-states), the other the people directly, which exercise their powers on the basis of the subsidiarity principle;

(*b*) trilateral decision-making structures (President–Senate–House of Representatives in the United States; Council–Commission–Parliament in the EU);

(*c*) executive bodies largely independent of legislative confidence (president independent of the Senate and the House in the United States; Commission independent of the Council and the Parliament in the EU);

(*d*) independent judiciaries with important roles in policy formation and implementation: judicial review by any kind of court in the United States; revision of national legislation by the European Court in Luxembourg;

(*e*) elections do not choose the government but encourage competition and ensure changes within parliamentary bodies;

(*f*) decision-making is dispersed among complex frameworks of governance, and the principle of government by minorities is upheld—which entails the accountability of the powerholders—rather than the principle of the collective responsibility of a majority government;

(*g*) political parties are nominal, fragmented and rather weak, whereas interest groups are very influential and their activities are intense at different entry points to the policymaking process; and

(*h*) separation of powers makes it difficult to ascertain accountability and to assess the responsibility of decision-makers.

These features also produce similar virtues and vices in the functioning logic of the two democracies. In both cases, the separation of powers is a fundamental guarantee against tyranny by the majority and executive abuses. But, on the other hand, it makes it more difficult to establish who is responsible for what decision, it obstructs interparty competition, and it fosters tyranny by organized minorities.

The similarities between the two unions should not, however, be exaggerated, for the differences are even more marked than the analogies. They concern:

(a) electoral systems and, consequently, the legislature's type of legitimacy: in the EU there is no single election for the executive body; many different voting procedures are used to elect both the member-states' legislatures and the EP;

(b) the scope of Union sovereignty: contrary to the United States, the EU lacks several essential elements of sovereignty: monopoly over legitimate violence through a united army and a united police force, a single foreign policy, and the right to levy taxes on citizens;

(c) the role of the president: this is very strong, although checked and balanced by the counterpower of Congress in the United States, and rather weak in the EU, where it is split between the Commission's president—who remains in office for five years but enjoys limited power—and the European Council's president who is a 'primus inter pares' and until now has rotated every six months, although according to the new constitution will serve a two-and-a-half-year term, which can be repeated for another term);

(d) the parties' strength at state level: it is weak in the United States (where parties are essentially electoral machines and are limited in their preroga-tives by such mechanisms as the primaries), but it is still strong in the EU (although in decline because of the growing influence of the media);

(e) political cultures and party ideologies: the key differences are the absence of socialist and religious parties in the United States and the different connotations of the political Left and the political Right on the two sides of the Atlantic;

(f) different conceptions of citizenship: European citizenship—as stated in the Maastricht Treaty—does not substitute for national citizenship but com-pletes it; and

(g) different roles of identity politics: in the EU the most important form of identity politics is still national, although regionalism and multicultural-ism exert growing influence, whereas in the United States race and ethnic politics have usually played a greater role.

These key differences spring from the fact that, whereas the United States was born as a modern nation made up of people sharing basic values, attitudes, and hopes in an underpopulated and resource-plentiful continent, the EU is a supranational union of fully independent nation-states with different genetic codes and histori-cal paths, although they share a common cultural heritage.

This interweaving of similarities and differences between the two unions requires two qualifications. First, similar traits often have different causes. Sec-ond, specific features at the union level go together with different patterns of internal differentiation in member-states. In order to examine these questions, the following comparative analysis will focus first on political parties and electoral cleavages, then on interest groups, and finally on political cultures in the United States and the EU.

5.4. **Political parties and electoral cleavages in the United States**

Political parties are weak in both the United States and the EU, but in different ways and for different reasons. In the United States the two national parties are loose locally dominated federations; although political campaigning is permanent, national parties do not have stable, powerful bureaucracies; they play a role in presidential and congressional elections, but candidates rely mostly on their electoral machines, staff, and professional consultants.

The contemporary American party system has a number of specific features, which I shall now briefly outline.

First, it is a rather simplified political system with two major parties, and with a resistance to third-party candidates due to an electoral system that maintains the 'winner-take-all' principle of a single-member, simple plurality system in every state. The United States is the world's longest-lived two party system: the Democratic and the Republican parties continue to dominate American elections and to organize government, in spite of periodic third-party insurgencies. The two largest parties have shared presidential election victories almost equally between them since World War II, while the Democrats have held a majority of seats both in the Senate and in the House of Representatives for more years than the Republicans, as Figure 5.3 and Table 5.1 show.

According to a view recently popularized by Stanley Greenberg, in the post–World War II era no party has been able to develop a sustainable political project for long periods (Greenberg 2004). All major presidential attempts to launch a long-lasting political program, like Kennedy's 'New Frontier', Johnson's 'Great Society', Reagan's 'New Right', and Clinton's 'Third Way', were unable to prove decisive at the polls or to command public opinion by their own party. Every effort by the Democrats and Republicans to become the leading party of the era has created new partisan loyalties but also contested groups, without forming a stable majority in the country. This interpretation of American politics, however, is only partially convincing.

It is true that in the sixteen presidential elections since World War II (between 1944 and 2004) the Republicans have won nine times and had six different presidents, and the Democrats have won seven times and had six different presidents. At the beginning of the twenty-first century, the politics of parity—that is a situation where the two parties are closely matched and each party has an equal chance of victory—seemed to have reached their apogee, with G. W. Bush contending for victory against Al Gore. As Table 5.2 shows, in the 2000 elections, the winning margin of the popular vote was small (543,000 votes) and in favor of the

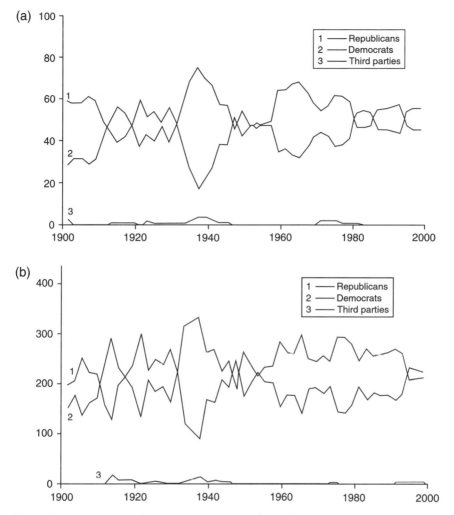

Figure 5.3. (a) US Senate (seats held by each party) and (b) US House of Representatives (seats held by each party)

Source: Caplow, Hicks, and Wattenberg (2001: 183)

defeated candidate—who obtained however a smaller number (five) of electoral votes—and the result itself required a decision by the Supreme Court because of contested popular votes in a few decisive states. In the 2004 elections, G. W. Bush's victory was less controversial (over 3 million more votes, or 50.73% against 48.27% for Kerry with a winning margin of 2.46%) but it reflected a vote markedly divided along regional, ethnic, occupational, and religious lines. Bush's victory went together with Republican control of both the House and the Senate. And Bush has been able to appoint two new judges and the new president of

Table 5.1. US Senate and House of Representatives 2004 and 2006 election results

Party	Breakdown			Total seats			Popular vote	
	Up	Elected	Not up	2004	2006	+/−	Vote	%
Democratic Party	17	22	27	44	49	+5	32,682,619	53.8
Republican Party	15	9	40	55	49	−6	25,784,256	42.5
Independents	1	2	0	1	2	+1	871,530	1.4
Libertarian Party	0	0	0	0	0	0	589,543	1.0
Green Party	0	0	0	0	0	0	373,314	0.6
Others	0	0	0	0	0	0	426,507	0.7
Total	33	33	67	100	100	0	60,727,769	100.0

United States Senate election results (2006)

Party	Seats				Popular vote		
	2004	2006	+/−	%	Vote	%	+/−
Democratic Party	202	232	+30		39,267,916	57.7	+11.1%
Republican Party	232	201	−31		28,464,092	41.8	−7.4%
Independents	1	0	−1		69,707	0.1	−0.5%
Others	0	0	0		255,876	0.4	−3.2%
Undecided seats	N/A	2	N/A	N/A	N/A	N/A	N/A
Total	435	435	0	100.0	68,057,591	100.0	0

United States House of Representatives election results (2006)

Source: The Associated Press

the Supreme Court, strengthening Republican hegemony in that key institution (Figure 5.4).

However, the gap between Republican and Democratic supporters continues to be rather small. As Table 5.1 shows, the 2006 midterm elections witnessed a resurgence of the Democrats, who now hold the majority in both chambers. In the House Democrats won a majority of thirty seats, in the Senate the Democratic Party has forty-nine seats but is considered to hold a majority with fifty-one seats because the two independents have indicated that they will caucus with the Democrats.

As Table 5.2 shows, the last presidential elections—with 17 million more voters than in 2000 and a total turnout rate among the voting-eligible population of 60 percent—marked a reversal in the trend toward lower participation consequent on growing concern for security and sharp conflicts on key moral issues. In fact, cleavages between the two parties on both domestic and foreign policy issues are widening. And even the terrorist attacks against American cities on September 11, 2001—which provoked a unanimous patriotic reaction—did not reduce differences in political preferences and policy options. The results of future elections will depend on the relative capacities of the two parties to mobilize nonvoters.

Although it is true today that there are two Americas and a potential political deadlock resulting from the politics of parity, this situation does not stem from the fact that either party has been unable to develop a sustainable political project for long periods; on the contrary, it is the result of a successful neoconservative revolution since the 1970s, which has put an end to the democratic hegemony supported by the social coalition originally formed in the New Deal and consolidated since

Table 5.2. Presidential election results, 2000 and 2004

Presidential candidate	Vice presidential candidate	Political party	Popular vote	Electoral vote
Presidential election results (2000)				
George W. Bush	Richard Cheney	Republican	50,460,110 (47.87%)	271 (50.37%)
Albert Gore Jr.	Joseph Lieberman	Democratic	51,003,926 (48.38%)	266 (49.44%)
Ralph Nader	Winona LaDuke	Green	2,883,105 (2.73%)	0 (0.00%)
Patrick Buchanan	Ezola Foster	Reform	449,225 (0.43%)	0 (0.00%)
Harry Browne	Art Olivier	Libertarian	384,516 (0.36%)	0 (0.00%)
Other (+)	—	—	236,593 (0.22%)	1 (0.19%)
Presidential election results (2004)				
George W. Bush	Richard Cheney	Republican	62,040,610 (50.73%)	286 (53.16%)
John Kerry	John Edwards	Democratic	59,028,439 (48.27%)	251 (46.65%)
Ralph Nader	Peter Camejo	Independent	463,655 (0.38%)	0 (0.00%)
Michael Badnarik	Richard Campagna	Libertarian	397,265 (0.32%)	0 (0.00%)
Other (+)	—	—	363,579 (0.30%)	1 (0.19%)

then. A new Republican majority was slowly formed as a reaction to New Deal liberalism and to the welfare and racial integration policies of Kennedy's 'New Frontier' and Johnson's 'Great Society'. The new Republican strategy built on this reaction and was able to integrate the two different and to some extent opposed streams of the political critique brought against liberal principles: populism and conservatism. The Trilateral Commission's theory of the crisis of democracy in terms of overloaded government (Crozier, Huntington, and Watanuki 1975) provided the analytical foundation for a political attack on organized interests and the federal bureaucracy, which were held responsible for the fiscal crisis of the state and government policy failures.

Democratic presidents from Roosevelt to Johnson favored the organization of disadvantaged social groups through federal programs of financial aid, legal recognition, and administrative protection. According to the neoconservative critique, Democrats had transformed the poor and disadvantaged groups, ethnic minorities, black women, and ghetto residents, from outsiders into insiders of federal policymaking, thus rebalancing a process traditionally weighted in favor of influential elites. Neoconservatives were thus able to give voice to the resentment of a white middle class aggrieved at both its tax burden and its exclusion from welfare benefits. Unlike in previous periods, however, the traditional populist argument against the big government of Washington politicians and bureaucrats was disconnected from the parallel critique against politics-corrupting big business, as brought by the early-twentieth-century populist movement, because business elites were able to present themselves as the true defenders of individual initiative and the free market against the hypertrophic federal government—which was blamed for the crisis of political authority (Micklethwaith and Wooldridge 2004). With a remarkable ideological turnaround, business elitism—which had been both the target and the adversary of populism—was able to acquire new legitimation through the latter (Fabbrini 2005). Middle-class populist stirrings of tax revolt against the federal government, and economically powerful elites often located in the fast developing southern and western regions, and active in

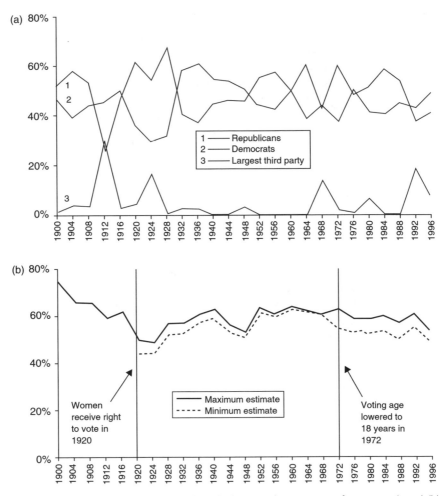

Figure 5.4. (a) Popular vote in presidential elections (percentage of votes cast) and (b) voter participation in presidential elections (percentage of eligible voters)

Source: Caplow, Hicks, and Wattenberg (2001: 181)

oil, weapons, aerospace, and other technologically advanced industries, formed the hardcore of the neoconservative social coalition, and the religious revival of Christian fundamentalism was its main ideological expression (Phillips 1983; Nye, Zelikow, and King 1997). This convergence of voting preferences does not, however, imply a rejection of the view that economic and cultural conservatism are often uneasy allies.

A second key feature of the American party system is the weakness of party organizations; they were at their strongest at the end of the nineteenth century, when the Progressive movement began, and then steadily declined largely as a consequence of policies of civil service protection and the use of primaries to select candidates. Given that the two principal resources on which parties depend to build their organizations are control over patronage in public employment and control over appointments to office, the unionization of the public sector by the AFL-CIO after World War II drastically curtailed the spoils system (today, with a much larger federal government, presidents personally control fewer than 4,000 appointments, whereas at the height of the spoils system they controlled over 100,000), and the spread of direct and open popular primaries democratized the parties and removed their decisive role in the electoral fortunes of political leaders. Electoral politics grew increasingly candidate-centered, and the two national parties have now become frameworks within which candidates compete with their own 'personal' parties, issue-oriented supporters and financers, and professional advisers. Once the presidential candidate has defeated the other contenders in the primaries, she or he uses the national party as a powerful technical machine, rather than as a political organization. Moreover, the advent of mass communication technologies has reduced the reliance of candidates on the traditional parties for the organization of consensus and fund-raising (Mayhew 1986). The decline of national parties has also attenuated the impact of great issues—like unemployment— to mobilize broad social coalitions (such as the New Deal coalition), and it has been responsible for diminishing voter participation, at least until the recent reversal of the trend. Indicative of this decline of the party organizations is the dwindling membership of both the Democratic and the Republican Party. Despite the recent revival of state and local party organizations, and an increase in party cohesion and presidential support in Congress, the American political parties have not regained their past strength and are weaker than those of the EU member-states.

We should not, however, exaggerate the weakness of the American parties. They have proved able to adapt to change, and they still perform an important political role in spite of ambivalent feelings in the American electorate (Epstein 1986). The Republican Party in particular became more militant and better organized after Reagan's presidency: a centralized congressional caucus was formed; the constellation of citizens' associations and committees, religious movements, and interest groups scattered throughout the country was more closely coordinated; the structures supporting candidates with fund-raising and political indoctrination became much more efficient; and, under Gingrich's leadership, congressional opposition to Clinton's policies was subject to much tighter discipline—which the Democratic opposition to Bush is now trying to emulate.

This last aspect introduces, and partially reduces the specificity of, the third feature of the American party system, namely that it is less polarized than in most other democracies. It is true that there has been a long-term balance between the two major parties and frequent bipartisan compromises whenever Congress majorities have not belonged to the same party as the president (and also when they have done). In the forty years between 1955 and 1994, the Democrats uninterruptedly held the majority of seats in the House of Representatives, they elected the Speaker, and they dominated the committees. In the 1994 elections a major turnaround took place: the Republicans gained fifty-four seats to take control of the House, control which they maintained in the following elections, with a majority in 2005 of thirty seats (232 to 202). In the 2006 midterm elections Democrats regained the majority. The Democrats have ruled the Senate, as well as most of the Congresses elected since World War II, electing the speakers and dominating the committees, but with two Republican intervals: in Reagan's 1980s and from 1994 to 2006. After the split Senate of 2001–3, the Republicans held a majority of eleven seats (55 to 44 and 1 independent), until the 2006 elections in which the Democrats regained a majority of two.

Republican control of Congress, the widening cleavages between Democratic and Republican voters, together with the organizational transformation of the two parties, had contributed to increase the polarization of the party system. But the return of divided government in a political system characterized by the institutional separation of the legislative and the executive branches of government fosters the tendency of American parties to cooperate.

The fourth most distinctive feature of the American party system is the remarkable absence of a socialist party, which is related in its turn to trade union exceptionalism: the United States has the weakest union movement in terms of density among the democratic developed countries. Sombart, in his famous 1905 work *Warum gibt es kein Sozialismus in den vereigneten Staaten?*, correctly pointed to the capitalist mentality of the American worker, the populist character of the electorate, the abundance of natural resources, the high standard of living, and the expectations of social mobility as the factors which combined to prevent the development of socialist ideology and organization. But he was wrong to predict that all these factors were about to disappear or to be converted into their opposite. Along the same lines, H. G. Wells in *The Future of America* (1906) argued that the United States had been the only country to introduce mass male suffrage before widespread industrial development, thus inducing Americans to recognize themselves as citizens before they recognized themselves as members of a specific class.

Building on Sombart's insights (1906), Lipset provided a similar interpretation which stressed the link between ideology and social structure:

the absence of a European aristocratic or feudal past, a relatively egalitarian-status structure, an achievement oriented value system, comparative affluence, and a history of political democracy prior to industrialization have all operated to produce a system which remains unreceptive to proposals for class-conscious leftism (Lipset 1979*b*: 109; Lipset and Marks 2000).

The greater importance of ethnic and racial differences with respect to class differences has also influenced the specific forms taken by the political action of the working class and underprivileged groups. A major consequence of the absence of a socialist political tradition has been that the Left–Right division is more blurred and less applicable in the United States than in the European democracies. However, widening cleavages on such issues as civil rights, abortion, welfare, and multilateralism in foreign policy have provoked confrontation between a predominantly liberal Democratic Party and a predominantly conservative Republican Party.

A fifth feature is the growing importance of ethnicity and religion in party politics, where they have played a role comparable to that of class politics in Europe, the difference being that while the importance of the latter has sharply diminished in Europe, the importance of ethnic politics and religious issues is growing in the United States. I will discuss the growing salience of religious issues in the last section. Here, I merely point out the close correlation between religion and party preferences: Republicans are preferred by Methodists, Lutherans, Presbyterians, Mormons, Christians, and Protestants with no specific denomination, while Democrats are preferred by nonreligious, Catholic, Baptist, and Jewish voters. Ethnicity is clearly correlated to party preferences, with African-Americans voting overwhelmingly for Democrats. The total number of black elected officials at all levels of government increased sixfold from 1,469 in 1970 to 8,868 in 1998 at the end of the century. Most of the country's largest cities have elected one or more black mayors. In 2004, the seats held by black representatives accounted for less than 10 percent of all seats in the House of Representatives. At the lower levels of elected government, such as school boards, sheriffs' offices, and county tax assessors, blacks are, however, significantly underrepresented. Another major instance of the importance of ethnic politics is the growing weight of Hispanics and multiculturalism in general. Scholars like Huntington fear that the growing influence of Hispanic America and the related identity politics may destroy the institutional fabric of American democracy and its Anglo-Saxon cultural foundations (Huntington 2004). Other scholars are concerned that multiculturalism may fragment American society (Schlesinger 1991) and that identity politics may endanger the commitment to common egalitarian ideals that marked the previous civil rights movement by emphasizing differences over commonality and by targeting group-specific political goals (Gitlin 1995).

Other key variables in interpreting party preferences, such as gender, geographical location and residence, and socioeconomic status, play a role in the United States which is not significantly different from that in Europe. Gender is important, not in the sense that it leads to the election of a sizable percentage of women (the percentage of US congresswomen is lower than in the EP despite a sharp increase in the final decade of the last century, as is shown in Figure 5.5), but in regard to electoral preferences, given that consistently more women than men have voted Democrat in the past twenty-five years. Socioeconomic status (with education more closely correlated with voting than wealth and income, and professional status) also matters, but it has a diminishing impact because of the growing importance of cultural issues which allies the suburban super-rich with blue-collar whites. Geopolitics also has an impact in the twofold sense of state location and residence: in the 2004 presidential elections the border states (coastal states both on the Atlantic and the Pacific and across the Canadian frontier preferred Kerry, while inland states—not only in the South and South-West— preferred Bush; residents of rural areas and outer metropolitan areas were more inclined to vote Republican than inhabitants of the big cities.

We may now turn to examination of the contemporary pattern of voting preferences in the United States in light of the neoconservative revolution of the past decades discussed above.

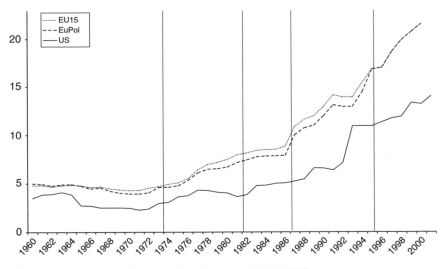

Figure 5.5. Percentage of women in parliaments (1960–2000)

Note: In bicameral systems data are taken for the lower house. Missing: Austria: 1996, 1997; Belgium: 1997, 1999; Greece: 1967–74; Ireland: 1996; Spain: 1996; USA: 1996. Adapted from: Armingeon, Beyeler, and Denegale (2000).

Source: Inter-Parliamentary Union 1995, Inter-Parliamentary Union, various years. For total population: OECD *Statistical Compendium*, various years. Period covered: 1960–2001. Percentage of women in parliaments data are weighted according to the month of election.

With some simplification, the following picture of voting preferences in the contemporary American party system can be drawn (Epstein 1986; Popkin 1994; Aldrich 1995; Bibby 1999; Greenberg 2004). Republicans draw heavily on the following groups: traditional, religious, well-disciplined, and patriotic voters, who share a belief that America is decaying morally because people do not practice their faith in their own lives, the family is under great pressure, and Christian values are under serious attack; the Deep South and the high-growth outer metropolitan areas in the South and South-West, which provide half of the electoral votes that the Republicans need to win nationally, are mostly white, with a majority living in small towns and suburbs but sizable numbers in the growing and modernizing South as well; voters in rural areas who, although they have declined to less than 20 percent of the voting population, still have geographical importance in the presidential election, are culturally conservative (but resent government policies favoring big business and are for this reason a potentially contestable ground for the Democrats); blue-collar married males, and male retirees, many of them veterans, who favor a hardline foreign policy; and upper income groups who favor the Republicans above all because of their tax cuts and pro-business economic policies. Republican loyalists are often the 'children of the Reagan revolution' and support his reaction against moral laxity, overreaching government, and disrespect for US military might.

As Reagan was the source of Republican loyalism, so Clinton's 'Third Way' political project created a sizable and sustainable bloc of partisan loyalists, although it fell short of creating a sustainable majority. The Democratic world centers on civil and human rights, on modern gender roles and secularism, and on government action to help the socially disadvantaged. Again with some simplification, one can argue that Democratic voters are recruited disproportionately from among the following groups: African-Americans, who are by far the most supportive group for the Democrats and have been stable in their support since the civil rights battles of the 1950s and 1960s; Hispanics (except for Florida Cubans), who represent the fastest-growing and most strategically distributed ethnic vote and include many economically vulnerable people greatly worried about jobs, education, health care, social security, and immigration issues; highly educated women, who criticize family and gender established relations, and trust the Democrats on the issues of closest concern to them, such as education, the environment, health, and social security; residents of the least religious and most cosmopolitan areas of the country, especially on the East and West coasts (California, New York, New Jersey, and the six states of New England), which display the growing ethnic diversity, new immigration, enhanced education, modern female roles, and secular attitudes which are characteristic of metropolitan areas and are committed to individual self-expression and autonomy and to minority self-determination; and unionized workers' families, who stand by the Democrats for material and ideological reasons, support a government able to control the power of business elites and provide for greater security, and share a trade union culture.

In addition to the social groups expressing a clear electoral preference for either party, there is a sizable minority, larger than one-third of the electorate, which either swings back and forth in elections, or is increasingly disengaged from politics, or wants political change to the point of being open to third-party protest politics. Instances of the contested groups forming this minority include people with both upper-middle and lower socioeconomic status; devout Catholics (of both gender and different ages) who are closer to the Republicans on issues like abortion and gay and lesbian marriages, but closer to the Democrats on markets, government, and individualism; the new professionals who enjoy upper and middle status in the information society and are attracted to the Democrats' positions on economic and world political issues, education, the environment, and quality of life issues, but are suspicious of their tax policy; and non-college-educated and blue-collar men and women attracted by the Republicans' policies on family and religion, but who, especially if aging and vulnerable, also want to raise their incomes, gain greater security, and obtain better schools, health care, and general care for their children and families.

Finally, different party preferences reflect different policy priorities. In most recent decades, the key policy issues in American politics have been the economy, national defense and international relations, race and ethnic inequalities, and social issues. The social and racial turmoil created by the Vietnam War and the civil rights revolution—which induced President Johnson to withdraw from the race in 1968—put an end to the New Deal party system and created the conditions for the so-called Republican 'lock' on the presidency in the following two decades (with the short intermission of Carter's administration). Traditionally, Americans have viewed the Democrats as the party of economic prosperity, while they have considered the Republicans to be more reliable and capable in international politics. But Johnson was blamed both for the way he was waging the war in Vietnam and for increasing government spending and the tax burden. Moreover, although his greatest achievements as president, symbolized by the signing in 1964 of the Civil Rights Act and by his 'Great Society' welfare programs, consolidated African-American support, they lost the Democrats their most loyal constituency in the Southern states. Reagan was successful both in domestic and foreign policies, but the Republican advantage evaporated in the early 1990s. Clinton owed his success to economic prosperity, and helped by the new economic boom, he was able to bring the federal budget under control while being cautious on controversial social issues such as health reform.

The cleavages between the two parties, and the increasingly cultural nature of key issues in recent years (equal rights, abortion, the role of women in the family, gays and lesbians, and gun control) besides the traditionally important ones of taxes and the role of the federal government, law and order, and foreign policy, have given rise to a culturally polarized country (the 'two Americas'). Religious and family issues have always been important, but they are increasingly provoking major cleavages. As became clear in the 2000 and 2004 presidential elections and in 2006 midterm elections, contemporary American society is politically polarized on major cultural issues.

Internal differentiation among states and groups of states is important in the American political system, as is the role of ethnic politics. But national politics outweigh state and local politics, and the party system is relatively simplified, with each of the two main parties striving to gain hegemony and dominate the polls. The European pattern is significantly different, and most of all with regard to the political systems of member-states.

5.5. The structuration and internal differentiation of the European party system

Parties are nominal, fragmented and rather weak in the EU as well, but for different reasons. Unlike in the United States, their weakness at the union level is related to the strength of the political parties in the member countries. Parties at the EU level, in fact, are nationally dominated transnational party federations or multiparty groups; and party politics at the union level is characterized by the dominance of national electoral cleavages, national political ideologies, and national policy issues over supranational politics.

A major difference between the European and American polities is the reversed relation of importance between elections at the level of the union and at the level of member-states. Amid the multitude of elections held in Europe there is no EU-wide election of the president, and the elections for the EP do not have a significance equal to those for the United States Congress; indeed, they

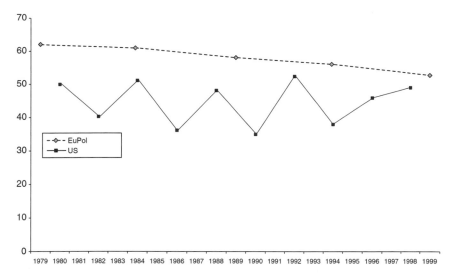

Figure 5.6. Voter turnout in parliamentary elections: European Parliament and US Congress

are perceived as less important than those for the parliaments of member-states. The still marginal institutional position of the EP, together with the absence of uniform electoral procedures for the EP (one for each of the twenty-seven member countries plus one more for Britain's Northern Ireland), accounts for the weakness of political parties at the union level, their lack of coordination, ideological and programmatic heterogeneity, and scant ability to develop a genuine European politics. It also accounts for a lower participation in the EP elections with respect to national elections. Average participation is however higher in the EU vis-à-vis the United States (Figures 5.6 and 5.7) although significant differences in participation rates exist among EU member countries (see Map 5.1 for the most recent elections).

The marginal position of Parliament is largely responsible for the weakness of parties at the EU level. The Parliament is the European institution that has evolved most in the past forty years: when the ECSC was created in 1952 also instituted was a Common Assembly of the six founding states, with seventy-eight members nominated by national parliaments in proportion to each country's population; but it was only in 1979 that the first EP was directly elected by the citizens of the European Community (as stated in the 1957 Treaty of Rome). It has been thus elected every five years since then, and its responsibilities and prerogatives have increased in time, in particular with the implementation of the 1987 Single European Act, which gave the EP the power to amend legislation directly (with the Commission's consent) and veto power over the accession or association of new states. A further prerogative—which makes the EP more similar to the US Senate—is the vote of confidence on the Commission president and individual commissioners, which (as the case of the formation of the Barroso Commission

Figure 5.7. Voter turnout in parliamentary elections: European country Parliament and US Congress

has shown) amounts to an outright power of veto. Moreover, the EP can force the Commission to resign, as it did in the case of the Santer Commission.

Notwithstanding the continuous enlargement of the EP's competence and responsibility, however, there is still an evident contradiction between its popular legitimization and its real powers. Although the Parliament has strengthened its role in the complex system of European governance, it still lacks many of the powers usually associated with parliaments and finds it hard to develop real party competition on important European issues and a genuine government/opposition dialectic (Hix and Lord 1997). As a result, party politics at the European level remain fragmented, a situation symbolized by the geographical dispersion of its activities among the three cities of Strasbourg, Brussels, and Luxembourg.

A further major consequence of the EP's lack of powers is the inability of European parties to appeal to the electorate on a genuinely supranational basis with distinct and coherent programs and policy proposals. As a result, European elections are often interpreted by political leaders, the media, and the voters themselves as more a test of public opinion on domestic issues than as a way to form a coherent majority in the EP (Blondel, Sinnott, and Svensson 1998). A vicious circle operates: the marginal position of the Parliament fosters the continuing dominance of national parties and their unwillingness to invest in European politics; the weakness of party federations and groups in the EP prevents them from forming coalitions which are ideologically and programmatically homogeneous and able to develop a genuinely supranational public discourse; and this, in turn, fosters low voter turnouts and lack of information on European issues among

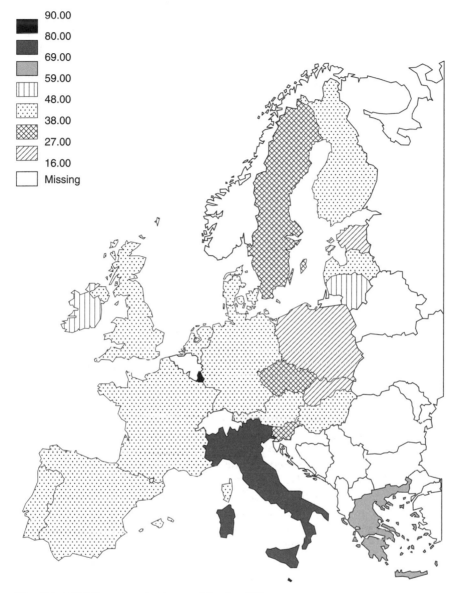

Map 5.1. 2004 European election participation (%)

Note: In Belgium election participation is mandatory
Source: European Parliament

European citizens, thus contributing to the democratic deficit of the EU. A further factor responsible for the weakness of parties is the influence of interest groups which conduct intense lobbying at various entry points to the policymaking process.

There are, however, signs that the original weaknesses of the EU party system are diminishing. In order to argue this point, I shall now briefly describe the evolution of the system since the first general elections of the EP in 1979.

Before looking at parties, it is worth remarking the better performance of the EP in terms of gender representation; the percentage of women in the EP has in fact steadily increased since the late 1970s with higher percentage increases than those of the US Congress, as Figure 5.5 shows.

As far as the EU party system is concerned, the two largest transnational party federations, the EPP–ED (Group of the European People's Party and European Democrats) and the PES (Group of the Party of the European Socialists)—which together with the ELDR (Group of the European Liberal, Democrat, and Reform Party) have been continuously present—have increasingly consolidated their power and now constitute the core of the euro-party system (Bardi and Ignazi 2004). In the 1999–2004 legislature, they accounted for about two-thirds (66%) of the Parliament's members and about three-fourths (74%) with the third largest. By contrast, the four multiparty groups—the Confederal Group of the European United Left/Nordic Green Left (EUL/NGL), the Group of the Greens/European Free Alliance (Greens/EFA), the Union of Europe of the Nations Group (UEN), and the Group for a Europe of Democracies and Diversities (EDD)—together fail to account for even one-fourth of the elected members.

The third variety of parliamentary groups besides the transnational party federations and multiparty groups—that is the mono-party group—was absent from the 1999–2004 legislature, but there were thirty-one nonattached members belonging to national groups unable or unwilling to join with others. Since the 2004 elections (Table 5.3), with the number of EP members rising to 732 to accommodate the representatives of the ten new member countries, the number of euro-parliamentary groups has remained the same—which is rather low if we consider the greater political and cultural heterogeneity (translations among the different EP languages involve 380 possible exchanges). The two largest transnational party federations—the EPP–ED with 279 members and the PES with 199—still represent around 65 percent of the total. With the third largest group, the ELDR—which has increased in size mainly as a result of the good performance by the British Liberals—the three main groups still account for almost 75 percent of the total. If we add to the three party federations the four multiparty groups we still reach 91 percent of the total in spite of the increased political heterogeneity of the EU at twenty-five.

Over the past fifteen years a new moderate party system founded on bipartisan cooperation has evolved in place of the previously polarized system based on strong ideological identities. The agreement index based on the voting behavior of members of Parliament shows greater cohesion both within parliamentary groups and for the Parliament as a whole (Raunio 1996). Instead of looking to their right and left for political support, the EPP and PES have shown a greater willingness to cooperate and compromise. 'This change in coalition patterns was a direct result of the institutional transformation of the European Parliament from a chamber of

Table 5.3. Composition of European Parliament, 2004

Country	EPP–ED	PES	ELDR	EUL/NGL	Greens/EFA	UEN	EDD	Others	Total
BE	7	7	5		2			3	24
CZ	11	2		6				5	24
DK	1	5	4	2		1	1		14
DE	49	23	7	7	13				99
EE	1	3	2						6
EL	11	8		4				1	24
ES	24	24	1	1	4				54
FR	28	31		3	6			10	78
IE	5	1				4		3	13
IT	28	15	9	7	2	9		8	78
CY	2		1	2				1	6
LV	3		1		1	4			9
LT	3	2	3					5	13
LU	3	1	1		1				6
HU	13	9	2						24
MT	2	3							5
NL	7	7	5	2	2		2	2	27
AT	6	7			2			3	18
PL	19	8	4			7		16	54
PT	7	12		2		2		1	24
SI	4	1	2						7
SK	8	3						3	14
FI	4	3	5	1	1				14
SE	5	5	3	2	1			3	19
UK	28	19	12		5		12	2	78
Total	279	199	67	39	40	27	15	66	732

Source: <http://www.europarl.eu.int/default.htm>

Note: EPP–ED: Group of the European People's Party (Christian Democrats) and European Democrats; PES: Group of the Party of European Socialists; ELDR: Group of the European Liberal, Democrat, and Reform Party; EUL/NGL: Confederal Group of the European United Left/Nordic Green Left; Greens/EFA: Group of the Greens/European Free Alliance; UEN: Union of Europe of the Nations Group; EDD: Group for a Europe of Democracies and Diversities.

debate to a legislative body' (Kreppel 2002: 151). As the EP has gained substantive direct legislative influence, the character of its internal organizational structures has changed from generally egalitarian to largely inegalitarian, the groups have assumed more and more responsibilities, while the powers of individual members have diminished correspondingly. After the Single European Act, the largest parties began to increase their power to the detriment of both other parties and nonaffiliated members. New rules were introduced with strict numerical requirements, and weighted voting was instituted within the newly created Conference of presidents. The new legislative procedures of the EP—specifically the rules requiring an absolute majority for amendments and proposals to be passed in later stages of the cooperation and co-decision procedures—favored the only two transnational party federations (the EPP and the PES) able to ensure their passage. Since neither a single party nor a durable ideological coalition has ever held an absolute majority, the only coalition able to guarantee the passage of most decisions has been the 'grand coalition' between the EPP and the PES. If the EP wants to participate effectively in the final stages of the legislative process, it must rely on cooperation between the two largest party federations. Sharp ideological proposals from the left or right would only serve to marginalize the EP, since they would be unacceptable to other EU institutions; first of all the European Council, where the balance between left and right is often different from that existing in the EU at a given time, owing to the different timing and outcomes of national and European elections. Given the divergent national interests and ideological views represented in the other institutions, the party groups are inclined to produce moderate proposals if they are to have any influence at all. This is not to say that ideology has no impact on the EP decision-making process, but EP party group members (and even more so the leaders) are constrained by EU institutions. The pattern of cooperation between the EPP and the PES has extended since the Single European Act and the Maastricht Treaty to encompass resolutions which do not require a special majority and which do not need to be adopted by the other EU institutions.

The future structuring of the party system of the EU will increasingly center on the two major federations, since the granting of legislative power to the EP has transformed it from a chamber of debate into a true legislative body, where power is centralized to the party groups capable of controlling the rules of the game. The central role of the EPP and the PES, and the cooperation between them, stem from the fact that they represent party families well established in all member-states and able to attract other similar forces. The third of the established transnational federations that comprise the Liberals and Democrats and the group of the Greens (which is close to becoming a stable and diffuse political actor), may also assume significant roles in the alternative model of an EP dominated by an ideological (center-left or center-right) coalition, rather than a 'grosse Koalition'. On the other hand, the groups on the radical left and the radical right, and the 'anti-Europe' groups, seem more volatile and, given the consensus-oriented moderate character of EP decision-making, they are more likely to be marginalized because of their smaller size and/or ideological extremism.

To summarize, the EU parties are fragmented and nominal like the American ones, but they are so for different reasons; they reflect the greater electoral complexity and internal diversification of member-states, where critical junctures and political cleavages related to nation-building and the Industrial Revolution have played a major role; and they suffer from the fact that politics at the member-state level is much more important than politics at the union level. For this reason, we need to focus briefly on the electoral preferences and the structuring of the party systems of EU member-states.

The diversity of EU member-state party systems has been traditionally interpreted in light of Rokkan's and Lipset's theory of critical junctures and political cleavages (Lipset and Rokkan 1967; Rokkan 1970). As political systems develop, cleavages emerge at critical junctures where basic decisions are made concerning external boundaries and internal structures. These cleavages are then frozen over long periods. Critical junctures are periods of radical change, which in Europe have historically taken the form of the national revolution and the Industrial Revolution. The theory envisages four basic types of cleavages produced by the interaction between these two types of revolution.

The first two cleavages are linked to the process of nation-building and to the historical consequences of the Reformation—the religious wars and the religious partition of Europe by the Peace of Westphalia (sixteenth century and first half of the seventeenth century)—and later of the French Revolution, which had immediate as well as long-term effects on all nineteenth-century national movements: (a) the cleavage between center and periphery, that is the resistance raised by peripheral regions, linguistic minorities, and culturally threatened population groups against the drive for centralization and standardization (mostly of language and national culture) by central national elites and their bureaucracies; and (b) the cleavage between state and church, that is the conflict, above all for control over education, between the aspirations of the nation-state and the corporate claims of the churches.

These older cleavages fed into the two new cleavages produced by the Industrial Revolution in the course of the nineteenth century: (c) the cleavage between the city and the countryside, that is the increasing conflict between rural and urban areas generated by the growth of the world market and industrial production and focused on free trade and protectionist policies; and (d) the cleavage between the bourgeoisie and the proletariat, that is the class conflicts between the rising masses of wage-earning workers and the industrial bourgeoisie and propertied classes in general—conflicts which usually developed later with the spread of industrial capitalism. The class character of the worker/capitalist cleavage was in its turn complicated by a further conflict, of an ideological nature, between proletarian internationalism and nation-accepting socialism and related to a further critical juncture: the 'International Revolution' in which the Bolshevik conquest of power in 1917 Russia played a key role and which gave rise to a fifth cleavage.

These various cleavages have generated a few ideal families of parties which have combined in various permutations in the various European democracies, to then 'freeze' their party systems in the following decades. These party families are: the liberal and radical parties and the conservative parties (these being secular bourgeois), the Socialist and Social-Democratic parties, and the Communist parties (all of which were originally workers' parties), the Christian-Democratic parties (mostly Catholic, but Protestant as well), the agrarian parties, the ethnoregionalist parties, and the parties of the radical right (Von Beyme 1982). The freezing of the traditional cleavages led to the consolidation of a limited number of reliable collective political actors which agreed on a set of basic rules of the game (concerning government and opposition roles, accepted strategies of mobilization, and arenas of political competition and policymaking) and thus regulated conflict.

At the birth of the European Community, the party systems of member countries reflected to a significant extent the cleavages identified by Rokkan and Lipset, with Christian parties and Socialist parties playing the major roles (with the notable exception of France, where De Gaulle's party did not have an open religious characterization, and can be better defined as a secular bourgeois party).

In the last part of the twentieth century the European party scenario changed (Ware 1996; Pennings and Lane 1998), again doing so because of two radical changes, one predominantly political (the collapse of the Soviet Union), the other predominantly socioeconomic (the advent of postindustrial society and the spread of globalization). The party articulations of the older cleavages declined in importance (in particular, the traditional ideological appeals of both religious and communist parties), while other cleavages and political preferences emerged in relation to postmaterialist values (Inglehart 1977) which fostered the growth of ecological parties (which obtained an average 4% of votes in the 1990s), as well as to local reactions to globalization trends which generated ethnoregional parties like the Catalan Party in Spain and the Northern League in Italy.

American political parties have had a much smaller number of party members than European ones (Katz and Kolodny 1994). However, party membership in EU member countries has steadily decreased in recent decades; party members in ten EU countries declined from 6 percent to 4 percent of the total population between 1960 and 1992 (Pennings and Lane 1998). The decrease was particularly intense in the case of communist and religious parties; voters became more volatile; and some parties saw significant decreases in their votes (religious parties declined from 22.4% in the 1940s to 14% percent in the 1990s, and communist parties from 11.7% to 5.7%) (Lane and Ersson 1999). However, the older parties resisted and they still today form the backbone of most party systems. Mair (1997) has analyzed average electoral preferences for traditional parties in fourteen European countries (eleven member-states of the EU plus Norway, Switzerland, and Iceland) between the early 1960s and late 1980s, finding that they did not decline by more than 15 percent (except in Belgium, Switzerland, and Sweden). There is, however, a striking exception: Italy, where both the Christian Democrats—the relative majority party which had ruled the country uninterruptedly for almost fifty years—and its allies (the Socialists, the Republicans, and the Liberals) were wiped out in the early 1990s by political scandals, the aggressive strategy of newcomers like the Northern League, and electoral reforms, their place being taken by new political formations like Forza Italia.

Significant differences exist between the European and American polities, first of all the reversed relation of importance between elections at the level of the union and at the level of member-states. And yet, if one makes the comparison at the level of the two political unions instead of comparing the United States with the EU member-states, once again American exceptionalism and European uniqueness are less pronounced. At the EP level, the party system is undergoing simplification despite the strongly proportional nature of the electoral system, which favors fragmentation (see tables on the EP): the European People's Party has joined with the European Democrats to become the largest political group, while the Party of European Socialists—the second largest group contending for leadership—is also considering change. No other group has more than 12 percent of the seats in the EP: neither the European Liberals and Democrats, nor the confederation of the European Left with some of the Greens, nor the Greens themselves, nor the right-wing nationalists, nor the Group for a Europe of Democracies and Diversities.

	Offices in Washington	Retains lobbyists in Washington
Corporations	20.6	45.7
Trade associations	30.6	17.9
Foreign corporations	0.5	6.5
Professional associations	14.8	6.9
Unions	3.3	1.7
Citizen groups	8.7	4.1
Civil rights/minorities	1.7	1.3
Social welfare and the poor	1.3	0.6
New entrants	2.5	1.1
Governmental units	1.4	4.2
Other unknown	14.6	10.2

Figure 5.8. Types of pressure groups in Washington, DC (percentage of total)

Source: <http://www.historylearningsite.co.uk, 2000>

5.6. **Interest groups and pressure politics**

A pronounced similarity between the United States and EU political systems is the intensity of interest group activity and the important role of pressure politics in policymaking (Figures 5.8 and 5.9), although the reasons for these features are slightly different between the two unions as a consequence of the different institutions of governance. In both cases, the involvement of interest groups is of a pluralist, open and competitive nature, rather than being corporatist, as also acknowledged by neocorporatist theoreticians like Schmitter (Schmitter and Streeck 1991). This is more clearly apparent in the United States, which is characterized by more conflict strategies and pluralist collective bargaining, and by lower levels of unionization than in Continental Europe, where remnants of neocorporatist structures still persist.

Most studies portray the EU decision-making system as pluralist in character: the large numbers of lobbyists alongside the growing power of European governance and the manifold access points make the establishment of monopoly positions impossible. The lack of direct participation by interest groups in binding decisions is another major argument in favor of the pluralist thesis. In fact, consultative committees, round tables, public hearings, and consultations exist, but their establishment is not consistently regulated, except for those few cases in which the European Commission is obliged to abide by the negotiated results (Pfeifer 1995; Van Schendelen 1998; Kohler-Koch 2000). However, some scholars, like Gorges (1996), find clear evidence of neocorporatism not at the macro but at the meso-level of relations between interest groups and EU governing bodies.

A third, interesting, position is that taken by Michalowitz, who argues that neither pluralism nor neocorporatism is completely compatible with EU structures, since both require the existence of a single point of reference: the state.

By contrast, at the European level several governmental structures possess equal weight and compete with a supranational umbrella organization, so that the involvement of nongovernmental actors is influenced by these structures at all levels of decision-making. Hence it is possible for rather pluralist patterns to prevail at one level and neocorporatist ones at another (2002: 42).

According to Michalowitz, a detailed analysis of the individual decision-making stages shows that the Parliament tends generally to be pluralist, while the Commission leans toward neocorporatism, and the Council is in general less open to interaction with interest groups. Michalowitz's view is interesting insofar as it calls for theoretical innovation based on the integration of different traditional approaches, given the very specific nature of the EU; but it tends to overemphasize the neocorporatist aspects because it employs a rather undemanding definition of neocorporatism based largely on the existence of general institutionalized procedures for the involvement of nongovernmental interests, without giving enough importance to other key features like direct and binding anticipation in decision-making, hierarchical organization, and monopoly position.

There is general agreement among scholars on the great number of interest groups active in the EU and lobbying the Commission, Parliament, national governments, and the courts, although estimates of the exact number vary from the 3,000 groups with about 10,000 employees calculated by a Commission study of the early 1990s (Mazey and Richardson 1993) to the 2,000 groups with offices in Brussels estimated by Fallik (1994) to the 1,678 groups calculated by Wessels (Figure 5.9).

The various interest groups are by no means equally represented. Business groups are much more active for many reasons: because corporations move more easily in a transnational space than other groups, they have greater financial and human resources, the priority given by the EU to market and financial integration, and the acceleration of European integration was primarily the outcome of an alliance between political and economic elites (Bornschier 2000).

But why are pressure politics so successful? First, as we have seen, because the EU's decision-making process is very slow and complicated, without a strong single executive, and it is based on an extended consensus which requires the consultation of organized interests (Ruzza in Fabbrini 2002). Moreover, the complex nature of many issues requires a high level of specialized competence and technical information. Furthermore, the pro-business culture of many EU policymakers and employees facilitates the formation of policy communities where representatives of organized business interests are steadily incorporated in the policymaking process. These are the main reasons for both the pervasiveness of interest groups and the privileged position of organized business. Other factors, stemming from the democratic deficit of the EU and the effort to cope with

Type of interest	Number
Individual companies	561
European interest associations	314
Private lobbyists (e.g. political consultants, public affairs, and law firms)	302
Miscellaneous interest groups (mostly public interest)	147
International organizations and non-EU state bodies	101
National interest associations	93
Regions	80
Chambers of commerce	47
Individual trade unions	21
Think tanks	12
Total	1,678

Figure 5.9. Types of pressure groups in the European Union

Source: Calculated from data in Wessels (1997)

the enlarged competencies of the Union after the Single European Act, also help explain the pervasiveness of interest groups but to some extent countervail the dominance of organized business.

The Single European Act has increased the EU's intervention in policy areas like the environment, research and development, and sectors of social policy—with the approval in subsequent years of more than 300 harmonization procedures—with the result that it has attracted a growing number of interest groups. Moreover, mounting criticism of the closed and nontransparent method of European policymaking has fostered demands for enlargement of the system of widespread consultations in order to remedy the democratic deficit of the EU, thereby enhancing the role of interest groups. The influence of business interest associations and unions at the EU level has induced authors like Crouch (1999) to speak of neocorporatist structures. In fact, unions and employers' associations, like the other EU interest groups, are typically pluralist in their nature—that is multiple, voluntary, competitive, and nonhierarchically ordered—because any neocorporatist attempt to grant a certifying role to EU institutions would be opposed by national governments.

Organized business still holds the dominant position. According to Mazey and Richardson (1994), in the early 1990s industrial and trade groups (general groups like Unice and Eurochambers, industry-specific like Cefic for chemicals and Acea for automobiles, and size-specific like the European Round Table) accounted for 50 percent of all interest groups, agriculture and food groups for 25 percent, services for 20 percent, and trade unions, environmental and consumer groups for the remaining 5 percent. The typology of pressure groups calculated from Wessels (Figure 5.9) shows a similar predominance of individual companies and European interest associations (many of them organized business associations). Public-interest groups are weaker than private ones also because they find it difficult to remain active throughout the long policymaking process of the EU (Paterson 1991). The influence of public interest groups is growing, however, because European institutions like the European Court of Justice (ECJ), the EP, and the Commission take closer consideration of their opinions and demands, and, as Majone (1996) points out, they enjoy a greater attention at the EU level than at the national level. As far as unions are concerned, they are still more influential in the member-states than at the EU level, and the EU has little control over the industrial relations strategies of national organizations (see European Industrial Relations Observatory, data on membership 1993–2003).

Interest groups have always been a very important component of American politics, and their influence is growing. However controversial the measurement of group membership may be (Baumgartner and Walker 1988; Smith 1990; Baumgartner and Leech 1998), Americans have long been considered a nation of 'joiners'. As Tocqueville remarked in the early nineteenth century, 'Americans... are forever forming associations. They are not only commercial and industrial associations...but thousands of other types—religious, moral, serious, futile, very general and very limited, immensely large and very minute' (Tocqueville 1835–40, Engl. tr. 2000: 513). Whereas little more than one-half of the adult population votes in presidential elections, more than three-quarters of Americans belong to at least one association: on average they belong to two, and they make financial contributions to four. Only some of these associations are openly political, although many of the apparently nonpolitical ones—like parent–teacher organizations and neighborhood associations—often engage in political activity. According to the data of the WVS (1993), when compared with the citizens of the five largest EU member countries, Americans record much higher percentages of belonging to four or more groups (19% vs. 9% in the UK, 8% in Germany, 4% in France and Italy, and 2% in Spain) and much lower percentages of belonging to no group at all (18% vs. 33% in Germany, 46% in the UK, 59% in Italy, 61% in France, and 70% in Spain).

Pluralism is a key feature of American society: it started as religious pluralism and developed into a pluralism of interests and cultural preferences. And pluralism constitutes a basic component of the American political system as well, through the formation of temporary, overlapping memberships and identities. Group formation in the United States has not been a steady and gradual process; rather, it has come about in waves, with major increases during the Progressive era (when large national associations like the National Association of Manufacturers and the American Farm Bureau Association were formed) and in the 1960s and 1970s (over 40% of the associations with Washington offices were founded after 1960). This latter period saw the formation not only of thousands of new economic groups with narrower bases than those of the previous period, but also numerous nonprofit organizations, ranging from those active in the public sector to various specialized professional associations, some of them actively and openly political—for example, the liberal National Organization of Women, the conservative Christian Coalition, and the many environmental, consumer and 'watchdog' groups—others not primarily political but concerned with politics insofar as they lobby for a specific policy—for instance, the 33-million strong American Association of Retired Persons, which is closely interested in Medicare and social security.

The main factors accounting for the recent growth of interest groups are advances in computer technology, which enables cheaper communications and easier mailing list formation, and the expansion of government activity, which fosters specialized lobbying by both new and transformed groups like the National Rifle Association (that with its 4.3 million members has been an important supporter of George W. Bush in national politics). Another factor in the proliferation of interest groups is the decline of large traditional organized interest associations like the trade unions: over the past fifty years, union membership has declined sharply from above 30 percent in 1950 to less than 15 percent in 2000 (Fiorina, Petersen, and Johnson 2002: 194).

According to the pluralist model, generally single-issue groups, with overlapping memberships and driven by utilitarian motives, compete with each other for government attention in the policymaking process. The interplay of the pressures exerted by groups in defense of their interests performs a key role in keeping democracy working, and in maintaining the political order. Government activity is a process of adaptation and optimal mediation among competing and countervailing interests. Interest groups, however, must cope with the difficult logic of collective action and the freerider problem (i.e. the fact that individuals who do not bear the costs of supporting the group can still enjoy the benefits delivered by the group). The problem can be overcome by encouraging emotional involvement or moral commitment to the group's cause, by using coercive measures, by offering selective incentives, or by deploying political entrepreneurs (Olson 1965).

Although the overall picture is that of organized pluralism, the interest-group system is biased, since some interest groups are endowed with greater resources and are more influential than others (Dahl 1956). Despite the large increase in the number of groups active in politics, business dominance of the Washington interest-group galaxy is even more pronounced than it was in the past (Schlozman and Tierney 1981; Fligstein 2001). As Figure 5.9 shows, corporations—the United States and foreign—account for more than 50 percent of total lobbyists in Washington, with trade associations adding a further 18 percent, whereas citizen groups account only for 4.1 percent, unions for 1.7 percent, civil minorities for 1.3 percent, and social welfare and the poor for 0.6 percent. Corporations and trade associations also account for more than 50 percent of total office space, with professional associations coming third with almost 15 percent. Even a policy domain such as foreign policy, where the public national interest should prevail over private sector interests, shows clear signs of privatization, owing to the great influence of specific interest groups on decisions concerning key sensitive areas like the Middle East and the oil and weapons industries. The Bush administration has provided evidence of the impact of the business interests of policymakers on policy decisions. Although some scholars, like Lowery and Brasher (2004), argue for a more open interest group politics in the United States, on the whole the thesis of the dominance of business interests seems convincing.

In this regard, the United States and the EU appear similar, although they differ with respect to the more important role played by trade unions in European politics. This role is more significant at the member-state level than at the supranational level, but trade unions' influence on national politics provides a basis for their influence on policymaking at the supranational level as well.

5.7. Political cultures

I have argued that the political institutions of the EU and the United States are less dissimilar than they may appear at first sight, although basic differences do exist. The same mix of similarities and differences applies to political cultures as well. First, comparative studies on political culture since Almond's and Verba's analysis of civic culture show that American and European citizens share fundamental beliefs and values concerning liberal democracy (civil and political rights, rule of law, representative government, adversarial politics, and information pluralism) and market competition (free trade, private property, and contract relations). This is no surprise, since American and European societies are different varieties of the same model of a capitalist economy, an open society and democratic government; they represent two different versions of Western modernity.

And yet basic differences exist in political cultures as well; differences considered so marked by scholars like Lipset (1996) and Bell (1988) that they speak of an American 'exceptionalism'. The American creed, according to Lipset, can be described in five terms: liberty, egalitarianism (involving equality of opportunity and respect, not of result or condition), individualism, populism, and laissez-faire.

Although American political culture today seems less homogeneous than it was in the past, in terms of its support for the values of the American creed, basic differences with respect to most EU states have been highlighted by numerous surveys on attitudes toward religion, individualism and various forms of government intervention, social attitudes, and confidence in institutions in the United States and in selected EU states.

The differences between the EU and the United States as a whole should not be allowed to obscure the fact that significant differences exist within each of the unions. In the United States, states and macro-regions differ in economic, cultural, ethnic, and political terms. The EU is even less homogeneous, owing to the different historical traditions of its member countries and regions. Various cleavages can be identified: Anglo-Saxon/Continental, Northern European/Mediterranean, Catholic/Protestant/Orthodox, old democracies/recent democracies, etc.

But there are some common features which differentiate the average political culture of the EU from that of the United States: first, less emphasis on the values of individualism and a greater emphasis on governmental responsibility because of socialist ideology and the Church's social doctrine; second, a conception of liberal democracy where the democratic component often appears stronger than the liberal one; third, a greater cosmopolitan orientation; and fourth, a more peace-oriented attitude toward global politics (this is probably the major difference between the present generations and those of the first half of the twentieth century).

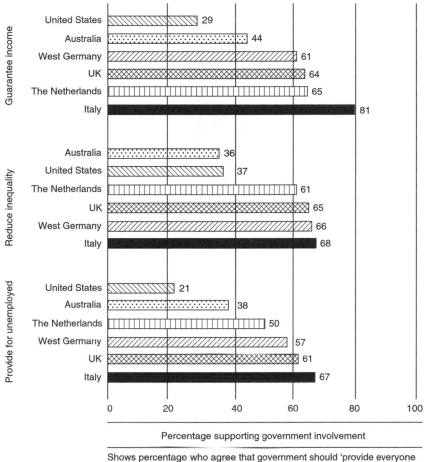

Figure 5.10. Percentage of people supporting government involvement

Source: Ladd (1994)

The first striking way in which Americans differ from Europeans concerns the balance between individual responsibility on the one hand and collective (especially governmental) responsibility on the other. Less than a quarter of US respondents completely agreed that 'It is the responsibility of the state ("government" in the United States) to take care of very poor people who cannot take care of themselves', whereas 50 percent of Germans, 62 percent of Britons and French, 66 percent of Italians, and 71 percent of Spaniards agreed (Ladd 1994).

As Figure 5.10 shows, similar differences exist with regard to support for government actions such as providing a guaranteed income (29% of Americans vs. 61% in Germany, 64% in the UK, and 81% in Italy), reducing economic inequality

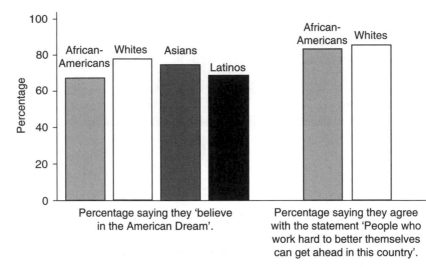

Figure 5.11. Percentage of US ethnic groups' agreement with individualistic values

Source: Fiorina, Petersen, and Johnson (2002: 108)

(36% of Americans vs. 65% in the UK, 66% in Germany, and 68% in Italy), and providing for the unemployed (21% of Americans vs. 57% of Germans, 61% of Britons, and 67% of Italians). It is worth noting that even less affluent Americans embrace widespread individualistic values. Americans are also more confident that they have better chances of getting ahead than are citizens of the EU: almost three Americans out of four declare this optimism, compared with 45 percent of Italians, 40 percent of Germans, and 37 percent of Britons (Ladd 1994).

Again it is worth noting that Asians and Latinos do not differ substantially from Whites in their belief in the American Dream, and that almost the same percentage of African-Americans as Whites agree with the statement 'People who work hard to better themselves can get ahead in this country' (Figure 5.11) (Fiorina, Petersen, and Johnson 2002). Americans are still much more individualistic, meritocratic, and antistatist than Europeans. The shift introduced by the Great Depression toward greater reliance on the state and acceptance of planning and welfare policies reverted to more individualistic attitudes and distrust of big government in the prosperous decades after World War II.

Different values are reflected in different policies as well. The EU policies and those of most member-states are much more closely concerned with social cohesion (as a necessary twofold goal of economic growth and competitiveness) and welfare. Comparative studies on welfare policies show that European choices are significantly different from American ones.

In terms of Esping-Andersen's typology of three welfare regimes—liberal, social democratic, and conservative—the liberal regime is typical of the United States (and of other Anglo-Saxon countries as well), while the social democratic and

conservative regimes are typical of the EU countries. The UK occupies an intermediate position between the Anglo-sphere and Continental Europe because, given
the significant role of the labor movement in social policymaking, its welfare
system is both market-oriented and comprehensive. 'Liberal welfare regimes in
their contemporary form reflect a political commitment to minimize the state,
to individualize risks, and to promote market solutions' (Esping-Andersen 1999:
74–75). Liberal welfare regimes are characterized by two core elements. First, they
are residual in two main senses: social guarantees are typically restricted to 'bad
risks' and a narrow definition of eligibility is used (a good indicator in this respect
is the relative weight of needs-based social assistance compared to rights-based
social policy programs); they embrace a narrow conception of what risks should
be considered 'social'—in the United States recognized social risks are Medicaid
benefits for the poor and Medicare services for the aged, subsidies for lone parents,
and tax credits for low-income child families, but there are no national health
care, sickness, and maternity benefits, nor parental leave provisions. The second
core element is encouragement of the market: the only 'bad risks' are welfare
dependents, citizens must deal with the other risks themselves, either individually
through life insurance and personal retirement programs or collectively through
occupational insurance plans (a good indicator in this respect is the amount of
private pensions as a share of total pensions).

The social democratic welfare regime operates on the principles of universalism
and egalitarianism and is committed to comprehensive risk coverage and generous
benefits which are not dependent on prior personal contributions. The original
legacy of nineteenth-century poor relief was gradually transformed into social
assistance, and then in the decade after World War II, into modern entitlement
programs. This is a state-dominated welfare regime which marginalizes the role of
the market and is typical of the Northern European countries.

The conservative welfare regime is mostly characterized by status segmentation
(status divisions permeate social security systems) and familialism (male breadwinner plus the family as caregiver and ultimately responsible for its members'
welfare). Its roots are monarchical *etatism* (especially in Germany, France, and
Austria, but still strong in the privileged treatment of the public civil service),
traditional corporatism, and the Catholic church's social doctrine and its notion
of subsidiarity. It is typical of Continental Europe. Given that it has evolved into a
conceptualization of the welfare society, according to the principle of subsidiarity,
it can be better defined as the familial or the societal welfare regime.

All three models have strengths and weaknesses: the liberal model reduces
female unemployment but is also characterized by greater employment precariousness and inequality; the social democratic model encourages the dual earner
family model and provides universal coverage, but it implies a higher tax level;
the conservative model stimulates family solidarity but has a strong female unemployment bias.

The welfare policies of EU countries continue to differ from that of the United
States, both because of their path-dependency and because European integration

has fostered interaction among the welfare systems of various EU countries, and EU regional development funds and employment initiatives have made them more similar. But the homogenizing market influence of globalization has reduced the differences among the three classic types of welfare regime, and at the same time it has increased the fragmentation and differentiation characteristic of postindustrial society. And, as it is argued in Chapter 6, differences in terms of public expenditure are less pronounced than it is commonly thought.

A second major difference between the European and the American political culture concerns religion and its relation to politics. Americans are more religious than Europeans, more likely to believe in God, to attend religious services, and to report that religion plays an important role in their lives: this is because of the deeply rooted religious pluralism of American society (much of the country's original settlement was by people seeking the freedom to practice their own religion), the dominance of religious sects over established churches, the consequent absence of a state religion, the clergy compete more vigorously for potential believers, and because religion can fill a gap in a liberal culture dominated by individualism, competition, this-worldly pragmatism, and relentless rationalism where people need a place of comfort (Fowler 1985). The importance of religion in American culture has also been seen as a factor contributing to the moralistic nature of US politics.

Fiorina, Petersen, and Johnson (2002) portray the United States as a study in contrasts. They stress the philosophical unity of Americans who share the fundamental beliefs of liberal political culture in spite of their great social and ethnic heterogeneity, and they speak of 'unity amidst diversity'. These fundamental beliefs grew out of the classical liberal philosophy that stresses the rights and liberties of individuals and is reflected in a greater emphasis on individual responsibility and hard work, and a greater suspicion of government. Contrary to what has happened in European countries, socialist, clerical, and royalist parties have never flourished in American politics.

This portrait somewhat underestimates the cleavages in contemporary American political culture. Contemporary debates on immigration, diversity, multiculturalism, religion and the family are not just the reemergence of debates conducted in earlier periods. There is concern that immigration is a threat to the distinctly American political culture and that the new immigrants are too different to fit easily into American society. A typical example of this concern is provided by Huntington (2004), who argues that the new bilingualism of Spanish-speaking Latin American immigrants may profoundly transform the American culture and model of society.

As far as attitudes toward religion (and family) are concerned, the situation has been dramatically changed by the terrorist attack of September 11, 2001 and by a new sense of insecurity mainly due to terrorism, but also to slower rates of economic growth. Different causes have contributed to a general sense of existential insecurity which gives a renewed significance to religious and moral issues. In the 2004 elections, the Republicans placed their emphasis on God, country, and the family—which are generally key conservative issues—while the Democrats were uncertain whether to take the same line or stick to the core American values of civil rights and individual freedoms. The present political split among American voters reflects two different views of society and the individual, and of what really matters in life. On the one hand, there are those who conceive society as made up of individuals with their natural rights to life, freedom and their own claims; they believe that sexual preferences and abortion are civil rights, that the key political issues concern personal freedoms and equal opportunities, and that politics is about 'who gets what and how'. On the other hand, there are those who conceive society as made up of families, held together by bonds of life and faith, that life is sacred because it is a gift of God, that religious values are the best guarantee against social disorder, and that politics is a fight of good against evil. Can this split be reconciled, or does the new conservative emphasis on family and religion threaten the traditional liberal values of American political culture?

A third major difference between the American and the European political cultures concerns the attitude toward war and peace. Americans claim that the United States is the redeeming nation, the bringer of freedom and democracy for the whole world, and contemplate recourse to war as a legitimate means to pursue a valuable end. This attitude has further intensified with George W. Bush's doctrine on the national security of the United States, based as it is on neoconservative thought: in a significant change with respect to the prevailing policy in the age of bipolarism, preventive war against rogue states and unilateral action are now affirmed as foreign policy guidelines.

The prevailing European attitude is different. At the roots of the project to build a united Europe, there was and still is the will to put a definitive end to European civil wars. The EU often gives the impression of having several foreign policies—these being the policies of the most important nation-states within it. In actual fact, Europe does have a foreign policy: what else can we call a policy of continuous enlargement which adds new peoples and territories? It is as if the myth of the frontier had traveled from the United States to Europe. And the EU has a widely shared foreign policy attitude amounting to the peaceful incorporation of new European countries, combined with the establishment of strong economic and commercial ties with neighboring countries (Russia and other post-Soviet states, the countries of the Southern coast of the Mediterranean, and the Middle East). Here again, in foreign policy as in welfare policy attitudes, the UK occupies a position midway between the Anglo-sphere and Continental Europe.

5.8. Conclusion: the quality of democracy on both sides of the Atlantic

Democratic values and institutions do not seem in real danger on either side of the Atlantic, but the quality of democracy gives some cause for concern. Worries stem from features common to both unions' logic of functioning and which can be related to their institutional similarities. These features are the difficult accountability of representative institutions, the impact of powerful minorities on policy formation and policy implementation, and interinstitutional conflict not mediated by weak and fragmented parties. They have been discussed in the foregoing analysis. Here, I shall briefly consider three other areas of actual and potential risk for democratic functioning, shifting the level of analysis from the EU to the political systems of its member states; one area is common to both the American and the European democracies, one is specific to the former and other is more applicable to most of the latter. These three areas are: the impact of the permanent campaign, the power of the media ('telecracy'), the increasing cost of electoral campaigns, the personalization of politics on democratic participation, and the quality of public discourse; the implications of the war on terror and the imperial ambitions of the present US administration for the quality of American democracy; the challenges raised by the multiculturalism and multiethnicity of European society for the quality of democracy in the EU.

Both the American and the European democracies are increasingly marked by the permanent campaign—that is, the fact that political campaigning literally never ends—and by the power of the media. The main factors responsible for the permanent campaign are (a) sociological and political factors, such as the decline of traditional party organizations and the explosion of interest groups and pressure politics which force candidates to build and maintain personal organizations rather than rely on a standing party organization; (b) institutional factors, such as, in the United States, the holding of separate federal, state, local, and other elections at different times, and the method of selecting candidates by means of primaries, which greatly increases the number of elections and shortens the intervals between them, so that the next election campaign starts as soon as the last one has ended, or even before; and in the EU, the holding of a great number of national, regional, and local elections in the twenty-five member-states at different times and with different electoral systems; and (c) technological changes in mass media and research techniques which foster the proliferation of polling and enable politicians to engage in continuous direct communication with potential voters and obtain constant feedback from polls on the electoral implications of their actions.

As a consequence of more election campaigns, more organization, more communications, and more opinion polls, the demand for money has greatly increased, forcing candidates and elected officials to engage in constant fundraising activities. The total cost of American elections has more than tripled in the past fifty years—from about $900 million in 1951–2 to over $3,000 million in 1999–2000—increasing dramatically (almost doubling) in the last decade of the twentieth century. Similar increases have taken place in European countries.

Another major effect of the permanent campaign is the declining percentages of voter turnouts. Presidential elections get higher percentages than local ones, but turnouts for both have steadily declined since the mid-1960s (although a reversal of the trend has taken place since the 2004 presidential elections). Americans are less likely to vote than are the citizens of EU member-states, although the differences are less pronounced when we compare elections for the US Congress and the EU Parliament.

The increasing cost of electoral campaigns, the declining percentages of voter turnouts, the growing impact of the mass media, the personalization of politics, and the uneven impact of interest groups on the policy process are all features which may reduce the role of direct involvement, the chances for deliberative democracy, and the influence of educated public opinion on electoral preferences.

A second source of actual and potential risks for democracy—and which specifically concerns the quality of American democracy—is US neoimperial foreign policy and the war on terror. In the United States, political and religious leaders and citizens in general have not transformed their response to the 2001 terrorist attack into ethnic and/or religious warfare. But, on the other hand, the post-September 11 syndrome has led to the enactment of rules that limit individual rights at home, and to the pursuit of aggressive policies against foreign countries in the name of the defense of freedom and democracy. The attitude to restrictions of individual freedom differs between the three Western countries which have suffered major terrorist attacks—the United States, Spain, and the UK—with higher percentages approving in the United States. However, those percentages decline sharply in the United States also when questions concern specific measures, like phone controls, and US citizens rather than foreigners. Although the mere definition of war as the struggle against international terrorism prompts an attitude in favor of exceptional measures by the government, commitment to civil liberties remains strong in the United States, and is not weaker than in the EU.

Contemporary American democracy does not only run the risk of imperial overstretching (Kennedy 1986). There are concerns that basic freedoms are in jeopardy, because US neoimperial foreign policy goes together with the growing weight of conservative moral and religious beliefs. The Republican Party's strategy of focusing on God and the family threatens individual rights (women's rights above all), personal moral preferences, and the freedom of scientific research. And ethnic politics may also threaten the core values of American liberal culture. But this culture is alive and well and continues to produce powerful antidotes to the violations of human rights.

A third source of actual and potential risks for democracy—and this specifically concerns the quality of European democracy—consists of populist reactions against the growing challenges of economic and cultural globalization. The treaty for adopting an EU constitution solemnly proclaims the core civic and political values of liberal democracy and multiculturalism, and most EU leaders have resisted vigorous attempts to establish Christianity as some sort of state religion. But, on the other hand, numerous opinion polls report shrinking confidence in democratic processes and institutions as a reaction to the challenges of the multiethnic society and the global market. The growing popularity of neopopulist forms of consensus which appeal to the many 'losers' in the globalization process, and the increasing reliance on technocratic elites, which appeal to the many 'winners', together reduce the space for democratic participation and accountability. Neopopulist trends toward local closure and the xenophobic fear of different peoples and cultures have found renewed life among political entrepreneurs in several Western democracies, notably France, Austria, Italy, Germany, and the Netherlands. These movements have gained the support of sizable minorities, and they may grow in the future if interethnic relations become more difficult to manage.

Democratic culture must be nurtured through the reaffirmation of the core elements of liberal democracy (civil rights, universal suffrage, free and recurrent elections, multiparty competition, multiple sources of information and free public opinion, and nonviolent methods of conflict resolution) and bold political innovations which foster public discourse, political participation and the creative adaptation of democracy to the needs of global governance—as in the case of the EU. By these means it will be possible not only to preserve the quality of political life, but also to strengthen the appeal of democracy for countries with authoritarian regimes to which it cannot be exported by force.

One gains the impression of a reversal or a crossover of trends between the EU and the United States on various aspects of modern polities. The US political system is becoming more polarized in terms of moral cleavages and political cultures, while the EU is becoming less so; the traditional American liberal ethos is under attack, while the EU upholds civil liberties as a basic requirement for membership, although xenophobic attitudes are present; the United States has become more belligerent, whereas the peoples and the nations of Europe have put an end to centuries of European civil wars and Europe-initiated world wars; the traditional Tocquevillian portrait of American society as a web of associations is countered by the image of Americans 'bowling alone', while European civil society is gaining strength. Although it is exaggerated to assert that the European dream is quietly eclipsing the American dream, as Rifkin argues, it is true that Europe's vision of the future is coming close to the first fully articulated vision of global consciousness.

6 Welfare

Gérard Cornilleau[1]

Welfare lies at the heart of the European political debate. The French and the Dutch rejection of the European constitution project in the spring of 2005 can largely be explained by the worries stirred by the return of the primacy of economics over the social aims of public intervention. It was because the constitution project gave too much precedence to the demands of 'competition' and the 'free circulation of goods and services' that eventually, and especially in France, a majority of citizens preferred to halt—at least momentarily—the political construction of Europe rather than question the 'European social model'. In the political debate, the social model referred to is only rarely defined with precision: it encapsulates implicitly all the dispositions which protect the status of workers on the labor market and the compulsory collective insurance systems which fund unemployment benefits, pensions, health care expenditures, and allowances for the disabled. It is generally admitted that in Europe the judicial system of workers' protection and the system of public insurance, which consists of welfare protection against the basic risks of existence (old age, illness, handicap, and unemployment), are more widespread than anywhere else in the world. It is claimed that an extension of European welfare leads to rigidities and, ultimately, to extra costs which impair economic productivity and account for the slow pace of economic growth. With respect to less developed countries, such as China, India, or Brazil, differences in welfare cannot provide a serious explanation, while differences in wage expenditures result directly from the gaps in lifestyles and are widely compensated for by differences in productivity which mostly restrain competition to low-quality products. However, the explanation may have some credibility when it comes to comparing the American and European situations.

In order to assess the relevance of these reasonings, the reality of the opposition between the European and the American welfare models should be tested.

A great deal of data is available, but interpreting it is a delicate matter. In particular, the impact of the different judicial dispositions is very difficult to evaluate. It is true that, at first sight, American—or more generally Anglo-Saxon—labor laws seem less constricting than the labor laws of Continental Europe. But antidiscrimination and equal opportunity laws impose constraints with respect to both hiring and dismissal procedures which are such that the judicial pressure over employment may actually prove to be as high in the United States as it is in Europe.

Moreover, the direct comparison of labor costs does not highlight a lasting gap in competitivity between the US and European economies. The external bilateral

---

[1] Translated from the French by Constance Bantman.

trade between Europe and the United States remains very favorable to Europe. The competition between the welfare models appears to have very little direct effect over the commercial competition between the European and American economic areas, and to date the international financial system has made it possible to transfer global financial surpluses toward the deficient United States without any particular strain.

The stakes of the debates over welfare models thus appear to revolve primarily around the internal consequences of these models. What is under discussion bears on the social consequences of the national systems: is well-being higher in liberal countries? Is it higher in America or Europe?

Welfare systems are designed to stabilize the individuals' incomes over their lifetimes, so as to prevent situations of absolute poverty from arising, and to contribute to stabilizing the economy by limiting the impact of macroeconomic fluctuations. The methods used to achieve such aims are very variable and the systems have numerous idiosyncrasies which make any comparison difficult. Moreover, the economic situations and the primary distribution of the growth returns also differ in each country and period. Of course, this is not without consequences for the welfare systems, which have to face different and changing challenges.

The macrosocial context and its evolution in Europe and the United States from 1970 to the present day will be introduced in turn (Section 6.1), followed by the traditional typology of the welfare systems founded on institutional comparisons. This typology is relatively robust, since observing the structural repartition of welfare expenditures roughly confirms institutional remarks (Section 6.3). It will then be seen that the efficiency of welfare systems from the viewpoint of the fight against poverty still depends heavily on public spending levels (Section 6.4). Finally, we will look at the shared challenges which the welfare systems will have to overcome over the next years, which mainly derive from the aging of the population (Section 6.5). The crisis of the welfare state is now a common theme and in this perspective it will be shown that the crisis affects private insurance systems just as much, and that an extra effort to redistribute incomes will prove indispensable in the future on both the Western and the Eastern shores of the Atlantic.

6.1. Primary income sharing between wages, employment, and profits: from the strong opposition between Europe and the United States in the 1970s to convergence in the 1990s

In order to analyze the modalities in primary income sharing, it will be convenient to break down the evolution of added value according to whether it can be attributed to a rise in employment, individual wages, or profits. Added value can indeed be broken down according to the following equation, in which AV stands for the added value, w for the average individual wage level, E for employment, P for the companies' profits, and Taxes, for indirect taxes.

$$AV = w \times E + P + \text{Taxes}$$

The added value's variation can then be broken down according to whether it is associated with the individual wages' variation (first term of following equation), to employment variation (second term), to the combination of the variations of individual wages and employment (third term), to the variation of profits (fourth term) and tax variation (fifth term).

$$1 = \frac{\Delta w \times E}{\Delta AV} + \frac{w \times \Delta E}{\Delta AV} + \frac{\Delta w \times \Delta E}{\Delta AV} + \frac{\Delta P}{\Delta AV} + \frac{\Delta \text{Taxes}}{\Delta AV}$$

Figures 6.1 to 6.3 retrace the evolution of the added value's growth sharing from the 1970s to the 1990s, between individual wages, employment, and profits. The term of covariation of employment and wages is of secondary importance and can be omitted. The term which can be attributed to taxes is weak in all countries, does not modify the conclusions of this general analysis, and can therefore be left aside.

In the 1970s, the United States and Europe were clearly opposed with respect to primary distribution of wealth creation (Figure 6.1). In the United States, work productivity was slow to evolve and individual wages did not increase by much. A very important part of wealth increases was thus affected by job creation. Also, the share attributed to profits was relatively high.

On the contrary, in Europe, in the four largest countries, the largest part of income growth was used to improve individual wages, while the share attributed to employment was very weak and that of profit slightly less important than in the United States. Sweden presented slightly different characteristics, with a primary income sharing more propitious to employment than in other European countries. Figure 6.1 highlights the very strong polarization of the European and the American models in the 1970s. There is a simple explanation for this configuration of income growth sharing, which rests on the gap in development between Europe and the United States. At the end of the war and up to the late 1970s, the United States was far ahead of Europe and individual wages were much higher. However, because it was at the cutting edge of technological development, and these years did not see any technical upheaval, the increase of work productivity was relatively low. In the same period, Europe was in a very different situation; it had to catch up from its technological shortcomings. Most of its employment growth resulted mainly from production increases, while a very sharp rise in work productivity made it possible for the purchasing power of individuals to gradually meet those of the United States. Moreover, a very steep increase in production ensured a sufficient progression in profits despite the weaker growth share attributed to it.

The disparity between the American and the European growth models gradually diminished from the 1980s onward (Figure 6.2). In France and Germany

Figure 6.1. Distribution in the 1970s: the strong opposition between the United States and Europe

the developments following the oil crises initially led to a major slowing down of wages, which saw the economic growth share of both countries brought down to the level as in the United States.

This change was accompanied by the attribution to companies' profits of most of the growth returns. In Germany, employment saw its contribution rise and the distribution scheme became almost identical with that of the United States, whereas in France job creation remained weak. In the United States, Italy, the UK, and Sweden, the primary income distribution pattern went through fewer changes than in the previous period. These facts were characteristic of a period of structural adjustment in Europe within the countries which had previously experienced a very high growth rate, which had made it possible to catch up on American productivity and provided for a strong wage increase. But the oil crises of mid-1970s and early 1980s had caused strong macroeconomic imbalances because wage increases had been increasing, white profits had been strangled by the rising energy costs. To some extent, the decrease of the wages' share and the increase of the profits' share in the distribution of growth returns therefore resulted from a delayed adaptation to the consequences of energy-related production costs. In this respect, the changes witnessed in Italy, the UK, and Sweden resulted from a longer adaptation lag. But, in addition to the necessity of adapting to changing energy costs, the modification of the European distribution pattern and its increasing

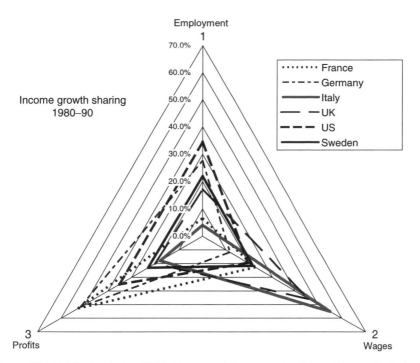

Figure 6.2. Distribution in the 1980s: France and Germany align themselves on the United States

similarity with the American model corresponded to a deeper maturation trend in the European economy which was completing a catching up phase with American development levels in the late 1980s. The European economy's newfound maturity thus translated into a lasting slowing down of the work productivity growth which, due to the threat of a widening of macroeconomic imbalances, prevented a quick increase of work returns from then on—all the more as the rise of unemployment made for a sharing of growth returns which was more favorable to job creation.

During the 1990s and early 2000s, distribution patterns in Europe and the United States became very close, while the Scandinavian model appeared increasingly autonomous.

With macroeconomic adjustments over in Europe, the single distribution pattern then became a very balanced sharing of the growth returns between wages, jobs, and profits. The share devoted to wages was slightly higher in the UK and the share to profits was slightly higher in Italy (where the adjustment had taken place later) and in Germany (where the reunification required a high level of investment and of productive capital accumulation), but the triangle of EU countries and that of the United States are exactly the same. On the contrary, in Sweden, the share corresponding to job creation became negative and the affect on individual wages became very prominent. This development resulted from the adjustment of

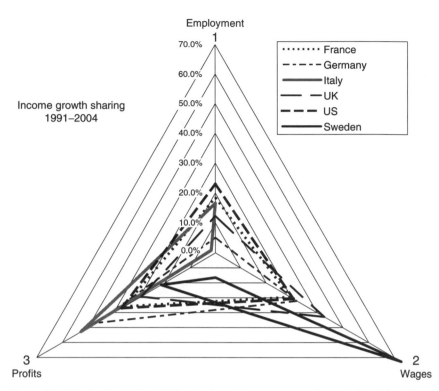

Figure 6.3. Distribution in the 1990s: the large European countries and the United States eventually converge, Sweden takes another direction

the Swedish job market through the lowering of workforce activity. The macro-economic shock of the early 1990s was very important in Scandinavia and led to strong employment cuts which could not be made up for in the early 2000s despite the increased competitivity in Sweden, made possible by an important and lasting monetary devaluation. In order to cut unemployment the only solution was to reduce the working population, which was provided for by social policies excluding the 'disabled' from the job market. These policies also made it possible to cut unemployment to a low level, but they also contributed to the rise of social contributions. The originality of the Scandinavian model stands out clearly: in the event of macroeconomic difficulties, the size of the countries involved makes it possible to find a solution through an increase in competitiveness founded on currency adaptation and important rises in productivity. These allowed for a wage increase, but the level of taxes has to be increased in order to finance social transfers for those excluded from the labor market.

The developments and changes in these primary distribution patterns have influenced social evolutions, the need for benefits, and the conditions of its funding. The primary sharing of the economic growth returns influences social advancement through its impact on employment and the growth of incomes. When the economy and work productivity rise quickly, full employment is another consequence, since many jobs are created due to the growth, as well as a quick income increase, since productivity gains make it possible to fund wage increases without inflation and without a reduction in profits. This situation, which was characteristic of Europe until the 1970s, is conducive to social progress in all its aspects: increase of individual purchasing power, reduction of working hours, possible lowering of the retirement age, etc. However, when the economy has joined a weaker long-term growth path, full employment can only rest on a strict sharing of wealth creation, which limits individual earnings and reserves an important part to job creation. Subsequently, even if wage levels and individual purchasing power are high, their growth can only be limited. Similarly, there is little leeway to improve work conditions or distribute extra social benefits. The prolongation for a relatively long time of the sharing pattern inherited from high growth, while the economy had slowed its progress because of the end of the catching up phase, accounts for the rise and then the maintaining of high level of unemployment in Europe. The lack of an efficient accompaniment to structural changes through relevant economic policies also explains the European difficulties. Restrictive policies were justified during the sharing pattern's first phase of adaptation to the slower rhythm of work productivity. Since the beginning of the 1990s the macroeconomic imbalances have been absorbed, as shown by the disappearance of inflation, and the profit level is now compatible again with the funding needs of capital accumulation in the long term.

Over the same period, the United States encountered far fewer difficulties, since it only had to overcome the effects of the oil crises, without having to profoundly modify its income sharing pattern. The transitory nature of macroeconomic difficulties can also be explained by a much better adaptation of economic policy, which was traditionally used more extensively and more quickly in the event of a rising unemployment.

The consequences of overall economic evolutions and of primary income sharing over welfare were important. In the United States, the emphasis on full employment made it possible to limit the need for unemployment benefits while wages–profits sharing remained stable. On the contrary, the existence of an important work pool has made it possible to implement social policies geared toward welfare-to-workfare initiatives and income support for the most disadvantaged (through the earning income tax credit). However, in the European countries where unemployment rose the most, as a result of macroeconomic maladjustments amplified by inappropriate responses, governments were forced to increase their income support spending for the unemployed and people involuntarily driven out of work.

6.2. **Institutional typology of the welfare systems**

The art of classification and typology relies on a reduction of the complexity of reality which evidences the distinctive features of 'opposite' models. In terms of welfare, there is a traditional opposition between 'Bismarckian' countries, in which insurance against the major social risks (illness, unemployment, and old age) is organized within the job sectors or activity branches and financed by contributions taken from wages, and, on the other hand, 'Beveridgian' models in which social protection comes from the state.

In Bismarckian systems, the guarantees given by social protection are delivered to workers and their families, whereas those who live outside the world of labor are excluded a priori and must either ensure personally that they have sufficient incomes, or fall back on the poor relief organizations generally granted by local authorities and financed by taxes.

In Beveridgian systems, the state guarantees to the resident population income minima in case of unemployment, illness, and during retirement. It also generally provides free health care.

Since Esping-Andersen (1990), these two basic models have usually been opposed to a Scandinavian model characterized by high levels of contributions and redistribution and by substantial state intervention. In this model, citizens have acquired rights, just as in the Beveridgian model, but they are far more important and go far beyond minimum protection against social risks.

These three basic welfare state models are coupled with economic organization regimes which are also different, so that, in the end, three broad social and economic models are defined:

- The 'liberal' model, which combines greater economic freedom (few regulations on the goods and services markets, few public companies, reduced state intervention), with a minimal welfare state of Beveridgian inspiration.
- The so-called 'conservative' or sometimes 'corporatist' model, in which the state plays a much greater part, and economic regulations are stronger (especially in the sphere of labor legislation) and the welfare state derives from Bismarckian inspiration.
- The Northern European countries' 'social democratic' model, in which the state plays an important—but different—role. Indeed, it is geared toward redistributing incomes and securing high social guarantees (especially in the event of unemployment) rather than market regulation.

This typology is helpful in understanding national debates about welfare. A liberal-leaning country will debate above all the sphere of application and the limits of welfare. Indeed, in such a system, the central questions hinge above all on determining the income level below which some intervention and state help are required, and the situations which must be covered by social intervention (unemployment type, family situation, etc.). In a country with a conservative tradition, the debate will naturally be more about judicial regulations and their simultaneous impact on the economy and workers' security. The question of the connection between welfare and employment costs will also be more emphasized because of the high level of social contributions. In social democratic countries, the question of the cost of social protection and of its consequences on competitiveness in an open world will logically fuel debates, as will the impact of benefits and contributions over economic behaviors.

Table 6.1. Welfare systems in Europe and the United States

	Liberal or residual	Social democratic	Conservative or corporatist	Mediterranean or familialist
Geographic situation	The US, UK, and Ireland	Scandinavia, and the Netherlands	Continental Europe (Austria, Germany, France, and Belgium)	Southern Europe (Italy, Spain, Portugal, and Greece)
Historical reference	Beveridge	Beveridge	Bismarck	Mixed. Often Beveridge since the reforms of the 1980s
Targets	Fight against poverty	Ensuring an income for everyone, egalitarian redistribution	Keeping up workers' incomes	Vary according to the systems. Fight against poverty, but also keeping up incomes
Level of social expenditures	Average	High	High	Low
Functioning principle	Selectivity	Universality	Contributivity	Selectivity/contributivity
Technique	Targeted benefits	Redistribution	Social insurances	Variable

As it is the case for all typologies, the one of Esping-Anderson simplifies the real world. On at least one point, it must be added to in order to cover roughly all the systems which may be encountered in developed Western countries. In the south of Europe, indeed, there are systems which often have a mixed inspiration, but are less developed than the northern countries. The Euro-Mediterranean systems are applicable to societies in which families often provide private welfare for their members, thus making the existence of a public system less necessary. There is no doubt that this is an original system which has its place within an enlarged typology of welfare system.

Finally, four broad models can be considered to structure the European and American welfare states (Table 6.1).

Their geography unambiguously evidences the fact that this opposition between Europe and the United States is not so clear-cut. Indeed, Great Britain is usually listed with the United States in the liberal type. On the contrary, Continental Europe appears to be divided into three, between the 'conservative', 'social democratic' and 'Mediterranean' countries. The analysis developed here leaves aside the Central European countries which have recently joined the European Community. Taking them into account would probably make the European map of welfare states even more complex. Therefore, this is very far from the opposition between the American model on one side and European model on the other. What is figured out by institutional analysis is mainly Europe's heterogeneity.

6.3. **Typology from quantitative data**

Beyond the institutional differences on which the above typologies are based, the welfare systems of developed countries fulfill identical functions. They aim to insure individuals and families against the four major risks of life, which are

- Childrearing, which affects families' income levels while wages do not vary according to family expenditure;
- Unemployment and poverty resulting from lack of work;
- Illness and handicap; and
- Old age.

Therefore, welfare states always include social advantages for families with children, some public unemployment benefit, a system of minimum income for the poor, public protection (more or less extensive), health care spending, public pensions, and complementary private systems.

What distinguishes one system from another is the extension of collective protection against risks. Some systems are more extensive on some risks, some others are more extensive on other risks. Other differences can be found in the modalities of benefits delivery: it could be centralized or decentralized. It could take the form of direct money transfers or free social services. It could be organized by public or private institutions. In order to compare European countries and the United States quantitatively, a seven-category nomenclature of social spending can be used:

- Public monetary benefits in favor of those in employment, including mainly unemployment benefits and income support for the poorest;
- Private monetary benefits for those in employment on top of the latter;
- Public health care benefits, monetary, or through services in kind;
- Public pensions;
- Private pensions; and
- Service expenditures in kind other than health care (which includes nursery spending among others).

Graphs 6.1–6.5 make it possible to visualize the importance and the distribution of welfare expenditures among the main Western European countries and in the United States.

The typology—based on a quantitive analysis of the actual distribution of social protection expenditure—outlines five models which overlap with those of the typology based on institutional analysis. However, while the American model can easily be paired off with the British liberal model, it appears much more isolated when a reference is made to the level and the distribution of actual expenditure.

The United States is therefore distinguished from the other models by the very low spending—whether public or private—on transfers in favor of those in work. The low level of this spending—unemployment benefits, family and housing benefits, transfers to deprived adults—is partly compensated for by 'tax' credits such as the earning income tax credit for those with a low work income. But it remains true that the American welfare system is little oriented toward the fight against

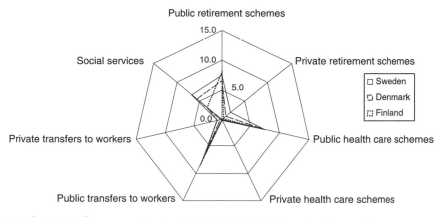

Graph 6.1. Welfare expenditure in GDP % in 2001, the Scandinavian model

Source: OECD

poverty and that there ensue, as we shall see, much more marked inequalities than in Europe and a much higher level of poverty.

For other countries, it is relatively easy to derive the traditional typology from welfare expenditure data. Scandinavian countries are grouped within a model characterized by a high level of overall spending and a very high share of social services. The 'Continental' model (Germany, Austria, Belgium, and France) is characterized by a significant share of pensions spending and, by comparison with Scandinavian countries, a small share of social services spending. The Mediterranean model (Spain and Italy) constitutes a zone with a low spending level, mostly public and almost restricted to pensions and health care expenditure. Finally, a 'British–Dutch' model emerges, characterized by a high level of private pension spending, which brings it closer to the North American model, but

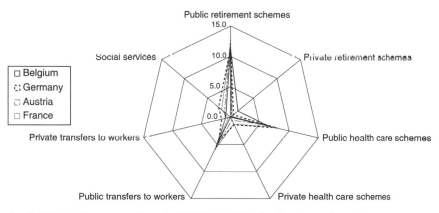

Graph 6.2. Welfare expenditure in GDP % in 2001, the Continental model

Source: OECD

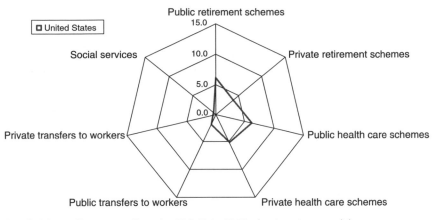

Graph 6.3. Welfare expenditure in GDP % in 2001, the American model

Source: OECD

which is distinguished from it by a much higher level of income support for the workers.

The institutional organization of the welfare state and the structure of welfare spending vary greatly according to the countries. However, the total amount of social protection expenditures ranges from 18.9 percent of GDP in Spain to 31.2 percent in France (except for Ireland which is an a typical small country); this is a small interval (Table 6.2). This comparison of the weight of welfare spending, both public and private, rests on assessing the rate of net welfare expenditure divided by GDP 'at factor cost'. It makes it possible to correct the results obtained by comparing untaxed spending levels which are biased, chiefly because in some countries a significant share of welfare expenditure takes the shape of a tax expenditure (such

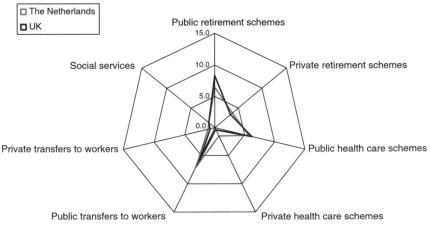

Graph 6.4. Welfare expenditure in GDP % in 2001, the Anglo-Dutch model

Source: OECD

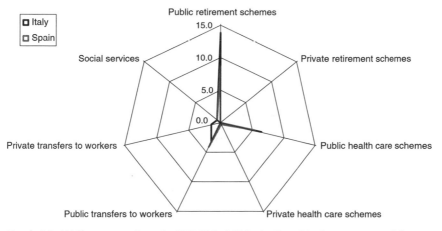

Graph 6.5. Welfare expenditure in GDP % in 2001, the Euro-Mediterranean model

Source: OECD

as the American Earning Income Tax Credit) and also because the variable level of contribution applied to outgoing benefits is very uneven. A country with a low rate of compulsory contributions may therefore provide low untaxed pensions, but whose purchasing power may be identical to those of a country with a much higher contribution rate providing more substantial untaxed benefits. Of course, it must be expected then that the redistribution of income between the highest and the lowest on the scale will be lower in the countries with a low contribution rates. By relating expenditure to the GDP at factor cost (i.e. by not taking into account the indirect taxes which put a strain on market prices), the actual economic impact of the contributions to be taken from producers in order to finance welfare expenditure can be measured. This comparison between the net rates of welfare expenditure in GDP reduces the differences between the countries and slightly modifies the hierarchy: once taxes are taken into account, Denmark, which is the

Table 6.2. Welfare expenditure in 2001 in GDP % at factor cost

	Gross public expenditure	Gross private expenditure	Gross total expenditure	Net total expenditure
Austria	29.6	1.8	31.4	24.8
Belgium	28.0	2.8	30.8	26.3
Denmark	34.2	1.5	35.7	26.4
Finland	28.0	1.3	29.3	22.6
France	33.0	2.3	35.3	31.2
Germany	30.6	3.9	34.5	30.8
Italy	28.3	1.7	30.0	25.3
Ireland	15.3	0.5	15.8	13.9
The Netherlands	24.3	7.1	31.4	25.0
Spain	21.7	0.3	22.0	18.9
UK	25.4	5.1	30.5	27.1
United States	15.7	9.8	25.5	24.5

Source: OECD

highest spending country, if taxes are taken into account, goes behind France and Germany. As for the United States, it joins the main European group: it overtakes Finland and finds itself just behind the Netherlands.

6.4. **A marked connection between poverty and public welfare spending**

If private welfare spending is taken into account and the impact of taxes is integrated, the United States matches the average of the main European group, with a level of welfare expenditure at 24.5 percent of GDP, placing it slightly below Denmark but above Finland. From this viewpoint, American citizens have access to welfare protection not unlike what is seen in Europe. It could be inferred from this overall observation that the nature of welfare, public or private, universal or category-based, centralized or decentralized, matters little. In reality, it appears that despite the convergence of welfare spending rates, important differences remain with respect to the eventual impact of welfare on income distribution and poverty. Therefore, the variation of public welfare rates in GDP accounts for more than a third of the variation of poverty rates observed in the United States and in a sample of European countries (Figure 6.4).

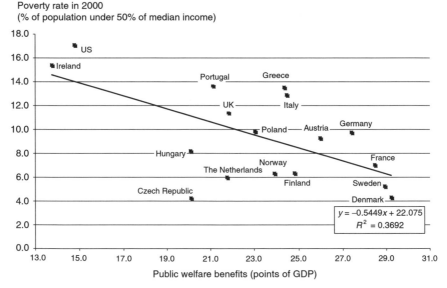

Figure 6.4. Poverty rate and public welfare benefits

Source: OECD and author's own calculation

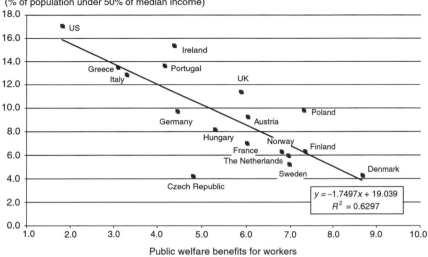

Figure 6.5. Poverty rates and income support public welfare benefits for the workers (author's calculation on OECD data)

With a more specific analysis, the reason for this statistical correlation can be identified. It can be explained by the large differences in social benefits targeted on workers in all countries. This specific welfare spending, which includes unemployment benefits, but also income support spending for the poorest, forms the basis of the redistribution which aims at reducing income inequalities and wiping out situations of extreme poverty as much as possible. On their own, they account for 63 percent of poverty rate variations in the sample of countries previously used (Figure 6.5). The United States is strongly at odds with the core of European countries, France, Germany, and the UK, and even more with the Scandinavian countries. The 'European social model' appears quite characteristic, and in this respect it is neatly contrasted with the North American model, through a high level of protection for the poorest which restricts poverty significantly. Only the South European countries are slightly closer to the United States. But even these countries spend more on workers and consequently have a lower poverty rate.

6.5. **A share challenge: population aging**

In all Western countries, the reform of welfare systems has been on the agenda since at least the early 1990s. These reforms are caused by several factors, the most important of which is population aging. Demographic evolutions in Europe and the United States will lead, without any major reform, to an increase of the financial burden linked to welfare funding, which is already heavy on the workforce—and will become increasingly so.

Three demographic events have led to the aging problem:

- The post-World War II baby boom (which took place slightly earlier in Germany for obvious reasons) constituted a demographic surge whose progress upset long-term demographic trends. Initially, up to the 1970s, it led to an important rejuvenation of the population, while also impairing the balance between the active and the nonactive part of the population: the baby boomers did not work yet. Then, from the 1970s to the noughties, it strongly diminished the ratio between workers and nonworkers: the baby boomers were in employment, they had fewer children than their parents, and the latter, who were gradually leaving work, were far less numerous. This phase was a boon for welfare, since pension spending was spontaneously contained, which made it possible to improve benefits with relatively weak contributions. Finally, since the early 1980s, the baby boomers' transition to retirement age has led to sudden aging population, and financing welfare benefits is becoming an increasingly heavy financial burden. The transition of the baby-boom wave has partly reversible consequences: once the wave is over, the working/nonworking ratio should return to its structural level which depends on average life expectancy and birth rate, and which is below the level reached during the baby boomers' retirement period. The degradation of welfare funding structures is therefore partly circumstantial (even if the duration of the 'cycle' stretches over thirty to forty years) and may as a result be compensated by a new immigration wave which is already well advanced in the United States.

- The extension of average life expectancy is the second factor of demographic aging. On average, in Western countries, life expectancy increases by a term every year. This is a structural movement whose end is difficult to forecast because of the great uncertainty relative to the asymptote that is the maximum duration of life (120 years?) and the difficulty of predicting the evolution of the population's health, as on the one hand it benefits from improved medical treatments and on the other, suffers from unfavorable behaviors (cigarette addiction, alcoholism, and poor eating habits), or even from the degradation of the natural environment. Nonetheless, the developments observed rather tend to confirm the hypothesis of the continued extension of life expectancy, which implies a structural adjustment of welfare. Contrary to the effects of the baby boom, which are transitory, this is a lasting constraint which cannot be bypassed by population movements (immigrants also age, and the duration of their retirement is on the increase too). The normal reaction to such aging through the extension of life consists in a proportional extension of the time spent in employment, so as to maintain the ratio between the number of those retired and those in work, and to avoid having to increase too much the contributions taken from workers' incomes. This balancing out is quite natural since, in addition to the fact that increased life expectancy extends retirement time, the latter tends to improve in quality since it is an increase of life expectancy in good health. All the countries have thus implemented reforms which encourage many people to postpone retirement age. Some, by pushing back minimal ages (United States, Germany, and the UK), others, by broadening individual freedom of choice through a reform guaranteeing the actuarial neutrality of the retirement age (Swedish, Italian, and French cases) and which, coupled with parameter changes (level of the replacement of employment income according to the time spent in employment), encourages individuals to postpone their departure from working life.

- The lowering of the birth rate is the third factor of population aging. This development is very negative in Europe, except for Ireland and France. As in the United States, the birth rate remains close to 2 (1.9 on average from 2000 to 2005 in France and 2.0 in the United States), which suggests that there is no risk of a population decrease. The situation in other European countries is especially critical, particularly as there is no guarantee that the situation will improve. Two groups can be ascertained: the first one, which includes the UK, Scandinavia, and Benelux, retains an average birth rate between 1.6 and 1.75; the second group, which comprises ex-communist Eastern European countries and all of Mediterranean Europe, shows an extremely weak birth rate ranging from 1.2 to 1.5 children per woman childbearing age. Such a low birth rate will have a delayed consequence on population that is not yet visible. But over the next twenty years, its consequences will be disastrous in countries like Italy and Spain. The decline of the birth rate will naturally make the funding of welfare more problematic, all the more as, just like the increase in life expectancy, it cannot permanently be made up for by immigration. And while the correction of this unfavorable evolution certainly implies an increase in the spending targeted at families, especially through an increase in child-minding services on offer, the only efficient way of making women's aspirations to work compatible with motherhood entail more public expense.

As a result of demographic aging, in the course of the twenty-first century, and from its early years, welfare systems in Europe and the United States will all face a sharp increase in the need for social transfers with respect to pensions and health care. Figure 6.6 shows the evolution of the ratio between population above 64 and those between 15 and 64 from 1970 to 2050. It clearly evidences the general character of the demographic challenge which concerns all countries, but with a very significant difference between the much degraded situation of Mediterranean countries and the more favourable evolution of the United States.

The increasing weight of pension benefits resulting from demographic evolutions may be partly contained by the gap between the retirement age and a certain rise in immigration, but the low European birth rate calls for an increase in health care spending. The latter, which is general, is especially significant in the United

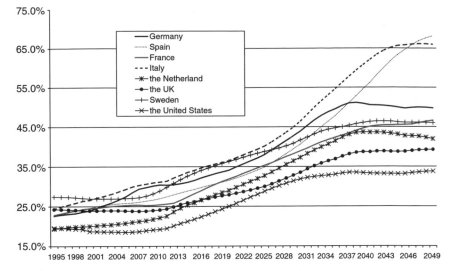

Figure 6.6. The ratio between the population above 64 and the population from 15 to 64

Source: UN population perspectives

States, partly as a result of the absence of any controls on medication prices. The projections of health care needs are uncertain, since the progression of the available therapeutics is hard to predict. However, recent-years observations show that the increase of life expectancy in good health and without any incapacity also results from the increase in health care costs.

If the demographic trends are extended, and supposing that the average benefits or refunding costs remain constant, future needs in terms of welfare in retirement and health care can be assessed. With a few simple hypotheses about the likely evolutions of spending for family and unemployment benefits, the projection of the share of all welfare expenditures in GDP can be made more complete (Table 6.3). These projections—carried out by the OFCE in 2004 for the *Conseil français d'orientation des retraites*—rest on the following hypotheses: for pensions, the actual age when work is stopped is maintained at the level reached in 2000 and the average pension allowance evolves like the average net salary; for health care, spending per person evolves like the GDP per head and increases according to population aging by supposing that the ratio of spending per age observed in early 2000 remains constant; spending for families is indexed on the population under 18; lastly, unemployment benefits evolve like unemployment whose rate is supposed to converge in the long term toward a uniform 5 percent level.

All EU countries and the United States thus have to face strongly growing welfare needs. Although the spending projections were carried out only for the large European countries and the United States, the orientation of demographic evolutions is identical in the other countries, so that the conclusions can be generalized to all EU countries. The differences in the demographic configurations play a relatively small part when the examination focuses only on the question of the

Table 6.3. Spontaneous evolution (i.e. before any reform) of the share of welfare expenditure in GDP between 2000 and 2050

% of GDP	2000 (%)					2050 (%)					Variation (2) − (1)
	Family	Unemployment	Pensions	Health care	Total* (1)	Family	Unemployment	Pensions	Health care	Total* (2)	
Germany	3.0	2.4	12.0	10.3	29.5	2.3	1.2	17.1	13.6	36.0	6.5
Spain	0.5	2.4	9.1	7.3	20.1	0.4	0.7	15.7	10.3	27.9	7.8
France	2.7	1.9	12.4	9.8	29.7	2.0	0.8	17.2	12.7	35.6	5.9
Italy	0.9	0.4	15.4	7.5	25.2	0.6	0.2	22.9	10.5	35.2	10.0
The Netherlands	1.2	1.3	10.9	0.6	27.4	0.9	1.3	16.6	13.8	36.0	8.6
UK	1.8	0.8	12.3	9.1	26.8	1.4	0.6	18.6	11.5	34.9	8.1
Sweden	3.3	2.0	11.8	11.8	30.9	2.6	1.4	16.4	14.1	36.5	5.6
United States	0.5	0.4	8.9	13.1	23.5	0.4	0.5	12.8	16.5	30.8	7.3

Source: OFCE calculations for the French 'Conseil d'orientation des retraites'

pressure of need. Therefore, the fact that the United States retains a higher birth rate and that the ratio between elderly nonworkers and workers is not degrading as much as it is in Europe, does not lead to a much more favorable relative situation. Many European countries, and particularly France, can make up for increasing pension and health care funding needs through a decrease in unemployment and family spending, while the United States already has full employment, fewer advanced retirement and family benefits, which therefore affords little leeway. It must be added that the funding needs of welfare depend little on the functioning of pension schemes. Thus, American companies' defined-contribution schemes have to deal with insufficient provisioning which has already reached $850 billion, and will entail the intervention of the federal pension guarantee and imply an increase in direct and added taxes. Similarly, British pension reform is called into question by the lack of voluntary contributions, which is likely to lead to an increase in compulsory contributions. In the countries which have implemented pay-as-you-go pension systems modeled on individual notional accounts (Sweden and Italy in particular), pension schemes may give out only very low pensions (especially in Italy, due to a very degraded demography), unless, as in some countries, the balance is reestablished through an increase in contributions. In fact, individual notional accounts simulate the functioning of a defined-contribution scheme in a defined-benefit pension system. Future benefits are not funded but the yielding of the subscriptions inscribed for each working individual depends on how the demographic ratio evolves, which ensures that the system remains stable. When life expectancy increases, if those in work retain the same retirement age, the amount of their pension benefit diminishes.

Ultimately, the current pension reforms have shared characteristics. Whereas, in the 1980s, the debate focused on systemic solutions to the aging population challenge (partial privatization of welfare and pensions, substitution of funding for pay-as-you-go systems), it seems that a parametric arbitration is increasingly favored: the point is to find out, today, while the baby boomers are drawing near retirement age, how to distribute the effort of financial adjustment between the age of retirement, the average pensions level, and the contribution level. The political debate on this question remains confused because the liberals have not relinquished the perspective of a systemic reform, especially in the United States. But it is now too late to apply it to the baby boomers, so that the solution will undoubtedly imply, at least partly, an increase in welfare contributions. This seems all the more likely as the funding needs of health care systems will probably not be contained over the coming years. The impact of population aging and increasing treatment costs will combine to increase the pressure, while in this sector the prospect of an efficient systemic reform is unlikely. Northern European countries may have achieved significant results over the past few years, but the American example of the HMO (i.e. the implementation of integrated care managed by insurers for the benefit of insurers) shows that the effects of the rationalization of health care provision are transitory and that, once they have been obtained, spending increases more quickly than incomes do.

How will the various European countries and the United States respond to this situation—all the more as welfare contribution levels are already high, and the dominant trend points toward liberalization, the reduction of the state's involvement, and competition between the nations and social systems? It is obviously very difficult to picture an opinion change today in favor of an extension of welfare provision. However, a strong resistance in public opinion against any substantial cut in public pensions and health care is also manifest. In the United States, it is therefore unlikely that the contemplated public pension reform which could lead to account individualization will see the light. Similarly, the British could quickly move toward a strengthening of the obligatory pillar of the pension system after having widely individualized the system in the 1980s. In France, as in Germany, the option for a parametric reform already forecasts a rise in contributions. In Italy, the transition to notional accounts is very slow and a contribution increase is certainly unavoidable. For now, no country seems to be able to take on the risks associated with a brutal reform without a contribution increase, which would lead to a massive impoverishment of pensioners in some countries (Italy), and a significant one in all the others.

The fact that all the countries are confronted with the same challenges almost at the same time makes it possible to contemplate a balanced reaction: a combination of parametric pension reforms and care efficiency improvement could limit, without canceling it out altogether, the necessary contribution increase. It is certainly possible, by lengthening the working life, resorting to immigration, and rationalizing health care systems, to cut by half the funding needs presented in Table 6.3. As a result, the progressive increase in social contributions, if it is also accompanied by a rationalization of other public spending, becomes absolutely likely. The neoliberal present could give way, under the pressure of needs, to a new extension of the welfare state. The United States, a homogeneous power protected by a strong and flexible currency, could deal with it easily enough. In Europe, the difficulty is no doubt much greater, because of the weakness of the institutions which weigh down the efficiency of economic policy and may lead some states to play on tax rate competition and, eventually, on social competition, to reestablish their economic and financial balances. This could lead to a paradox: because they fail to coordinate efficiently, the European states could yet, through competition, destroy the social balances which they are all trying to reach. The cost of this 'non-Europe' could thus become exorbitant. Fortunately, there exists a more favorable scenario in which the shared constraints linked to population aging and the attachment to the welfare systems' value of solidarity lead to balanced reforms. Which of these two scenarios will prevail? The arguments in favor of one or the other's success seem to balance out at present. The next few years will be crucial for Europe. More than ever, institutional reform is a sine qua non to enable the debate to develop clearly.

Comparing welfare systems on both sides of the Atlantic shows that while solutions differ, the problems to be solved are widely shared: population aging is a major challenge everywhere. The growth of inequalities made worse by globalization and bitter competition mean greater income redistribution everywhere. The growth of age-related health care spending, but also, and above all else, improved medical techniques, increase mutualization needs everywhere. Overall, these evolutions all imply an increase in welfare spending in a context of tensions over public spending linked to reluctance to taxes and the search for competitive labor costs. Over the last decade, new solutions have emerged, which mix a hidden rise of contributions through the privatization of elements of welfare protection (such as the increase in health care funding by private insurances or the reduction of public pension systems and incentives to individual pension benefits), the refocusing of social transfers on the most deprived sections of the population, often paired with the activation of passive spending (work incentives). These measures, which in the end amount to a cut in welfare, do not avoid an increase in compulsory or voluntary contributions linked to the growth of welfare needs. On the one hand, these measures appear to be justified above all by the various notions in each country of the place of the state, rather than by the necessities of improving the systems' efficiency. In this debate, the United States seems quite far from Europe, while public opinion there is much more receptive to the liberal theses than European opinion (see Chapter 7 on values, and Chapter 10 on American and European models of society). But beyond ideology, welfare systems prove enduring, and they should not regress, whether in the United States or in Europe, because they appear to be indispensable in modern societies. In this respect, the promotion of the Scandinavian flexi-security model (which in reality is restricted to Denmark), which mingles economic liberalism and a strong individual protection against social and economic risks, only reemphasizes the original mission assigned to welfare protection: enabling the market economy to function while warranting the citizens' welfare.

7 Value change

Michel Forsé and Maxime Parodi

Shared values are part of what is needed to make up a society. Constituting a society certainly implies the establishment of collective institutions and norms but they would have little political, social, or moral legitimacy if they were not based on shared values. To take this into account, it is necessary to focus on the actors and their reasons; for example it is clear that there is no democracy in a country with no democrats. If we examine the social foundations of Europe in this way while allowing that it is not a society like, say, the United States, we can ask ourselves if Europe actually amounts to a society, or is at least on its way to becoming one. In other words, is what Henri Mendras (1997) calls 'the Europeans' Europe' a reality or not?

Nonetheless, there are two ways of agreeing on values. There may be a strong consensus on conceptions of the good. But major disagreements may subsist, as happens in any modern society. Here, what counts is for actors to accept a pluralism of reasonable conceptions of the good rather than for them to all hold exactly the same values. However, this assumes actors endeavor to be impartial toward each other by allowing each one the freedom to think. Obviously, this does not mean 'anything goes' or 'who cares anyway?'—it simply means ensuring that an actor's freedom is only curtailed where it infringes on another's, that is actors agree on a *reasonable* framework within which differing and even conflicting values may flourish. Now we can begin answering our question not only by asking ourselves if Europe exhibits any degree of unanimity on certain values but more importantly, by seeing if Europeans share any common reasonable viewpoint that goes beyond all the subsisting differences and serves as a framework for both personal judgment and acceptance of pluralism about the good life.

Because values do not suffer direct observation, we shall try to answer our dual question by examining the personal opinions of Europeans. However, this means diagnosing both opinion levels and trends because any consensus can increase or taper off and we need to take that into account. Europeans may also be converging on some values even in the absence of any consensus. Differences may widen or hold fast. The temporal and spatial perspectives should stand side-by-side because we need to see if a given difference in one context also appears in another that irrefutably qualifies as a society. Thus, we chose the United States for purposes of comparison.

7.1. **Data**

We used representative surveys because the general nature of the questions requires data that allow inference of Continental magnitude. However, we realize the extreme difficulty, if not impossibility of comparing survey questions that were not asked in identical terms at different times and/or places. This left us with precious little usable data. In fact, all we have are the 1981, 1990, and 1999 waves of the World Values Survey, that is the European Values Survey for Europe. The latter covered Belgium, Denmark, France, Germany, Ireland, Italy, the Netherlands, Spain, Sweden, and the UK. Today we have data from more countries but it is unusable for comparison purposes. Nonetheless, the data cover major countries of Western Europe and much of its geography (Stoetzel 1983; Riffault 1994; Bréchon 2000; *Futuribles*, No. 177, 2002; Bréchon 2002; Galland and Roudet 2005). We also noted changes from one questionnaire to the next and discrepancies between the European and US versions. Therefore, we restricted our comparison to only those questions asked simultaneously in all three waves and on both continents. For the sake of clarity, these opinions will be clustered into the seven main blocks we have identified: lifestyles, civic spirit, social selectivity, religion, work, family, and childrearing.

We shall then individually review every question in the three waves spanning all the countries except for two questions we cover later in the discussion on postmaterialism because their results challenge that theory. The first such question asks if money should be given less importance while the second covers the government's most important responsibility (with highly controversial response choices). Technically, in addition to the weighting factors provided by each country, each sample will be weighted to take account of the size of the 15+ year age group in each country at the time of the survey (source: OECD). This operation does not affect the total number of respondents for each date. That number is then adjusted to allow for actual demographic growth between 1980 and 2000. The same is done for the US data. Postweighted European sample sizes are 13,441, 14,625, and 15,494 for each of the three years against 1,627, 1,779, and 1,959 for the United States.

That said, the 1999 version of the European questionnaire was more extensive (and in the United States the survey also took place in 2000). Thus, we shall sketch out a preliminary overview on the basis of the most recent opinion results (two more blocs can then be added: democracy and economy) before going on to examine the opinions for the trends, differences, and any convergences while bearing in mind the restrictions described.

7.2. **The domains of consensus in 2000**

We shall begin with values enjoying broad consensus. To that end, we list answers supported by four-fifth of respondents ('strong majority') and then those supported by two-thirds of respondents ('broad majority'). This gives us a 1999–2000 snapshot of values shared by Europeans, along with any differences from those shared by Americans.

7.2.1. ATTITUDES TO DEMOCRACY

Over 80 percent of respondents on both sides of the Atlantic believe democracy is 'good' or 'very good'; a strong majority find it 'better than any other form of government'. They overwhelmingly reject the idea that a military government is good. Likewise, over two-thirds of respondents think it would be 'bad' or 'very bad' for a nation to have a strong leader who could ignore its legislature and elections.

Some 86 percent of Europeans and 75 percent of Americans believe that society needs reform, not radical change or more of the status quo. Another broad majority on both continents think that their countries have 'some' or 'a lot' of respect for individual human rights'; both also disagree with 'the economic system runs badly in a democracy'.

7.2.2. COMPETITION AND THE MARKET ECONOMY

Should individuals or government take more responsibility in providing for the needs of the individual? Some 66 percent of Europeans and 69 percent of Americans sooner feel that responsibility is individual. Moreover, 76 percent of Europeans and 80 percent of Americans think competition is good because it stimulates hard work and new ideas. In a context of high unemployment, people should not be choosy: 69 percent of Europeans agree that the jobless should be forced to accept any job available under pain of forfeiting unemployment benefits.

Americans accept capitalism fairly well. A strong majority there agree that owners should run their companies and appoint the management or at least that management should be appointed by owners and workers jointly. They strongly reject the view that government or workers alone should appoint management. Likewise, 83 percent of Americans think that private ownership, not nationalization, of business and industry should be encouraged. These questions were not asked consistently within some European countries or even asked at all in others. Nonetheless, in France, Germany, the UK, and elsewhere asked, 78 percent of respondents sooner support the encouragement of private enterprise. Thus, it appears that Europeans very broadly accept capitalism.

However, 68 percent of Europeans and 65 percent of Americans would like to see less emphasis on money and material possessions. There is nice consensus about respect for nature, with a strong majority of Europeans wanting a 'simple, more natural lifestyle' and a strong majority of Americans preferring coexistence with nature to domination thereof. Behind these responses lie concerns about the environment but each continent differs on how best to fight pollution. Some 69 percent of Americans are open to 'giving part of their income' to prevent pollution, against 54 percent of Europeans, while 57 percent of Americans feel that government should prevent it 'at no extra personal cost', against 74 percent of Europeans.

1. *Attitudes to Freedom*—Some 74 percent of Europeans and 89 percent of Americans feel they exercise free choice and control over their lives. And a strong majority are quite 'satisfied' with their lives. There is also greater allowance for free choice in other people: abortion, divorce, homosexuality, and other practices are no longer widely condemned. This reflects changing attitudes to which we shall return, but we notice that with too much focus on evolutions, the risk is to forget the levels. On the other hand, the indicators of 'permissiveness' confirm consensus against lying, joyriding, hash/marijuana consumption, and drink-driving. A strong majority consider suicide quite unjustified.

2. *Civic Spirit and Confidence in Institutions*—While a strong majority of Europeans think it would be good to see more emphasis on self-fulfillment, they also show concern for the community and stress the need to obey the law, that is the need for civic-mindedness. They clearly condemn free riders. A strong majority find it unjustified to claim benefits to which they are not entitled, to evade tax or to take bribes in the line of duty. A broad majority trust the police to enforce law and order and say they would report any information that might 'help justice be done'.

Americans show greater respect for authority: 70 percent versus 58 percent for Europeans. The higher crime rates that prevail in the United States may explain the gap; rates partly due to the fact that the US federal government does not (yet) have a monopoly on lawful violence—or at least less so than European central governments (these opinions are unstable as we shall see in the trends analysis below). But attitudes to national security give a different picture: Americans are very confident about their armed forces—most unlike Europeans. Moreover, 73 percent of Americans are ready to fight for their country in the event of war, against only 56 percent of Europeans (results predate September 11, 2001 and the Iraq War).

At all events, dissonance transpires between civic spirit and confidence in government institutions or leaders. A broad majority of Americans have no confidence in their political parties, television, or the press. While below a two-thirds majority, levels of mistrust in trade unions, political parties, and legislatures run high on both continents. Citizens do not like delegating powers to officials without having watchdog rights. They give politicians no blank checks; they are mistrustful and prepared to demonstrate if needed. Thus, Americans have a distinct affinity for petitions—81 percent report having signed them. But if the affinity for demonstrations is growing, protest is not sufficiently widespread to build any wider consensus: today a broad majority of Europeans still refuse to join a wildcat strike as a matter of pure principle. And a broad majority on each continent would not help occupy an office or factory.

3. *Nondiscrimination of Neighbors*—Queried about what neighbors they might find objectionable, respondents on both continents usually present as quite tolerant. A strong majority uphold the democratic criterion and will not reject a neighbor on the basis of race, foreign nationality, religion, or sexual orientation. We also find strong tolerance of big families, HIV/AIDS sufferers, and broad tolerance of left-wing extremists and the emotionally unstable.

4. *Teetering Religion*—Americans award more importance to religion than Europeans: 83 percent say religion is 'quite' or 'very' important in their lives, which only 46 percent of Europeans agree with. As Alexis de Tocqueville noted, Americans are attached to religion because, unlike Europeans, they never had to live under a (single) church with a (spiritual) monopoly and have always had lots of churches to choose from. This observation remains relevant because, very plainly, when you mention religion, Europeans relate the word to an institution while Americans link it to their personal belief system. The survey asked if 'your church' gives 'adequate' answers to 'moral problems and needs of the individual, problems of family life, people's spiritual needs, and social problems facing our country today'. Well, a broad majority of Europeans say their 'church/the churches' fail to do so while a majority of Americans say they succeed. Other responses obtain no broad majorities. In fact, a broad majority of Europeans fret over the spillover between religion and politics. They do not want religious leaders to influence either voters or governments. A broad European majority also disagree that people who 'do not believe in God are unfit for public office'. Americans ring no such alarms: their responses show no consensus on this issue and a broad majority trust their churches.

This issue is not just a matter of historical legacy: the two continents diverge sharply on faith in God and the meaningfulness of religion. Some 94 percent of Americans believe in God and in the existence of the soul, 84 percent in the existence of heaven, 75 percent in life after death, and 71 percent in hell. Here, Europeans are far more skeptical, registering distinctly higher 'Don't know' and 'Don't believe' scores than Americans. Only 70 percent believe in God, 45 percent in life after death, 40 percent in heaven and 27 percent in hell. At heart, Europe differs from the United States by her declining faith: 82 percent of Americans qualify themselves as 'religious' against 60 percent of Europeans. Nonetheless, Europeans remain attached to the religious ceremonies because a broad majority find them important to birth, marriage, and death.

5. *Attitudes to Work*—A strong majority consider work an important or very important part of their lives. The idea that work has lost its importance is manifestly a dead conventional wisdom. Nonetheless, Americans and Europeans have differing job expectations. In general, Americans are more demanding and stress job involvement. Thus, 'good pay' is important to 89 percent of Americans and 77 percent of Europeans. Consensus here is broad but differing levels of job involvement probably account for the gap in wage expectations. Although a

broad majority of Europeans believe in merit-based pay, the corresponding US majority is massive (the question used to evaluate support for merit-based pay asks: 'Imagine two secretaries, of the same age, doing practically the same job. One finds out that the other earns considerably more than she does. The better paid secretary, however, is quicker, more efficient and more reliable at her job. In your opinion, is it fair or not fair that one secretary is paid more than the other?'). Additionally, 84 percent of Americans think it important for their jobs to give them a sense of achievement, against only 57 percent of Europeans. Likewise, 81 percent of Americans stress the need to find their jobs 'interesting', against 66 percent for Europeans. Finally, Americans express a slightly greater need for job security—72 percent versus 64 percent for Europeans.

For their part, Europeans express a preference for 'pleasant people to work with', a question omitted from the US survey. More significantly, they scarcely chose 'not too much pressure' or 'generous holidays' from among the job quality items. Europeans mirror Americans in wanting more job involvement. Finally, 68 percent of Europeans find that they need a job to 'achieve something', against only 48 percent of Americans.

6. *Family and Social Lives*—The surveys almost unanimously affirm that respondents consider family important to their lives and want 'more emphasis' on it: 90 percent of Americans and 76 percent of Europeans say that marriage is not an 'outdated institution'. In Europe, where such questions were asked, the responses emphasized the issues of faithfulness, mutual respect, and tolerance; results show Europeans consider them all essential to a successful marriage and rate them highly. Here we see the effects of radical change in the family as an institution. We also see rejection of marriage as an indestructible bond and of adultery as a way of developing extra emotional bonds in favor of a more 'romantic' model where matrimony sincerely reflects the emotional attachment of one person to other. However, this makes for a more fragile bond, which may explain why respondents consider it important to be 'willing to discuss the problems that come up between husband and wife'. Finally, a broad majority of Europeans consider that differing political beliefs are not a serious impediment to a 'successful' marriage.

The premium value on intimacy and conviviality extends beyond the couple. Respondents rate socializing with friends and recreational activities as 'important' or 'very important'; a strong majority report spending time with friends over twice a month. Responses to a question asked of Americans show that these values do not reflect narcissistic withdrawal: a large majority found it more important to understand the other person's personal preferences than to be able to clearly express one's own (the question is artificially asymmetric however). A broad majority of Europeans also report feeling 'concerned about the living conditions of the elderly' and feel 'a moral duty' to help them. These two questions were not asked of Americans.

7. *Women's Status and Child Rearing*—Despite unusually pronounced national differences in Europe, broad majorities now agree on the vanishing of

gender roles. Today a broad majority of Europeans think that both the wife and husband 'should contribute to household income' and that 'a job is the best way for a woman to be an independent person'. Europeans also want a readjustment of parental roles. While a broad majority agree that 'a working mother can establish just as warm and secure a relationship with her children as a nonworking mother', another equally broad majority agree that 'in general, fathers are just as suited to look after their children as mothers'.

But Europeans and Americans diverge over the role model of the house-wife. Some 80 percent of Americans and only 56 percent of Europeans feel that 'being a housewife is just as fulfilling as working for pay'. To explain the gap, we hypothesize that Europeans are probably reading the housewife's role along a scale of values that runs from 'traditional' to 'modern' while Americans are likely reading it on a scale that goes from 'coercion' to 'free choice'. Thus, the issue for European 'modernists' is the abolition of the traditional model, whereas Americans have no issue with this model *if freely chosen*. This would explain why Americans reject gender discrimination more resolutely: they focus more on the procedures than the results. For example, 82 percent reject the idea that 'when jobs are scarce, men should have more right to a job than women'. Europeans are distinctly softer on this point and only 65 percent disavow such discrimination. A strong majority of Americans also disagree that higher edu-cation is more important for boys than girls. Two-thirds of Americans think that men do not necessarily make better political leaders than women and they have confidence in feminist organizations. These questions were not asked of Europeans.

More generally, the idea of gender roles is weaker in the United States. Some 85 percent of Americans versus 55 percent of Europeans feel 'a woman has to have children to be fulfilled'. Yet 82 percent of Europeans versus 64 percent of Americans think 'a child needs a home with both a father and a mother to grow up happily'.

Children are a bi-Continental priority: 85 percent of Americans and 72 percent of Europeans hold that 'parents' duty is to do their best for their children even at the expense of their own well-being'. Reciprocally, broad majorities concur that 'regardless of what the qualities and faults of one's parents are, one must always love and respect them'.

Finally, respondents were asked to select five top qualities that children should learn out of a possible eleven (i.e. good manners, independence, hard work, feeling of responsibility, imagination, tolerance and respect for other people, thrift/saving money and things, determination and perseverance, religious faith, unselfishness, and obedience). Tolerance/respect ranked first at 79 percent for Americans and 81 percent for Europeans. A broad majority also ranked responsi-bility high on their list. Europeans also insist on good manners, an item omit-ted from the US questionnaire. Certain minor qualities also attracted nega-tive broad majorities. Imagination interests neither population. Hard work and religious faith thrill few Europeans while thrift and obedience hardly inspire Americans.

7.3. **Change over 1980–2000**

After this review of current consensus, we can proceed to look at the changes. Different approaches are possible. We can look at average change in Europe for a given value or look for convergence and divergence in opinion among European countries. We can also compare opinion in Europe and the United States to see if transatlantic gaps are widening or narrowing. We shall begin with average change in Europe and the United States over 1980–2000, as presented in four categories (see Tables 7A.1 and 7A.2). First it lists opinions for which net change over twenty years exceeds 5 percent, with increases shown first, declines second. Next come opinions showing less than 5 percent change and termed 'stable'. Finally, the tables list opinions that escape these categories and are termed 'unstable'. We drew the line at 5 percent because (*a*) we needed a figure above the standard threshold of statistical significance and (*b*) the figure turned out to distribute the data fairly evenly among the four rows of the tables, thus making it a good criterion to distinguish bundles of trends with respect to each other.

1. *From Condemnation to Individual Responsibility*—Over the past twenty years, Europeans have perceived a growing feeling of control over their lives and greater self-fulfillment, but below US levels. The exercise of free choice is therefore on the rise, with a tendency to take a deeper hold in people's minds. The idea is gaining ground that you can do as you like so long as you do not disturb the peace. We often hear talk of 'rising individualism' in the sense of greater emphasis on self-fulfillment. Indeed, ever-greater numbers of Europeans feel this would be a good thing. At all events, consensus was already strong at 81 percent in 1981, before rising to 86 percent for both 1990 and 1999.

We shall return to this question later but for now, we underscore that the trend on the upswing here is actually the liberal notion that the individual decides what makes her or him feel happy and fulfilled but with no entitlement to erect one's own conception of happiness into a platform for condemning others. This is the least we can infer from the growing tolerance of soft drug abuse, abortion, homosexuality or euthanasia. These questions ask for responses on a scale of 1 (never justified) to 10 (always justified); as a rule, we report change in the proportion of responses between 1 and 5, that is the negatives, or between 6 and 10, that is the positives, but we also report separately on those who selected '1' (never justified) or '10' (always justified). From this point of view, attitudes toward abortion appear somewhat different. The opinion that it 'can never be justified' climbed back up to 26 percent in 1999 after a 1980 high of 32 percent and 1990 low of 21 percent. Against the backdrop of increasing tolerance, a core of opinion here has become more radical. But abortion is considered increasingly acceptable for single mothers and couples not wanting more children.

However, what we are seeing is far from a simple increase in 'permissiveness' and recognizing the individual's right to a personal definition of happiness hardly grants exemption from condemnation. Fellow citizens may well make value judgments and criticize; they may express disapproval, ask for explanations, and demand justifications. And it is tempting to read the results on attitudes to suicide and lying in this way. As for abortion, they show two trends: a strong majority of Europeans still find it more or less unjustified while the core that finds it 'never justified' has shrunk. Thus, the individual's right to use personal judgment and end his life finds increasing acceptance, but European opinion still maintains that suicide is a decision she or he ought to reconsider. Ditto for lying. On the one hand, Europeans find 'lying in your own interest' more or less unjustified but on the other hand, the condemnation is milder and the share of Europeans voting 'never justified' has fallen. Which probably means that lying is not altogether damnable. It is a matter of personal judgment—carefully weighed judgment— without forgetting that, *as a rule*, lying is disrespectful of others. US results show the same trends at comparable levels.

On the choice between freedom and equality, half of Europeans still prefer freedom, with the remainder either choosing equality or remaining undecided. That said, these two ideals go hand-in-hand in a democracy, which makes the question meaningless because when you ask a respondent for a snap choice, you tend to obtain a random 50/50 outcome. The slight European preference for freedom probably means that they would still rather have freedom without equality than the other way around.

2. *The Rise of Civil Society and Mistrust of Political Leaders*—The proportion of Europeans who frequently or occasionally discuss politics has remained remarkably stable over the time frame whereas that of Americans who follow and/or discuss politics among friends has risen somewhat. It was already higher in the United States in 1981 and here we see a wider gap today. Nonetheless, membership in private voluntary and activist organizations is on the rise in Europe, especially those involved with developing countries, human rights, and the environment. Also expanding are grassroots organizations active in poverty reduction, jobs, housing, and racial equality. Rising numbers of Europeans report having attended a lawful demonstration or joined a boycott, or at least declare they 'might' do so. The same holds for petitions: more Europeans say they have signed one—so many so that there is a dip in the number of respondents who have not signed one but 'might'. Inversely, although few Europeans report having occupied buildings or factories or joined wildcat strikes, more now declare they 'might' do so.

Another yardstick for the vitality of a civil society is people's confidence in each other. The confidence level for Europeans is stable throughout the time frame and well below that for the United States. A rough third of Europeans and half of Americans trust their fellow citizens '*in general*'. Nonetheless, the WVS shows a drop to 36 percent in this confidence for the United States in 2000. However, the 1998 ISSP survey found no such drop and the WVS for 2000 reports that 62 percent of Americans think that if someone had a chance to cheat them, she or he would not exploit it and behave decently. Thus, the 36 percent drop looks questionable.

Americans and Europeans remain as quick to condemn tax dodging and bribe taking today as twenty-five years ago. An equally large share of Europeans condemns claiming state benefits abusively but less adamantly because fewer respondents rate it as 'never justified'. In other words, there is ambivalence here. Such condemnation is even somewhat milder in the United States. That said, lawbreaking still attracts strong condemnation on both continents, regardless of hearsay about galloping permissiveness and plummeting moral standards. This transpires from the fact that 85 percent of Europeans still consider auto theft for a joyride unjustified, practically the same score as in 1981. Last, both continents show unstable support for the idea that 'greater respect for authority' would be a good thing.

If civic values continue to thrive, so do mistrust for political leaders and disaffection with political parties and trade unions. Thus, confidence in legislatures is headed downhill in both Europe and the United States. Meanwhile, membership in political parties is down in Europe but up in the United States. This result is consistent with the trends cited earlier for political discussions among friends and general interest in 'following' politics. Finally, union membership is falling in Europe but fluctuating in the United States while confidence in trade unions remains persistently low.

We should point out, however, that these low European confidence levels specifically target elected officials, not law enforcement agencies. There is stable confidence in the police, government agencies, and civil service. Only confidence in the armed forces seems unstable. Confidence in the school system is even slowly climbing. And that in media is holding up.

3. *Rising Social Selectivity?*—The question about personal taste in neighbors serves to measure social selectivity. Now as before, Europeans will not reject people on discriminatory criteria and only a steady 10 percent or so of respondents would reject someone on the basis of race, ethnic origin, or nationality.

Rejection of left-wing extremists is stable at a high 32 percent. However, the undesirability of right-wing extremists has grown from 29 percent in 1981 to 44 percent today. Part of the explanation is the growing popularity of ultra right-wing parties in several European countries.

Greater numbers of Europeans would not like a neighbor who is emotionally unstable or an ex-convict. Here, we can assume respondents just want to safeguard their peace and quiet. At the same time, any general trend becomes hard to detect in light of the rejection facing heavy drinkers, which is unstable yet already particularly high—half of Europeans do not want one next door. The American picture is equally fuzzy: ex-convicts and the emotionally unpredictable go unwanted there too while levels for others remain stable. And rejection has been softening for some categories first included in the 1990 WVS, that is HIV/AIDS sufferers, drug abusers, and homosexuals.

4. *Secularization*—Religion continues losing its appeal. In 1981, 67 percent of Europeans called themselves 'religious' against only 60 percent in 1999. For those two years, 54 and 48 percent of people identified themselves as Catholics

respectively, and 30 and 23 percent for Protestants. Those reporting not 'belonging to a religious denomination' rose from 15 to 28 percent. Likewise, ever fewer Europeans say they belong to any religious organization. The overall trend for belief in God is down despite the slight 1999 upturn. In the United States, belief in God and self-identification as a 'religious' person remains high while membership in religious organizations seems unstable.

Institutional religions are the primary target of the decline in Europe and mis-trust of Christian churches continues mounting. In particular, church positions on the 'problems of family life' seem increasingly 'inadequate', although agreement levels remain stable about the ability of the church to meet 'the moral problems and needs of the individual'. Yet opinion wavers about its ability to meet 'people's spiritual needs': 56, 62, and 60 percent in timeline order. For the United States, this line of questioning points up sagging expectations—fewer Americans than before now say their religious institution adequately meets their moral, family, social, or even spiritual needs.

That said, belief in God remains firm. The results show stable shares for Europeans who find God rather 'important' or who 'get comfort and strength from religion'. In fact, religiousness exists with or without supporting institutions because there is no change in the proportion of Europeans who report devoting time to prayer, meditation, or other spiritual equivalent. Belief in heaven and 'life after death' are stable; it fluctuates when it comes to hell and it is falling somewhat for sin. In the United States, where all these beliefs are largely shared, they remain stable, except for the belief in hell which shows mild fluctuation from a plateau of much higher mean values.

Although belief in sin continues its decline, the past twenty-five years have seen an increase in the conviction that 'there are absolutely clear guidelines about what is good and evil'. Today 33 percent of Europeans believe so, against 27 percent in 1981 while the share of those who feel that 'what is good and evil depends entirely on the circumstances' has slipped from 66 to 60 percent. Responses to this question on good or evil are hard to interpret. It is tempting to look to Weber's distinction between an ethics of conviction versus an ethics of responsibility. In this context, choosing that circumstances determine good or evil is a way of reserving judgment and postponing responsibility until the appropriate moment. Meanwhile, opting for clear guidelines may mean that there is no reason to pass any individual judgment on what is good or evil because the definitions are all already known and irrefutable. Ideally, this question should detect transition from a religious community to a modern society, that is from a community with a single set of rules about good and evil for all its members to a liberal society which recognizes each member first and foremost as an individual judge of good and evil. In this context, the level of identification with 'personal responsibility' should be following the trend for, say, civil society indicators such as that for activism. So how do you account for the downswing in the 'ethics of responsibility' choice just as civil society is showing more activism? In short, Weber is not helpful here. Respondents may be interpreting this good or evil question in the opposite sense in order to mean that if everything depends *entirely* on circumstances, then the rules of society lose their general validity and therefore 'anything goes'. So we must realize that if modern people today are reserving an individual right to judge good and evil, it also means that they are not surrendering that right to circumstances—but the word 'entirely' in the question implies just that! Actually, modern respondents ought to refuse choosing between 'depends entirely on' and 'absolutely clear guidelines', as 6 to 7 percent did.

The same dilemma appears in the US results. Agreement on 'absolutely clear guidelines' rose even more there from 37 percent in 1981 to 50 percent in 1990 and 49 percent in 2000, while religious opinions show remarkable stability. All these elements argue for careful interpretation on the question of good and evil, heavily supported by a broad range of evidence.

5. *Higher Job Hopes and Expectations*—Europeans definitely expect more from employment today than twenty years ago. From a list of conditions of a 'good job', they cited more items in 1999 than in 1981. And they are more demanding about most items they select, whether working conditions, chances for promotion, social atmosphere, or job satisfaction. More Europeans say a 'good' job should carry 'good pay' (+13%), make you feel 'you can achieve something' (+10%), be 'interesting' (+10%), offer 'good hours' (+10%), be 'respected by people in general' (+9%), offer chances of 'meeting people' (+9%), be a 'responsible job' (+9%), with 'pleasant people to work with' (+8%) but 'without too much pressure' (+7%). 'Job security' wobbles from 59 percent in 1981 to 56 percent in 1990 and 65 percent in 1999. Demand is also rising for jobs that 'meet one's abilities' (+6%), provide 'an opportunity to use initiative' (+5%), with 'good chances for promotion' (+5%), and which are 'useful for society' (+5%). The most sluggish increase was 'good holidays' (4%).

Europeans want greater job autonomy. In 1981, 21 percent said they had to be 'convinced first' before executing a superior's 'instruction' they did not 'fully agree' with. In 1999, 34 percent felt that way. Acceptance of merit-based pay is also rising in Europe. Trends for the United States are comparable except that mean levels have long been higher.

6. *Demise of the Traditional Family Model*—The opinion that family life deserves 'more emphasis' remains very widespread, but not in the traditional sense of the term 'family'. This is visible from the fact that ever fewer Europeans feel the churches offer 'adequate answers' to family problems or from the increasing acceptability of divorce. There is also deep change in the prerequisite conditions of a 'successful marriage'. Conditions boosting the social and material dimensions of marriage at the expense of emotional conditions are down. Ever fewer Europeans prioritize 'adequate income', 'same social background', 'good housing', and 'shared religious beliefs'.

However, the modern family is having trouble working out a new package deal, if indeed it really needs one. Agreement that marriage is an 'outdated institution' fluctuates mildly from 20 to 18 percent and 23 percent, as it does for 'love and respect' of parents 'regardless of (their) qualities and faults', which scores 68, 71, and 66 percent. Opinion that a woman 'needs children' to be 'fulfilled' remains flat at 44, 47, and 46 percent. In some cases, we are probably witnessing a reversal of values that prevailed throughout the 1960s. Since 1981, the number of Europeans disapproving of a woman who 'wants to have a child as a single parent' has climbed from 24 to 26 percent and 32 percent. Despite the fluctuations, strong majorities of 84, 89, and 83 percent of Europeans feel 'a child needs a home with both a mother and father to grow up happily'. Another trend probably in reverse is that a 'happy sexual relationship' is important to a 'successful marriage', which has been falling since 1981.

Interestingly, no condition listed of a successful marriage seems more important today than before. 'Faithfulness', 'mutual respect and appreciation', and 'understanding and tolerance' hold their rankings but have always enjoyed broad consensus. Other conditions that also remain stable include 'agreement on politics', 'sharing household chores', and 'living apart from your in-laws'. 'Children' are another condition still deemed of equal importance. Attitudes to adultery remain stable too. This all shows that there is no quantum jump from a 'bourgeois' marriage into a 'romantic' one: emotional bonds are not upstaging the social dimension. Finally, the data show hesitation about the 'right' balance between the emotional and social dimensions.

No single model is preeminent in the United States either. The results show the same fluctuations around an average value, but these averages are at different levels than in Europe, for example 17, 20, and 15 percent for a woman's fulfillment through children or 63, 73, and 64 percent for a child's need of both parents. And marriage remains the rule: only 10 percent of Americans find it 'outdated' today, barely more than the 8 percent registered in 1981. Meanwhile, Americans are more tolerant of divorce than Europeans, and marriage seems to be a more flexible institution in American eyes.

7. *More Autonomous Offspring*—Although 70 percent of Europeans feel parents must put their children ahead of their own well-being, the share who feel that 'parents have a life of their own and should not sacrifice their own well-being for the sake of their children' jumped from 8 percent in 1981 to 18 percent in 1999. Respondents are definitely not ignoring the innate vulnerability of children, but opinion is drifting toward a family setup that takes greater account of each member's hopes and needs. This trend turns up in questions about childrearing. Parents obviously want to hand down a maximum of positive character traits and the question asks respondents to choose five out of a list of eleven (but seventeen in the 1981 version). Here, one good way of trend-spotting is to look at the change in trait rankings between waves. Thus, for the time frame, we find determination/perseverance is up 3 notches and generosity, up 2; thrift/saving on money and things, up 1; and imagination, up 1 too. Unchanged rankings were found for independence, feeling of responsibility, and good manners while hard work is down 1 as both obedience and religious faith are each down 2.

As seen, the new rankings reflect weak change of social values. The values in the lead are especially stable: 'tolerance' retains first place while 'feeling of responsibility' and 'good manners' vie for second and third position, with 'independence' still fourth. This is surely no fluke and it is noteworthy that 'independence', the hallmark of individualism, comes *after* 'tolerance' and 'feeling of responsibility'—a key point we shall return to later.

That said, we see change further down. Traits on the rise are those that help children 'cope' with unexpected situations, that is in relating to others, they will need to demonstrate 'perseverance/determination', 'imagination' and 'generosity'. Inversely, 'obedience' in the passive sense of the word is losing appeal. And, as already seen in the trends for religion, 'religious faith' is losing ground too. For the United States, the trends are heading the same way, but with differences in the initial order of rankings. In 1981, 'religious faith' stood higher but 'thrift', far lower; the differences have since become more marked. 'Determination and perseverance' and 'hard work' are up 2; 'imagination', up 1; 'obedience', down 3; 'religious faith', down 2 and 'thrift', down 1. So here too, we see a rise in traits that help *cope* and a fall for those less helpful. In short, children on both sides of the Atlantic are being brought up with a view to preparing their autonomy.

7.4. The diversity and uniformity of European opinion in 2000

Trend averages do not suffice to diagnose value change. We also need to take account of the levels in differences between individual nations and then reexamine the differences to detect any trends. But we cannot establish a comparison with the United States on these two points because of the geographic variable: the breakdown of US data is by large region while the European data are by country. Any comparison would therefore prove contrived. For statistical purposes, we shall use regressions (analysis of variance). Fisher's F distribution is adequate to assess diversity, along with Cramer's φ for qualitative variables. We use F to divide opinion into two groups of fairly equal size: the first group is where opinion of European nations differs barely at most (low F for a given number of degrees of freedom) and the second, where it differs more (high F). We shall first review the distribution of European opinion in 1999 before moving to Section 7.5 and assessing convergence or divergence by tracking changes in F over the three waves of the WVS.

1. *The Limits of Free Choice*—Europe pretty much agrees on the need for more emphasis on self-fulfillment, that is responses to this question suggest that no single European nation is more 'individualistic' than any other. Opinion is also fairly similar on how 'satisfied' people are with their lives 'on the whole'. However, opinion on 'free choice and control' over how one's life 'turns out' varies between countries. Scores are high for Denmark, Germany, Ireland, and the UK and lower for Belgium, France, and Italy.

Country variations appear in opinions about tolerance of other people's behavior, especially where life is at stake. Thus, opinion gaps are fairly small for rejection of lying, soft drug abuse, and homosexuality but widen on abortion and suicide; even more so on euthanasia. Euthanasia and suicide are more acceptable in Denmark, France, and Holland but rejected in Ireland, Italy, and Spain. Abortion is better accepted in Denmark and Sweden but rejected in Ireland and Spain; reasons for an abortion do not narrow the gaps. Homosexuality finds greater tolerance in Northern than Southern Europe, with Ireland among the latter as often happens.

However, not all country opinions call as hard for 'greater respect for authority' to offset individual freedom. France, Ireland, and the UK find it significantly more important than Denmark and Sweden. The choice of freedom versus equality divides Europeans relatively little.

2. *Civil Societies*—European countries show strong disparities over confidence in fellow citizens. This comes out in the frequency of political discussions or confidence in the press.

However, the civil societies stand closer together on 'attending lawful demonstrations', 'joining unofficial strikes', 'occupying offices or factories', or 'joining a boycott'. Only 'signing a petition' shows strong country variations. Country opinions are fairly similar about joining a political party or community action program, that is almost equally few people are active here in any European country sampled. However, noticeable country differences arise for belonging to organizations involved in 'education, arts, music, or cultural activities', 'third world development or human rights' or 'conservation, environment, ecology, animal rights', or 'trade unions'.

Confidence in public institutions stands at very similar levels throughout Europe. Although institutions do not match country-by-country, opinion has confidence in the police, trade unions, legislature, government agencies, civil service, and school system; strong variations are seen only for the armed forces.

All European countries also show comparable disapproval of unlawful behavior. The level is the same for 'accepting a bribe in the course of duty', 'cheating on tax', and 'joyriding'. However, there are bigger country variations about 'claiming state benefits which you are not entitled to'.

3. *Open-Arm Welcome and Personal Sensitivities*—Country opinions show general agreement about not rejecting a neighbor on discriminatory criteria. We can arrange the desirability of neighbors by degree of similarity between countries. This approach obtains a motley assortment of preferences: foreigners and immigrants, non-Caucasians, and alcoholics. Then there are country-specific sensitivities and, in decreasing order of preference, we find the emotionally unstable, left-wing extremists, ex-convicts, and right-wing extremists.

4. *Religious Discord*—Europeans clearly disagree on all religious issues except one: that 'your church/the churches are giving adequate answers to people's spiritual needs'. Elsewhere disparities are strong and numerous, whether it comes to membership in a denomination (Catholic, Protestant, Other, and None), the importance of God in one's life, qualifying oneself as 'a religious person', finding 'strength and comfort' in religion, prayer/meditation, or the importance of

instilling 'religious faith' in one's children. The disparities hold for all manner of beliefs: in God, heaven, hell, life after death, and sin. Membership in religious organizations varies very widely as does confidence in religious institutions or their ability to furnish 'adequate answers to . . . moral and family problems'.

Beyond all the contradictions, a gap appears that pits religiously skeptical France and the Nordic countries against Southern Europe and Ireland, more devoted to Christianity and the Church of Rome. Germany and the UK usually fall somewhere in-between.

Countries are little divided on the problematic question of good and evil, which argues for a de-linked reading of religious trends.

5. *Differences on Working Conditions; Agreement on More Job Autonomy*— Europeans pretty much agree about whether to just 'follow instructions' or 'be convinced first' nor is merit-based pay an issue. Countries agree en masse about 'opportunity to use initiative'.

Arranging the aspects of a 'good' job from the most to least generally shared among nations, we obtain: 'pleasant people to work with', 'good chances for promotion', 'a job that is interesting', 'good holidays', and 'a responsible job'. Beyond this point, countries diverge. In the same order, we see: 'good pay', 'meeting people', 'opportunity to use initiative', 'a job in which you feel you can achieve something', 'good hours', 'a job that meets one's abilities', 'a useful job for society', 'a job respected by people in general', and 'good job security'. The most divisive aspect is 'not too much pressure'. In summary, there is *Europewide* consensus about self-fulfillment at the workplace, which is an extension of a wish for more personal autonomy while the aspects that countries disagree on concern working conditions, which probably reflects differences in national institutions or job markets. Note that qualifications such as 'useful to society' and 'respected by people in general' are external features of a job that do not enhance how interesting or fulfilling a job may be.

Turning to the controversial aspects of employment, at the extremes we see that only 11 percent of French find 'not too much pressure' important against 61 percent of Italians. In between but nearer the French figure, low-job pressure ranks high for 28 percent of British subjects and 24 percent of Germans. 'Good job security' inspires only 45 percent of Belgians, 46 percent of French, 50 percent of Danes, and 51 percent of Swedes against 79 percent of Germans, 76 percent of Italians, and 75 percent of Spaniards. And the British again fall in-between at 65 percent. Finally, 61 percent of Italians want a 'respected' job against only 11 percent of Danes, 25 percent of British, 26 percent of French, and 29 percent of Swedes.

6. *Family Ambivalences* —All Europeans support 'more emphasis on family life' and say that marriage is not an 'outdated' institution but they are not talking about the same form of marriage because country opinions disagree over divorce. The question of what makes a 'successful' marriage also underscores the different forms in which marriage exists between countries. The features that Europeans agree over most are in descending order: 'understanding and tolerance', 'faithfulness', 'shared religious beliefs', 'mutual respect and appreciation' and 'same

social background'. And also in descending order, the features they disagree over are: 'agreement on politics', 'adequate income', 'children', 'happy sexual relationship', 'good housing', 'sharing household chores', and 'living apart from in-laws'. In summary, Europeans disagree over everything except the romance of marriage that fosters emotional bonding in the home. They condemn adultery in varying degrees but within a fairly narrow range. In our opinion, the attitude to these variations is understandable because it concerns the sincerity of a spouse's commitment to the couple (a bonding feature) and her or his attitude to marriage (a divisive feature).

Europeans go on to disagree deeply on the role of women. This was plain when it came to 'sharing household chores' as an ingredient of a 'successful' marriage. Gaps are also wide about a woman's need for fulfillment through children or a child's need for two parents. Thus, 68 percent of Danes and 65 percent of French say women need fulfillment through children but only 7 percent of Dutch, 14 percent of Irish, and 18 percent of British concur. Disagreement also reigns over whether a woman should raise a child alone.

7. *Varying Angles on Instilling Respect for Others*—Two issues of discord are whether parents deserve love and respect 'regardless' of their 'qualities and faults' and whether parents should put children first 'even at the expense of their own well-being'. The same holds for childrearing and traits to instill in children. Europeans agree on some points. From general consensus to general discord, the traits are: 'thrift/not wasting money or things', 'determination and perseverance' and 'tolerance and respect for others'. Listed in the same order, country opinion varies for the remainder, that is 'imagination', 'good manners', 'feeling of responsibility', 'hard work', 'independence' and 'generosity'. On the last three, 60 percent of British and 56 percent of Danes mention 'generosity' against only 3 percent of Spaniards and 6 percent of Germans. Independence is important to 80 percent of Danes, 70 percent of Germans, and 69 percent of Swedes but just 29 percent of French and 34 percent of Spaniards. Obedience find favor with 11 percent of Germans, 13 percent of Swedes and 14 percent of Danes but soars to 49 percent of British, 48 percent of Spaniards, and 47 percent of Irish.

7.5. Country convergence and divergence in Western Europe

Our review of 1999 country differences now leaves us to evaluate any convergence in European opinions. To that end, we wanted Fisher F and Cramer φ thresholds that would neatly divide responses into four groups, that is convergence, divergence, stable scattering, and unstable scattering over the full twenty-year time frame.

1. *Fuzzy Convergence on Free Choice*—'More emphasis on the development of the individual' is as undivisive as before to Europeans. Country differences

on the feeling of 'freedom of choice and control' over one's life were unstable over the time frame while gaps narrowed when it came to 'how satisfied' people were with their lives. Opinion also converges on the choice between freedom and equality.

We have convergence over acceptance of homosexuality, divergence over suicide, and stable acceptance of lying. Instability prevails over euthanasia, soft drug abuse, and abortion (usually acceptable in unmarried women and families wanting no additional children). Finally, we see unstable gaps concerning 'greater respect for authority'. The bottom line is that each country is going its own way here.

2. *Civil Society: More Agreement on the Importance of Rules, Less on the Means to Produce Them*—Europe shows convergence in disapproval of bribe taking and tax dodging. Opinions about abusively claiming state benefits and joyriding remain unchanged. These data suggest greater agreement on the importance of civic spirit.

However, we see almost no change regarding the 'standard' ways and means of running civil society. Distribution remains unchanged for the frequency of political discussions, membership in political parties, joining lawful demonstrations, or confidence in fellow citizens. But country gaps have widened on the other means. Thus, trade union membership distinguishes countries more than before. As does membership in private voluntary organizations dealing with the Third World, environment, human rights and, to a lesser extent, cultural associations. Distribution becomes unstable when we look at grassroots organizations fighting poverty, unemployment, housing deficiencies, and racism. Country differences further appear over signing petitions, joining boycotts, and occupying factories or offices. And there is no clear gap change on the issue of wildcat strikes.

European countries diverge somewhat more today over confidence in the press. However, they converge over confidence in government and public services while retaining stable confidence levels in the police and trade unions, but school systems and armed forces only rate unstable levels. That said, there is converging mistrust of national legislatures: we have general, deepening Europewide mistrust in political leaders.

3. *Varying Gaps Over Neighbors*—Social discrimination shows country gaps that do not add up to any European model. While witnessing converging acceptance as neighbors of immigrants or foreigners, we see divergence over non-Caucasians. We also see converging acceptance of left-wing radicals but divergence over right-wing radicals. For others, Europewide convergence lies even further out of focus: we have convergence on hard drinkers and stability on ex-convicts but no visible trend at all for the emotionally unstable.

4. *Convergence on the Demise of Religion but Divergence on Religiousness*—Due to the falling numbers identifying themselves as 'a religious person', country gaps are narrowing mildly on religious membership. Narrower gaps also characterize distrust of religious institutions while membership of

religious organizations remains quite stable. In short, the decline of institutional religion brings European countries closer together. However, Europeans diverge over the role of these institutions. There is sustained divergence over whether they supply 'adequate answers' to family problems, which aggravates when it comes to the individual's 'moral problems and needs' and 'spiritual needs'.

The impact on religiousness is helter-skelter. Country figures diverge over defining oneself as a 'religious person'. Divergence persists over any importance of God to one's life or a perception that God gives 'strength and comfort'. That said, country gaps subsist at stable levels for moments of prayer, meditation, or any rough equivalent thereof. Belief in God, heaven, and sin also hold up but diverge on hell and life after death while distribution remains stable about good and evil.

5. *Convergence on Workplace Initiative and Divergence over Job Organization*—European opinion converges on whether to just 'follow instructions' or 'be convinced first'. Opinion gaps on merit-based pay have been unstable but narrow on what defines a 'good job': it consists of 'pleasant' coworkers, 'responsibility', 'interesting' duties, and 'good chances for promotion'. Other gaps remain constant, for example 'good pay', 'opportunity to use initiative', feeling one 'can achieve something', 'good holidays', and functions that 'meet one's abilities'. Gaps widen for 'not too much pressure', 'good job security', 'useful for society', and 'meeting people'. And we see no real pattern for a 'job respected by people in general' or 'good hours'.

6. *The Nonmodel of the European Family*—Country gaps remain stable about 'more emphasis on family life', whether marriage is 'outdated' and 'adequate answers to . . . the problems of family life' are offered by the church(es). But gaps over the acceptability of divorce are unstable. So no European model of the family has emerged in the past twenty-five years, but there is greater consensus about a woman who intends to become a single mother.

There is some convergence on what makes a 'successful' marriage: 'faithfulness', 'understanding', and 'children'. Stability characterizes 'mutual respect', 'sharing of household chores', 'good income', 'same social background', 'sharing religious beliefs', 'good housing', and 'happy sexual relationship'. Only 'agreement on politics' and 'living apart from your in-laws' fluctuate. On the whole, stability prevails, which means we have no more of a European family model today than in the early 1980s. That said, disapproval of adultery is less divisive between European countries today.

7. *Raising More Autonomous Children*—Country gaps are unstable over a woman's need for fulfillment through children or that parents deserve love and respect 'regardless of their qualities and faults'. There are stable gaps and no new trend on the parental duty to 'do their best for their children even at the expense of their own well-being' or on a child's need for both parents.

On the list of 'qualities to be encouraged at home', country gaps show strong differences. They have narrowed for qualities such as 'independence', 'obedience', 'imagination', and 'religious faith', 'tolerance and respect for other people', 'thrift', and 'good manners' but remain stable for 'generosity'. They wobble for 'feeling of responsibility', 'hard work', and 'determination and perseverance'.

7.6. Individualism or greater reasonableness?

Does this analysis of consensus, trends, and convergence in seven broad domains of values offer a global model that describes the general direction of United States or Western European opinion since 1980? Actually, the literature already contains such models but are they satisfactory? Prolific research on value trends has been published worldwide based on the same set of surveys (see the websites of the WVS or European Values Survey for a bibliography of hundreds of articles and publications triggered by these surveys) and the most common conclusion is that, if anything, the surveys simply show an increase in individualism. This conclusion is so unsurprising that we regret to see it pass for a statement of the obvious and go unchallenged as the only common denominator of all the changes. Although some authors lay more stress on the secularization or on development of 'modern' and 'rational' values at the expense of traditional ones, they are essentially still using individualism as their baseline. The conclusion is not wrong but the baseline contains ambiguities. Actually, most research into the opinions and values lumps together a wide range of definitions of 'individualism' that overlap most imperfectly.

In speaking of individualism, many authors correctly refer to Tocqueville. As he saw it, democracy goes hand-in-hand with withdrawal on oneself, which he (Tocqueville 1835–40, II, II, 2, p. 585) defined as a 'reflective and tranquil sentiment that disposes each citizen to cut himself off from the mass of his fellow men and withdraw into the circle of family and friends, so that, having created a little society for his own use, he gladly leaves the larger society to take care of itself.' But this can induce two distinct and, indeed, opposing forms of individualism (Lamberti 1986–7). In the United States, individualistic withdrawal does not involve illusions of any total self-sufficiency of the individual and it does not compromise the vitality of civil society. The individual does not ignore his civic duties. His 'enlightened' self-interest incites him to take part in local affairs and voluntary associations. Such well-tempered individualism is therefore equally compatible with both liberty and law and order. However, there is a second form of individualism, whose dangers to France Tocqueville noted, where liberty is reduced to a mere right while becoming less and less of a civic duty to participate in public life. Here each person lives as 'a foreigner to everyone else's fate' and soon concludes that self-interest can be defended without due regard for law and order. In this case, withdrawal exceeds the limits of reasonableness and rejects any authority other than one's own. Subverting public virtue, it turns into pure egoism. But, as Tocqueville points out, personal liberty can never be total. It can never be absolute independence without engendering a risk of anarchy or despotism. Thus, we have an individualism that can exist within the limits of reasonableness, and another which ignores it.

Along similar lines, Durkheim (1898) distinguishes between utilitarian individualism driven exclusively by personal interest and humanistic individualism that goes beyond egoistic interests to embrace 'the quality of man *in abstracto*'. Borrowing from Kant and Rousseau to pin down the trait of this humanism, Durkheim stresses the practical reason but unfortunately fails to distinguish it from a religion of humanity. Yet an essential feature of this form of reasonable, 'humanistic' individualism is to make man an end in himself, which stands in opposition both to 'undifferentiated' or egoistic individualism and to altruistic, or saintly humanism. Kant sums this up nicely in his *Metaphysics of Morals* (*Doctrine of Virtue* 1791, I, I, Para. 11):

Man as a person, i.e., as the subject of a morally-practical reason, is exalted above all price. For such a one (*homo noumenon*) he is not to be valued merely as a means to the ends of other people, or even to his own ends, but is to be prized as an end in himself. This is to say, he possesses a *dignity* (an absolute inner worth) whereby he exacts the *respect* of all other reasonable beings in the world, can measure himself against each member of his species, and can esteem himself on a footing of equality with them. The humanity in one's own person is the object of the respect which he can require of every other being, but which he also must not forfeit.

To further clarify this distinction, let us emphasize that if we are to dignify the individual by asserting that everyone is at the origin of any evaluation, then we are taking into account the role of *subjectivity* toward reaching consensus. Against that, if we glorify the individual by placing an absolute value on the ego, then *individuality* becomes the baseline. In the first case, evaluation is freely based on recognition of membership in a common humanity and proceeds from the *subject's autonomy*. In the second case, the baseline is the mere fact of being a separate entity and proceeds from the *individual's independence*. In the first case, 'individualism' thrives *within the limits* of the reasonable while the second definition describes *undifferentiated* or *unrestrained* individualism.

Let us use the example of a school cafeteria to understand the difference between the undifferentiated individualism from the autonomous subject who is a free co-creator of the norms that govern her or him and, as such, only expresses herself or himself within the bounds of reason. Given that legitimacy is based on tradition and/or charisma, the chef lays down the daily menu with little consideration for individual preferences. Transition to a modern society demands freedom from such submission. Adopting reason as the framework, the first issue is to win recognition for each person's right to suggest menu items and negotiate them with the chef. Each person chooses her or his meal according to personal preferences and distinguishes herself or himself through that exercise of free choice. The first simple fact to note is that if everyone has his or her own taste and if nothing else interferes to govern meal choices, reasonableness boils down to simple individualism. But as soon as everyone's preferences cannot be satisfied, as often happens in daily life, reasonableness clashes with undifferentiated individualism. So each participant seeks a reasonable solution by deciding which preferences not to satisfy through a discussion in which each one accepts to limit his or her wishes in function of *general and context-pertinent* principles that are approved by everyone involved in meals (these principles are universal). In other words, they need to develop a *reasonable* menu because reason is about exercising the power of principles. Individualism trespasses outside the framework of the reasonable as soon as the individual refuses to limit his or her wishes and demands exactly what she or he feels like having, even at the expense of others. Such a demand becomes unreasonable because it elects to ignore the needs of others and, as such, others will reject it on the principle of equal consideration for all (that is the principle of universality).

As seen, the unreasonable individual remains rational: in defending her or his personal interest, she or he is optimizing an asset. And it may even evolve into altruism if the individual then uses the asset to better serve others. Nonetheless, the reasoning remains that of someone following her or his own nature. But once constraints enter the picture, participants must renounce trying to maximize their utility functions, as an economist might put it, and the reasonable attitude is to start by trying to reach agreement on a rule that will apply to everyone and win their general approval because it respects every member's freedom equally. The attitude of reasonableness is thus based on recognizing that every other person is also a free and reasonable being, with whom it is possible to reach agreement on a set of principles for communal living, which are justified in everyone's eyes because they deny equal freedom to none (Rawls 1971). The drive behind this attitude is the will to build a society.

To better grasp this point, we have to assume that individuals have good reasons for the actions or opinions they choose. On the one hand, the individual has reasons that are merely relative to him or her, that is they affect her or his personal interests or conception of the good life. Such reasons are merely empirical, or rational in a narrow-minded way. On the other hand, there are neutral reasons, defined as such by their power of conviction over others, even those not sharing the same interests or conception of the good life (Nagel 1991). Reasons are neutral because they are shared; they have thoughtfully integrated everyone's personal considerations into a common view deemed reasonable by all. Alternatively, neutralization relates to Kant's concept of pure practical reason. He says the personal inclinations and desires *affect*, but *do not determine* the individual, who has personal reasons for action that meet *other ends*, ends that must be thought through for coexistence. 'Other ends' means other people and 'neutral reasons' means reasons capable of securing unanimous approval, which assumes fair treatment of every individual as an end. In other words, a given opinion or course of action is reasonable because its terms are deemed acceptable by one and all and because it carries no preference for the personal interests or ethics of any particular individual. Actors making such a choice place fairness before personal interests and act or think in a manner that lends itself to unanimous approval (Forsé and Parodi 2004).

Depending on whether we stress the subject or intersubjectivity, this principle finds different forms of expression within the reflective process that leads to the reasonable choice. For example, we can note that neutral reasons are in tune with the general will (Rousseau 1762) or are reasons which prevail in the context of the discourse ethics (Apel 1988; Habermas 1991). Or we can hold that they are the reasons of a subject are behind a veil of ignorance (Rawls 1971). If we allow that, at any event, subjectivity and intersubjectivity are reciprocal concepts, the implications may be of methodological importance, but not fundamentally so. In any case, the reasonable choice amounts to a maxim that everyone wants to pass into a universal law, that is the categorical imperative (Kant 1785): 'Act in such a way that you always treat humanity, whether in your own person or in the person of any other, at the same time, never simply as a means, but always at the same time as an end'.

If we now confront this theory of the reasonable with the empirical data, then it seems hasty to settle for a conclusion of 'increasing individualism', which obtains a superficial modelization of value changes that fails to explain why individualism is growing in some areas but shrinking elsewhere. Some data even invalidate the model. In practice, pure individualism happens when everyone ends up eating home-made sandwiches by themselves and the socializing that comes with breaking bread together loses all value. Any expansion of such undifferentiated individualism should be appearing in the data through, say, a fall in membership in voluntary organizations, which is happening neither in Europe nor in the United States. The opinion data should be showing a general rise in 'permissiveness', whereby we should have an open-ended menu of lifestyles. Anything would go: divorce, adultery, homosexuality, lying, corruption, soft drug abuse, and more. Here again, the data definitely disagrees. Using another example, we noticed that people want more autonomy on the job, which explains the 'must be convinced first' before following instructions (block 5: work). Yet that hardly means they want more 'independence'—people like togetherness, as seen in the importance awarded to 'meeting people' and having 'pleasant people to work with'. Fellow researchers have already noticed these points. But is it not worth seeking an alternate modelization of the underlying reasons instead of settling for the ambivalent proposition of irresistibly rising individualism?

Our alternate model says that individualism only grows so long as it remains within the limits of the reasonable. And it grows because of differing conceptions of good and evil. So what we are actually witnessing is sooner the *rise of reasonableness*. The quest for self-fulfillment only meets approval so long as it does not encroach on the self-fulfillment of others. The cornerstone of change primarily concerns the limits of the reasonable, which creates new leeway for the expression of individual preferences as its limits become increasingly refined.

Under this model—which is intrinsically connected to moral liberalism and does not seek to narrow pluralism in attitudes about good and evil by invoking any single conception of good and evil—we can elect to stress the liberalism so long as we do not misunderstand 'liberalism' to mean 'freedom from rules'.

Liberalism is no moral advocate of 'absolutely anything goes'. It says that 'anything goes within the limits of the reasonable' or, stated otherwise more precisely, 'do as you like insofar as you have a reason and can justify your behavior in anybody else's eyes'. In short, moral liberalism advocates both freedom *and* the rules to safeguard it.

Empirically speaking, it is not easy to verify such a model because it makes two phenomena embedded: in this case, individualism into reasonableness. We are not just seeking opinion trends but *opinion rankings* as well. However, only by adopting such a perspective can we hope to escape interpretations that classify an opinion as 'altruistic' by default as soon as it does not qualify as 'egoistic'. Or automatically classify another opinion as 'communitarian' simply because it is not 'individualistic'. The actual issue is to realize that people know how to go beyond black and white alternatives in order to recognize each other without forgetting themselves; that is people work toward solutions that seem reasonable to one and all. From this standpoint, they are speaking neither as egoists or altruists nor as individualists or communitarians, but as citizens of a modern society.

We shall start by considering religion (block 4). Freedom of religion appears in the models of undifferentiated individualism and the reasonable, which each offer its own interpretation for the irrefutable rise of secularism in Europe. However, undifferentiated individualism should imply falling membership in religious organizations and a corresponding dissipation of feelings of religiousness that holy services serve to reinforce and intensify. For its part, reasonableness implies nothing on this point because it only implies religious autonomy, not independence; this model does not rule out religious association on condition that membership or attendance is both voluntary and revocable. What do we see? The trends do fit the predictions of undifferentiated individualism but they are also a possible outcome of rising reasonableness. However, religious individualism (strict definition) runs into trouble in the United States because feelings of religiousness remain quite stable there and membership in religious organizations has been fluctuating but definitely not declining over the past twenty years.

Other domains offer more striking conclusions and childrearing stands among them (block 7). Rankings for qualities to encourage in children have hardly budged over the time frame. We immediately notice more insistence on those qualities that help children 'look out for themselves'. This trend is compatible with both models. However, the individualism-based model should imply that people would rank 'independence' topmost. The data say otherwise. 'Independence' still sits tight in fourth place after 'tolerance and respect for other people', 'feeling of responsibility' and even 'good manners'. The reasonability model finds this order telling. It holds that independence would essentially find encouragement *within the limits of* broad respect for others, that is through higher rankings for 'tolerance and respect' or 'feeling of responsibility'. And if we accept with Simmel (1910: 130) 'that the sense of tact is of such special significance in society, for it guides the self-regulation of the individual in his personal relations to others where no outer or directly egoistic interests provide regulation', the ranking of 'good manners' would also be telling. Here the data clearly argue in one direction when we examine the hierarchical relationships between qualities, not just the rankings themselves. Although we admit having no clear picture for 1981, the fact that respondents had to pick five qualities to encourage in their children out of a possible seventeen (not eleven as in subsequent waves) probably scattered responses and masked any structure. That said, in both 1990 and 1999, 'independence' is nested into 'feeling of responsibility' and 'tolerance'. This stands out clearly on a two-level Guttman scale where 'independence' gets included in 'tolerance and respect for others' and 'feeling of responsibility'. In other words, 'independence' is generally cited only after selection of the other two qualities. This proves that independence is only encouraged within the limits of reasonability. Survey responses lean heavily in the direction of the reasonability-based model, not that of undifferentiated individualism.

In the rules of daily life, the situation is simpler. Individualism itself admits of no rules or restrictions. The fact that both continents continue to firmly disapprove of tax dodging, bribe-taking, joyriding, or falsely claiming state benefits proves the opposite and suffices to show that individualism is never unrestrained—nor altruism unrestrained for that matter. All these abuses are simply perceived as unreasonable (block 2: civic spirit). For its part, the increase in activism primarily shows growing concern for the law because if citizens thought the law worthless, they would not press for its reform. We do indeed see greater participation in *lawful* demonstrations, boycotts, and petition signing while *unlawful* occupation of offices/factories and unofficial strikes attract few participants and high disapproval. Nonetheless, respondents are now more willing than before to resort to illegal forms of protest. This means that people still respect the (positive) law but greater numbers are reserving an option on civil disobedience for whenever they find it warranted—perhaps for the day this positive law clashes too strongly with the most fundamental rights deriving from the reasonable.

Going further, what is at stake is the citizen's relationship to politics. Undifferentiated individualism translates into radical indifference about politics because, by definition, the architecture of law is a senseless, unjustifiable limitation. Rising reasonableness predicts that interest in politics does not wane but that the exercise of policy formulation requires increasing attention to the broadest range of individual viewpoints and that it is more vulnerable to public criticism than before. In practice, we are still far from witnessing the end of politics. Lower confidence in political leaders reflects that (*a*) citizens are asserting their right to a say in public affairs, an integral feature of democracy, as Amartya Sen (1999) stresses, and (*b*) elected officials cannot ignore voter views between elections. Yet again, the trends confirm the proposition of rising reasonableness.

More generally, undifferentiated individualism should obtain growing rejection of all normative tendencies while reasonableness merely says that norms will become increasingly considerate of others, their differences and personal conceptions of what makes a good life. Both theories explain greater acceptance of homosexuality and soft drug abuse (so long as respondents perceive the abuse is not damaging the abuser's mental and physical health). However, the persistent disapproval of lying clearly validates the reasonability model.

We also see firmer priority of the individual over the group in the data showing higher acceptance of divorce, abortion, and euthanasia. These examples would appear to reflect a desire for greater independence that fits exclusively into the model of undifferentiated individualism. However, this will is linked to personal circumstances deemed unfortunate. Moreover, it does not close doors to the future: divorcees are free to remarry and couples can procreate again at a later date (block 6: family). And euthanasia is acceptable exactly because it applies to the desperation of a 'no-future' patient. Thus, independence is simply momentary and what the trends sooner reflect is the freedom to choose one's company. From this standpoint, a reasonability-based model fits the trends. It also fits suicide: as already seen, suicide finds no more approval today than twenty-five years ago because it is mainly about persons with a future who commit the irrevocable. While the trends rather reflect recognition of a person's right to make her or his own judgments, they do not preclude criticism of suicide.

On the whole, undifferentiated individualism may explain a given number of specific trends but fails to map out an overall framework for the interpretation of opinion trends. A reasonability-based model does this—perhaps with exceptions! We do not have space here to review the entire questionnaire but such a review would bear out our diagnosis and we invite readers to consult the trends table in the appendix. At all events, we are not seeing in the value trends for either continent any personal withdrawal or a quest for more independence, as supported by the data for voluntary organization membership, confidence in others, the near statically high level of tolerance for, and preferences in neighbors (block 3: social selectivity). What we are seeing is the assertion of the freedom to make value judgments for oneself with respect for those of others. People are only rejecting self-contradictory rules that negate the respect due to one and all: self-fulfillment is approved but only within the strict limits of the reasonable. It is not 'loose morals' but moral liberalism in the strict sense of the term, that is acceptance by all that each is free to make judgments and to create his or her set of personal, but reasonable morals, insofar as any rule approved by all applies to all. There is no blind rigidity here. This is not about obeying a rule because it is a rule on the pretext that, say, 'the law says so'. On the contrary, this is about grasping the reasons that legitimize the rule (see 'must be convinced first' responses).

Nor is there any return to authority here. Moreover, some sociologists sooner stress a loss of authority (Caplow 1994) that Inglehart (1999) associates with 'postmaterialistic' individualism (we shall return to this issue). Empirically, the trends do indeed show contrast. In Europe, 'greater respect for authority' goes from 60 percent in 1981 to 52 percent in 1990 and 57 percent in 1999, while 'obedience' has lost ranking under childrearing and 'always follow instructions' remains stable throughout the time frame. In the United States, respect for authority declined by 15 percent between 1980 and 2000 but, at its lowest level of 70 percent, it remains far higher than in Europe; the importance of teaching children to be obedient has also fallen while that of 'always following instructions at work' has shown erratic variations. From another standpoint, confidence in the political authorities is on the wane (more so in the United States than in Europe) but confidence in democracy (block 0) remains very high on both sides of the Atlantic. This means there is no clear-cut conclusion to be drawn about any broad resurgence or decline of authority (Wroe 2002). But a closer look says this is normal and that opinion is not incoherent because it all depends on the definition of 'authority'. Unreasonable, arbitrary, and unilateral authority (now) stands little chance of finding favor while reasonable, justified authority by delegation is not rejected when exercised within a framework of renegotiable rules, laid down with the consent of one and all and which apply to one and all.

Adoption of this standpoint lends coherence to the responses by elucidating the reasons behind them. And it appears indeed that the responses articulate around an axis of increased reasonableness. The model therefore needs not label seemingly contradictory responses as 'incoherent'—they were only so at first glance. There is no individualism, 'permissiveness', relativism, or decline of authority in one corner with a call for greater authority and coercive rules or such from the other. At both ends, there is a quest for a reasonable opinion. The battery of questions on 'permissiveness' (block 1) provides a perfect illustration thereof. Tolerance is broadly rising on issues concerning personal life, for example homosexuality, while intolerance remains high and stable for those concerning public life or relations to others, for example tax dodging and lying. It therefore seems clear that no general explanatory model is to be found from concepts like a return to/rejection of authority, individualism, or relativism. Either we conclude that respondents are incoherent or we admit that such a model is incomplete. It would be just an ad hoc model. And of course it is unfulfilling to have to work with a different model for each type of opinion because, in the end, very little is really explained. One only has to conclude that individualism is expanding in some cases and contracting in others. Against that, the proposition of rising reasonableness advantageously proposes a general explanatory model for all the trends. The differences stop being contradictory and fall in with a single line of thought. Still on the same example, it is normal to see homosexuality rating more tolerance (so long as homosexuals respect others; only imposing one's own conception of virtue can explain intolerance) while tax dodging faces strong sustained disapproval (freeriding is unreasonable because it cannot be universalized). Both trends point to greater reasonableness. By avoiding ad hoc explanations, the reasonability-based model is more general and parsimonious than any other. And in models, parsimony is a virtue.

That said, while undifferentiated individualism, its variants and alternatives lack parsimony, other theories striving for general validity have been suggested. The most famous is postmaterialism. Inglehart (1990), one of its leading proponents, maintains that advanced industrial societies have been in a phase of cultural transition from materialistic to postmaterialistic values since the early 1970s. He ascribes this to the new generations being less motivated to accumulate material wealth than their elders because they grew up in an environment of material abundance where nothing was really wanting. Thus, he continues, they place value not on physical and material needs ('survival' values) but have moved on to seek self-fulfillment and aesthetic satisfaction ('self-expression'). Visibly, this is another way of arguing a rise in undifferentiated individualism by anchoring it securely to freedom from basic needs.

This theory owes much to prophetic 1970s discourse about educated US youth. It recycles appealing ideas under a coat of fresh theoretical varnish. Yet Inglehart stands above his colleagues of that decade because of the survey apparatus he set up to validate his theory: it was a most highly commendable enterprise. But how do you defend this theory in light of the WVS data and other data now available? And how do some scholars still find it valid?

Let us look at some facts, starting with responses to a question asked in Europe once and in the United States, never. It is hard to speak of postmaterialism when, in 1999, 91 percent of twenty-five European national populations say that a society is 'just' when it is 'guaranteeing that basic needs are met for all in terms of food, housing, clothes, education, health'! And this item outranks two other usual criteria of social justice: 'recognizing people on their merits' and 'eliminating big inequalities in income between citizens'. When it comes to social justice, the very foundation of living in society, almost all Europeans thus neatly reject any postmaterialism or other postmodernism. Moreover, Inglehart's theory implicitly suggests we should award less importance to money, which is materialism in its most elementary form, but the question was actually asked in that way in the surveys we are examining. And there has been no change in response levels to that question since 1980! Inglehart's theory faces many further stumbling blocks. The architecture of the indicator of postmaterialism seems odd. Respondents have to choose two priorities out of four for the nation: (1) law and order, (2) greater involvement of citizens in government decisions, (3) fighting inflation, and (4) safeguarding freedom of speech. Respondents are classified as 'materialists' if they choose (1) and (3) and 'postmaterialists' for picking (2) and (4)—everyone else is qualified as 'mixed'. But what justifies such architecture? We immediately wonder if there is a sense in itself to rank these options. And we simply fail to grasp any relationship between the (2) + (4) choice and postmaterialism, which is about fulfilling spiritual needs, aesthetic satisfaction and such. Choices (2) and (4) sooner relate to civic values and citizenship. We find the (1) + (3) choice equally perplexing: What do the maintenance of law and order have to do with materialism? These criticisms alone should have sufficed to torpedo the theory, and they were first expressed long ago, yet the theory is still afloat. So the criticism continued. Davis and Davenport (1999) ran a very systematic study of limpid outcome: far from reflecting an underlying dimension that orientates responses, the postmaterialism indicator is hardly worth more than a set of random answers. We can therefore no longer be satisfied with a few scattered cases that 'conveniently' lean in the direction of the model and ignore the rest. And even if, after this demonstration, we still see any value in the indicator, it turns out that the theory of rising postmaterialism does not fit the trend of the past thirty years. From this standpoint, the 'materialistic' choice of fighting inflation poses an obvious problem (Haller 2002). Europe experienced a stretch of high inflation spanning 1970 to the early 1980s, followed by competitive deflation that led into exceptionally low inflation in the 1990s: the swings in European opinion simply cloned the curve for the economy. The postmaterialism index varies inversely with the cost of living index and Inglehart's 'generation effect' only reflects the state of the economy (it is also paradoxical to defend rising postmaterialism in generations of youth facing high unemployment and low job security). We can now safely predict that materialism will rise with inflation. Worse still, Clarke, Dutt, and Rapkin (1997) have not only demonstrated that the state of the economy exerts decisive impact on the Inglehart index but that if we adjust his model for inflation and use it anyhow, postmaterialism has been on the wane since the 1970s.

More recently, Inglehart has employed other methods to propose a similar theory, holding that economic growth induces displacement toward 'rational' values, as opposed to 'traditional' ones (Inglehart and Baker 2000). But here again, we have an 'appealing' theory validated with a hasty assortment of correlations—from a factorial analysis whose results are available online. But in reality, this theory is just as equivocal. To defend it tooth and nail, we have to allow that 'traditional' values are all irrational, which means ignoring that traditional values are based on reasons as solid as today's. It is wrong to imagine that reason is always on the side of the most recent. This belief is not limited to the sociology of values and Boudon (1990) nicely demonstrates why this misconception lives on, even in scientific discourse. At all events, any rationality to which today's world may lay claim usually remains vaguely defined, so we can still play wordgames and hold that, say, rejection of marriage is rational and acceptance, irrational. But that would be a shortcut with at least two flaws. First, it presupposes straightforward antagonism between the 'modern' and 'traditional' value systems. This misunderstands that modernism is about imposing only a strict minimum of values and recognizing the individual's freedom of choice. Rejecting marriage does not make you modern: you are modern because you make your own assessment of the value to you of marriage, without being a blind heir to the choices of the past. The second, more serious flaw is the idea that today's Western values are rational. As if the Ancients (or, today, the people living in less-developed countries) were foolish and irrational enough to systematically get every choice wrong. Or opted only into evil. But going further, a person would have to reject marriage to qualify as rational. As usual, the underlying evolutionism of this proposition remains content to tell us that today's values are spreading worldwide because they are rational, and that they are rational because they are spreading. Unless we remain alert, this remarkable piece of circular reasoning may become dogma.

The real difference is of course not the presence or absence of reason but the fact that the modern values promoted at least since the Age of Enlightenment are both reasonable and rational while traditional values are only rational. Traditional values result from reason within a framework of customs above reproach while modern values also apply reason to questioning that framework. That questioning begins with recognition that one and all are reasonable and proceeds to seek out common principles capable of establishing a framework acceptable to one and all. We see this difference in law: each member of a traditional society acts rationally in function of a legal framework she or he does not question while each member of a modern society acts rationally and reasonably by questioning the legitimacy of the legal framework.

Change on both continents over the past two decades thus fits inside a trend of rising reasonableness happening over a much longer timespan. In other words, behind the conflict between those values that probably prevailed fifty years ago and those that prevail today, or are about to do so, the essential issue is entirely included in this trend of greater reasonableness. The rise of individualism as we have redefined it argues in favor of this trend. This individualism has little value for Americans and Europeans as long as it is not embedded into reasonableness.

7.7. **Conclusion**

Europeans certainly consider themselves far less European than Americans, American. But like Americans, they prefer keeping things close to home and show a certain mistrust of European institutions. From the range of values we have just reviewed, it appears there are no divisions such that they could prevent Europe from constituting a society, even in the absence of common, well-defined fiscal and foreign policies. As in the United States, divergences subsist on various points but we also found convergences and areas of strong consensus. The essential point is that we have a strong consensus on democracy and that there is a firmer resolve to ensure that what is legal must also be legitimate. Today's baseline for the constitution of a society is not high adherence to a single set of standard values but shared tolerance of differing values, so long as they are reasonable. So we needed to see more reasonableness, which is indeed what we found in the countries studied. This is what gives meaning to the shared moral liberalism on both continents, a liberalism with the function of circumscribing individualism.

While the rise of open-minded reason is of far greater importance than any alignment of opinion along one single set of values if Europe is to qualify as a modern society, this is just one necessary but insufficient criterion. The elements of a foundation are moving into place, although backsliding of shorter or longer duration may still occur. But to constitute a society of one institutional form or other (Habermas 1998), the reasonable must go beyond national allegiances to reflect a common will, which is an altogether different matter.

Appendix

Table 7A.1. Value change and convergence in Western Europe

More shared	Stable	Less shared	Unstable
Increasing			
Education = thrift	Aims of this country 1: more say	Education = imagination	Confidence education system
Follow instructions at work: be convinced	Belief in god: no	Good job = job security	Education = determination and perseverance
Follow instructions at work: depends	Education = unselfishness	Good job = meeting people	Good job = good hours
Good job = chances for promotion	Good job = achieving something	Good job = not too much pressure	Good job = respected job
Good job = interesting job	Good job = good pay	Good job = useful for society	Member local community
Good job = pleasant people	Good job = meeting abilities	Joining boycotts: have done	Neighbors = emotionally unstable
Good job = responsible job	Good job = use initiative	Joining boycotts: might do	Secretary: fair
No religion	Good and evil: clear guidelines	Locality	Unofficial strike: might do
Woman single parent: disapprove	Lawful demonstration: have done	Member cultural activities	Decrease importance of work: good
	Lawful demonstration: might do	Member environment	
	More emphasis on individual: good	Member Third World, human rights	
	Neighbors = record criminal	Neighbors = right wing	
	Parents resp.: no sacrifice	Not a religious person	
		Occupying buildings: might do	
		Signing petition: have done	
Stable			
Accepting a bribe (1 to 5)	Aims of this country 2: maintain order	Belief in life after death	Education = responsibility
Adultery (1 to 5)	Aims of this country 2: more say	Church and moral problems: yes	Successful marriage = apart from in-laws
Cheating on tax (1 to 5)	Belief in heaven	Confidence press	Successful marriage = politics
Confidence civil service	Claim state benefits (1 to 5)	Comfort and strength from religion	Unofficial strike: have done
Education = good manners	Confidence police	Country	Women need children: yes
Education = tolerance	Confidence trade unions	Education = independence	Decrease importance of work: bad
Follow instructions at work: always	Discuss politics: frequently	Europe	More respect on authority: bad
Freedom or equality: freedom	Discuss politics: occasionally	Importance of god in life (1 to 5)	
Woman single parent: approve	Discuss politics: never	Convinced atheist	
Neighbors = immigrant	Good job = generous holidays	Neighbors = different race	
Neighbors = left wing	Joyriding (1 to 5)	Occupying buildings: have done	
Other religions	Less emphasis on money (all items)	Region	
Successful marriage = children	Lying (1 to 5)	Suicide (1 to 5)	
Successful marriage = faithfulness	More emphasis on family life (all items)	World	

(cont.)

Table 7A.1. (Continued)

More shared	Stable	Less Shared	unstable
Successful marriage = understanding	More emphasis on technology (all items) Most people can be trusted More emphasis on individual: bad More emphasis on individual: don't mind Belief in god: do not know Parents resp.: best for children Good and evil: neither clear or unclear Prayer and meditation Successful marriage = household chores Successful marriage = respect		Abortion (1 to 5) Abortion if no more children: disapprove Abortion if not married: disapprove Control over life (1 to 5) Divorce (1 to 5) Education = hard work Euthanasia (1 to 5) Decrease importance of work: don't mind Taking soft drugs (1 to 5) Unofficial strike: never
Decreasing Catholic Confidence church Confidence parliament Homosexuality (1 to 5) Protestant Satisfaction (1 to 5) Woman single parent: depends	Aims of this country 1: fighting rising prices Aims of this country 2: fighting rising prices Belief in sin Church and family life: yes Good and evil: not clear Member political parties Member religious organization Lawful demonstration: never Successful marriage = adequate income Parents resp.: neither of them Successful marriage = good housing Successful marriage = happy sexual life Successful marriage = religious beliefs Successful marriage = social background	Education = obedience Education = religious faith Member trade unions Religious person Signing petition: might do Signing petition: never Joining boycotts: never Occupying buildings: never	
Unstable Neighbors = heavy drinker	Aims of this country 1: maintain order Aims of this country 1: protect freedom of speech Aims of this country 2: protect freedom of speech Belief in god: yes Children need both parents: yes Marriage outdated: yes	Belief in hell Church and spiritual needs: yes	Confidence armed forces Love and respect parents: always More respect on authority: good More respect on authority: don't mind

Table 7A.2. Value change in the United States

Increasing	Stable	Decreasing	Unstable
Discuss politics: often	Discuss politics: at times	Discuss politics: never	Member religious org.
Member social welfare	Neighbors: other races	Neighbors: Aids*	Member trade unions
Member culture	Neighbors: drinkers	Neighbors: addicts*	Member Third World
Member political parties	Neighbors: Muslims*	Neighbors: homosexuals*	People trusted
Member community action	Neighbors: foreigners		Child need parents: agree
Member environment	Neighbors: Jews*	Church and moral problems	Thrift
Member professional assoc.	Religious person (all items)	Church and family life	Obedience
Member youth work	Marriage outdated: yes	Church and spiritual needs	Confidence press
Member sports/recreation*	Both contribute: agree*	Church and social problems*	Following instructions
Member women's group*	Respect parents: always	Woman needs child: yes	
Member peace mvt*	Unofficial strikes: have done	Petition: might do	
Member health org.*	Accept bribe	Petition: never	
Neighbors: criminals	Cheating on tax	Lawful demonstration: never	
Neighbors: unstable	Claim state benefits	Unofficial strikes: never	
Secretaries: fair	North America	Confidence parliament	
Men more right to job: disagree*	Belief in god	Avoid transport fare	
Working mother: agree*	Belief in hell	Homosexuality	
Housewife fulfilled: agree*	Belief in heaven	Abortion	
Independence	Belief in life after death	Divorce	
Hard work	Good and evil: neither clear or unclear	Euthanasia	
Responsibility		Suicide	
Imagination		More emphasis on authority: good	
Tolerance		Town	
Determination		Region	
Religious faith		Good and evil: circumstances	
Unselfishness			
Petition: have done			
Lawful demonstration: have done			
Lawful demonstration: might do			
Unofficial strikes: might do			
Good and evil: guidelines			
Country			
World			

*No data available for 1981.

Note: For more readability, tables only list one choice where respondents had two. We have no space for full citation of responses. Readers can access the EVS and WVS questionnaires online for details of the abbreviations used herein.

8 Religion

Mathias Bös and Kai Hebel

> 'When I arrived in the United States, it was the country's religious aspect that first captured my attention. The longer I stayed, the more I became aware that this novel situation had important political consequences. In France, I knew, the spirit of religion and the spirit of liberty almost always pulled in opposite directions. In the United States I found them intimately intertwined: together they ruled the same territory.'
>
> (Tocqueville [1835] 2004: 340–1)

Through the centuries, numerous observers have been struck by the differences in the role religion plays in European and US-American life. This is especially noteworthy since both societies are, from a structural point of view, Christian despite an increasing number of non-Christian denominations and atheists in both societies, three quarters of the populations are Christians (the EU about 75% and United States 80%, see Barret, Kurian, and Johnson 2001). As early as the 1830s, Alexis de Tocqueville uncovered one of the key differences: in the United States, religion symbolizes the unity of the US-American society, whereas in Europe religious discourse evokes the disunity of the European people (Tocqueville 1835). It is one of the founding myths of the United States that the American people are unified by the desire to live their religious faith freely; in contrast, political culture in Europe is still shaped by the long history of devastating religious conflicts between different Christian faiths.

The aim of this chapter is twofold. First, we intend to analyze the basic trends and patterns in church–society–state relations in Europe and the United States. Second, we attempt to explore how these trends influenced the reaction to the rise of militant Islamic fundamentalism in both societies. The analysis proceeds in three steps. We start with some basic considerations on the concept of religion and describe long-term religious trends on both sides of the Atlantic. We then give a short sketch of the main impact of Islamic fundamentalism on US-American and European societies and conclude with a summary of the main religious differences between both societies.

8.1. Religious structures and trends

Looking at the role of Christianity, one is inclined to modify an old saying: Europe and the United States are divided by a common religion. Although both societies are strongholds of the Christian faith, the relation between religion and the state differs significantly. In order to shed light on this situation, we start with some conceptual ideas on religion and proceed with a sketch of historical developments essential to understanding the multiple differences in the social organization of church–society–state relations between the United States and the EU. We end with a few remarks on today's religious landscape in Europe and the United States.

8.1.1. THE CONCEPT OF RELIGION

The term religion is a distinctly European invention. It was first used to describe differences in faith within the population of Europe. The very term 'Europe' itself came into use to substitute the notion of Christianity, which, after the Age of Reformation and the beginning of the Enlightenment, could no longer serve as a unifying idea of the people inhabiting a small portion of the Asian continent (Davies 1998: 7). The term religion is quite vague and conveys changing, sometimes even contradictory notions. There is no consensus within sociology about the definition of religion (for a short discussion, see McKinnon 2002).

Nevertheless, we can collect some aspects, which are most common among different definitions. Two basic types of conceptualization can be found: religions are either defined by the meaning structure shared by participating individuals (substantial definition) or by their functions for a group or society (functional definition). The shared meaning is the belief in something sacred, transcendent; that is in God.

In respect to different social functions, religion contributes to the cohesion of society through rituals, organizations, common values and beliefs. This functional view of religion is often associated with the work of Emile Durkheim (1912). In his famous analysis of the clans of Australian aborigines, he argued that the idea of the collective is reflected in the religious totem—an animal, for example—which represents the worshiped forefathers of all members of the clan. The totem symbolizes the God and the community, hence Durkheim's often-cited idea that religion is a fundamental way for society to express itself to its members. Religious beliefs and rituals integrate the clan. Durkheim analyzed another feature of religion, which is of prime importance: religion is a way to coordinate social action. This chance of 'acting together', exemplified in rituals, is an important way to generate an emotional bond not only between single members of a group but also between members of a group to the group itself (for a more elaborate version of this argument, see Bös 2004). Whether Durkheim's analysis of Australian aborigines was accurate or not, his concept of religion still serves as a popular tool to examine the role of religion in Western societies. In a sense, Durkheim's analysis of religion epitomizes the Western dream of a society integrated by shared values, where all people share the same notion of what is sacred and what is profane. Compared to this mythical vision of a religiously over-integrated society in the past, every contemporary Western society seems to disintegrate; religion seems less important than it once was and social cohesion is in danger.

Like the idea that religion is capable of unifying entire societies, the very idea of religion is unique. One can rightfully argue that the dominant definitions of modern religions in sociology derive from the ideal-type of a close family of monotheistic religions that emerged in the Levant: Judaism, Christianity, and Islam. Christianity and Islam forcefully proselytized many parts of the world. As a result, not only the majority of Europeans and North Americans, but also more than half of the world's population belong to that family of religions. But one has to keep in mind that the very idea of exclusive membership is an idea not all religions share, that is Buddhism may be much more widespread than suggested since many people are Buddhists and something else.

Hence a general definition of religion emerged out of that idiosyncratic context. Max Weber (1920) called Christianity and Islam (as well as Confucianism, Taoism, Buddhism, and Hinduism) world religions. Like most religions, world religions offer salvation from suffering in the world, which, in principle, is open to everybody.

'A religion' is of course no homogeneous block. All world religions are subdivided into many strands, and although the differences between different versions of Christianity or Islam often seem small for the external observer, they are nevertheless of extreme importance for some groups of adherents. It is not possible to account for the hostility between, say, Sunnis and Shias or Anglicans and Independents by referring simply to their dogmatic differences. Dogmatic differences between these religious doctrines are nearly invisible compared to disparities between Christianity and Buddhism or Islam and Shinto. There are many more factors needed until some members of one religious group feel forced to bomb holy places or to emigrate to another continent, but we return to that at the end of this chapter.

These religious subdivisions can be differentiated according to their organizational form. It is common to distinguish between churches, denominations, sects, and cults (Johnstone 2001). The prototype of a church is the Roman Catholic Church. Churches assume that their doctrines form the only 'true' religion. They are characterized by an organizational hierarchy that is used to dominate the religious orientation of a majority of people within an area. Denominations, sometimes also called churches, have a much lower level of societal dominance. The Protestant denominations in North America, which have by and large learned to tolerate each other's doctrines, can serve as an example in that respect. This structural feature of US-American society, aptly called 'the denominational society' by Greeley (1972), constitutes one of the most evident discrepancies between Europe and the United States. Sects and cults refer to religious groupings, which are usually in tension with mainstream society. Whereas sects are often characterized by a more fundamentalist 'back to the roots' ideology, cults are typically much less rigid. Both heretic forms are quite common in Islam and Christianity, although the number of their adherents is rather small compared to churches and denominations.

Fundamentalism is a term often used today for Christian and Islamic sect-like movements (the key work on fundamentalism as a general category is Lawrence

1989). It was first utilized to describe a conservative Protestant movement in the United States between 1870 and 1925 (Marsden 1980), and later on applied to some Shiite movements (Riesebrodt 1990). Though notoriously difficult to define, fundamentalism is seen as a reaction to modernity by most scholars (for a comprehensive overview, see Emerson and Hartman 2006: 128). Here modernity is perceived not only in its 'master trends' of increasing differentiation, rationalization, industrialization, and urbanization but also as a threat to morality, community life, and traditional patriarchal ideas of social order. In this context, fundamentalism can be defined as 'a discernible pattern of religious militancy by which self-styled "true believers" attempt to arrest the erosion of religious identity, fortify the borders of the religious community, and create viable alternatives to secular institutions and behaviors' (Almond, in Emerson and Hartman 2006: 130). Like the concept of religion itself, the term fundamentalism developed within Christianity and was later on applied to other religious contexts.

8.1.2. SELECTED HISTORICAL TRENDS

As already mentioned, present-day United States and Europe are dominated by Christianity. Christianity emerged as a Jewish cult in the first century AD and expanded dramatically over the course of 500 years until it dominated the Levant, Asia Minor, Northern Africa, and Europe. Since 600 AD, the Muslim faith expanded into large parts of Northern Africa, the whole of Asia Minor, and the Hispanic Peninsula. In 1054 AD, the first important schism within Christianity emerged between the Byzantine Orthodox and Roman Catholic Christianity. Christianity's first step toward the establishment of 'state churches' was the declaration of the Orthodox Church in Russia and its secession from Constantinople in 1448 AD.

The struggle between different power centers and religious movements led to extremely violent conflicts within European society (Tilly 1990). One first effort to resolve these conflicts was the Peace of Westphalia (1648), which legitimized and promoted the segmentary differentiation of European society into sovereign units. One expression of the sovereignty of the units within the Westphalian system was a reinvigoration of the ancient principle of *Cuius regio, eius religio*, thereby authorizing each state or kingdom to determine the religion its subjects had to practice.

The British colonies, which later became the United States, started from the same model. As Pyle and Davidson (2003) point out, all colonies had laws on which religions were accepted within each colony and which were not. Most colonies did not tolerate Catholics at least in some phases in their history. Furthermore, many colonies formed a religiously homogeneous ruling class, mostly Anglican or Congregational. The legal situation changed with the First Amendment to the Constitution of the newly formed United States in 1791: 'Congress shall make no law respecting an establishment of religion, or prohibiting the free exercise thereof.' In order to unify the different states with their various

Christian churches, the separation between state and religious organizations was established. The United States became a single nation-state with a set of heterogeneous denominations.

European history took a more twisted path; epitomized by the French Revolution and its opposition, the cleavage between churches and the developing nation-states started to be one of the bitterest and deepest in European society. As Stein Rokkan puts it:

> The decisive battle came to stand between *the aspirations of the mobilizing nation-state and the corporate claims of the churches.* The Church, whether Roman Catholic, Lutheran, or Reformed, had for centuries claimed the right to represent man's 'spiritual estate' and to control the education of children in the right faith. (Rokkan 1999: 286)

In the course of the nineteenth and twentieth centuries, European nation-states increasingly claimed the right to influence the individual citizen directly, forcing churches to redefine their role. This process led to the various models of church–state relations in European society. Protestant and Orthodox countries tended to establish national churches: four successions of autocephalous churches took place: Greece (1833), Romania (1864), Bulgaria (1871), and Serbia (1879). In contrast, Catholic countries either tried to separate church and state or to redefine Catholicism into a special form of a national church. Dissimilar as these arrangements were, they led to the typically European religious landscape where every nation-state is characterized by one, sometimes two confessions, often closely related with different national identities.

The educational system is one of the key arenas in which the direct influence of nation-states manifests itself. In Europe and the United States, schools are one of the major institutions promoting identification with the nation-state through the teaching of national languages and histories as well as a standardized canon of knowledge. Yet in Europe education is mostly centralized and secularized, whereas in the United States education is organized locally and hence much more susceptible to religious influences (Berger 2005).

Another historical difference between Europe and the United States lies in the different paths the state–church relationship has taken over the past two centuries. In the United States, the former colonies switched to a model which assumed no congruency between one special kind of Christianity and the central government. In contrast, most states in Western Europe kept to that pattern (Schilling 2001) leading to a close, often highly strained relationship between churches and states in Europe. In the age of Absolutism, the King or the central government often assumed 'church-like' authority, evident, for example, in the British monarch's title as the 'Supreme Governor of the Church of England'. With the increasing separation between churches and states, this moral authority remained with the central government, but it was increasingly considered inappropriate to use religious references to support that authority. The structural reason for this process was that, in most European states, a reference to religion implied the reference to the one former state religion, thus reinforcing the connection modern nation-states typically seek to diminish. The historical connection between the central government and a church was equally problematic for the church. Tocqueville pointed out that the separation between state and church is especially important for churches because it is dangerous for them to be identified with one political regime that may change. The prime example of this process is France, where Catholicism was traditionally associated with the *ancien régime*.

In the United States, the central government was never seen as a moral authority in the European sense. And since churches in the United States never stabilized the central government directly, it was not necessary for the political establishment to separate from the church symbolically. Using religious arguments and rhetoric was therefore seen as unproblematic. In the United States, governmental authority was never religious authority, which made the use of religious symbols and discourses as a symbol for American societal unity much easier than in its European counterpart. This extensive exploitation of religious symbols in American political life can be seen as an indicator of a religious–cultural complex that Robert Bellah (1967) called 'civil religion'. On the one hand, civil religion means that the United States as a nation-state 'uses' religious symbols, but on the other hand—and even more importantly—that the shared ethical principles of all Americans transcend the nation-state. In this sense American civil religion is Janus-faced: its rhetoric can potentially be used to manipulate the electorate, but it also provides for the possibility to judge American social practices and leaders by 'higher' standards than, for example, by the benchmark of national interests defined in purely secular terms. While every nation-state may develop its own kind of civil religion as a (quasi-)religious self-understanding, American civil religion is surely exceptional in its power and decisiveness. It continues to inform American politics to this day (see below).

8.1.3. THE MODERN RELIGIOUS LANDSCAPE IN EUROPE AND THE UNITED STATES

Although the major historical trends in the European and US-American religious landscape are well known, precise data on churches and religiosity are relatively few compared to information on economic or political processes. This is partially due to the fact that the religious sphere of society does not share the same obsession with figures and lists which is quite common in the economic or political realm. Churches and denominations tend to produce a much smaller stock of data about themselves than other organizations do. Especially long-term data are often gathered by groups interested in proselytizing and thus have to be taken with a pinch of salt. Data collected by the churches themselves are mostly focused on one church in a given country and are therefore hardly comparable. There are only a few official data on religion in the United States. Laws (i.e. Public Law 94-521, 1976) prohibit the Bureau of the Census from asking questions on religious affiliation on a mandatory basis. Most data published by the Bureau of the Census are based on Gallup polls. The validity of these data is often very weak

Table 8.1. Religious preferences from 1957 to 2002 in the United States (%)

Year	Religious preference						
	Protestant	Catholic	Jewish	Orthodox	Mormon	Other specific	None
1957	66	26	3	NA	NA	3	3
1967	67	25	3	NA	NA	4	2
1975	62	27	2	NA	NA	2	6
1980	61	28	2	NA	NA	2	7
1990	56	25	2	NA	NA	6	11
1995	56	27	2	1	1	5	8[a]
2000	56	27	2	1	1	5	8[a]
2002	53	25	2	1	2	8	9[a]

Note: Data cover civilian noninstitutional population, 18 years old and over. Data represent averages of the combined results of several surveys during year or period indicated. Data are subject to sampling variability, see source.

NA: Not available.

[a] Includes those respondents who did not designate.

Source: Statistical Abstracts of the United States 2004 (Table 80) and 1994 (Table 85)

so they can only be seen as a rough estimate (Caplow 1998). Since the 1970s, the interest of more quantitative-orientated social sciences in religion has grown so that more data on religion have been produced.

Table 8.1 shows that the United States is a predominantly Protestant society; only in a few states in the northeast does the proportion of Catholics get close to 50 percent. Since the 1960s, American society has witnessed a slight decrease in Christian religious preferences from 90 percent Christians to about 80 percent, mainly due to a slight increase in non-Christian adherents. The Catholic and Orthodox proportions of Christianity in the United States are rather stable; the sinking number of Protestants explains the slight decrease of Christians. Compared to Europe, the Muslim community is relatively small. According to conservative estimates, it accounts for less than 1 percent (exceptions are Illinois 1.01 percent, Maryland 1 percent, New Jersey 1.43 percent, and New York 1.18 percent). However, estimates vary widely and these are especially conservative figures, which should be seen as the absolute base line. The Muslim community could be almost triple the size in some states.

As already mentioned, the most noteworthy feature of the US-American religious landscape is the high level of fragmentation especially among Protestants. The American Religious Data Archive informs us that 'Mainline Protestants' are divided in 23 denominations and the group of 'Evangelical Protestants' consists of 127 denominations from 'The Advent Christian Church' to 'The Wesleyan Church'. (For Christian Orthodox 23 denominations are listed as well, for Muslims no subdivisions are mentioned.) Some observers argue that such a plurality of different groups led to a kind of religious market in US-American society (Stark and Bainbridge [1987] 1996: 187pp.). The different 'religious offers' in that marketplace enable individuals to choose the denomination which fits best to her or his needs. This flexibility of the religious market in the United States can be seen as strengthening American religion, whereas in Europe one may speak at best of

Table 8.2. The distribution of nation-states and religions in European society (based on figures of the mid-1990s)

	Main religious orientation of at least 70% of the population	Count of all countries in the EU
Current member-states	1957: *Belgium* (Cath), *France* (Cath), *Germany* (Pr, Cath), *Italy* (Cath), *Luxembourg* (Cath), *Netherlands* (Cath, Pr, nonr). 1973: *Ireland* (Cath), *Denmark* (Pr), *United Kingdom* (Ang, nonr, Cath, Pr). 1981: *Greece* (Orth). 1986: *Portugal* (Cath), *Spain* (Cath). 1995: *Austria* (Cath), *Finland* (Pr), *Sweden* (Pr)	*One religion:* 12, Cath = 8, Pr = 3, Orth = 1 *Two religions:* 2, Pr & Cath = 2[a] *More religions:* 1, Ang & Cath & Pr
Enlargement 2004	*Cyprus* (Orth), *Czech Republic* (Cath, Nonr), *Estonia* (Pr, Orth, nonr), *Hungary* (Cath, Pr), *Latvia* (Pr, Orth, Cath), *Lithuania* (Cath), *Malta* (Cath), *Poland* (Cath), *Slovakia* (Cath, Pr), *Slovenia* (Cath)	*One religion:* 17, Cath = 12, Pr = 3, Orth = 2 *Two religions:* 6, Pr & Cath = 4, Pr & Orth = 2 *More religions:* 2, Ang & Cath & Pr, Pr & Orth & Cath

[a] In the case of Germany after reunification the figure dropped slightly under 70% and has since remained stable at about 65%.

Cath: Catholic, Pr: Protestant, Orth: Orthodox, Ang: Anglican, nonr: nonreligious.

an oligopolistic market of religions and denominations. Thus religions tend not to be sufficiently 'consumer oriented', and thus not as high on demand as in the United States.

Religious diversity in Europe, defined as the internal variation within Christianity, seems to be in decline. In Europe, recent studies show that there is a tendency to reduce denominational differences. On the one hand, more and more adherents consider differences between different forms of Christianity as unimportant (Dubach and Campiche 1993); on the other hand, some (Protestant) denominations tend to form unified umbrella organizations like the Lutherans and Calvinists in Germany ('Evangelical Church in Germany').

Contemporary European society is predominantly Catholic, with some mainly Protestant parts in the north and a few Orthodox areas in the east (Table 8.2). The enlargement of the EU in 2004 led to an increase of the Protestant and Orthodox populations of Europe, but it did not change the basic structure: one Christian religion in Europe characterized by different Christian faiths. Islam is the only non-Christian denomination which increased in considerable numbers after World War II. The possible future inclusion of Turkey—as a dominantly Islamic country—would change the traditional religious landscape of the EU dramatically.

Table 8.2 shows basically the same pattern before and after enlargement in 2004; the majority of countries are dominated by one denomination, mostly Catholicism, with the exception of a few Protestant or Orthodox cases. The enlargement of 2004 raised the number of countries dominated by two and more religions to eight, so in general enlargement increased the religious heterogeneity of the European society.

Table 8.3. Religious landscape of the European Union (all twenty-five countries, figures in million)

	Protestants		Catholics		Orthodox		Muslims		Pop.
	Mill.	%	Mill.	%	Mill.	%	Mill.	%	Mill.
1970	72	17.59	243	59.59	12	2.95	2	0.69	407
1990	64	14.49	261	59.35	14	3.20	10	2.31	440
2000	64	14.26	265	58.85	14	3.27	12	2.62	450

Source: Own calculations based on Barret, Kurian, and Johnson (2001). In view of the difficulties associated with gathering data on the size of Muslim communities in European countries, it should be noted that these figures probably underestimate the number of Muslims in the EU.

In spite of the aforementioned change, the religious landscape of Europe shows some stability: about 80 percent of the European population is Christian as the figures for the EU of twenty-five member-states indicate (Table 8.3). The main shift can be seen in the proportion of Muslims, which quadrupled between 1970 and 2000. The growth of the Muslim minority is largely connected to recent immigration to Europe and took place within the 'founding nations' of the EU, especially France and Germany. In this perspective, Europe faces a major change in its religious landscape. One has to take into account that the Muslim community is very heterogeneous concerning different denominations within Islam, but since about half of the people in the Muslim community are born in Europe (Savage 2004), we face the emergence of a new kind of European Islam.

8.1.4. PERSONAL RELIGION IN EUROPE AND THE UNITED STATES

It is difficult to give reliable numbers on the trends in religious affiliations and institutional settings, but it is even more difficult to analyze the personal dimension of religion in both societies. Here the United States and Europe show remarkable differences. At least in this respect the phrase 'Secular Europe, religious America' (Anderson 2004) may fit. One of the few sources on this topic is the European and the World Value Survey. In the following figures, we compare the second wave 1990 (country surveys conducted in 1990) and the fourth wave 2004 (country surveys conducted in 1999–2000). Data for the second wave includes the EU15 without Greece and Luxembourg. Data for the fourth wave includes the EU25 without Cyprus. Sometimes the first wave (1981–4) is mentioned for the United States, but for this wave not enough countries were included to calculate figures for the EU. The percentages are calculated with 'don't know' and 'no answer' included (own calculation with the ASEP/JDS database accessed at http://www.jdsurvey.net, November 12, 2006).

Asked 'how important is God in your life?', about 58 percent of US-American respondents considered God as very important (on a ten-point scale from 'not at all important' to 'very important'). This proportion increased over the past ten years (53% in 1990). In the EU25, only one-fifth of the population feels that God is very important for their life. Although there are some variations within Europe, the only two 'outliers' are Malta with 67 percent and Poland with 51 percent. In general, the enlargement of the EU in 2004 did not change this picture. A 1990 survey of the EU15 established that only about 17 percent ascribed a central role to God in their life; here, Ireland was the exception with 40 percent.

On the other hand, both of our societies have a remarkable number of non-religious persons and convinced atheists. In the United States (1999) they add up to 17 percent (atheists well above 1%, nonreligious persons 16%), with a slight increase over the past ten years in the nonreligious persons (13% in 1990). Considering data like this, one has to take into account that America is not homogeneous when it comes to personal religion (Berger 2005). As a rule of thumb, Americans living on the East and West coasts are closer to the European pattern than their fellow citizens in the mid-west or the south of the United States. In the EU25 today with 31 percent, the percentage of convinced atheists (5%) and nonreligious persons (26%) is nearly twice as high as in the United States; in the EU15 in 1990 the proportions were about the same. Here the variance between the different countries is high. Poland and Portugal range on the lower level of the scale with 6 and 11 percent of convinced atheists and nonreligious persons. In contrast, these groups make up between 51 and 58 percent in the Czech Republic, France, Great Britain, and Sweden.

Questions related to the actual content of Christian beliefs show basically the same pattern. One of the items used was the question 'Do you believe in hell?' 71 percent of Americans answered affirmatively, a proportion that has remained rather stable over the past ten years. In the EU25 member-states, only 27 percent think hell exists, again with Malta (76%) and Poland (57%) as the usual outliers; in general, Catholic countries rate higher than Protestant EU member-states. This number has slightly increased since 1990 when approximately 20 percent believed in hell (Ireland 50%).

The disparity between the US-American society and Europe is less pronounced when it comes to church attendance. About 45 percent of US-Americans attend religious services once a week or more, the same proportion as ten years ago. In the EU25, only half of that proportion (23%) participate in religious services once a week or more (Malta 82%, Poland 59%, and Ireland 59%). This was almost the same in the EU15 with 24 percent in 1990 (Ireland 81%).

One of the most remarkable differences pertains to the question about politicians and their religiosity. Nearly 38 percent of US-Americans agree or strongly agree that 'politicians who don't believe in God are unfit for public office'. In the EU25, only 14 percent agree or strongly agree with that statement. Here Poland is no exception at all: only 16 percent of Polish respondents concur with the statement. Only the Maltese (40%) and Greeks (37%) are more in line with US-American attitudes.

However, one should not overestimate the differences between both sides of the Atlantic either. Europe's secularism and America's religiousness are a reaction to the same trends of social change; both societies are marked by pluralism. No single religion dominates exclusively in the public sphere, traditionally not in the United States but increasingly not in Europe. Of course, there are European nations where one religion dominates, like Catholicism in France. Yet hardly anyone would argue that Catholicism is taken for granted in the public sphere in France. Since no religion dominates in both societies, the main feature is that people are free to choose. In the United States, they chose between different denominations; in Europe, there is a choice between being religious and nonreligious (Berger 2005).

At the end, a caveat especially for our European readers is necessary. Many observers argue that America is somehow an exception with its high levels of religiosity, but on a global scale we find a totally different picture:

Much has been written to the effect that religion is a part of "American exceptionalism." But in reality, most of the world, not just the United States, is characterized by an explosion of passionate religious movements. The real exception is Europe. Explaining European secularity, especially its contrast with America, is one of the most interesting topics for the study of contemporary religion (Berger 2005: 112p).

8.2. The (re-)politicization of religion

Since its inception US-American political culture has been marked by an idiosyncratic blend of the religious and the political. As already noted above, this gave rise to an ideology of unity, which provides social cohesion to an extraordinarily fragmented society—a distinctly American 'civil religion', as famously called by Robert Bellah. His notion of civil religion as a 'religious dimension' (1967: 1) is somewhat broader than our usage here in which we focus solely on the unifying effects of civil religion.

In this section, we argue that the (re-)politicization of religion in the United States following the terrorist attacks of September 11, 2001 was channeled by, and in turn radicalized, the traditional patterns of American civil religion. Following its initial reaction of shock and widespread empathy with the victims of the attacks as well as the United States in general, European society reacted in an increasingly estranged fashion to the radicalization of American civil religious rhetoric and the essentially unilateralist foreign policy it legitimated. Despite a considerable convergence of attitudes toward Islamist terrorism, fusing into Islamophobia in both societies, the blend of the religious and the political, so essential to US-American culture and politics, is bound to remain a source of considerable tension in transatlantic relations.

This section is divided into three parts. The first one provides a brief sketch of American civil religion and its radicalization after September 11. This is followed by an analysis of European responses to this development in US-American society as well as to the rise of Islamist fundamentalism. Finally, we briefly discuss some similarities in the way both societies face the challenge represented by violent Islamist fundamentalism. We predict that the shared fear of Islamist terrorism will probably serve as an Other against which the construct of a transatlantic community can keep (re-)creating itself. Yet the different role of religion in both societies will also provide a continuous source of irritation.

8.2.1. THE RADICALIZATION OF AMERICAN CIVIL RELIGION

American civil religion is an ideology, which is religious insofar as it employs Judeo-Christian symbols, Old Testament metaphors and narratives, and borrows heavily from the Puritan sense of mission. These religious components nevertheless serve essentially political ends; they are a way of constructing political unity. Despite the constitutional separation of church and state, American civil religion bestows a transcendental quality on national identity. It thus allows for a quasi-religious reading of the American political project, which is characterized by the notion of exceptionalism and the universal advancement of materialist individualism, free-trade economics, and Western-style democracy. Civil religious discourse constructs the act of implementing this project as a sacred duty of all those who choose to be Americans. This nonsecular quality of national identity contributes to the exceptional vigor of American patriotism. The United States has consistently topped national pride indices. One of the most recent surveys again ranked the United States as the number one in 'domain-specific pride' and a close second (after Venezuela) in 'general national pride' (Kim and Smith 2006). The at times Manichean way in which dissent to specific policies, such as the war in Iraq of 2003, is charged as 'un-American' heresy, as well as the 'paranoid style' in US-American politics (Hofstadter [1964] 1996) are instances of the vigor of national pride. Civil religion is also crucial in providing the basis for the foundational mythology, which stresses the exceptional character of the American project. This narrative portrays the American people as being 'chosen' by divine providence and given the chance (and obligation) to start civilization from anew in a 'promised land', removed from the sins of the European continent, and as an exemplar to the world. The latter aspect—the notion of being removed from, while acting as a model to the rest of the world—is crucial because it explains the somewhat paradoxical belief that American political and social values are unique as well as universal. While American political leaders have disagreed sharply between different options to spread these (non-)secular values—the ideal-type alternatives being the model of America as a beacon (the isolationist stance) and America as a crusader (the Wilsonian and neoconservative variant)—none of them questioned the righteousness of the project as such.

The terrorist attacks of September 11, 2001 had a radicalizing effect on American political culture at the mass as well as at the elite level. Although the long-term consequences of this trend are hard to assess as of now, we do maintain that 9/11 had a profound effect on American civil religion. In line with the key features of civil religion, the immediate response of many Americans was an idiosyncratic mix of the religious as well as the political. On the one hand, church attendance soared, President Bush proclaimed a 'National Day of Prayer and Remembrance' and termed the 'war on terrorism' a 'crusade' (Bush 2002). Tellingly, the locus from which the president declared this 'crusade' was the pulpit of the National Cathedral—a civil religious gesture par excellence. On the other hand, despite the Islamist agenda of the attackers, September 11 was at least as much perceived an assault on the more secular trademarks of American society and its polity: the World Trade Center as a symbol of American economic prowess, the Pentagon as one of military might.

Interestingly, the impact of September 11 on purely religious indicators was more short-lived than on civil religious ones. In fact, a Gallup/CNN/USA Today poll shows that the upsurge in religious practices fell most dramatically, while civil religious responses to the attacks declined the least; indicators of intimate interpersonal relations occupied a middle ground (for a very useful compilation of the initial data set, see Vorländer 2004). Respondents were asked whether, 'as a direct result of September 11', they prayed more than usual, showed more affection for loved ones, or personally displayed an American flag. Over the course of one year, percentages dropped respectively from 74 to 41 percent (more prayers), 77 to 47 percent (more affection for loved ones), and 82 to 66 percent (display of an American flag). The latter indicator not only started from a higher point, it also remained fairly constant compared to the others.

On the elite level, the Bush administration radicalized American civil religion in two interconnected ways. First, American civil religion was increasingly robbed of its potentially self-critical quality. The more liberal variants of civil religion advocated by John F. Kennedy, Martin Luther King, and others are based on the belief that God-given values transcend the nation and its political system (Bellah 1967: 4). Civil religion thereby provides benchmarks against which to judge the actions of each American citizen, including those who carry political responsibility. According to this belief, the American people are 'chosen' by God, but they can also fail to carry out His will on earth. This self-reflexive element is fundamental to American civil religion and increasingly less significant in the fundamentalist version the Bush administration has put forward. Its reinterpretation of civil religion has important ramifications in regard to the second way in which this ideology was radicalized. Bush radicalized American civil religion by explicitly projecting it onto the global stage. Core symbols like the American flag are cast as universal rallying points: 'The American flag stands (...) for the cause of human dignity. (...) This ideal of America is the hope of all mankind' (Bush 2002). The belief in the uniqueness and universalism of American values is nothing new, of course. However, in the absence of its potentially self-reflexive quality, American civil religious beliefs assume a new quality. As a consequence, statements like these, packed with religious quotations, do not merely represent yet another general expression of American exceptionalist universalism; they not only express the belief that intervention can be justified whenever 'human dignity' is seen at risk—they also assume that America's political responses to September 11 are almost automatically sanctioned by divine authority. Jim Wallis points out how Bush's speechwriters frequently distort religious texts by using them out of context and substituting God or Jesus for the United States or the American people (Wallis 2003). One of Wallis's examples is the aforementioned quote from Bush's speech commemorating the first anniversary of 9/11: 'This ideal of America is the hope of all mankind. (...) That hope still lights our way. And the light shines in the darkness. And the darkness has not overcome it' (Bush 2002). Identifying the last two lines as direct quotes from John's gospel, Wallis notes that 'in the gospel the light shining in the darkness is the Word of God, and the light is the light of Christ. It's not about America and its values'. Hence Wallis's conclusion that Bush's 'theology is more American civil religion than Christian faith' (Wallis 2003). In view of the importance of American civil religion as an ideology of integration and the potential to win votes by tapping into it (Wimberley 1980; Wimberley and Christenson 1982), this highly selective usage of religion in the president's speeches is more likely to be a deliberate move rather than simply 'a mistake' as Wallis asserts. 'Either you are with us, or you are with the terrorists'—Bush's most often-cited statement—can be seen as the logical result of a stance which treats the righteousness of the United States and its moral leadership role in regard to the rest of the 'civilized' world as a given. It also shows the degree to which an ideology that fuses political and religious discourses can be used to legitimate contingent policy choices.

8.2.2. EUROPEAN RESPONSES

The initial response of a majority of Europeans to the attacks of September 11 was characterized by a mixture of shock at the massacre and support for the United States, memorably captured by Le Monde's solemn declaration 'Nous sommes tous Américains' (Colombani 2001). However, the numerous European pledges of, in German Chancellor Schröder's words, 'unlimited solidarity' (Schröder 2001), were soon joined by a growing sense of uneasiness about precipitate US retaliation and its potential consequences. Europe 'cringed' at the stark religious rhetoric when President Bush declared the launch of a global 'crusade' against terrorism (Ford 2001), which would bring the perpetrators to 'infinite justice'. The influential French policy analyst Dominique Moïsi commented: 'This confusion between politics and religion (...) risks encouraging a clash of civilizations' (quoted in Ford 2001). This warning should not be downplayed as typically French recalcitrance; on the contrary, it reflects concerns throughout European society, harbored even by nations with highly sympathetic attitudes toward Americans. In the UK, the self-declared 'transatlantic bridge' between the United States and Europe (Hebel 2006), an opinion poll of 3,200 Britons found out that 32 percent of the respondents believe George W. Bush to 'pose a greater threat to world peace' than Saddam Hussein. On the borders of Europe, mass opinion was even less benign: in Turkey, a potential candidate for EU accession, a majority of participants in a Pew Research Center poll subscribed to the view that the US-led campaign against Saddam formed part of 'a general war against unfriendly Muslim countries' (Borger 2002). The highly volatile situation in Iraq and Afghanistan and the continuing presence of American troops in these states are bound to further solidify this opinion. However, concern over specific policy choices of a particular administration should not be construed as abysmal divides between entire societies (Hebel 2005). This is especially the case since a whole string of events which reinforced fear of Islamist fundamentalism is likely to increase a feeling of solidarity on both sides of the Atlantic. The most important of these events were the bombings in Madrid and London, but other events such as the ritualistic slaughter of film director Theo Van Gogh in November 2004 (Schümer 2004) and the attempted train bombings in Germany in the summer of 2006 also attracted a high-level of media coverage.

Although European society widely shares the fear of violent Islamist fundamentalism with its comparator on the opposite side of the Atlantic, the European response was largely devoid of religious rhetoric and symbolism. In contrast to the radicalization of civil religious discourse by political elites in the United States, many European leaders deliberately used essentially secular narratives in their reaction to the rise of Islamist fundamentalism. The British response to the London bombings may serve as an example in that regard. Fearing that religiously charged rhetoric may further divide British society, Tony Blair invoked the memory of World War II. By likening the terrorist attacks in the capital to the Nazi bombings during the 'Blitz' (Manthorpe 2006), the prime minister sought to provide a secular rallying point for all Britons and, by extension, for all Europeans. Framed in this way, the fundamentalist threat challenges secular values such as the unity of British society and the European political project. The latter arose out of a rejection of political totalitarianism, German Nazism in particular, and the long history of intra-European warfare. In contrast to US-American society, whose foundational mythology is inextricably bound up with religion via the narrative of the Pilgrim Fathers seeking religious freedom and fulfilling God's designs, European society invoked its own political history to deal with the new threat. European leaders were thereby able to deal with the Islamist challenge largely without desecularizing European public discourse and European foundational narratives.

Of course, this is not to imply that religion plays an insignificant role in European politics. Political culture in Europe has been deeply affected by Islamist fundamentalist violence. For example, there is a growing tendency to exploit fear of Islamist terrorism for political ends by framing events as having an Islamist background. One illustration of this development is the treatment of the civil unrest in Paris of October–November 2005 (Becker et al. 2006). The then French Ministre d'État, Nicolas Sarkozy, was very quick to claim an Islamist background to the riots, although the French intelligence agency and several newspapers had denied such a link (Smith 2005). It seems likely that Sarkozy invoked Islamist fundamentalism in order to drum up support for the government's controversial management of the crisis.

European leaders are likely to follow Sarkozy's example as fear of Islam is rising within European society. Another incident, which at first was unrelated to the riots in the French capital, illustrates that point. Ten days before the unrests, *El Fagr*, a newsweekly based in Cairo, published a selection of cartoons featuring the Prophet Mohammad, which had initially been printed by the Danish newspaper *Jyllands Posten*. A probably targeted campaign induced a series of protests and even violent demonstrations in Europe, the Middle East, Asia, and Africa. This gave rise to fears of new riots in Paris and elsewhere. On the mass level, the 'cartoon riots' certainly increased fears of Islamism and the Muslim faith in general by reinforcing the view of Islam as a 'backward' religion hostile to freedom and prone to violence, a belief deeply ingrained not only on the European side of the Atlantic. It thus helped to consolidate the Huntingtonian dystopia of the 'West against the Rest' (Huntington 1993, 1996) as part of the collective political imagination. On the elite level, it reinvigorated the debate about the integration of the growing Muslim community into European society, the results of which are yet to be seen.

In sum, examples like the Paris riots and the cartoon controversy provide evidence for what one may call a repoliticization of religion in Europe in a 'narrow' sense. Religion, in the form of Islamist fundamentalism, remains a top priority on the European agenda, and European leaders are prepared to use fears in European society and a growing sense of Islamophobia for political purposes. However, European elites have done so without challenging the secular cornerstones of the European political project. The refusal of a reference to Christianity in the preamble of the constitutional treaty underlines this point. Even in the face of a considerable challenge such as Islamist fundamentalism, the political integration of European society remains an essentially secular undertaking. To further increase the credibility of the EU in that regard, many European politicians and intellectuals have called for the inclusion of Turkey into the Union. This move would shield the EU against the charges of being a de facto 'Christian club' and establish the Union as a truly multicultural and multireligious 'bridge-builder' between the Orient and the Occident.

8.2.3. US-AMERICAN AND EUROPEAN SOCIETY AND THE CHALLENGE OF ISLAMIST FUNDAMENTALISM

This section has sketched ongoing trends in American and European societies, which are difficult to assess at this point in time. It would therefore be misplaced to draw overly specific conclusions. However, it does seem safe to assert that the Huntingtonian assessment of a 'clash of civilizations', and especially its crude dystopia of a Western 'showdown' with Islam, assumes a front place in both popular political cultures. The American-led 'war on terrorism', initiated by an administration headed by a born-again Christian and legitimated by a radicalized quasi-religious ideology, runs the risk of solidifying this horrific scenario. The internal dimension of this campaign seems to cast blanket suspicion on Muslim Americans (American Civil Liberties Union 2004) while, externally, predominantly Muslim countries such as Afghanistan, Iraq, and Iran are targeted. This is not to deny that the administration of George W. Bush has made gestures of goodwill toward the Muslim community. The *Iftaar* dinners at the White House to which Muslim leaders are invited are a case in point. However, instances like the 2003 dinner show how Bush's dealings with the Christian right undermine these efforts. That year, several Muslim leaders declined the invitation in protest over Bush's handling of the Boykin controversy. Lt. Gen. William Boykin, the Pentagon's Deputy Undersecretary of Defense for Intelligence, had been criticized for publicly depicting the 'war on terrorism' as forming part of an ongoing battle with Satan, and for his assertion that the Christian faith is superior to Islam.

In European society, the cartoon controversy nurtured preexisting fears of Islamism and Muslim 'parallel societies'. However, the fact that the cartoon riots had to be deliberately triggered and orchestrated should not be seen as evidence of the existence of the Muslim community as a coherent, politically active, and overly sensitive transnational community, let alone of Islam as a unitary actor as Huntington assumes. It does show, however, that it can be instantiated under certain circumstances. As a consequence, a 'clash of civilizations' between Islam and the two variants of Western civilization embodied in US-American and European society remains unlikely and certainly far from inevitable. After all, civilizations are far from being unitary actors or, to use Huntington's metaphor, 'tectonic plates' destined to collide due to *exogenous* forces beyond their control. Yet given sufficiently powerful *endogenous* trends and forces, such highly suggestive imagery does have the potential to be turned into a self-fulfilling prophecy. Indeed, trends pointing in this direction are observable in American and European societies as the rise of Islamophobia suggests. The increasing political importance of Christian fundamentalism in the United States is another worrisome development, though its salience may decrease somewhat after the presidency of George W. Bush. In any case, at this point in time, both American and European societies have all the means at their disposal to prevent those forces from within from realizing this bleak scenario.

8.3. **Two models of Christianity**

Alexis de Tocqueville observed that religion, freedom, and democracy are seen as intrinsically connected to each other in the United States, whereas this link is much more ambivalent in Europe. This section summarizes similarities and differences in church–society–state relations in Europe and the United States and argues that religious practices tend to be 'post-Durkheimian' in the former and 'neo-Durkheimian' in the latter.

Since the French Revolution, a European political tradition emerged, which tends to portray religion, especially Catholicism, as antidemocratic and at odds with personal freedom. In this line of thinking, one can argue that 'post-Christian Europe' (Anderson 2004) derives its secularism from the dominant 'French version' of Enlightenment, which sees religion as irrational and outdated, whereas the US-American Enlightenment modernized religion and established it as an essential part of modernity. This is reflected in the fact that a highly individualized society like the United States also displays high levels of religiosity, whereas in Europe increasing individualism tends to weaken religiosity, and most of all church membership.

The main divergence lies in the US-American tradition of denominations, that is the idea that none of the many Christian religions can claim to be the only true faith. Denominations modernized American religious life quite early and led to the institutionalization of religious tolerance. This process, coupled with the lower impact of secular intellectuals, stabilized a religious plural society (Berger 2004). In this regard, the institutionalization of religiosity is rather dissimilar in America and Europe, although this can be seen as different reactions to a common trend toward more individualism (Berger 2004). In the United States, individual spiritual needs are being met by the extraordinarily large variety of denominations; in contrast, European individualism displays the tendency to express spirituality outside any church.

Nonetheless, the differences in substance between the two societies, especially in regard to the role of religion in public life, are considerable. These divergences are epitomized in the simple fact that Europe is largely a Catholic society, whereas the United States is a Protestant one. One should not engage too much in religious stereotyping, but it may be no coincidence that Catholic Europe has gone especially far in recognizing its past 'sinfulness' in respect to its history of religious violence. On the other side of the Atlantic, the predominantly Protestant United States sees its prosperity as a sign of 'divine providence' and as an incentive to assert the universal rightfulness of its belief.

In addition to these divergences in church–society relations the church–state relations are different as well. The fundamental contrast between the United States and Europe is *not* the separation between church and state, as this can be observed in both societies. In terms of long-term historical trends, it can be observed that in the United States, the separation between church and state was implemented early and has remained relatively stable. This division generated the somewhat paradoxical effect that religious narratives, symbolism, and rhetoric remain an important part of America's political life. The heterogeneous relation between the churches and the states in Europe, which often erupted in devastating warfare, put a taboo on the intrusion of religious discourses into the national political systems and the supranational and intergovernmental project of European integration.

Yet the growing structural similarities are obvious: with the unification of Europe, the EU increasingly resembles the United States when it was founded. It was the highly diverse setting of different state–religion relations in the countries of Europe that contributed to the strong separation between Europe as a political organization and its different churches. This can be seen in the aforementioned debate about a reference to Christianity in the European Constitution.

In view of these similarities and differences, how did the trends analyzed above influence the reaction to the rise of militant Islamist fundamentalism? In both the United States and Europe, a repoliticization of religion took place in the aftermath of 9/11, although in different ways. This trend mainly manifests itself through a radicalization of civil religious discourse in the United States, and a growing willingness to exploit heightened fears of Islam for political purposes in Europe.

But it is not only the changing function of Christianity in both societies which defies simple conclusions. The analytical construct of civil religion shows that the political use of religious symbols is, of course, related to, but also distinct from religion. As suggested above, the religious conduct of Americans after 9/11 soon went back to 'normal', that is back to the patterns before this event. It was the civil religion that changed more permanently, and it was this change in political discourse and the policies it legitimated that contributed to the alienation between Europe and the United States.

Contrary to traditional patterns in both societies, different forms of fundamentalism, mainly Christian and Islamic, are increasing. The highly individualized societies in Europe and the United States have no means to stop people from acting according to their individual religious beliefs in the public sphere. Hence the increasing demands for the 'deprivatization of religion' (Casanova 1994), be it the intrusion of Christian fundamentalism into school boards to promote 'nonevolutionary' approaches in biology or the attempts to display private religious symbols in schools.

In addition to these endogenous trends in church–state–society relations, the (re-)politicization of religion, that is its reinsertion into the public sphere in Europe and its increasingly powerful articulation in US-American society, is also due to exogenous factors. Post–9/11 discourse on Muslim minorities is drifting toward latent Islamophobia in both societies. Despite this converging trend, which is fueled by the construction of a common enemy, the different traditions of religious–political discourses in the United States and Europe have generated different reactions and legitimization strategies in the 'war on terrorism'. This is likely to remain an important source of tension in transatlantic relations for the years to come.

In this chapter, we suggested that recent trends in American politics should be understood within the context of shifting patterns of America's civil religion. While the often-cited influence of Christian fundamentalism should not be downplayed, it is important to see that the US-American reaction to Islamic fundamentalism is not simply a 'clash of fundamentalisms'. The Christian right is of course well organized and wields considerable political power, but it is also constrained by its integration into the larger structure of American democracy and its civil religious creed (Leggewie 2005).

Charles Taylor famously suggested that the patterns of religious practices in Europe tend to be 'post-Durkheimian' as opposed to 'neo-Durkheimian' ones in the United States (Taylor 2002). Europe is post-Durkheimian because religion no longer functions as the main structure of meaning in which society or the nation-state expresses itself. In contrast, the United States possesses neo-Durkheimian qualities, as the radically individualized Christianity of the majority of Americans is used to express the commonality of all Americans. These developments in both societies represent idiosyncratic reactions to the common challenges of modernity.

9 Cities

Patrick Le Galès and Mathieu Zagrodzki

From the integrated medieval European cities surrounded by walls, to the colonial Boston or the rapidly growing Phoenix, Las Vegas, or South East London, the category 'city' comprises different densities, borders, and dimensions; for instance: *the material city* of walls, squares, houses, roads, lights, utilities, buildings, waste, and physical infrastructure; *the cultural city* in terms of imagination, difference, representations, ideas, symbols, art, texts, senses, religion, and aesthetics; *the politics and policies of the city* in terms of domination, power, government, mobilization, welfare, and education; *the social city* of riots, ethnic, economic, or gender inequalities, everyday life and social movements; *the economy of the city*: division of labor, scale, production, consumption, trade . . . . Urban areas are robust beasts. Despite ups and downs, contrasting evolution over time, most of them have considerable amounts of resources which have been accumulated and which, in due course, may be mobilized for a new period of growth. This does not exclude periods or sequences of rapid changes, but less often.

Comparing US and European cities is a classic exercise of urban sociology. Urban sociology has long privileged analytical models of the convergence of cities, either based on models of urban ecology inspired by writers from the University of Chicago, or in the context of the Marxist and neo-Marxist tradition that privileges the decisive influence of uneven development and capitalism on social structures, modes of government, and urban policies. This tradition is still alive and constitutes an important body of research about global cities (Sassen 1991), metropolises, and flows (Castells 1996). This implicit convergence is massively at play in the postmodernist representation of fragmented incoherent urban space and is widespread all over the world (Scott and Soja 1996). In theoretical terms, if the urban is growing everywhere, there are several urban models different types of social, political, cultural, and economic structures. That does not mean that all these models will not follow the same path to some extent. The comparison between European and American cities in this chapter is done in this spirit.

There is however now a clear move in urban sociology to deal at the same time with issues of convergence related in one way or another to globalization issues (see the excellent collection edited by Marcuse and Van Kempen 2000). Any analysis of cities faces the challenge of taking into account at the same time the dynamics of the cities, often in comparative terms, at the risk of neglecting their profound embeddedness within national societies. Within the European context, the issue is particularly important as the category 'European cities' was coined for the Middle Ages, but vanished later as national states became the main crucible for the forming of societies, meaning national societies. For more than a century, in some cases much longer, the concept of European cities was illustrated by the aggregation of Finnish, British, Spanish, German, Italian, Dutch, and French cities. Only the creation of the EU and erosion of national societies allowed the category 'European cities' to make sense again (see Le Galès 2002). European societies have been, in particular, characterized by the following features: the institutionalization of social and economic life, the importance of the state and the welfare state in particular, the territorialization of the economy, politics, and society. American cities and metropolises are by contrast part of the remarkable success story of the United States over the past two centuries, part of a highly mobile and less hierarchized society where a powerful state has traditionally played a more regulatory than redistributive role, where privatism largely exceeds the public domain, and where the common good is understood more in terms of aggregation of individual interests than a holistic general interest in the European context.

After comparing the creation of the urban map in the two continents, the chapter then characterizes recent urban growth but emphasizes the contrasting dynamics of cities and metropolises. Two points are explored further, economic dynamics and ethnic dynamics. By contrast, key issues of social segregation, social structure, and urban politics are not addressed for lack of comparative data and lack of space.

Overall the chapter argues that in the United States and Europe, cities and metropolises are back in town.

9.1. **Robust ancient European cities versus dynamic American metropolises**

In the nineteenth and twentieth centuries, the contrast between 'new America' and 'old Europe' was particularly striking in urban matters. The understanding of cities usually relies both on long-term change and evolution on the one hand, and massive surge and rapid growth cycle on the other. Most sociologists of the time contrasted not only US and European cities but more importantly the new huge metropolises (Paris, London, Berlin, and Vienna) with the old medieval 'European' city.

9.1.1. MEDIEVAL EUROPEAN CITIES AND COLONIAL AMERICAN CITIES

The urban map of Europe has been mainly structured by three influences: the trade-led development of the Middle Ages (Table 9.1) and Renaissance, the State, and the Industrial Revolution.

Table 9.1. European cities in 1400 (based on Hohenberg and Lees 1992)

City	Population
Paris	275,000
Milan	125,000
Bruges	125,000
Venice	100,000
Granada	100,000
Genoa	100,000

In Western Europe, cities emerged at the turn of the first millennium, insinuating themselves into the gaps of the feudal system. In *The City*, Max Weber portrays the medieval Western city as having the following characteristics: a fortification, a market, and a specifically urban economy of consumption, exchange, and production; a court of law and the ability to ordain a set of rules and laws; rules relating to landed property (since cities were not subjected to the taxes and constraints of feudalism); a structure based on associations (of guilds) and—at least partial—political autonomy, expressed in particular through the existence of an administrative body and the participation of the burghers in local government, and sometimes even through the existence of an army and an actual policy of foreign expansion; and citizenship associated with affiliation to a guild and with relative freedom.

The medieval city was the crucible of European societies, in which new cultural and political models developed, along with new social relations and cultural and organizational innovations, furthered by interactions between the various populations thus promoting mechanisms for learning a collective way of life, for innovation and spreading innovation, rapid accumulation, transformation of behaviors, interplay of competition and cooperation, and processes of social differentiation engendered by proximity. The Europe of cities was not just the Europe of early capitalism and of merchants, but also the Europe of intellectuals, universities, and culture which launched the Renaissance. The current urban map of Europe massively reflects this Europe of cities which then grew progressively, and are even now at the forefront of urban growth in Europe (Le Galès 2002). The great age of European cities and the relative stability of the urban system (what Cattan, Pumain, and Rozenblat (1999) call 'metastability') therefore constitute a specific feature of European cities.

9.1.2. US COLONIAL CITIES

Urban United States started with the first settlements on the East Coast. The first cities emerged and started to develop with immigration and the early days of industrialization. During the eighteenth century, the first American cities were organized by Britain, France, or even Spain as part of their respective colonial empire and hence organized around their military and economic requirements.

Table 9.2. 1820: Five leading colonial cities

New York	152,000
Philadelphia	65,000
Baltimore	63,000
Boston	43,000
New Orleans	27,000

British trade dynamism in particular guaranteed the rapid expansion of its American cities. New York had about 33,000 inhabitants in 1790, but 515,500 in 1850 and similarly Baltimore grew from 135,000 to 169,000 (Table 9.2). In relation to trade, wealth had accumulated over the eighteenth century and the revolutionary war against the British Empire was started and financed by the bourgeoisie of the main cities, Boston to start with. However, in comparative terms, those cities of a new country were far behind their European counterparts in terms of size and development ... but not for long.

As Gottdiener and Hutchinson (2006) remind us, the colonial period had in particular three major consequences for American cities which sharply contrast with their European counterparts: (*a*) the absence of city walls, that is the fact that locations within and beyond the city were remarkably free of various constraints; (*b*) the absence of independent economic privileges or rights specific to the city and therefore the freedom for various groups to split for whatever reasons and to develop new settlements, hence a pattern of fragmentation, privatism, and weak political power attached to the city to this day; and (*c*) the crucial role of land development: the fact that land was so freely available and cheap and the competition between coalitions or networks to organize land development were a major source of wealth creation, and a distinctive pattern of boosterism, i.e. of creation of new towns in the expansion of the American West.

9.1.3. INDUSTRIAL DEVELOPMENT AND MASSIVE IMMIGRATION IN EUROPE AND THE UNITED STATES

The Industrial Revolution led to the formation of industrial societies and a new wave of urbanization (Table 9.3). Concentration in great metropolises and large industrial areas lent a different dynamic to cities, changing them both socially and physically: a new type of industrial city emerged in the nineteenth century—most often around coal mining, textiles, or iron and steel, then later chemicals, electricity, and mechanical engineering—enjoying an extraordinarily rapid growth fueled by immigration. This led to very dense industrial regions and industrial centers in Britain, the northeast of the United States, the German Ruhr or the northeast of France, 'Coketowns' as Mumford (1961) put it. The 'tyranny of fixed cost' (transport) also supported the rise of industrial ports, the creation of canals and railways, and the pace of concentration in large industrial cities both in the

Table 9.3. European cities during the Industrial Revolution (1850)

City	Population
1. London	2,320,000
2. Paris	1,314,000
3. St Petersburg	502,000
4. Berlin	446,000
5. Vienna	426,000
6. Liverpool	422,000
7. Naples	416,000
8. Manchester	412,000
9. Moscow	373,000
10. Glasgow	346,000
11. Birmingham	294,000
12. Dublin	263,000
13. Madrid	263,000
14. Lisbon	257,000
15. Lyon	254,000

UK and in Germany, as well as in large US cities from the East Coast, such as New York, but most importantly the Midwestern Great Lake cities such as Chicago, Pittsburgh or Cleveland, and Detroit. Cities became places where capital was tied up in major fixed assets, with labor forces that varied in composition and size, and with a high level of internal diversity. Phenomenal urban growth first in Manchester (UK) and then in Chicago made those cities the ideal types of this new breed of cities.

At the time of massive expansion of industrial capitalism, in two very different contexts, the creation of the urban map followed very similar lines in both the United States and Europe—a mix of industrialization and immigration. In both cases, the impact was massive in some parts of the continent (northwest Europe and northeast United States) but was only one influence to have a lasting impact on cities and metropolises on both sides of the Atlantic.

9.1.4. DEVELOPMENT, DIVERSIFICATION, SPECIALIZATION: THE RISE OF TWENTIETH-CENTURY METROPOLIS

For observers of the late nineteenth, early twentieth century (Simmel in particular), the development of large cities and metropolises is a major phenomenon, both in Europe and then in the United States, as centers of experiment in

Table 9.4. US 1870: six big cities

New York	1,478,000
Philadelphia	674,000
St Louis	311,000
Chicago	299,000 (but 2,701 million in 1920)
Baltimore	267,000
Boston	251,000

Table 9.5. Population of European capital cities and major US cities in the nineteenth century

	1800	1910
Vienna	231,000	2 million
Berlin	172,000	2.071 million
Prague	70,000	0.6 million
Paris	835,000 (1831 estimate)	2.888 million
London	959,000	4.522 million
The United States	1820	1920
New York	123,700	5,620,000
Chicago		2,701,000
Philadelphia	63,800	1,823,800
Detroit		993,100
Cleveland		796,000

Sources: Moriconi-Ebrard (2000) and Hohenberg and Lees (1992), and Gottdiener and Hutchinson using Campbell Gibson (1998)

modern lives. Although this trend was at work on both continents, the major contrast remained central.

Capital cities in Europe in particular benefited from the consolidation of states, the shift of political life onto the national level, and the strengthening of the capacity of states—and therefore bureaucracies, including the army—for control, as well as from industrial development and colonization. They absorbed a large part of the flow of migration, thus providing sizable reserves of labor. They were the first beneficiaries of the transport revolution, from tramways to road and rail networks. Opening up to the world in an era that saw increasing numbers of different kinds of exchanges, discoveries, and technical innovations, they established their role by organizing universal exhibitions and great fairs. Concerned with public health and safety, governments organized major improvement works, created wide avenues, and constructed new public buildings; stations, squares, and monuments that symbolized their dynamism and technical progress. These cities were also places of speculation, public and private investment in housing, and financial capital. Their cultural influence changed scale because of more rapid diffusion, transport, and colonial empires. London, Paris, Berlin, and Vienna in particular were the theatre of extraordinary physical and cultural transformations. As university cities and cultural centers, they were the focus of unrest and the sites of the political and social revolts that punctuated the nineteenth century. The great metropolis became the site of consumption, department stores and wide avenues; overstimulation which changed the urban cultural experience. This led also to physical transformation with the ever-increasing diffusion of urbanization around these large metropolises, hence the rise of suburbs, either working class ones the red belt in Paris or bourgeois suburbs where the middle classes abandoned the center. At that time, Chicago, Detroit, or Cleveland were small places, with under 10,000 inhabitants.

The figures give a sense of the phenomenal rise and dissemination of the large metropolis model which became an American feature (Table 9.5): New York,

Chicago, and later Los Angeles in particular gradually replaced European cities in the urban imagination of the modernist metropolis. They grew thanks to stunning economic development and massive immigration.

9.2. City versus metropolis

One way to think about urban development in the United States and Europe alike is to defend the idea of the end of cities and the triumph of urban sprawl; in other words the suburbanization of cities and the urbanization of suburbs, what Dear and his colleagues in Los Angeles sometimes call the Los Angelization of the world (2000). This makes sense as suburbs are more and more diverse in the United States and cases of sprawls are rapidly growing in Europe . . . but that does not undermine the strength of cities. 'Sprawl is a land development pattern that spreads residential units over a large area . . . sprawl also encompasses the separation of residential from commercial land uses, the absence of clustered development of town centers, and reliance on the automobile' (Dreier, Mollenkopf, and Swanstromm 2005: 59). In that line of analysis, the dissolution of the city is taking place within a large fragmented, chaotic, and unstable urban world.

Let us first look at figures for cities and metropolitan areas on the two continents.

9.2.1. CONTRASTING URBANIZATION IN THE UNITED STATES AND EUROPE

At first glance, two features make those two continents more or less comparable. First, both continents are now massively urbanized, more than 80 percent of inhabitants live in cities. As shown in previous figures, the dynamics are staggering in the US case while more progressive in the European case. For most Southern European countries and some Nordic European countries, general urbanization only took place in the postwar period, while rural populations and interests were still very strong and organized. Second, if one takes as a measure, the number of urban agglomerations comprising more than a million inhabitants, one will find a more or less comparable number of urban agglomerations, around thirty-five (Table 9.6). However, this does not suffice, and those averages mask profound differences.

Europe and the United States are distinct not only because of the 'longue durée' of European cities but also the relative stability of the urban map made of medium-sized cities. Beyond London and Paris, other European cities of this size are rare. Thanks to their work in building databases on European and world cities (Moriconi-Ebrard 1993), Cattan et al. are able to highlight the factors that distinguish Europe. With a degree of urbanization comparable to that of the United States, Europe is characterized first by its very large number of cities and

Table 9.6. Fifty largest US (2000) and European cities (2003)

Rank	City	Population (census 2000)	Rank	City	Country	Population (2003)
1	New York	8,008,278	1	London	UK	7,074,000
2	Los Angeles	3,694,820	2	Berlin	Germany	3,387,000
3	Chicago	2,896,016	3	Madrid	Spain	2,824,000
4	Houston	1,953,631	4	Rome	Italy	2,649,000
5	Philadelphia	1,517,550	5	Paris	France	2,152,000
6	Phoenix	1,321,045	6	Hamburg	Germany	1,705,000
7	San Diego	1,223,400	7	Vienna	Austria	1,540,000
8	Dallas	1,188,580	8	Barcelona	Spain	1,455,000
9	San Antonio	1,144,646	9	Milan	Italy	1,306,000
10	Detroit	951,270	10	Munchen	Germany	1,195,000
11	San Jose	894,943	11	Naples	Italy	1,047,000
12	Indianapolis	791,926	12	Birmingham	UK	1,021,000
13	San Francisco	776,733	13	Köln	Germany	963,000
14	Jacksonville	735,617	14	Turin	Italy	921,000
15	Columbus	711,470	15	Marseille	France	800,000
16	Austin	656,562	16	Athens	Greece	772,000
17	Baltimore	651,154	17	Salonika	Greece	749,000
18	Memphis	650,100	18	Stockholm	Sweden	744,000
19	Milwaukee	596,974	19	Valencia	Spain	736,000
20	Boston	589,141	20	Amsterdam	The Netherlands	729,000
21	Washington, DC	572,059	21	Leeds	UK	727,000
22	Nashville-Davidson	569,891	22	Seville	Spain	695,000
23	El Paso	563,662	23	Palermo	Italy	689,000
24	Seattle	563,374	24	Genova	Italy	656,000
25	Denver	554,636	25	Frankfurt/Main	Germany	644,000
26	Charlotte	540,828	26	Glasgow	UK	616,000
27	Fort Worth	535,694	27	Saragossa	Spain	601,000
28	Portland	529,121	28	Essen	Germany	600,000
29	Oklahoma City	506,132	29	Rotterdam	The Netherlands	593,000
30	Tucson	486,699	30	Dortmund	Germany	590,000
31	New Orleans	484,674	31	Stuttgart	Germany	582,000
32	Las Vegas	478,434	32	Düsseldorf	Germany	569,000
33	Cleveland	478,403	33	Lisbon	Portugal	563,000
34	Long Beach	461,522	34	Helsinki	Finland	549,000
35	Albuquerque	448,607	35	Malaga	Spain	543,000
36	Kansas City	441,545	36	Bremen	Germany	540,000
37	Fresno	427,652	37	Sheffield	UK	530,000
38	Virginia Beach	425,257	38	Duisburg	Germany	520,000
39	Atlanta	416,474	39	Hanover	Germany	515,000
40	Sacramento	407,018	40	Oslo	Norway	505,000
41	Oakland	399,484	41	Copenhagen	Denmark	499,000
42	Mesa	396,375	42	Leipzig	Germany	490,000
43	Tulsa	393,049	43	Nuremberg	Germany	487,000
44	Omaha	390,007	44	Bradford	UK	483,000
45	Minneapolis	382,618	45	Dublin	Ireland	482,000
46	Honolulu	371,657	46	Dresden	Germany	477,000
47	Miami	362,470	47	Liverpool	UK	468,000
48	Colorado Springs	360,890	48	Antwerpen	Belgium	468,000
49	St Louis	348,189	49	Gothenburg	Sweden	462,000
50	Wichita	344,284	50	Edinburgh	UK	449,000

Sources: US Census Bureau, www.citymayors.com

Table 9.7. Fifty largest US and European metropolitan areas in 2000

Rank	Metropolitan area	Population	Rank	Metropolitan area	Population
1	New York	21,199,865	1	Essen	9,962,743
2	Los Angeles	16,373,645	2	Paris	9,849,666
3	Chicago	9,157,540	3	London	9,160,487
4	Washington	7,608,070	4	Madrid	4,658,427
5	San Francisco	7,039,362	5	Brussels	4,423,523
6	Philadelphia	6,188,463	6	Barcelona	3,988,393
7	Boston	5,819,100	7	Manchester	3,976,124
8	Detroit	5,456,428	8	Milan	3,890,644
9	Dallas	5,221,801	9	Berlin	3,755,223
10	Houston	4,669,571	10	Athens	3,349,716
11	Atlanta	4,112,198	11	Rotterdam	3,116,490
12	Miami	3,876,380	12	Naples	2,973,487
13	Seattle	3,554,760	13	Rome	2,897,788
14	Phoenix	3,251,876	14	Birmingham	2,456,183
15	Minneapolis	2,968,806	15	Lisbon	2,344,824
16	Cleveland	2,945,831	16	Hamburg	2,195,830
17	San Diego	2,813,833	17	Vienna	1,928,221
18	St Louis	2,603,607	18	Lille	1,800,000
19	Denver	2,581,506	19	Kortrijk	1,696,813
20	San Juan	2,450,292	20	Leeds	1,659,893
21	Tampa	2,395,997	21	Munich	1,576,104
22	Pittsburgh	2,358,695	22	Frankfurt am Main	1,439,695
23	Portland	2,265,223	23	Lyon	1,416,093
24	Cincinnati	1,979,202	24	Turin	1,400,320
25	Sacramento	1,796,857	25	Copenhagen	1,396,666
26	Kansas City	1,776,062	26	Marseille	1,354,571
27	Milwaukee	1,689,572	27	Stockholm	1,346,291
28	Orlando	1,644,561	28	Valence	1,332,319
29	Indianapolis	1,607,486	29	Glasgow	1,317,411
30	San Antonio	1,592,383	30	Porto	1,258,077
31	Norfolk	1,569,541	31	Stuttgart	1,210,544
32	Las Vegas	1,563,282	32	Douai	N/A
33	Columbus	1,540,157	33	Peruwelz	1,202,742
34	Charlotte	1,499,293	34	Newcastle	1,178,500
35	New Orleans	1,337,726	35	Amsterdam	1,158,310
36	Salt Lake City	1,333,914	36	Bielefeld	1,118,606
37	Greensboro	1,251,509	37	Seville	1,050,941
38	Austin	1,249,763	38	Helsinki	1,037,958
39	Nashville	1,231,311	39	Zurich	985,624
40	Providence	1,188,613	40	Dublin	978,282
41	Raleigh	1,187,941	41	Bilboa	944,527
42	Hartford	1,183,110	42	Florence	924,858
43	Buffalo	1,170,111	43	Southampton	904,278
44	Memphis	1,135,614	44	Nice	893,366
45	West Palm Beach	1,131,184	45	Mannheim	891,244
46	Jacksonville	1,100,491	46	Bremen	838,710
47	Rochester	1,098,201	47	Genes	826,163
48	Grand Rapids	1,088,514	48	Salonika	805,645
49	Oklahoma City	1,083,346	49	Oslo	778,998
50	Louisville	1,025,598	50	Toulouse	775,512

Sources: US Census Bureau, Moriconi-Ebrard (2000), and Géopolis data-base

their marked proximity to one another (Cattan et al. 1999: 23); second, by the fact that the major cities of Europe are not huge: large metropolises with a population of over 2 or 3 million are rare (Table 9.7), and 'if one compares the total number of urban areas of over 200,000, the average size is of the order of 800,000 in Europe, as against 1.3 million in the United States and Japan ... the top thirty American cities are markedly larger than the top thirty European cities' (Cattan et al. 1994: 26); and third, by the relative importance of small and medium-sized cities: Europe distinguishes itself by its relatively large number of urban areas of between 200,000 and 1 or 2 million. In 1990, the EU contained 225 urban areas of 200,000 or more, 40 or so of these exceeding 1 million and a very small number exceeding 2 million.

Given that to some extent size goes with social, political, and economic diversity and complexity, these facts provide a very important contextual element for the analysis of European cities: one that is accounted for partly by the age of cities that came into being before the development of different forms of transport. The relatively stable core of Europe's urban system is made up of medium-sized and reasonably large cities, which are fairly close to one another, and a few metropolises. This importance of regional capital cities, of medium-sized cities (200,000 to 2 million inhabitants), remains a major feature of contemporary European societies (Therborn 1985; Crouch 1999). But are those features under threat?

9.2.2. CITY VERSUS METROPOLIS: THE LOS ANGELIZATION OF THE WORLD?

In the 1970s, cities in the United States and Europe, like many cities and urban areas lost population and were destined to disappear. Many prophets, including sociologists announced the end of cities as we knew it; the coming age of a post-city era, or the final crisis of cities organized by capitalism.

The loss of population includes two different phenomenons: (*a*) the departure of populations from both the city and metropolitan area because of deindustrialization, for instance, or the decline of the city because of suburbanization, and (*b*) the rise of the metropolitan area (Paris, Brussels, Milan, Marseille, or Lisbon for instance). Again, similar dynamics in the two continents had very different outcomes.

'Born to run' Americans left the cities in huge numbers for the suburbs but also the industrial northeast, where 'born to stay' Europeans only left the more industrial cities to a lesser extent. Those individual choices are largely influenced by collective strategies: European welfare states and urban policies contributed to the regeneration and quick growth of medium-sized cities when the absence of regional or urban policy and a less generous welfare state encouraged adjustments by mobility.

In the European context, the economic crisis of the 1970s marked the decline of the once symbol of economic development: industrial cities. Large-scale economic restructuring processes took place and contributed to the relative or absolute decline of the most industrial regions, particularly the oldest, and of industrial ports. Northern cities in the UK in particular lost hundreds of thousands of inhabitants. The decline was even more pronounced in small industrial cities. They all experienced the effects of deindustrialization, the urban crisis, loss of population (especially the most highly skilled), and the departure of firms, followed by attempts to renew the fabric of enterprise, either by attracting businesses or by creating them (see the Urban Audit 2000). The scale of urban decline was extensive in UK cities, industrial Belgian cities, Rurh Germany, industrial harbors, and in the industrial triangle of northwest Italy.

However, this was not the dominant pattern for European cities: industrialization and then deindustrialization were important dynamics but overall represented a parenthesis in the structuring of urban Europe. The powerful images of urban decay together with the dominance of British literature gave the overall impression that cities were in decline across Europe. Also, beyond the urban industrial crisis, the rise of post-1968 antiurban ideology by the European greens and the left gave rise to powerful images of the coming age of a post-city period. Numerous accounts of the 'end of the city' prophecy developed all over Europe, for example in the north in relation to ecological disasters or the final crisis of capitalism.

From the 1960s onwards, the American debate on cities has also been dominated by the image of a crisis which links three elements. Cities like St Louis, Pittsburgh, and Philadelphia have lost more than half of their population, a figure which in Europe is only comparable to the worst British cases of urban decline—Liverpool, Manchester, Glasgow—and hardly known elsewhere on the western part of the continent.

First, the image of the urban crisis was shaped by the series of riots in the 1960s in New York, Los Angeles, and a few others. The obsession with race became even more central in urban America. The question of the ghetto, ethnic, and spatial segregation of the black population became fundamental. Second, the industrial economic crisis led to the accelerated decline of industrial cities from the northeast which has been underlined. The classic image of the metropolis/city in the United States became associated with crime, social problems, and violence. The departure or collapse of firms led to major financial difficulties epitomized by the bankruptcy of New York in the 1970s. Third, the state-supported boom of new houses in suburbs fed the 'white flight', the massive suburbanization of the United States—what observers have called the rise of 'edge cities'. White middle classes fled from the inner cities and the metropolis for either the suburbs or rapidly growing cities in the south and the west, leaving the Rust Belt. The cultural divide between city and suburb grew, and the political support for the needs of cities and their poorer inhabitants declined. After Nixon declared that the urban crisis was over, the 1970s and 1980s became a period of increasing cuts for urban and social policies; in other words another transfer of resources at the expense of the poorest.

The gloomy picture of the marginalization of cities and metropolises remained both politically and empirically accurate in the 1980s in the United States when booming cities were at last identified in the European context. By the 1980s, there

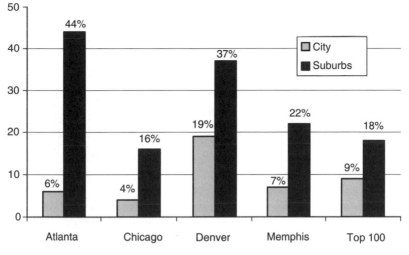

Figure 9.1. Cities' and suburbs' population growth, 1990–2000

Source: US Census Bureau, Brookings Institution

was a remarkable revival of not only large but also medium-sized, classic European cities and urban agglomerations, regional capitals for instance, in particular in northern Europe, the Netherlands, parts of Germany, France, Austria, and to a lesser extent in Italy, and only much later in the UK. On average, this dynamic was marked by one feature which confused many analysts: the growth concerned both city and urban agglomeration. In most cities, urban growth took the dynamics of suburbanization. However, in most cases the city center also enjoyed growth or gentle decline, in marked difference with the UK and the United States. Timing is essential here: by the late 1980s, medium-sized European cities/urban agglomerations were enjoying growth and dynamism while gloom prevailed in the American context. In the United States the 1990s presented the strongest urban growth (Figure 9.1) in four decades (Katz 2005). Urban America was striking back; for the first time in decades, the census showed the revival of urban agglomerations: cities are back in town.

The contrast is, of course, not just about the timing: the remarkable feature of Europe was the long-term stability, that is the revival of medieval cities or regional and national capitals with a strong identification and public role for the city center. By contrast in the United States, beyond New York and Los Angeles, the fastest growing cities and urban agglomerations are to be found in the sunbelt—Las Vegas, Austin, Dallas, Atlanta, Miami, or Phoenix—which epitomize the urban growth of sprawled, polycentric, and low-density cities.

Increasing urban concentration has been accompanied by apparently inescapable, unlimited dispersal into conurbations and urban regions with fluctuating outlines. Cities have expanded, fragmented, and organized into networks like those in Northern Italy or the Netherlands, and this is said to be rendering traditional spatial representations obsolete. Many writers stress

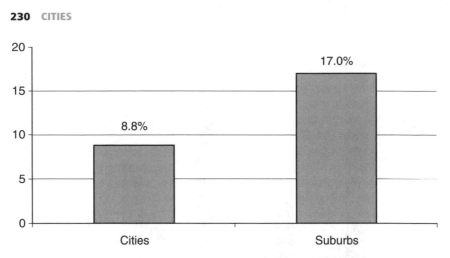

Figure 9.2. Population growth, 100 largest cities and suburbs, 1990–2000

Source: US Census Bureau, Brookings Institution

the unending extension of the suburbs, the development of 'non-places' (Augé 1992), anonymous similar urban spaces (motorway slip roads, shopping centers, residential developments, areas of commodified leisure facilities, car parks, railway stations, airports, office blocks, and leisure parks), and megalopolises ('post-cities') in different parts of the world. In short, this is the time of 'citizens without cities' (Agier 1999), where new forms and experiences are being invented.

Physically, the medieval European city was characterized by a citadel, an enclosing wall and marketplace, a built-up area around a focal point, administrative and public buildings, churches, monuments, squares, areas for commerce and trade, and development radiating out from the center revealing the centralization of power, the relative integration, if not coherence of the city; unlike American cities, which are organized around a geometric plan. The medieval city evolved little by little, partly as a result of the development of such towns and partly because walls and identifiable town boundaries gradually disappeared to make way for faubourgs, that is districts beyond the walls, and peripheral urban spaces.

By contrast, the US model was constructed around the industrial city with its low-income neighborhoods linked to manufacturing districts, and close to commercial cores and the middle-income neighborhoods beyond. The theme of the physical breakup of the city is classic in American literature, because of the exodus into residential suburbs (Figure 9.2) and the decline of the centers of big cities. This vision of breakup has been strengthened by the political marginalization of cities, the creation of fortified districts on their margin, and the development of secessionist movements, for example in Los Angeles or Toronto (Boudreau and Keil 2001). In the American experience, privately owned, fragmented technical networks have promoted urban sprawl and the breakup of cities, giving rise to urban regions with several focal points defined in contrast to the city center.

This built-up town model, characteristic of the medieval city, has not remained unchanged. The logic of the metropolis exerted a strong influence on the way in which the urban space broke up and became increasingly complex. Revolutions in technology, starting with roads and railways, had an impact on the development of cities and the forms they took. Finally, every state made its mark, in the shape of public buildings, networks, forms of urban planning, and the development of housing. It was a mark that varied considerably according to country: the ascendancy of the Jacobin French state, with its prefectures and stations, had little in common with that of Italian or Swedish states. Despite these significant differences, the historic center continues to hold meaning in most European cities and has preserved its traditional influence—for example, as a place for citizens to gather for protest meetings. The way authority is organized also still has meaning in relation to the center. European cities have remained relatively built-up in nature, even though important developments have taken place, and the imagined picture of the city is still a reality.

American cities were organized around a particular type of urban planning model, 'the grid', with low density, an essential role given to cars, zoning, and sur-burbanization. After 1945, mobility became even more the distinctive character-istic of Americans within a dynamic society where a large middle class was in the making. The postwar period marks the triumph of highways, trucks, flights, and air freight (Warner 1995). Moving people and commodities became inexpensive. The rise of ports and trading centers in all four corners of the United States led to major urban development. Progressively cities in the west and the south of the United States started to grow—Houston, Dallas, San Antonio but also Memphis, New Orleans, Seattle, Phoenix and Los Angeles. The rise of a large number of widespread metropolises was accompanied by the dispersal of population from the central city.

In the United States, the 1990s were characterized by the following elements: sprawl, continuous decline of the poorest industrial cities, and revival of central districts within metropolitan areas. Out of the suburban migration of the middle classes, accentuated after World War II, emerged the prototypical metropolis with its central city ringed by suburban enclaves. In the best cases, the commercial core became dominant. In the worst cases, along with manufacturing districts, it was in decline. The dynamics of development were horizontal, with activities deconcentrated and decentralized from the center, creating secondary centers in the urban region, hence the image of the polycentric metropolis.

The 1990s saw, as has been the case for at least fifty years, a continuous sprawl of metropolitan areas. A study of the fifty largest American cities during that period shows that they grew faster than in the 1970s and 1980s: 9.8 percent according to the 2000 census, whereas this rate was 6.3 percent in the 1980s and 1.6 percent in the 1970s. Several cities, such as Atlanta, Chicago, Denver, and Memphis, gained population after a decrease in the 1980s. Nevertheless, suburbs grew even faster: the population growth in the 100 largest cities during the 1990s was 8.8 percent, in the 100 largest suburbs it was 17 percent. In Atlanta for instance, the central city's population growth was 6 percent, and 44 percent in its suburbs. The analysis of the 2000 census for US cities with populations greater than 100,000 also reveals that the median growth rate for cities in the 1990s was 8.7 percent, more than double the median growth rate of the 1980s (Glaeser and Shapiro 2001). Old industrial metropolitan areas with high unemployment rates are growing slower and have not yet entirely recovered after a period of economic decline. By contrast, the cities with less social and economic problems are growing faster: levels of residents' education and income are consistent predictors of urban growth (Glaeser and Shapiro 2001). Also, foreign-born residents contributed to strong city growth rates. Manville and Storper (2005) rightly distinguish between two different processes: the return of metropolitan areas which had lost investment and population on the one hand, and the revival of central cities on the other. The return of various groups to city centres, and enjoying city life was seen as a major shift.

9.2.3. EUROPE: INCREASE OF SPRAWL BUT NOT THE DECLINE OF CITIES

The European context is shaped by a few declining cities, many dynamic medium-sized and large cities, and two dynamic, large, global cities, whatever that means.

European cities make a fairly general category of urban space, relatively original forms of compromise, and aggregation of interest and culture which brings together local social groups, associations, organized interests, private firms, and urban governments. The pressures created by property developers, major groups in the urban services sector, and cultural and economic globalization processes provoke reactions and adaptation processes of actors within European cities, defending the idea of a fairly particular type of city that is not yet in terminal decline. The modernized myth of the European city remains a very strongly mobilized resource, and is strengthened by growing political autonomy and transverse mobilizations.

The long-term metastability of the European urban structure has been central in the making and development of European societies but that does not lead to a conservative view of the urbanity of the European city—balanced, welcoming, innovative, and dynamic, isolated from any restructuring of the labor market, from globalization processes, social conflicts, reorganized power relations, new forms of domination, deregulation of transport, telecommunications, and energy services, as well as from pollution and from persistent and developing forms of poverty. This stability goes together with its original structure (the high concentration of medium-sized cities) and the remains of its physical form. European cities (if we set London and Paris apart), although they are gaining more autonomy, are still structured and organized within European states—in particular, welfare states. The ongoing restructuring process does represent a threat, but—for the time being—European cities are supported and to some extent protected by the state, including in terms of resources. European cities are becoming more European, in the sense that the institutionalization of the EU is creating rules, norms, procedures, repertoires, and public policies that have an impact on most, if not all, cities.

The EU also is a powerful agent of legitimation. By designing urban public policies and agreeing (under the influence of city interests) to mention the idea of 'a Europe of cities' as one of the components of the EU, it is giving a boost to cities to act and behave as actors within EU governance. This also, to some extent, leads other actors—for instance, firms—to take European cities more seriously. Another point relates to their economic and social structure. European cities are characterized by a mix of public services and private firms, including a robust body of middle-class and lower-middle-class public sector workers, who constitute a firm pillar of the social structure, despite increasing social tensions, inequalities, even riots at times. There is no ideal world of European cities but the remains of a less unequal social structure than in most cities in the world. The more important the welfare state and the scale of redistribution (northern Europe), the lesser the level of inequality and poverty. From the form of the city, the existence of public spaces, the mix of social groups, and despite powerful social segregation mechanisms, one can suggest the idea of continuing sense of 'urbanity' still characterizing European cities (Zijderveld 1998). Despite sprawling movements in most European cities, the resistance of the old city centers epitomizes their peculiarity. The example of large public collective transport (in particular the tramway) together with pedestrian areas and cycling paths to demonstrates the remaining strength of the idea of European cities. Finally, there is a continuing representation of the city as a whole; Crouch (1999) suggests a 'Durkheimian' view of the city which still exists in Europe. The increased legitimacy of political urban elites sustains and reinvents this presentation. European cities are still strongly regulated by public authorities and complex arrangements of public and private actors. European cities appear to be relatively robust, despite pressures from economic actors, individuals, and states (including welfare states) being reshaped within the EU. Processes of exclusion, strengthening and transformation of inequalities, segregation, and domination are also unfolding in these cities. The development of residential suburbs and polycentric cities separated from the city, the isolation of disadvantaged districts, the development of cultural complexes, leisure facilities, and shopping centers, as well as diverse cultural models and migrations, all clearly demonstrate the pressures exerted on the traditional medium-sized city. The urban regions of Milan in Italy or the Ranstadt (in the Netherlands) are good examples of a more polycentric structure and interdependent dynamics between the city center and other cities. Finally—and this point is vital to our analysis—actors within cities have been strongly mobilized to direct the future of cities.

Yet focusing on European cities today goes hand in hand with an analysis of forms of interdependence between scales, levels of government, multilevel strategies of social actors, and linkages between forms of mobility and local societies. It would be a vain exercise to work on European cities without applying oneself at all to the global strategies of major firms, from private developers to utilities and leisure firms, to the transnational communities that weave links on both sides of the Mediterranean or toward the Rast, to the competition rules drawn up and then imposed by the EU, or the restructuring of welfare states.

Since the mid-1980s, cities (those that are not old industrial cities), and above all the largest cities, have felt the full benefits of growth. In centralized countries, it seems to be mainly the region around the capital city that absorbs the strongest forces and economic dynamism: this is true not only of London, Paris, Rome, and Berlin, the capitals of the leading member-states, but also of Madrid, Dublin, Stockholm, Helsinki, Copenhagen, and Lisbon. In the lower echelons of the hierarchy of cities, some regional capitals and other medium-sized European cities have also experienced strong growth: Bologna, Strasbourg, Lyon, Grenoble, Nice, Montpellier, Toulouse, Bordeaux, Nantes, Rennes, Munich, Cologne, Frankfurt, Geneva, Valencia, Seville, Saragossa, Norwich, Bristol, Swindon, Leicester, and Turku. In some cases, however, economic dynamism has actually combined with population losses to release the grip previously exerted by certain metropolises; a development that has been particularly spectacular in Northern Italy, where medium-sized cities from Milan to Venice have seen very strong growth. A new feature has been that a number of cities have undergone economic development disconnected from the regions surrounding them. The movement of concentration/dispersal of activities favors smaller cities and rural spaces around cities. By contrast, others—especially smaller cities (which, from a French point of view, might be described as medium-sized cities)—are experiencing changes that tend more toward decline, as if regional metropolises in their turn are largely absorbing the economic dynamism of their region, as in Tuscany, Emilia-Romagna, Languedoc-Roussillon, and Midi-Pyrénées.

9.3. Economic dynamics and social structure: the coming of age of the global city?

In both Europe and the United States, the gloomy view of cities in the 1970s has now changed in favor of 'resurgent metropolis' and 'dynamic cities'. Two main factors have been put forward: the pressure of globalization processes and the need for agglomeration raised by new forms of economic development. On both sides of the Atlantic, issues of social segregation and immigration are central in the making of the urban fabric.

9.3.1. A NEW WAVE OF METROPOLIZATION OR THE COMING OF AGE OF THE GLOBAL CITY IN EUROPE AND THE UNITED STATES: ECONOMIC ENGINES OF CITIES

In Europe and in the United States alike, the rise of what was named global cities (Sassen 1991) associated to the rise of increasingly globalized capitalism became the new paradigm to analyze metropolises and their rise. Booming city centers, ambitious city center redevelopments, most spectacularly in New York, the rise and fall and rise again of large-scale office development projects, booming house prices and office prices, the demographic growth of the city centers—all those elements have signaled that something was going on in the largest and most powerful metropolises. Many observers have therefore taken globalization trends and increasing networks and exchanges as the main factor behind the resurgence of cities.

Urbanization is reaching a new high in the contemporary world with the rise of megacities above 15 million inhabitants, such as Calcutta, Los Angeles, Cairo, Tokyo, New York, Bombay, and Seoul. Beyond the modern metropolis, researchers try to make sense of those large urban areas: postmetropolises, global cities, and global city regions.

In Europe and the United States alike, the first point which took the analysts by surprise in the 1980s was the rise of the largest metropolises, what became known as the global cities. The Paris metropolitan area absorbed half the French population growth in the 1980s; London enjoyed accelerated growth while Los Angeles, Tokyo, and more spectacularly New York, enjoyed remarkable levels of demographic and economic growth. The growth of those large cities was put in parallel with the rise of economic exchanges at a global level. Processes of globalization, including transnational migration, architecture, financial transactions, transport flux, or dissemination of technological innovations, contributed to the rise of megacities in different parts of the globe. The traditional idea of the city, the modern metropolis or the industrial city were therefore replaced by contradictory images of those megacities, where one either emphasizes cultural diversity and an infinite range of interactions or the strength of control and capital accumulation by dominant groups. Those metropolises seemed to be reshaped by local groups and culture interacting, adapting, or protesting against globalized flows. As a symbol of the times, Shanghai with its extraordinary rapid growth represented the urban future in a somehow functionalist way of thinking.

In other words, within that paradigm, the urban world is becoming determined by globalization trends and the rise of mega, hyper, and super urban areas. For instance:

- The US East Coast: Boston, New York, Baltimore, Philadelphia down to Washington
- The Cleveland, Pittsburgh, Detroit, and Chicago area
- California, that is San Diego, Los Angeles, San Francisco—one could even go up to Seattle and Vancouver

In Europe too, some urban scholars are also trying to map out huge urban areas:

- The southeast of England, around London
- Paris Ile de France (some suggest to take the triangle London/Paris/Brussels as the right unit of analysis)
- The Delta metropolis, that is the four cities of the south of the Netherlands

- Lombardia around Milan
- The Ruhr region in Germany

In principle, several consequences follow for our comparison:

1. Comparison between cities should be organized first around the issue of globalization at the expense of the national framework. The same process is supposed to play at full strength in different contexts.

2. Large cities are the engine of growth, whereas medium-sized cities, in particular in Europe are being marginalized, they become museums of ancient history (Castells 1996). Urban Europe in the classic sense is bound to disappear.

3. Politics and classical social groups do not matter anymore, and a new sociology is needed in terms of mobility and migration (Urry 2000).

Their development is related first to the pressure and incentives of globalization trends. They are seen as the new motors of the global economy: issues of competitiveness are central to this notion. They result from the amalgamation of existing localities to construct interterritorial organizations for collective action which are more or less functionally dependent. Some can be organized around a major urban center as in the classic model of the metropolis, some may be a network of urban centers (Delta metropolis in Holland), some may go beyond regional boundaries such as Copenhagen, Malmöe, or San Diego Tijuana. The basic argument behind this version of the megacity is from economic geography: those global city regions are the center of dense networks of transnational firms, they 'thrive on the productivity—and innovation enhancing effects of dense and multifaceted urban milieux that are simultaneously embedded in worldwide distribution networks' (Scott 2001: 4). Administrative boundaries are, of course, becoming irrelevant.

The focus on global cities does not resist empirical analysis. There is no evidence so far of the creation of a megacity within the European context beyond the cases of London and Paris. If one brings together a series of cities in England, in the Netherlands, Benelux, or the north of Germany, there is always the possibility for 'discovering' other megacities ... but that does not change the existing framework. Over the past two decades, there was no particular rapid growth of Paris or London at the expense of European medium-sized cities. The scenario of 'obsolete European cities', is not on the cards, for now.

In fact, most trends characterizing global cities are also taking place in most European cities. There is little evidence to suggest that, in the European context, global or world cities are a particular category of cities beyond the concentration of networks, headquarters, more diverse interests, more fragmentation of ethnic minorities. In Europe, urban flagship projects are emblematic of this desire for cities to reaffirm their importance and to take their place in European and globalized networks, as witnessed by the rebuilding of the Potzdamer Platz in Berlin or the regeneration of the London Docklands, but that is also true in most regional capitals in Europe. The contradiction of capitalism is more marked in global cities; there are more interests, less capacity to integrate, a fragmented governance (Préteceille 2000; Scott 2001).

In economic terms, therefore, the rise of the so-called global cities is to be related to the more general renewal and acceleration of metropolization trends which are also valid for medium-sized cities in the United States and Europe alike. There is indeed more to economic development than just the leading services, for instance the financial services. Following Veltz (1996) we would argue that dynamics of metropolization can be used to account for both the growth of a good number of European cities, notably regional capitals, and the effects of acceleration and accentuation of these dynamics in the largest of them. Differences are of degree, not nature, reflecting the hierarchies of cities. Many European and American cities are economically dynamic without being global cities.

What remains unclear is the extent to which there is a direct link between the concentration of headquarters, networks of various sorts, advanced services, diverse skilled professionals, knowledge complexes, and economic development, or in other words, is there a clear size effect which has some impact on the rate of economic development? It may be the case that global city regions are the genuine motor of economic growth and have a major comparative advantage. It may also be the case that different patterns of metropolization may lead to the same result because the combination of networks, mobility, and diffusion of innovation can take different forms. The density of medium-sized cities in Europe may be a functional equivalent to the concentration within a large metropolis. Some of the debate is rather rhetorical when it concentrates on the size and location of network. Access and mobility are also central. Links between German cities or Paris and regional capitals (around two hour) are equivalent to a drive from the east to the west of Los Angeles for example. It may be the case that there is a distinct type and rate of economic development in global/world cities, but that is still an open debate, at least within the European context. One suspects the dream of 'one best way' which is often implicit in regional economist literature.

In a different way, the revival or growth of metropolis on both sides of the Atlantic is explained by the demands of the 'new economy'. Storper and Manville eloquently suggest that

the New Economy's demands for proximity are stimulated by information, which often requires that people work in close quarters with one another . . . soft-input economies are found more in big cities with diverse economies—precisely the sorts of places we see resurging. In such places it is the diversity of the economy that both sustains and is sustained by the easy movement of knowledge. Information spills from one industry to another, creates agglomerations in new branches of the economy; the talent and knowledge from Hollywood, for example, have flowed out and helped sustain LA's fashion, design, and advertising industries.

(quoted in Manville and Storper (2005))

In that reading of the return of cities and metropolises, the level of education and available diverse skills has been seen as crucial. Cities are seen as 'metropolitan hubs' as argued by Veltz, in other words giant matrices for recombining resources in order to generate innovations. That works if the right sort of people and their interaction aggregate, exchange, combine.

As Katz (2005) points out, the 1990s in the United States were affected by major economic restructuring, mostly by the development of service-related jobs (19% of jobs in 1970 and 32% in 2000). Education skills vary a lot depending on cities and ethnic groups. The rate of adults with a bachelor's degree is around 35 percent in Minneapolis-St Paul and Atlanta, less than 10 percent in Newark. Furthermore, in the top 100 US cities, only 10 percent of Hispanics and 14 percent of blacks have a college education, whereas 37 percent of whites and 39 percent of Asians do. In addition to this, we can see a decentralization of work: one-third of jobs in the United States are located in an area of ten miles or more around central cities. On different indicators in Europe, the numbers of company headquarters have increased in two-thirds of cities. The productivity gap in favor of cities in comparison to the national average applies more to Paris and London but is also true for many other European cities. It therefore follows that from an economic development point of view, the focus on 'global cities' may not be crucial to understanding the development of cities on both sides of the Atlantic.

In the United States, recent fast developing cities include not only Los Angeles but San Jose (Silicon Valley), San Diego, Seattle, Portland, Phoenix, Minneapolis, Indianapolis, Charloot, and Columbus, comprising a mix of high tech, defense industry, tourism ... with low level of black inhabitants (Dreier, Mollenkopf, and Swanstrom 2005).

9.3.2. SEGREGATION, GENTRIFICATION, INEQUALITIES, RACE, AND MIGRATION

Within the space of this chapter, there is no room for a detailed analysis of the social structure, the key social cleavages, and the dynamics of inequalities. Some major features are however briefly reviewed, the data available for comparison is also problematic.

A classic question is however: to what extent are cities/metropolises becoming more polarized? 'Polarization' refers to a process by which the poles of the richest and the poorest are reinforced at the expense of the middle of society, in terms of society's various inequalities (occupation, income, social mobility, and consumption). In urban sociology terms, this polarization can be observed spatially, in the reinforcement of the wealth of the richest areas and the poverty of the poorest areas. In the United States, large-city households represent a high proportion of the bottom tiers of the national income distribution, whereas only one-sixth of them are part of the nation's top income quintile. Beyond an inadequate 'dual city' model, areas of intense poverty and areas of intense wealth exist and are increasing within cities, thus recreating a mosaic of spatial inequalities and conflicts. According to Berube and Thatcher (2004), census data on households in

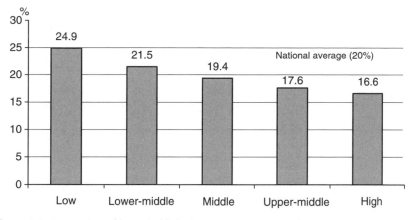

Figure 9.3. Proportion of households by income category, 100 largest cities, 1999

Sources: Brookings Institution, Census 2000 data

100 largest American cities between 1979 and 1999 (Figure 9.3) shows that large American cities can be divided into different basic household income distribution patterns, reflecting a more subtle reality than the 'dual city model'.

The proportion of households with high incomes declined in 79 of the 100 largest cities between 1979 and 1999, especially in the northeast and the Rust Belt, where 'stressed cities' proliferated the most. This fact confirms the assertions about declining industrial cities in those areas, in a context of globalization and service-based economy. By contrast, 25 percent of suburban households occupy the highest-income quintile, even though the relative numbers of high-income households in suburbs declined (Berube and Thatcher 2004). However, European cities saw the same social problems: increasing inequalities, rising poverty levels, and housing a crisis in. As the Urban Audit demonstrates around a quarter of European households have less than 50 percent of the average national household income. The average median weekly household income for the 32 cities for which data was available was 347 euros. The proportion of households receiving less than half of the national average income averaged at 23.2 percent, whereas 19.4 percent of households relied on social security.

In general in the United States, poor people live in city centres, except in places like Seattle, Boston, or New York, where low-income families are pushed away to the suburbs (Dreier, Mollenkopf, and Swanstrom 2005). In 1960, per capita income for cities was bigger than that of suburbs. Today, per capita income in cities represents 83 percent of the per capita income of suburbs. However, this decline stabilized in the 1990s. Miami, San Francisco, Seattle, Chicago, and Atlanta reduced the income gap with their suburbs. At the same time, the geography of poverty in US metropolitan areas has shifted (Katz 2005). The number of poor people in US metros has increased over the past two decades (19.3 million in 1980 and 25.8 million in 2000). Still, poverty rates have gone down during the 1990s in city centres: 19 percent in 1990, 17 percent in 2002, while they have remained the same (9%) in suburbs. Although in suburbs the share of people who live in poor areas (suburbs with per capita incomes of less than 75% of its metro area) saw a 10 percent increase between 1980 and 2000 (8.4% to 18.1%), the number of people living in high poverty neighborhoods declined during the 1990s (Jargowsky 2003).

The pattern is more diverse in European cities. On average, poor people live on the outskirts in outer-city developments because the center has remained more middle class and has benefited from high levels of public investment. However there are many exceptions. There are no clear patterns of poverty concentration in the Italian case, whereas in Brussels, the pattern is similar to the American one.

9.3.3. IMMIGRATION, ETHNICITY, AND RACE

In the 1990s, more than 2 million people immigrated to just New York and Los Angeles. With the exception of London, there is no equivalent in Europe. On the one hand, immigration remains a dividing feature between Europe, with regular increase of immigrant intake at a relatively slow rate, and the United States where cities, Los Angeles and New York in particular, are boosted by high levels of immigration. On the other hand, what was once a massive difference also signals some convergence. In European cities, immigrant groups are now present in most cities and metropolises; politics of ethnicity is on the rise in many places, first in the UK, then Northern European cities and gradually Southern Europe. In that sense, the ethnic diversity of European cities progressively resembles that of American cities. Similarly, even in remote cities and metropolises, more diverse ethnic groups are gaining ground all over the United States. However, urban politics is increasingly defined in the United States as the aggregation and coalition of different ethnic groups to an extent which is not known in Europe (Jones-Corea 2001).

Every European country has seen waves of immigration, frequently a long time ago, with their geographical origins often linked to a colonial empire: Pakistan, India, the Caribbean, and Central Africa for the UK; Indonesia and Surinam for the Netherlands; Italy, Poland, Spain, Portugal, then Algeria, Morocco, Tunisia, and Black Africa for France; and Turkey for Germany. For the traditional countries of immigration in Europe, the percentage of the population from abroad varies from 5 to 10 percent in the Netherlands, Germany, France, the UK, Belgium, and Austria. More favorable legal provisions and an unemployment rate that remained low during the 1980s have made Sweden the European country with the highest proportion of immigrants (11.5%). In contrast, immigration is a recent phenomenon in Southern Europe, but is rapidly reaching similar levels. For the EU, border closure policies have meant that the flow of immigration into Europe has stabilized at a level that is not very high and includes the immigration movements of highly skilled individuals, which somewhat blur the image of an immigrant. The high density and wide variety of immigrant populations is more a distinctive characteristic of the largest European cities, notably London and

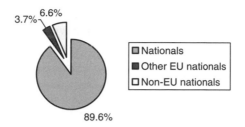

Figure 9.4. Nationality in all Urban Audit cities (%, 1996)

Source: Urban Audit

Paris but also Frankfurt (25%), Rotterdam (20%), Brussels (just under 30% of the city center population), and Stockholm. However, immigrant populations in medium-sized European cities increased during the 'Thirty Glorious Years' from 1947 to 1976 and again from the 1980s, as well an increased diversity of their countries of origin. Although not a large-scale phenomenon, the presence of populations foreign has become the norm for medium-sized European cities, even though, of course, there are wide variations. European urban areas, especially central cities, have seen a huge flow of nonnationals from outside Europe over the past few years (the Urban Audit). Around 10 percent of their residents are nonnationals (Figures 9.4 and 9.5), mostly (two-thirds) from outside the EU. In over 90 percent of cities, the proportions of non-EU nationals have increased. Ports such as Liverpool, Rotterdam, Marseille, Genoa, and Naples, for example, are cities that have long played host to immigrant populations. This means that, although cities that are now called 'global' are distinguished by a wide variety and high density of populations from abroad, medium-sized European cities are also affected, but to a lesser extent.

What are the implications for European cities? Most of what has been analyzed is more visible and seemed more obvious in the larger cities, in London in particular, than in other European cities. The concentration of the trend underlined seems to be clear although there is lack of clear comparable empirical data to

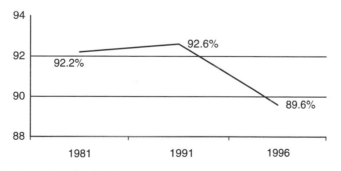

Figure 9.5. Proportion of nationals

Source: Urban Audit

be sure. However, most European cities are also concerned about segregation, the rise of the mobile middle classes, migration, cultural diversity, and social exclusion. From a sociological point of view, there is not much of a particular social structure to identify the global cities. The main point remains a question of scale, of concentration and diversity of groups, which makes more difficult the question of integration and aggregation of interest.

9.3.4. ETHNIC URBAN AMERICA

American cities remain symbols of diversity and a haven for hundreds of thousands of immigrants from around the world. Most of the largest American cities are shaped by immigration. One of the conclusions we can draw from the 2000 census is increasing diversity in metropolitan areas (Katz 2005). Inner cities saw a dramatic growth of minority populations, especially Hispanics (+42.6%) and Asians (+38.3%). Some cities like New York, Minneapolis-St Paul, and Boston would actually have lost population without the massive flow of immigrants. This trend made the minorities a majority in the top 100 US cities: the share of white residents is only 44 percent in those cities, whereas white residents represented 53 percent of their population in 1990 (Brookings Institution Center on Urban and Metropolitan Policy 2001). Almost half of the largest cities no longer have majority white populations.

Again, suburbs are also effected by this phenomenon. The share of ethnic minority groups living in suburbia has grown significantly since 1990: 39 percent of blacks (33% in 1990), 55 percent of Asians (51%), and 50 percent (46%) of Hispanics live outside central cities. Ethnically mixed metros like Los Angeles, Chicago, Washington, DC, Houston, and New York have the highest minority suburban populations. The number of predominantly white neighborhoods fell by 30 percent in the 1990s (Booza, Fasenfest, and Metzger 2004). Mixed white/Hispanic or white/Asian neighborhoods are now the most common ones. Fifty percent of suburban populations live in 'at-risk' suburbs, which are extensions of city ghettos, but often located far away from the city limits (Dreier, Mollenkopf, and Swanstrom 2005). Those 'at-risk' areas are characterized by an important minority population, low racial integration, and low tax bases compared to rich low-density suburbs with commercial space.

9.3.5. NEW IMMIGRANTS, NEW DESTINATIONS

As Audrey Singer (2004) explains, not only the US foreign-born population grew in the 1990s, but also new destinations for migrants, mostly from Asia and Mexico, emerged—states like Colorado, Georgia, Nevada, and North Carolina, and cities like Dallas and Washington, DC. However, large metropolitan areas like New York, Los Angeles, San Francisco, Chicago, Washington, and Miami remain the main

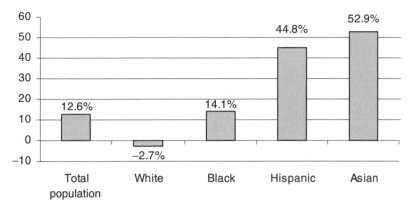

Figure 9.6. Population change by race/ethnicity, ten largest metropolitan areas, 1990–2000

Source: The Brookings Institution, Census 2000 data

magnets for foreign migrants (Frey 2003). They gained 3 million foreign migrants between 1995 and 2000, but at the same time, those areas lose more residents (2.1 million), from various ethnic backgrounds (Figure 9.6), who move to other parts of the country. Western and southern metropolitan areas (Phoenix, Atlanta, and Las Vegas) attracted most of those in-migrants, who tend to move to suburban areas.

Another interesting detail to note in terms of migration and ethnicity is domestic migrations of black citizens (Frey 2004). During the late 1990s, the south scored net gains of black migrants. At the same time, New York, Chicago, San Francisco, and Los Angeles experienced the biggest loss of black residents. Atlanta and Washington, DC have replaced California as the main destinations for black migrants, mostly college-educated.

9.4. **Conclusion**

This chapter answers some questions of the United States/Europe comparison but did not address all the key issues.

First of all, the comparative analysis of European cities shows the originality of European societies despite elements of diversity. The issue of European cities came back in the 1980s for two reasons. First, the growing field of comparative empirical urban research stressed the growth and dynamism of middle-sized cities all over Europe; they were even booming in some countries such as France and Scandinavia. Second, it was related to the question of how European societies emerged because of the acceleration of the political project of European integration and increased interdependence between national societies and the vigorous development of European networks of cities. We argue that common changes within European cities, the impact of EU norms, the dynamism of horizontal networks of cities, increasing urban tourism, and the privatization of utilities rather supports the view of the slow emergence of a European society.

European cities are characterized by the following features. They are part of an old urban system, consituted in the Middle Ages and which has remained more or less stable over time. Both the form of the city, the existence of public spaces and the mix of social groups, suggest the idea of a continuing sense of 'urbanity' still characterizing European cities (Zijderveld 1997). Despite sprawling movements the resistance of the old city centers epitomizes their peculiarity. One can take the example of large public collective transport (in particular the tramway) together with pedestrian areas and cycling paths to demonstrate the remaining strength of the idea of the European city.

The empirical elements we have analyzed in this chapter show the specificity of European cities. Obviously, European and US cities share common trends in a context of a globalized capitalist economy: growing inequalities, segregation, increasing poverty rates, housing crises, cultural diversity, but also a renaissance of cities symbolized by growth, metropolization, and economic dynamism. But behind those undeniable common points lie deep differences, generated by all the above mentioned historical and political reasons. European welfare states and regional policies softened the effects of industrial decline during the 1980s, preventing the exodus of the 'born to stay' middle classes to the suburbs that occurred in the United States, where 'born to run' Americans accelerated the suburbanization and metropolization of their country. Inner cities, despite improvements in their economic situation during the 1990s, remain symbols of poverty and social exclusion on the other side of the Atlantic, whereas old European downtowns have kept their economic and political leadership. Another example of these differences is immigration and ethnic diversity: even though many European cities have become highly multicultural, this aspect is—not yet?—comparable to diversity in American cities, where growth is sustained mostly by immigration. Finally, European cities remain firmly rooted within national welfare systems (on average, for the former fifteen members of the EU, state expenditure still represents about 45% of GDP against less than 30% in the United States; a massive difference in terms of public policies, employment, availability of social services, and income redistribution through welfare mechanisms).

Second, our analysis does not provide much support for the 'globalization leads to convergence' paradigm. For instance, the convergence of metropolises worldwide sometimes implied by the global city theory does not seem obvious after what we have seen. The national framework is still relevant in the European context, where medium-sized cities remain dynamic and have not yet become museums . . . . In the United States, the emergence of new urban magnets in the south and the west seem to contradict the idea that global cities such as New York or Los Angeles grow at the expense of smaller ones. Actually, cities of all kinds are back in town . . . .

Third, both the United States and Europe are large units with scope for diversity. Any systematic comparison is torn between the characterization of societies at that level, and the diversity it masks. This chapter does not avoid that trap.

Fourth, both European and American cities/metropolises are part of a globalizing capitalist system. Without espousing the more functionalist views, there is a robust tradition of research showing the impact of changes on urban labor markets and the role of private developers and utility firms for the creation of urban societies and cities. In the second part of the 1990s, the EU has played a decisive role to introduce more competition in different sectors: energy, transport, water, post offices .... More or less reluctantly, member-states have had to adapt and comply to this new set of rules. Large firms in those sectors have reorganized at a global scale and ferociously compete to buy or manage services and infrastructure in European cities. The change is even more striking for private developers and nowadays for housing provision or privatization. The long-term impact of those privatizations can take different forms according to the institutions within which they operate but it makes sense to imagine there will be some impact in terms of inequalities, access to services, control and surveillance in public spaces, and capacity to govern urban societies. In political terms, a point which was not considered in this chapter, there are now in Europe 'urban growth coalitions' of private and public actors investing resources to promote growth in a competitive way. The parallel with US cities is both useful and misleading as the political resources of the European urban elite make them far less dependent from private sector interests, but the priority given to economic development, large urban projects, and consumption spaces clearly indicates some common factors of change with the US. Cities do develop strategies on the 'international marketplace'; there is clearly room for comparison too (Kantor and Savitch 2002).

Fifth, urban and ethnic segregation on the one hand, issues of poverty and upper-middle-class segregation on the other hand are still reflecting different histories and dynamics of social change in US and European cities. However, in terms of public policies and urban politics, similar conflicts of interests emerge: issues of gated communities, increasing competition between social and ethnic groups, new inequalities, salience of the school issue, and integration of immigrant populations. There are no major cities/metropolises in Europe where an ethnic minority mayor is likely to be elected in the short term and no urban politics looks like that of Miami or Los Angeles. However ethnic minorities are progressively becoming more active, organized, and present in urban politics despite some fierce resistance, for instance in France or Italy, and despite the extreme right vote in cities such as Antwerp Marseilles or small industrial towns in the UK or the north of Italy. More diverse, competitive cities/metropolises are on the rise both in the United States and in Europe.

10 The American and the European models of society: not so different after all

Alberto Martinelli

The aim of this concluding chapter is to discuss the basic questions of this work in light of the findings of the various chapters. More specifically: (*a*) What kind of society do the United States and the European Union constitute? How similar and how different are they? Are they two variants of Western modernity or two wholly distinct models of society (American exceptionalism and European uniqueness)? Are the two societal models converging or diverging? (*b*) Which are the distinctive features of the American model of society? Is it departing from its core culture and institutions? (*c*) Is there a European society in the making? How diverse are the member countries of the EU? What shape is taking the European project of building unity through diversity? and (*d*) Which model of society seems more reactive to the challenges of globalization?

In the first part of this concluding chapter, I discuss salient similarities and differences and interpret trends of convergence and divergence in selected aspects of European and American societies, building on the analyses of previous chapters. In the second part, I outline the organizing principles of American society and analyze how and to what extent its basic values and institutions are changing. In the third, I discuss whether a European society is in the making; most European societies appear to share a significant number of common traits which make them less and less specific, shared values, and common supranational institutions foster the slow construction of a European society, in spite of continuing great structural, cultural, and institutional diversity at the national level, but is this enough to identify a specific European model of society? I conclude by focusing on the implications of globalization for the two societies and on US and EU roles of cooperation and competition in global governance.

10.1. Major similarities and differences: the European Union and the United States as two variants of Western modernity

In Chapter 1 I argued, on the one hand, that the United States and the EU are two variants of Western modernity and, on the other, that they are two specific models of society, although not so 'exceptional' and 'unique' as some scholars seem to think. The EU and the United States do not only have a common heritage, but are becoming more and more interdependent and interconnected in contemporary globalization. Within the context of multiple modernities, the modern societies of Europe and the United States are by far the most similar.

To put it in a different way, the United States constitutes the single biggest comparator for European society. At times, differences have been exaggerated according to a mental picture of Europe as the opposite of America—as in Parkes (1947). At other times, similarities have been overstressed to the point of considering the United States just as an instance of a 'Europe outside Europe'. In the historical cycle, which began with the three modern revolutions—the English, the American, and the French—and ended with the twentieth-century triumph of American power and European decline, the consciousness of Americans was characterized by two opposite conceptions of their relationship with the old continent, in search of a difficult synthesis: on the one hand, the conception of Europe and America as two expressions of the same Western civilization, on the other, the conception of America as the new promised land. These comparisons between the United States and Europe as two fictitious entities have progressively given way to more empirically based comparisons, such as those conducted in this volume.

The characteristics that render European countries similar to each other—and likewise the different regions of a single country—and different from most others are often also those which they share with the United States: a common cultural heritage ('Western civilization') with the classical legacy of Greek philosophy and rationality and Roman law, and a strong Judeo-Christian base; a lengthy history of market industrial capitalism and a related system of social stratification; the institutions of modern science and technology; the separation of spiritual and temporal authority, representative bodies, limited government, and the rule of law; and democratic citizenship and civil rights, social pluralism, and individualism. These characteristics are all common to both Europe and the United States, except for the multiplicity of languages (a feature, however, of great importance, as I shall argue later). Some authors like Huntington (1997) maintain that most of the core features of Western civilization predate the process of modernization. Contrary to this view, I argue in Chapter 1 that, indeed, these characteristics originated before the modern era and made modernization possible, but they changed significantly because of it and through it. Europe is the cradle of modernity and the United States is the radical embodiment of modernity (Martinelli 2005). American and

European societies are two variants of the same Western civilization, both similar and different.

Their similarities stem from a variety of factors: they are both modern post-industrial societies, complex market economies, and representative democracies; there is intense cultural cross-fertilization between the EU and the United States; the earlier Europeanization of America has echoed back to Europe (Giner 1994) through an American cultural hegemony in several domains.

Moreover, there are specific reasons for them to grow more similar than they have been in the past. First, US cultural hegemony was able to develop in the institutional vacuum left in Continental Europe by the defeated Nazi power in 1945: mass media, educational and research infrastructures, and intellectual disciplines were reconstructed under strong American influence, and so were the democratic institutions after Fascism. The crucial American decision to 'win the peace' after winning the war, by helping the economic and democratic recovery of the defeated European nations and guaranteeing their military defense, put an end to the *Sonderweg* of Germany and other European nations outside the Soviet bloc. American hegemony after World War II changed the attitude of the United States toward Europe as well: while nineteenth-century America had defined itself as different from and opposed to Europe, as the twentieth-century United States strove for leadership on the world scene, it developed a closer sense of identity with Europe and defined itself the leader of the West.

A second reason is the 'gatekeeper' role played by the UK: the UK is both part of Europe and part of the Anglo-sphere. On the one hand, there are the deep cultural and linguistic ties and the 'special relationship' with the United States. On the other, the UK is strongly attracted by—and gravitates to—the continent. Political cooperation draws it toward the West and the ocean, economic integration draws it toward the East and the mainland. For this reason, the UK plays a rather complex and ambivalent role in the unification of Europe: it acts as a gatekeeper and guarantees the alliance between Continental Europe and North America; and at the same time it slows down the process of unification and aims at limiting it to a mostly economic integration among sovereign nation-states. This cultural affinity and special relationship implicitly helps to explain the peculiar choice made by Huntington (1997) when drawing his map of major civilizations (although strangely enough he does not mention the Anglo-sphere): he distinguishes a Western civilization (including Europe, North America, plus other settler countries such as Australia and New Zealand), from the Orthodox civilization—which is centered on Russia and characterized by a distinct religion and a tradition of bureaucratic despotism, and from the Latin American civilization—which incorporates indigenous cultures.

Third, and related to the previous point, is the fundamental role performed by the English language: it is the lingua franca of the contemporary world, but like any language it is also a major vehicle for the diffusion of ideas and information, cultural codes, and models of behavior. English—including its hybrid versions— is the fastest growing language in the contemporary world and it owns a number of words which by far exceeds all other spoken languages. English is the language of science, finance, the media, and international relations.

Fourth, the more recent spread of certain American characteristics has been fostered by the growth of the global deregulated market and the strengthening of the power and scope of the largest transnational corporations, through the diffusion of homogeneous products, patterns of consumption, and lifestyles. It is true that the homogenizing impact of global corporations on styles of life and consumption patterns is counterbalanced by the increasing hybridization of cultural traits and the staunch defense of specific identities; but Europeans and Americans buy goods and services in closely interconnected markets, are exposed to the same types of advertising and marketing strategies, and are closely interconnected by webs of material and symbolic communications.

The fact that they are two variants of the same modern Western civilization, and that they are influenced by the same global processes, provide a first answer to the question of what kind of society the United States and the EU constitute, in the direction of a growing similarity. In previous chapters there is abundant evidence for this thesis.

On the other hand, I also argue that the EU and the United States are two specific models of society, although less 'exceptional' and less 'unique' than some scholars think, and in previous chapters there is abundant evidence for this thesis as well. The two unions share the values and the institutions of scientific innovation, market economy, and representative democracy, but have institutionalized them in different ways. They become more integrated in terms of economy and trade, more similar in terms of consumption patterns and lifestyles, but continue to differ or become even more different in terms of values and attitudes toward religiosity, patriotism, risk taking and the state role in solving social problems, and the use of force in international relations and criminal justice.

There are several factors pushing toward a greater diversity between American society and the EU society. A first set of factors stems from the fact that core cultural and institutional elements which have contributed to defining identity of both Europe and the United States do not form a coherent system: they have in fact conflicted with each other, as in the cases of market and democracy, religious beliefs and scientific research, nationalism and peace. Each of the two variants has therefore stressed some aspect more than the other and tried to reach a precarious balance between contradictory elements. Let us take the notion of freedom and the relation between democracy and religion. Americans tend to associate freedom with autonomy; Europeans tend to associate it with solidarity and embeddedness. In the United States, democracy and religion are strictly connected, in most EU countries they are not.

A second set of factors contributing to diversity lies in the different histories of the societies on the two sides of the Atlantic and on the different patterns of path dependency. As I remarked in Chapter 1, American society has not been plagued by religious wars. American democracy has never been seriously threatened by totalitarian movements. American patriotism is of a blend different from many European nationalisms. And the religiosity of Americans is different from that of the Europeans. Individual faith is more widespread and religion is becoming more important politically among the former. European secularism went together with anticlericalism because it had to fight against a monolithic church and fostered— together with the utilitarian version of classical liberalism—a materialistic culture and the subordination of moral considerations to economic ones. More recently religious beliefs have been challenged by such diverse phenomena as skepticism about beliefs, permissiveness of lifestyles, maximization of wants and claims, and multiculturalism. American secularism, by contrast, was built on Christian moral institutions and fostered a widespread moral consensus which only in recent decades has been challenged, opening a cleavage between the defenders of individual rights and the believers in God and the family.

A third of set of factors contributing to differentiate the United States and the EU has to do with political and demographic implications of contemporary globalization. For the United States, the most important differentiating features are related to the unique character of American hegemony in a uni-multipolar world, the growing interdependence with Asia, and the increasing non-European stock in the ethnic mix of the American population. For Europe, the most relevant differentiating feature is that European identity is not only the product of a common cultural heritage but also, and mostly, the outcome of a project of society in the making that is specific with regard to America and is intended as a response to the challenges of globalization. A common identity, in fact, does not only need a common memory to build on; it must be constructed on the future as well, given that it is the realization of an open-ended project rather than the passive conservation of past values; and it is actively fostered day-by-day through institutional building (the EP, the euro). Europe's identity is being made possible by a common cultural heritage which, in various ways and to varying degrees, cuts across the several European *ethnos*, but it can develop only through the growth of a European *demos* defined in terms of shared rights and obligations and is capable of consolidating the ties of citizenship within freely chosen democratic institutions.

European society and American society are variants of the same modern Western civilization and at the same time two specific societal models. Differences between them are diminishing in some areas, but they are stable or even growing in others. Similarities and differences also vary according to the various parts of the EU we compare. As Crouch (1999: 404–5) remarks,

it is the 'northern' Europe of the welfare state, muted social inequalities, and rather regulated capitalism that mostly contrasts with contemporary North America. However, these are the very parts of Europe that in other respect most resemble the USA: for example, a high level of general education, technological sophistication, increasingly egalitarian gender relations. The 'southern' Europe that contrasts with the USA on these points is more similar to the latter country on questions of greater social inequality, weak welfare state development, and relatively small manufacturing sectors.

Let us now discuss the main similarities and differences between the two models of society, with regard to the selected areas we chose to investigate in this book:

1. Varieties of capitalism
2. Patterns of social inequality and social mobility
3. Demographic trends and the family
4. Politics and institutional architectures
5. Welfare models
6. Cultural values and attitudes
7. Religiosity and state–church relations
8. Forms of the city

10.1.1. VARIETIES OF CAPITALISM

First, two different models of capitalism are institutionalized in Continental Europe and the United States: 'market-led capitalism' versus 'social market economy'. The American economy is the champion and paradigm of market-driven capitalism, which differs from Continental Europe's social market economy (or *rheinische Kapitalismus*). In the former, the market economy is more competitive and dynamic, but with fewer guarantees for workers in terms of job security and union representation (although other stakeholders of the firms—like consumers and investors—receive special protection from antitrust and consumer protection laws). In the latter, greater efforts are made to combine economic growth with social cohesion through the development of a welfare state—that is, a system of public services and income transfers for social security, health care, education, unemployment, minimum wage—in response to claims for social citizenship as well as legal and political citizenship (workers have been integrated into the democratic polity, exchanging their loyalty to democratic institutions and values for the granting of full citizenship rights through welfare policies). The United States can be seen as a typical example of the liberal market economy where firms coordinate their activities through competitive markets and by top management authority, while most EU countries—with the notable partial exception of the UK—are instances of the coordinated market economy where firms' activities are based on a set of strategic institutionalized interactions among entrepreneurs, workers, banks, and government institutions (Hall and Soskice 2001).

Other differences concern economic structures and institutions of the two models, with the UK more on the American than the European side: the United States began much earlier to develop a large tertiary sector of employment than the economies of Continental Europe which maintain longer a larger manufacturing sector (Kaelble 1987). Moreover, the American economy has tended to develop giant corporations on a larger scale than Continental Europe, mostly because of the greater role played by financial markets in fostering asset acquisitions and company takeovers. The American financial system with its concentration on short-term asset flows favors rapid flexibility and the growth of companies through the acquisition of other firms, while in the EU companies tend to favor more long-term institutional stability, and growth through acquisition is made more difficult by government hostility.

There are recent trends in convergence between the two models, because of globalization. In Europe too industrialism is losing ground; there are many more opportunities for financial investment in the unregulated global market, and a wave of acquisitions is under way because companies realize that global competition requires larger size and more aggressive financial strategies (Crouch and Streeck 1997).

Identifying two models must not obscure the fact that both the European economy and the American economy are internally differentiated, although not in the same way. The economies of the EU member-states have been very different, due to their diverse origins, their different pace of development and their different position in the international division of labor. Nevertheless, the long process of economic unification has brought an increasing integration into a common market, although the role of the state in the economy, and especially the welfare regimes are still inspired by different models. As Chapter 2 shows, the economies of the EU member-states have become more similar in terms of market size, sectors of the economy, work, public expenditure, household well-being, and consumption. Actually economic integration proved easier than political integration and was perceived more and more as a major way to foster the latter.

The economy of the United States is also differentiated in the fifty states, but unlike the European one, is characterized by the same institutions and legal framework. Moreover, while the United States could enjoy earlier of a common, although diversified economy, the most important steps of European economic integration took place only recently.

In the last decade of the twentieth century, it became more and more clear that the original reasons for European unification had been turned to the new challenges and opportunities created by the processes of globalization (Castells 1998) and by the new geo-political configuration of Europe stemming from the collapse of the Soviet Union, the reunification of Germany, and the entering into the EU of former Soviet bloc countries from Eastern Europe. Questions were raised about the specific nature of the European variety of capitalism (Soskice 1989; Albert 1991; Esping-Andersen 1999), and its capacity to face global competition and grant increasing and widespread welfare for its citizens.

The EU countries (mostly the euro countries which had to respect the Maastricht parameters in order to join the Economic and Monetary Union) introduced a variety of structural reforms by partially or entirely abolishing government subsidies to firms, deregulating the labor market, restructuring the bank system, and opening protected sectors to competition. Differences among national EU economies—as with differences in the American economy—have been gradually reduced, because the single market requires norms, regulations, and controls able to create a level playing field for all firms, while the Monetary Union fosters European financial integration (Schmidt 2002).

During the Lisbon meeting in 2000, the European Council adopted a more comprehensive strategy for modernizing the economy of the EU, in order to face competition on the world market with other major players such as the United States and the emerging industrialized countries. The aim has been to open up all sectors of the economy to competition, encouraging innovation and business investment, and modernizing Europe's education systems to meet the needs of the information society. On the other side, unemployment and the rising cost of pensions are both putting pressure on the member-states' economies, and this makes reform all the more necessary.

These changes have reduced, but not eliminated, the differences with respect to American capitalism. They result not only from the need to compete in the global market but also from EU laws and policies favoring competition, and they tend to produce a new form of Continental European capitalism through the harmonization of the economic policies of different EU countries. This is a capitalism that differs both from the American economy and from the different national varieties of capitalism. It further differs from the American economy in its greater concern with social cohesion and cooperation. In general terms, as the debate on the Bolkestein directive on the liberalization of services has shown, the Continental European model is put under growing strain by the contradiction between increasing liberalization and continuing social protection.

10.1.2. PATTERNS OF SOCIAL INEQUALITY AND SOCIAL MOBILITY

There are fewer social inequalities in the EU than in the United States (also by virtue of the welfare state), but there is also less social mobility. To put it in different terms, in the United States there is more inequality of results (in living conditions), but somehow less inequality of opportunities (chances to get ahead or fall behind). In terms of inequality of results, the differences between the United States and the EU countries are consistent, so that it is appropriate to speak of two distinct social models, though this has not always been the case. As Chapter 3 argues, by all measures, the United States is now more unequal than Europe. This difference largely reflects the dismal conditions of the poor in America. The GINI standard measure of income dispersion was slightly above 0.46 for the United States in 1999, while the average for the EU countries was 0.31 in the mid-1990s. Although every single EU nation was significantly more egalitarian than the United States, the EU countries displayed greater divergence in their inequality (the coefficient of variation was 0.13) than the American states (where the coefficient of variation was 0.10). Moreover, while in the United States the top fifth in income distribution accounts for 46 percent of the total, and the bottom fifth for 5 percent, the European average is 38.4 and 8.3 percent, which is about half the American ratio. As regards relative poverty, a substantially larger proportion of Americans than their European counterparts are excluded from the social mainstream. Since the late 1970s, levels of social inequality—in terms of both incomes deriving from labor markets and incomes after taxes and welfare benefits—have been rising in the United States (and in the UK), in contrast to a more egalitarian trend in Continental Europe. More recently, however, European societies, and in particular the UK, have grown less egalitarian as well.

On gender inequality, the United States is on the 'progressive' side of the European range—which shows considerable variation—but not very different in terms of women's empowerment.

As far as social mobility is concerned, American society appears to be more open than most European societies for both intergenerational and intra-generational mobility, but not to the point of justifying the American exceptionalism thesis that the United States is the country of equality of opportunities. The greater social mobility helps to explain why Americans are more likely to perceive their society as less unequal than Europeans, when in fact the opposite is the case.

No doubt, class has played a greater role in Europe than in the United States, while the reverse is true for ethnicity. But the impact of social classes is diminishing in Europe as well. As Hondrich and Caplow remark in *Convergence and Divergence* (1994), 'today major political conflicts are no longer defined by the antagonism of social classes but by concurrent interests'. And ethnicity is increasingly important in Europe too. The United States is an immigrant, multicultural, multiethnic society open to newcomers, whereas the EU has become a multicultural and multiethnic society by virtue of two different processes. The first process is the formation of a union made of different nation-states —which for the most part were ethnically heterogeneous since the very process of nation-building took place through the progressive homogenization of linguistic and cultural minorities. The second reason is that an increasing number of EU member-states are receiving a growing rate of immigrant workers and refugees. Alongside the traditionally labor importing countries like England, France, and Germany, in the past decades countries which traditionally exported labor, like Italy, Portugal, and Spain have also received large flows of immigrants. Although less open to immigrants than the US, European society is becoming increasingly multiethnic and multicultural too.

In general terms, one can contrast a European diversity which is ordered, limited, and structured with American unstructured and pluralistic diversity bounded by a framework of overall national and market homogeneity (Hradil and Immerfall 1997; Crouch 1999).

Related to this feature is the tendency for European social life to be segregated into different occupationally based milieux which establish boundaries of social intercourse and delineate cultural styles (Kaelble 1987). The growth of mass consumption has greatly reduced status-based distinctions in terms of lifestyles, family relations, leisure, and daily language, mostly among the younger generations. And yet, the thesis argued by Bourdieu in *La distinction* (1979) that cultural capital (inherited by the family and acquired through education) and social capital (stemming from networks of social relations) combine with wealth and income in shaping the specific *habitus* of different status groups, that is the set of dispositions and orientations which manifest themselves in lifestyles and consumption patterns (aesthetic standards, cultural activities, house furnishings, food preferences, etc.), is still valid although to a more limited extent.

There are also different ways to cope with social conflict and multiethnic society: in Europe with class compromise and the welfare state (the virtuous circle of social citizenship), in the United States with greater social mobility and individual achievement; whence, the American 'melting pot' or 'salad bowl' with hegemonic liberal (Anglo-Saxon) culture, and the European attempt to build a multicultural society out of different national identities (and to achieve unity through diversity), together with different responses to the challenge of immigration (French republican citizenship, German Gastarbeiter, and English and Swedish multiculturalism).

On the whole, European society is more class aware, elitist, law-abiding, statist, collective-oriented and particularistic (status-oriented) than is American society. The analysis in Chapter 3 showed that differences exist in various dimensions of inequality, but there is 'no overriding cultural distinction, nor overarching trend toward convergence'.

The portrait drawn by the theorists of American exceptionalism of a relatively classless society—despite evident inequalities in material conditions—that is in sharp contrast with European societies—which are structured by class and characterized by social hierarchies and distinctions—still holds, but to a much lesser extent than is maintained in much public discourse. In addition to this, some convergence is taking place.

10.1.3. DEMOGRAPHIC TRENDS AND THE FAMILY

Both the European and American societies experienced the demographic changes which are typical of modernization. Modernization and the gradual progress of equality transformed family life in both the EU and the United States between 1960 and 2000.

The direct effects of modernization include the steady decline in infant mortality rates (deaths of infants in the first year of life), dramatic declines in fertility, corresponding decreases in average household size, and a vast improvement in the material equipment of family households.

The gradual progress of equality greatly reduced the long-standing differences between men and women in sexual opportunity, access to the labor market, occupational careers, control of property, freedom to divorce, and relationships with children.

In both the EU and the United States, the families of 1960 functioned within a legal and customary framework wherein the mutual obligations of husbands and wives, the authority of parents over children, the obligations of kinship, the disadvantages of extramarital births, the rules of inheritance and adoption, and the prevailing sexual taboos were mostly of long standing, and perceived as part of the natural order. As pointed out in Chapter 4, that framework was changed beyond recognition in the ensuing four decades, on both sides of the Atlantic.

It goes without saying that the prevailing trends interacted with each other and with other events so that the causal sequences are not easily untangled. The decline of fertility and household size seems to have been both cause and effect of the entry of married women into the labor force which, in turn, seems to have been both cause and effect of the feminist movement and of the rise in divorce. The introduction of oral contraception in the 1960s and the legalization of abortion in the United States and in most of the EU states accounted for declining fertility but did not account for the great increase of extramarital births that followed.

While similar trends in family relations were recorded in the EU and the United States, they started and ended at different levels and their consequences were never identical. Moreover, differences among the EU member-states are often greater than those between the EU and the United States, so that they often explain EU internal diversity rather than differentiating European from American society.

The decline of fertility appears to be a normal consequence of modernization and is adequately explained by the declining value of children's labor, the rising status of women, the mechanization and simplification of housework, the increasing cost of child-raising, and the availability of means for the voluntary control of conception. In the past thirty years fertility rates have, however, diverged, being lower for the EU in general and specifically for some EU countries than for the United States. Fertility has hovered close to the replacement level since 1980 in the United States (two children for fertile women on average) and France (1.9%), whereas in the UK and the Scandinavian countries fertility has gone below the replacement level, and in countries such as Germany, Italy, and Spain, and the former communist Eastern European countries, fertility has plunged far below the replacement level in the same interval of time (between 1.2% and 1.5%). As remarked in Chapter 4, such differences are not easy to explain, since throughout the world, the most powerful depressants of fertility are higher education for women and the labor market participation of married women; and yet the United States has relatively more women with university educations and more married women in the labor force than the three low-fertility countries just mentioned. In order to interpret such sharp differences in fertility among EU countries, one has actually to take into account other variables, first of all welfare policies: countries with early welfare developments, like the Northern European ones, and countries with effective government policies of family support, like France, have higher fertility rates.

On both sides of the Atlantic, the great majority of 1960 babies were born to married couples. That began to change in the 1970s and changed a good deal more in the 1980s and 1990s. By 2000, more than one in four births in the EU (with 45% in Denmark and 56% in Sweden) were extramarital, with similar percentages in the United States among white Americans, but with a much higher figure (70%) among African-Americans. Moreover, while the extramarital births of 1960 were presumed to be unwanted, the extramarital births of 2000 were largely voluntary, given the availability of reliable contraception and legal abortion. Extensive family obligations and strong local communities, as they are more easily found in Southern European countries and in some ethnic groups, are relevant variables in this respect. The Protestant–Catholic division also plays a role in explaining differences between Northern and Southern Europe.

Another major difference between the United States and the EU is the higher number of single-parent families. By 2000, over 21 million US citizens lived in households consisting of a single parent and children under 18. In the great majority of these households, the single parent was a woman, and a great many of them were poor. The corresponding figure for the EU in 1999 was much lower, over 11 million in 2000.

The great recent changes in family structure that we have just reviewed suggest that we ought to look for correspondingly important changes in family attitudes and values, but they turn out to be rather elusive. One reason is that the traditional attitudes and values are both persistent and flexible. Contemporary Americans and Europeans continue to disapprove of divorce in general while accepting and even welcoming the divorces of their relatives and friends. Parents favor adolescent chastity but discover as little as they possibly can about the sexual activities of their adolescent children. Unmarried mothers, whose own mothers were unmarried, express as much attachment to the ideal of a happy marriage as long-married women.

On the whole, the age structures of Europe and the United States reflect the nature of developed countries, but are on the other hand rather different. The same factors have been at work on the two sides of the Atlantic in raising the percentage of elderly people in society, as argued in Chapter 6: the exhaustion after World War II baby boom, the lengthening of the average life span—due to medical progress and betterment in the quality of life—and the lower fertility of women—due to the changing role of women in society. The problems of an aging society are present in all developed countries, but are more acute in the EU (although with significant differences among member countries).

European society is, on the whole, getting much older than American society: the percentage of persons aged 60 and over in the total population has always been higher in the EU than in the United States over the past half-century, and has been steadily growing for the EU countries, while it has been steady for the United States in the past three decades. While in the United States the median age will remain about 35 for the next half century, in the EU the median age will jump from 38 to 53, with the likely consequence that its culture will be dominated by people more averse to risk and innovation and less youthful in their approach to the world.

As a consequence of demographic and family trends, there is a similar need to increase expenditures for social policies, but significant differences exist in the respective weight of pensions and health care as Chapter 6 shows. The United States is spending and will spend more on health, whereas the EU member-states are spending and will spend more on pensions.

10.1.4. POLITICS AND INSTITUTIONAL ARCHITECTURES

The United States and the EU have significantly different polities and institutional architectures which spring from the fact that, whereas the United States was born as a modern nation made up of people sharing basic values, attitudes, and hopes in an underpopulated and resource-plentiful continent, the EU is a supranational union of independent nation-states with different origins and historical paths, although they share a common cultural heritage.

Key differences concern, first of all, the nature of union sovereignty, since the EU lacks several essential elements, such as the right to levy taxes on citizens, a united foreign policy and a united army, and a united police force. Second, the legitimacy of the legislature, since in the EU there is no single election for the executive body and many different voting procedures are used to elect both the member-states' legislatures and the EP. Third, the role of the president, which is very strong, although checked and balanced by the counterpower of Congress, in the United States, and rather weak in the EU. Fourth, much greater power of member-states and much greater institutional diversity among them in the EU vis-à-vis more extensive responsibilities and prerogatives for the central government in the United States. Fifth, much greater strength of parties at state level in the EU than in the United States. Sixth, different social and ideological connotations of the political Left and the political Right on the two sides of the Atlantic. Seventh, different conceptions of citizenship, since European citizenship—as stated in the Maastricht Treaty—does not substitute for national citizenship but completes it. Eighth, different roles played by nationalism and ethnicity in identity politics. Finally, differences in government policies with regard to the depth of the institutionalization of welfare policies, the level of state intervention in general, and the level of formal involvement in international economic consortia; in the EU, the situation is still one of a dense network of well-organized, self-governing interest associations with multiple institutional arrangements for negotiating and mediating between public and private interests.

However, American federalism and European supranational governance are less different than assumed. Analogies are less marked than differences, but they are significant, since, as I argued in Chapter 5, they can be viewed as different versions of the compound republic, the pluralist model of democracy which differs from the parliamentary model institutionalized in most EU member-states.

Key similarities concern, first of all, both the vertical and horizontal separation of democratic powers, insofar as legitimate authority has different bases in the two legislative bodies, one representing the subsystems (the fifty US states and the twenty-five EU member-states), the other the people directly, which exercise their powers on the basis of the subsidiarity principle, and decision-making takes place in a trilateral structure (President–Senate–House of Representatives in the United States; Council–Commission–Parliament in the EU), with president independent of the Senate and the House in the United States and the Commission independent of the Council and the Parliament in the EU.

Second, independent judiciaries with important roles in policy formation and implementation: judicial review by any kind of court in the United States; revision of national legislation by the European Court in Luxemburg. Third, decision-making is dispersed among complex frameworks of governance, and the principle of government by minorities is upheld. Fourth, political parties are nominal, fragmented, and rather weak, whereas interest groups are very influential and their activities are intense at different entry points to the policymaking process.

Another aspect where the United States seems more similar to the EU than to most member-states is in government regulation of the economy. The American market economy is by no means an unregulated market, but the US government has different priorities than that of most EU member-states, insofar as it aims to protect the consumers rather than the workers, and it protects the consumers by fighting monopoly. The EU Commission has often showed a similar determination to defend competition, as in the recent cases of General Electric and Microsoft.

Similar traits often have different causes, and specific features at the union level go together with different patterns of internal differentiation in member-states, but as for other aspects of our comparative analysis, the United States and the EU appear less unique than one might think.

These similar features also produce similar virtues and vices in the functioning logic of the two democracies. In both cases, the separation of powers is a fundamental guarantee against tyranny by the majority and executive abuses. But, on the other hand, it makes it more difficult to establish who is responsible and accountable for what decision, it obstructs interparty competition, and it fosters tyranny by organized minorities. One of the main questions concerning the future of the EU is whether its political institutions will become more similar to the federal model of the other union or to the parliamentary model of most member-states.

10.1.5. WELFARE MODELS

The welfare state is considered one of the most important institutional innovations of the twentieth century, an innovation which is markedly European. The welfare state has been the main instrument for the virtuous circle of social citizenship. It guarantees social security and is aimed at correcting market failures. Here lies one of the main differences between the American and European social models, with two caveats, however. First, the issues of social protection are not unknown to American policy and social expenditures are sizable, although lower than in most EU member-states. Similar demographic trends, first of all the aging population, foster growing expenditures for health care and pensions on both sides of the Atlantic, so that we can say that the EU and the United States are less different than usually thought, as argued in Chapter 6. Differences do exist, but they lie in different institutional arrangements—and more specifically in the greater role of the state—more than in the percentage of GNP invested. Second, there is significant diversity within the EU, where we find a variety of welfare systems, as a vast literature shows. The country essays in our CCSC Group volume *Leviathan Transformed* (2001) clearly portray the different systems. Whatever the diversity of European models of welfare state, however, they are all significantly different from the American model. Let us briefly recall the main factors accounting for higher expenditures in social policy and then outline the key institutional differences in the welfare systems of the United States and the EU member-states.

The exhaustion after World War II baby boom and the baby boomers' reaching of the pension age have altered the ratio between the working population and pension holders, and contributed to a great increase in the financial burden for social security. This demographic cycle will last about thirty to forty years and has less severe consequences in the United States, because of higher immigration rates and higher fertility rates. The lengthening of the average life span—due to medical progress and betterment in the quality of life—is a second major factor, which influences both social security and health care expenses. Its impact is greater in most EU countries than in the United States because of higher immigration rates. A possible remedy to this trend is lengthening the working life, which however runs into widespread opposition in several EU countries. The lower fertility of women—due first of all to the changing role of women in society—is a third major factor which influences both social security and health care expenses, since it contributes to reduce the percentage of workers with regard to pension holders and puts a greater burden on institutional care with respect to family care. A fourth factor is represented by changes in family structure, with more one-parent families than before, and more women and children living in poverty.

Both the EU member-states and the United States have to face major, although different, increases in the expenditures for pensions and health care (as Table 6.3 in Chapter 6 shows). The widespread resistance to significant changes in welfare policies both in the United States and in EU countries makes political leaders unwilling to run the political risks of thorough reform. In most EU countries, taxes and the nonwage component of labor costs are already very high and there are few chances for extending welfare in the context of increasing competition in the global market. Lengthening of the working life, immigration, and forms of rationalization of health institutions are possible remedies, but also have social and political costs.

Although difficult and potentially costly for political consensus, reforms are attempted and will be attempted, according to the specific institutional arrangements and social policies of the United States and the EU.

Traditional typologies of welfare state (Esping-Andersen 1990; Crouch 1999) usually distinguish three main models, in terms of rules and range of entitlement to benefits (more or less detached from prior work experience and past financial contributions), income replacement standards (more or less close to employment earnings): the liberal (or market oriented), the social democratic (or full citizenship), and the conservative (or communitarian). In the first model, there is a development of welfare provision, but of a very basic, needs-related kind, and more targeted policies designed specifically to interfere as little as possible with workers' performance in the labor market and implying lower taxation levels. The United States fits well into this type, as do other Anglo-Saxon countries, and to a lesser extent the UK, at least after the Thatcher government. The second is a universalistic model of social assistance that offers high standard state services on a more or less equal basis provided by the state itself through high taxes. Scandinavian countries come closer to this ideal type. The third model mainly takes the form of occupation-based social insurance schemes; it was initially associated with Bismarck's reform and largely restricted to male breadwinners. It gradually extended its coverage but maintained its status-based structures rather than developing universal national social security schemes. It is influenced by the role of communitarian institutions, first of all the family, the church and professional associations and by government's intention of not interfering too much with them. The welfare systems of France, Germany, Italy, Spain, and Austria have features which can be referred to this model, but the diversity is such that other authors prefer to split this type in two, distinguishing a Central European and a Mediterranean version, with the former based mainly on payroll contributions and the latter depending heavily on provisions from the family (Ferrera 2005).

In Chapter 6, these typologies are reformulated on the basis of available data and five models of social policy expenditures are identified: the US model and four types of European model. The US model is characterized by low expenditures, both public and private, for the active population (whereas assistance is targeted to unemployment compensation, benefits for families and housing aid, and social transfers to the poor), which is only partially compensated by the earning income tax credit. This type of policy contributes to higher social inequalities in American society. The British–Dutch model is closest to the American one because of the high level of private expenditure for pensions funds, but differs from the latter because of a much higher expenditure for sustaining the income of the active population. The Northern European or Scandinavian model is characterized by a high level of social expenditure in general and for social services in particular. The Continental model of countries like France, Germany, Austria, and Belgium is marked by relevant expenditure for pensions and lower expenditure for social services in comparison with the previous model. Finally, the Mediterranean model of countries like Italy and Spain is characterized by high and essentially public expenditure for pensions and health with very low expenditures in other social policy.

A few conclusions can be drawn: first, in spite of the great diversity of welfare systems, the most basic difference is the one between the more market-oriented US model on the one side and the more social cohesion-oriented EU member-states, on the other—which imply different institutional mixes between public and private actors. Second, the impact of the same structural factors (both worldwide as intensifying globalization, and specific to the EU because of the aging of the population) makes the societies of EU member-states more similar to each other and more in need of a common European social policy. Third, in spite of partially similar factors, differences between the EU and the United States are significant, mostly with regard to the different roles played by public and private institutions.

Europe's welfare state is not 'European' in the sense that is standardized or uniform across the EU, but in the sense that it involves a much greater role for the public sector in daily life than Americans are comfortable with. Public transit systems are much more pervasive in the EU than in the United States, as are public medical systems, public universities, public housing, and public art.

10.1.6. CULTURAL VALUES AND ATTITUDES: INDIVIDUALISM AND THE PROGRESS OF REASON

In Chapter 1, European society and American society are interpreted as two variants of Western modernity, and individualism/subjectivity and rationalism are identified as a core set of values of this type of civilization. Chapter 7 argues that these values are indeed important and common to both Europeans and Americans who are both individualistic and rational in a specific reasonable way. European and American attitudes diverge on some important issues, such as religiousness, family models, and conceptions of social justice, but, on the whole, they tend to agree on core values, and particularly on democracy. They show an evident propensity to uphold what is not only legal but legitimate and to tolerate a reasonable range of opinions and attitudes among themselves. A necessary condition for a democratic society to exist in the contemporary world is not so much a strong and widespread consensus on the same values, but rather a high degree of acceptance of cultural pluralism within the limits of the rule of law.

This common cultural attitude is defined as 'moral liberalism' and is contrasted with 'undifferentiated individualism'. On the whole, the latter may explain a given number of specific trends, but fails to map out an overall framework for the interpretation of opinion trends. Individualism has little value for Americans and Europeans as long as it is not embedded into reasonableness. Self-fulfillment is approved but only within the strict limits of the reasonable. It is not 'loose morals' but moral liberalism in the strict sense of the term; that is acceptance by all that each is free to make judgments and create his or her set of personal, but reasonable morals, insofar as any rule approved by all applies to all. Evidence for rising reasonableness is provided in such domains as childrearing, daily life, attitudes toward politics, and membership in voluntary associations. Among the values considered most important in childrearing, for instance, independence (that is those qualities that help children to 'look out for themselves') comes after 'tolerance and respect for other people', 'feeling of responsibility', and even 'good manners'. In the rules of daily life, the fact that both continents continue to firmly disapprove of tax dodging, bribe-taking, joyriding, or falsely claiming state benefits shows that individualism is never unrestrained. As far as the citizen's relationship to politics is concerned, the prevailing attitude both in the United States and the EU is not radical indifference about politics but rather an increasing attention to a citizen's right to a say in public affairs and a greater demand for political accountability. Confidence in political authorities is on the wane (more so in the United States than in Europe), but confidence in democracy remains very high on both sides of the Atlantic.

On the other hand, there are significant differences in the values and attitudes prevailing among Europeans and Americans, particularly in political cultures, as argued in Chapter 5: first, less emphasis on the values of individual responsibility and a greater emphasis on governmental responsibility, as well as related differences with regard to support for government actions such as providing a guaranteed income, reducing economic inequality, and providing for the unemployed, because of socialist ideology and the Catholic Church's social doctrine.

Second, a conception of liberal democracy where the democratic component often appears stronger than the liberal one, although, as we will see later, the core civil liberties of the American tradition are under growing stress because of the war on terror and the religious fundamentalism of the New Right.

Third, a greater cosmopolitan orientation, which is favored by geopolitics and the greater internal cultural diversity of Europe, and a more peace-oriented attitude toward global politics which is the result of the tragic experiences of the two twentieth-century world wars (this is probably the major difference between the present generations and those of the first half of the twentieth century).

Fourth, a different attitude toward global governance: most EU states are in favor of a multilateral order and a greater role for the UN aiming at binding Gulliver down, whereas the United States—mostly under the Republican administration—has responded to the collapse of the USSR and September 11 with a unilateral, 'imperial' foreign policy, little inclined to share power with other actors.

Finally, respect for authority, in both societies has declined but there is a striking difference in attitudes toward crime and punishment. The imprisonment rate has quadrupled in the past thirty years in the United States, and it is now five times the proportion in Britain, the toughest sentencer in the EU. It is a major indicator of inequality, being much higher among some ethnic groups (nearly one black man in five has been to prison, and one in three has been convicted for a felony). It is the Republican Party which successfully pushed for tougher policies, but Democrats did not oppose since Americans are far more censorious than Europeans and law and order issues are a reliable vote getter.

In Chapter 7, we also discussed whether a European shared culture is in the making and to what extent it has progressed in the past twenty years, through the systematic analysis and comparison of EU citizens' values and attitudes since 1980 with those of American citizens in the same period: attitudes toward democracy, individual responsibility, and the competitive market (the various manifestations of freedom, civic culture and confidence in democratic institutions, attitudes toward neighbors, evaluation of work, attitudes toward family life and conviviality, the role of women, patterns of children's education, the role of religion on society, etc.). From this detailed analysis of survey trends the conclusion can be drawn that although European citizens identify with the EU much less than American citizens identify with the United States—since they prefer what is closer to them and maintain a certain degree of detachment from EU institutions—they share to a significant degree a basic core of values. There are two ways of agreeing on values. There may be a strong consensus on conceptions of the good, but major disagreements may subsist, as happens in any modern society. Here, what counts is for actors to accept a pluralism of reasonable conceptions of the good rather than for them to all hold exactly the same values. This attitude assumes actors endeavor to be impartial toward each other by allowing each one the freedom to think. Obviously, this does not mean 'anything goes' or 'who cares anyway?', it simply means ensuring that an actor's freedom is only curtailed where it infringes on another's according to J. S. Mill's famous thesis, that is actors agree on a reasonable framework within which differing and even conflicting values may flourish.

In this sense, a European shared culture has significantly progressed in the past twenty years, and Europeans already 'make society', even if the EU still lacks basic requirements of state sovereignty like a common fiscal system and a common foreign policy, according to the data analyzed.

This shared culture still runs up against powerful counterforces, such as nationalistic feelings and even xenophobic closures, and it still has to build a strong European identity and common will, but progress is taking place.

In the comparative analysis of values and attitudes, our two hypotheses—that significant but not overriding cultural differences exist between the EU and the United States and that the cultural attitudes of EU member-states are growing more similar—seem verified.

10.1.7. RELIGIOSITY AND STATE–CHURCH RELATIONS

The area where differences both between the EU and the United States and within the EU are more striking is that of religion, that is the various ways in which religious values and beliefs penetrate institutions and orient collective and individual behavior.

The main difference consists in the higher levels of religious belief and religious practice in the United States compared with most EU states (apart from a few exceptions, like Poland). In some cases, for example the Scandinavian countries, the decline has been steady and gradual; in others, like Spain, it has been sharp and rapid. In America 95 percent of the people believe in God, against 76 percent of Britons, 62 percent of French, and 52 percent of Swedes. More than three in four Americans belong to a church, 40 percent go to a church once a week, and one in ten goes several times a week, compared with much lower percentages in most EU states.

Closely related to diminishing religious practice is the declining authority of religion over peoples' lives in most EU countries, where one witnesses the declining capacity of churches to enforce their authority in matters concerning sexuality, and on individual choices in general (Langlois et al. 1994). This trend is in sharp contrast with the American experience of growing church membership and participation as well as greater obedience to religious norms; and it challenges the interpretations of authors like Davie and Hervieu-Léger (1994) and Hallman and Patterson (1994) who maintain that the most significant factors accounting for the decline of religious institutions are the individualization and subjectivization of many aspects of life and the drive for autonomy, which foster the avoidance of collective and authoritative constraints. Individualism and religiosity are both in fact key elements of American culture.

A second basic difference resides in the fact that virtually all European societies have for centuries displayed a low degree of religious and ethnic diversity: usually, a dominant ethnic group has coexisted with a few minorities; each country has had only one, or at most two, dominant established Christian churches; a state church has often existed because religion has been the source of fundamental cleavages and of separated national identities, cases in point being the North/South cleavage between Catholics and Protestants, and the East/West cleavage between Orthodox and Catholics. By reverse, in the United States and despite White, Anglo-Saxon, and Protestant (WASP) hegemony, there is a real religious pluralism and a real ethnic mix; there is no state religion, and it is difficult to say who the true Americans are, and who are the foreigners.

A third major difference is that the United States is predominantly Protestant and the EU is predominantly Catholic: the former provides a greater legitimation for individual economic success, while the latter is more concerned with the protection and relief of underprivileged groups. Once the impact of immigration into the United States from strongly Catholic countries is taken into account, however, the two societies look rather less different than they are sometimes made to appear (Norris and Inglehart 2004).

A fourth major difference between the EU and the United States concerns the relation between religion and politics. American history has been characterized by religious freedom, whereas most European nations developed state churches according to the principle of *cuius region, eius religio*. In the latter, although political allegiance is now declining, it is still rooted in certain major religious (and class) cleavages, even though the parties thereby formed then reach out to wider sectors of the population and transform themselves into 'catch-all parties'. In the United States, religion is playing an increasingly prominent role in politics, but the overall pattern is far more complex, subtle, and incoherent.

As argued in Chapter 8, the separation between churches and state was implemented early in the United States and remained relatively stable. Whereas this division generated the somewhat paradoxical effect that religious rhetoric remained a part of American political life, the heterogeneous and problematic relation between church and state in Europe put a form of taboo on the intrusion of religious discourses into the political systems. Within this context a set of different converging and diverging trends in religious behavior and religiosity can be explored for both societies. Taylor (2002) suggests that the patterns of religious practice in Europe were post-Durkheimian as opposed to neo-Durkheimian ones in the United States. In this line of thinking, Europe is post-Durkheimian since here religion no longer functions as the main structure of meaning in which society or the nation-state expresses itself, whereas the United States possesses neo-Durkheimian qualities since the radically individualized Christianity of the majority of Americans is used to express the commonality of all Americans.

In America religion has always played an important part in political public discourse. Both openly religious presidents, like Carter and Reagan, and others who were not, like Franklin Roosevelt and Eisenhower, have made frequent references to God, divine providence, and the Scriptures (Bonazzi 2004). It is apparently paradoxical that the country whose constitution proclaims the principle of the separation between church and state should exhibit such a strong presence of religious beliefs in public discourse. But in actual fact the principle was introduced to defend religious freedom against the constraints of a state church. In the United States, religion is first and foremost a question of individual choice, and this helps explain why the American people are more religious than most Europeans. As Bellah argued (1967, 1986), religious faith provided the foundation for a civil religion which, through the selection of certain aspects of the religious tradition, was a basic nation-building element able to construct powerful symbols of national solidarity. The national symbols have a religious character and the respect for the constitution looks like religious awe. The history of the United States is reminiscent of episodes in the Bible: the Exodus, the new Israel, and the providential destiny of the United States as the redeemer nation (Tuveson 1968). According to the American Constitution, the people of the United States are specific people like all others, but at the same time they have universal characteristics and realize the universal ideal of liberty. The free act of becoming an American citizen is an act of liberation like the act of choosing the path to religious salvation. A basic aspect of American exceptionalism, therefore, is the fact that the American people are both specific and universal, and have a unique destiny. Whence derives the special importance of American patriotism and its difference from the nationalisms of the European people, although it is a universalism that is inherently contradictory because of the barriers raised against Native Americans and blacks, and the tendency to interpret history as a battle between good and evil.

We assist today to explain the growing politicization of religion, that is its reinsertion into the public sphere in Europe and its increasingly powerful articulation in American society, as we pointed out in Chapter 5. In America, Christian fundamentalism is a basic component of the New Right and is rapidly on the rise: 39 percent of Americans describe themselves as born-again Christians, about one-third of voters are Evangelical Protestants, compared with less than a quarter twenty years ago. American churches are in a state of permanent boom, the Left Behind series of books, which deal with 'the Rapture'—the moment when true Christians will be taken up to heaven—have sold 55 million copies in ten years. Focusing on such hot issues as abortion and Darwin's theory of evolution, and building powerful organizations like the Christian Coalition (with almost 2,000,000 members in the late 1990s) and think-tanks like the American Enterprise Institute, the Heritage Foundation, and the Cato Institute, and building on the Americans' fondness for arguing about fundamentals, the Republican right was able to make the fight against secularism a central issue in political competition. The reinsertion of religion into the public sphere takes place in most European states too, although to a more limited extent than in the United States; different forms of fundamentalism (mainly Christian and Islamic) together with new forms of transnational religiosity are increasing, but on the whole religious issues are less relevant in politics than in the United States.

10.1.8. DIFFERENT FORMS OF THE CITY

A final area of comparison between the EU and the United States, where differences are significant, is the city. The similarities between American and European cities are more apparent than they are real: the EU and the United States resemble each other in their levels of urbanization, but they differ in the form of their cities, in the relationships between the centers and the peripheries, and in the quality of urban life. In most of the EU member-states, the typical city has a center (not a 'downtown') expressing historical and civic identity and continuity, and which has remained relatively immune (except for war damage) to the major subsequent waves of urban transformation responding to market forces and ethnic segregation which have been vividly depicted as a metaphor of modernity by Berman (1982).

The two most important differentiating factors are, first, the existence of a medieval urban heritage and the continuity of a historical urban identity, and second, the experience of regulatory policies of urban development and of city planning in most European cities.

Cities have played a very important, multifunctional role throughout European history, from the Roman *civitates* to medieval towns and modern cities. The Roman *civitates* were commercial, religious, and administrative centers, the sites of magnificent public and private buildings. Medieval towns experienced various forms of self-governance many centuries after the ancient Greek city states: their artisans, merchants, and proto-bourgeois fought against, and were able to obtain special prerogatives from, central authorities (popes, emperors, and kings); and they developed their own statutes, councils, courts of justice, police forces, and sometimes urban armed forces. The classical and medieval urban heritage left its mark on the architecture, the organization of the urban space, and relations with the surrounding countryside. This imprinting, although modified by the process of modernization, made European cities unique and entirely different from American cities and from modern cities in other parts of the world.

Unlike American cities, most contemporary European cities have developed various forms of urban planning and regulation, the purpose being to preserve historic monuments, safeguard public spaces, set standards for private buildings, and perpetuate the distinctive European urban form that arose in a belt of cities in Northern and Central Italy, Germany, Switzerland, Burgundy, and the Low Countries, which long escaped the centralized power of wider territorial states and now roughly correspond to the 'blue banana' (the uninterrupted line of urban lights to be seen from the sky at night above a territory stretching from greater London to Northern Italy).

As argued in Chapter 9, the long-term metastability of the European urban structure has been central in the creation and development of European societies. This stability goes together with its original structure (the high concentration of medium-sized cities) and the remains of its physical form (Le Galès 2002). European cities (if we set London and Paris apart), although they are gaining more autonomy, are still structured and organized within European states— in particular, welfare states. The ongoing restructuring process does represent a threat, but—for the time being—European cities are supported and to some extent protected by the state, including in terms of resources.

European cities are becoming more European, in the sense that the institutionalization of the EU is creating rules, norms, procedures, repertoires, and public policies that have an impact on most, if not all, cities. The EU itself is a powerful agent of legitimation. By designing urban public policies and agreeing (under the influence of city interests) to mention the idea of 'a Europe of cities' as one of the components of the EU, it is giving a boost to cities to act and behave as actors within EU governance. This also, to some extent, leads other actors—for instance, firms—to take European cities more seriously.

Another specific feature relates to their economic and social structure. European cities are characterized by a mix of public services and private firms, including a robust body of middle-class and lower-middle-class public and private tertiary workers, who constitute a firm pillar of the social structure despite increasing social tensions, inequalities, and even riots at times. There is no ideal world of European cities but the remains of a less unequal social structure than in most cities in the world. The more important the welfare state and the scale of redistribution (north of Europe), the lesser the level of inequality and poverty. Both the form of the city, the existence of public spaces, the mix of social groups, and despite powerful social segregation mechanisms, one can suggest the idea of a continuing sense of 'urbanity' still characterizing European cities (Zijderveld 1997). Despite sprawling movements in most European cities, the resistance of the old city centers epitomizes their peculiarity. The enduring strength of a specific model of the European city is also exemplified by the continuing importance of large collective public transport (in particular the tramway) together with pedestrian areas and cycling paths.

Finally, there is a continuing representation of the city as a whole; Crouch (1999) suggests a 'Durkheimian' view of the city which still exists in Europe. The increased legitimacy of political urban elites sustain and reinvent this presentation. European cities are still strongly regulated by public authorities and a complex arrangement of public and private actors. European cities appear to be relatively autonomous, despite pressures from economic actors, collective movements, and states.

In all these domains, significant differences exist between most EU countries and the United States and in areas like demographic patterns and religious attitudes differences not only persist but are even growing.

In other domains, however, differences are declining, and a process of 'Americanization' is taking shape in many EU metropolitan areas. The Continental European model of the social market economy has made room for more privatization, less state intervention, and greater flexibility of labor markets. European social relations are becoming less egalitarian, and ethnicity is becoming more important and classless as a criterion of social inequality. European metropolitan areas are witnessing the growth of peri-urban space consisting of commercial malls and residential neighborhoods far from the center, the number of private cars is increasing, criminality intensifies and there is a growing neglect of public service and space and of the environment. Hradil and Immerfall (1997) stress that Americanization is the next stage in any modernization process, and that it is characterized by greater institutional flexibility, growing market individualization, and more informal social relations. Crouch (1999) points out that the convergence of most European societies takes the form of the spread of certain American characteristics, which in their turn are fostered by the growth of the global deregulated market and the strengthening of the power and scope of the largest transnational corporations and the most homogeneous products.

The decline of differences is, however, not only resulting from a process of Americanization but from various forms of cross-cultural fertilization which is taking place in different aspects of life such as architecture, music, the performing arts, fashion, and lifestyles. Cross-cultural fertilization works both ways: as a matter of fact there are various instances of a counter trend of 'Europeanization' of some neighborhoods and districts in American cities like New York, Boston, and San Francisco, where one can identify clear signs of a specifically European urban way of life.

10.2. **Two models of society**

The appraisal of the similarities between the EU and the United States in key selected areas supports the thesis that American and European societies are two variants of the same civilization of Western modernity. The appraisal of the differences, however, also provides evidence for outlining two distinct models of society.

A model is both an analytical construct—which abstracts from the complexity of empirical reality those elements which can form a coherent whole—and the blueprint for a desirable project. Those who talk of American exceptionalism or European uniqueness use the term predominantly in the former sense, but they also make reference to a model to be achieved. In other words, they develop a positive analysis of American or European society that contains some normative elements as well.

I shall outline the basic elements of the two models, also on the basis of the similarities and differences previously identified, and discuss their sustainability with regard to present challenges. Major challenges for the EU come from increasing competition in the global economy, increasing ethnic and cultural diversity, resurgent nationalism, and the protectionism of vested interests. Major challenges for the United States come from its hegemonic role and the risk of imperial overstretching, the rising economic and political power of countries like China and India, and the ideological conflict between the religious fundamentalism of the New Right and the liberal culture which upheld the ideology of American exceptionalism.

Both the EU and the United States try to provide responses to those challenges building on the core values and distinctive institutions of their societal models (freedom and competition, democratic patriotism, the redeemer nation, for the United States, and social market economy, achieving unity through diversity, and passive aggression, for the EU).

10.2.1. THE AMERICAN MODEL OF SOCIETY

Identification of the key normative and institutional features of society-making is relatively straightforward for the United States, and more complex and controversial for the EU.

The United States is one of the most complex social systems that has ever existed. It is characterized by extraordinary ethnic and cultural heterogeneity, continuous flows of economic innovation and cultural change, fierce competition and intense social mobility, sharp inequalities and individual precariousness, high levels of collective conflict and individual litigation, multiple tensions and contradictions. And yet, the American political system is one of the most stable in the world. During the two centuries of its history, it has evolved significantly, adapting to the dramatic transformation of American society from a nation of thirteen states on the Atlantic coast to a continent-wide federation of fifty states with 300 million people. But it has not changed its institutional foundations, which have protected individual rights and provided a remarkable degree of continuity, social consensus, and political stability.

These institutional foundations have been so stable because, although the founding fathers were convinced that the United States would be the providential nation, the one whose dedication to liberty and individual worth would be the cornerstone of a new moral society, they did not seek dogmatically to impose their own model of the perfect society. Rather, they pragmatically chose to protect individual, inalienable rights and to define the rules of the game for social interaction and the free development of individuals and groups. Each immigrant was free to 'make himself' and could hope to succeed, being free from wars and famines, feudal bonds and aristocratic privileges, the despotism of kings and the intolerance of established religions. Every religious community that arrived in the new world could endeavor to realize its own model of the good society within the limits set by the rule of law; but the model was not imposed by the rulers as revolutionary ideologists and religious fundamentalists aspire. From the outset, the United States was a rejection of the old social order, an open society for a

mass of *homines novi*, religious dissidents, adventurers, outcasts, and poor peasants and artisans fleeing famine and political oppression. On comparing the two
great eighteenth-century revolutions, one can argue that while the French one—
at least in its more radical version—attempted to achieve a social revolution that
would create the new man and institute the religion of humanity, the American
political revolution more pragmatically and less ambitiously aimed at creating
new institutional conditions for the deployment of individual freedom, leaving
the economic order alone and thus giving men an outlet for their passions while
the political order mediated their interests.

This new societal model has its own dark sides: the de facto ethnic cleansing
of the Native Americans, the slavery of African-Americans and following the
Civil War the continuing racism against them, and the discrimination of recently
immigrated ethnic minorities were all phenomena in sharp contradiction with
the principles and the institutions of a free society and a democratic culture.
Moreover, although not a colonial power in the strict sense of the word, the
United States exercised various forms of neocolonial rule. During the cold war,
US foreign policy has sometimes justified—or even contributed to—violations of
democratic principles and the rule of law abroad, while upholding them at home.
The stability of institutions has been paid for to some extent in terms of mass
conformism and political manipulation (Molnar 1978). But, on the whole, liberal
values and democratic institutions have proved strong and stable in American
society.

The American institutional system has demonstrated a remarkable capacity
to adapt to industrial capitalism and mass society, to the growth of large private and public organizations, to postindustrial society and the global economy,
and throughout its history, to an increasingly multiethnic society. Today, it is
increasingly placed under strain by the contradictions stemming from imperial
overstretching and the hegemonic role of the United States in world politics, but
it nevertheless still holds firm. America is not in any danger of breaking apart.

Historical processes have worked to solidify and stabilize powerful central institutions, while suppressing possible sources of resistance and alternative societal
models. The gradual forging of a powerful national political structure took place
through a complex history. Hall and Lindholm (1999) stress four major turning
points: the first moment of genuine division was at the end of the eighteenth
century, when it seemed that federalists favoring a greater power of the state were
prepared to act with force against their Jeffersonian political opponents; but power
was peacefully transferred and conflict regulated by means of a stable and flexible
dual party system and the institutionalization of a loyal opposition. However,
the newfound unity of the nation was made fragile by the social and economic
distinctiveness of the South and the question of slavery; in the second turning
point the union was preserved only through a civil war, the result of which was a
more solidified and homogenized nation. The third turning point was the failure
of workers' radicalism against industrial capitalism at the end of the nineteenth
century because of the combined effect of social mobility and cultural individualism with violent repression. Finally, American hegemonic power fostered the

challenges posed by black protest, civil rights and antiwar movements in the 1960s, but again the institutional fabric was able to resist through policy innovation and at least partial political inclusion.

The institutions of American democracy were outlined and discussed in Chapter 5 as exemplifying the 'compound republic', and they need only to be briefly recalled here. The 'compound republic' involves both a vertical and a horizontal separation of powers. First, power is divided between the federal center and the states through the double principle of representation in Congress (territorial, so that states have equal representation in the Senate; and individual, so that representatives are elected in proportion to the population in the House). Second, the legislative and the executive branches are institutionally separated, reciprocally independent in terms of electoral legitimization, and therefore forced to cooperate. The key federal principle of subsidiarity is applied in that the powers attributed to the federal center are carefully defined and circumscribed, with the justifying principle that they can be better performed at that level of government. All the other powers are left to the member-states. Since the Civil War, however, the national government has grown steadily more powerful in relation to the states. Congress and the judiciary have expanded the federal role in many areas formerly reserved to the states, such as crime control, education, health care, environmental protection, and product safety. And yet local authorities and states still wield significant autonomous power.

Stable and enduring political institutions are closely related to widely shared values and beliefs. It may be, as Walzer points out, that Americans have no need of a common cultural identity because they are protected from moral anarchy by a shared reverence for the constitution (Walzer 1990). But solid institutions must be grounded in widely shared beliefs, mostly in multiethnic and multicultural societies. As argued in Chapter 5, American society can be portrayed as a study in contrasts, as a country of 'unity amidst diversity' where the great majority of Americans, old-comers and newcomers alike, share the fundamental beliefs of liberal political culture notwithstanding their great social and ethnic heterogeneity (Fiorina, Peterson, and Johnson 2002).

Individualism is a core value of American culture, that is praised as a guarantee of freedom and criticized as selfishness. But individualism goes together with communal action. In Tocqueville's (1835–9) famous account of American democracy, an active associational life is seen as the remedy for the risk that isolated individuals will acquiesce passively in the tyranny of the majority and the despotism of the state. In Weber's less famous, but equally insightful, study of American sects (1920), the legacy of the Protestant ethic links radical individualism with principled and self-aware voluntary participation in the larger moral community. Individualism and communal action often go together, as political equality and social inequality. American culture is not a homogeneous whole, it is torn by the contradictory implications of its core values, as in many other societies. Nor should it be neglected that the consensus of American culture was not predetermined at the start, but intense conflict over interpreting core principles took place and sometimes rather genuine societal alternatives were defeated by violent means.

Contrary to what one might think, in fact, the high level of consensus on core values does not spring from the absence of conflict. The reverse is true: American history has been marked by widespread and intense conflict among ethnic and social groups, heated morally based confrontation on public policy, and high levels of violence. However, conflict can both cause a society to break apart and help to foster consensus. Conflict can intensify and lead to disaster the more that different struggles become layered on top of one another. But in American society the recognition and regulation of conflict has successfully managed to avoid such divisive layering of region, class, ethnicity, and race.

Moreover, with very few exceptions, protest movements and radical critics do not uphold alternative ideological models but they have made appeal to the principles of the American Constitution and denounced their violation. An episode of the 1960s epitomizes this attitude: Jerry Rubin, the leader of the hippy antiwar movement accused of anti-patriotic activities, went to court symbolically dressed as an eighteenth-century soldier of the American War of Independence. More intense conflicts reflect antagonistic interests as they do everywhere, but in the United States they also tend to be defined in moral terms, whereas in Europe they tend to be framed within a political ideology (Martinelli 1974). The two most important collective movements of the second half of the twentieth century—the civil rights movement and the anti-Vietnam War movement—did not contest (with a few notable exceptions) the basic political principles, but rather the ways in which they were being interpreted and applied. Martin Luther King fought injustice not only in the name of Christian love but also as a violation of the American creed. As Lipset puts it, Americans fight each other in their efforts to defend or expand the American creed. Stable institutions and an enduring political culture help explain why the serious crises undergone by American society—as at the time of the Vietnam War—have never turned into systemic crises endangering the country's political order.

Traditional explanations of the homogeneous political culture of American citizens, from Tocqueville (1835) to Parrington (1927), Hartz (1955), and Lipset (1996), argue that the liberal beliefs which early settlers brought with them did not meet resistance in the American social structure. Unlike in Europe, there were no landed aristocracy and oppressed peasantry, nor a monarchy, established state church, and feudal traditions. By contrast, there was a plentiful supply of land and scarcity of labor, which enabled ambitious and capable men to get ahead and fostered the myth of the frontier and the ideology of personal responsibility for one's successes and failures.

Political socialization played an important role in the cultural assimilation of successive waves of immigrants, most of them from countries with authoritarian political traditions. The assimilation of core liberal values fostered, and was favored by, the remarkable continuity of political institutions. And the self-selection of immigrants guaranteed both rejuvenation and consolidation. With the notable exception of African-Americans, immigrants came to America voluntarily. Push-factors—like economic poverty, religious discrimination, and political oppression—certainly played a major role; but, since only a minority of the population chose to emigrate, even from countries with severe economic and political conditions, it is likely that those who immigrated were—relative to their own societies—unusually individualistic, and they had a kind of predisposition for free institutions and values, or at least they were willing to embrace those beliefs and lifestyles.

For Baudrillard (1988), the success of the American model of society has sprung from the difference between democracy and egalitarianism, and from the fact that freedom and equality only exist when they are present at the outset. Democracy presupposes equality at the beginning, while egalitarianism presupposes it at the end; democracy demands that all citizens begin equal, egalitarianism insists that they all finish equal. Whereas Europe has remained stuck in the old pattern of social difference and has been constantly dragged back into the history of its bourgeois culture, America, by contrast, has achieved a state of radical modernity which can be described as a perpetual present, a kind of achieved utopia where everything is exactly what it appears to be. It is worthwhile considering whether and to what extent the presently prevailing conservative mood, with its stress on God and the family, contradicts this radically modern attitude.

The peculiar nature of American culture was affirmed in the writings of Frederick Turner and other historians of the American Studies School of the 1930s. They stressed the American culture's continuous and privileged relationships with the frontier and the great open spaces of a continent where European heritage was of little use. This return to the roots of human nature fostered the distinctive American traits of individualism, love of freedom and spirit of independence, ability to adapt to change and diversity, nondogmatic view of religion, and pragmatic and nonideological attitude toward social life, which in their turn made the American melting pot possible.

The emphasis on the uniqueness of the American experience and the American national character performed an important role in freeing Americans from an 'Oedipus complex' toward Europe (Boorstin 1960): that is, Americans no longer needed to compare themselves with Europe in order to define their own identity. This emphasis on uniqueness seems in sharp opposition to the view which I have expounded of American society as a variant of a common Western modernity. Indeed, it is not, because this is not the way it was perceived; in the years of World War II and the cold war against the Soviet Union, the United States was seen as bypassing and more completely realizing Western civilization (Bonazzi 2004). The idea of American uniqueness was reconciled with that of a common Western heritage, so that America continued and completed in the present the long journey of European civilization. This was an ideologically loaded view which provided legitimacy for American hegemony in the fight against communism and gave historical depth to the relationship between Europe (the past) and America (the present). And it is a view still widely present in contemporary American society, as exemplified by the courses in Western civilization taught at American universities (Segal 2000). When stripped of its ideological overtones, however, the conceptualization of American society as a specific version of

Western culture and institutions is theoretically sound and empirically grounded; it is one of the main theses of this volume.

10.2.2. AMERICAN EXCEPTIONALISM?

The unique character of the American model of society has induced scholars like Lipset (1979*a* and 1996) and Bell (1988) to speak of an American 'exceptionalism'. For Lipset, 'the United States is exceptional in starting from a revolutionary event, in being "the first new nation", the first colony . . . to become independent. It has defined its *raison d'être* ideologically' (1996: 18). In a much quoted definition, Hofstadter remarked that it has been 'our fate as a nation not to have ideologies, but to be one' (1948). Political leaders like Lincoln and writers like Waldo Emerson have emphasized the country's political religion. And because of their distinctive history, many Americans share the belief that they are the redeemer nation, which is another key dimension of American exceptionalism (Tuveson 1968).

The cornerstone of exceptionalism is what Myrdal (1944) termed the American creed. According to Lipset, the creed can be described in five terms: liberty, egalitarianism (which is equality of opportunity and respect, not equality of result or social condition), individualism, populism, and laissez-faire. These values reflect the absence of feudal structures, monarchies, and aristocracies. The United States has been the chosen country for millions of immigrants seeking not only better life chances but also greater individual and institutional freedom. The United States is the most religious, optimistic, patriotic, rights oriented, and individualistic country. Lipset draws binary comparisons between the United States and Canada (1990), and between the exceptionalism of the United States, the most individualistic nation, and the uniqueness of Japan, the most group-oriented society (1996). But the comparison with Europe is constantly in the background of his books.

Compared with Europe, American society is wealthier in per capita income and purchasing power, much more job-creating, more individualistic, less committed to welfare and government regulation, more committed to higher education and meritocracy, more religious, more patriotic, more prone to divorce, less law-abiding, more populist and antielitist, more favorable to private initiative and business success, and with greater social inequalities, lower voting rates, and a greater willingness to join associations. Lipset points out that the various seemingly contradictory aspects of American society are intimately related:

'the lack of respect for authority, anti-elitism and populism contribute to higher crime rates, school indiscipline and low election turnouts. The emphasis on achievement, on meritocracy, is also tied to higher levels of deviant behavior and less support for the underprivileged. . . . Concern for the legal rights of accused persons and civil liberties in general is tied to opposition to gun control and difficulty in applying crime-control measures'.

(Lipset 1996: 290)

In his essay 'The Hegelian secret: civil society and American exceptionalism' (1988), Bell identifies the essence of United States exceptionalism in the strength of civil society vis-à-vis the state. Bell challenges Hegel's view of the United States as the embodiment of modernity ('the land of the future... the land of desire for all those who are weary of the historical lumber-room of old Europe') and of England as the bourgeois nation that exemplifies civil society in its self-interest and its utilitarian character; and argues that it is the United States which embodies the complete civil society, since it is there that individual self-interest and passion for liberty go together with the absence of a unified rational will of the state. 'In every European nation (with the partial exception of England), the state ruled over society, exercising a unitary or quasi unitary power (enforced by a military class and a bureaucracy); and the state itself was the locus of power' (Bell 1988: 21). In Europe, therefore, revolution has meant the seizing of state power, whereas in the United States, despite acute and widespread social conflicts, class struggles, ethnic and racial violence, there have been no contests for state power. Rather than 'state', 'government' or 'administration' is the appropriate word for American politics defined as a political arena in which interests—with different capacities and influences in pressure politics—contend against each other, and where deals are constantly made and compromises are constantly reached.

Both Lipset and Bell and the other theorists of exceptionalism, although providing interesting insights, overemphasize the distinctiveness of the United States model of society and neglect the fact that the United States and Europe are not so different after all. They ignore the fact that American society may have been exceptional but for many decades has been no longer 'new', 'young', with a 'moving frontier' and 'isolated' from the rest of the world. They neglect to acknowledge that American society combines political equality with a structure of social inequality and that, as Hall and Lindholm (1999) argue 'the greatest problem of American culture is its inability to conceptualize and deal with inequality'.

Moreover, Bell's account, in particular, overemphasizes the role of civil society (which according to other, more recent, studies like Putnam's seems to have sharply declined), and it underplays the growing power of the state in the contemporary United States. In the United States, as elsewhere, the state is not only the arena of pluralist politics, but also the monopolist of legitimate force both in the domestic sphere and in the international arena. Bell acknowledges the rise of the state since Roosevelt's New Deal but argues that it was 'unplanned and not at all consistently ideological, but a response, during crisis, to three elements: the changes in the "scale" of the society; the outcome of changing political realignments; and the logic of mobilization for war' (Bell 1988: 27). It may be true that it was unplanned and not coherent with the American creed, but what matters is that the powers of the US president and his or her administration have been steadily growing since the 1930s as a result of both domestic and international factors.

By 1930, the United States had become a national society with national markets and national corporations, fostered by a modern transportation system. The New Deal was a 'matching of scale' which created national political institutions (like the

National Industrial Recovery Administration) to establish national industry codes and price-fixing schemes in the major industries, and regulatory mechanisms to control markets (like the Security and Exchange Commission) in order to match national economic power. The redistributive effects of New Deal policies built a political coalition in which labor, farmers, and disadvantaged groups swung over to the Democratic camp, asking for and finding protection against economic and social hazards.

Finally, the need to mobilize human and material resources, first for World War II and later in the confrontation with the Soviet Union for world hegemony, helped strengthen the role of the federal government, increasing the size of government, the number of public sector employees, the incidence of taxation, and the growth of state expenditure as a percentage of GDP, to the point of creating the huge national debt of recent decades. At times, domestic pressures and foreign policy pressures go together in strengthening federal administration—as in the period of Johnson's Great Society and the Vietnam War and at times they do not—as when Reagan expanded defense budgets for the military and reduced subsidies and entitlements. Countervailing political power was distributed among the states, but not very effectively. After the New Deal and World War II, American society looked less exceptional with regard to other Western democracies in terms of economic and social policies.

Since the 1970s, however, with the vanishing of the 'New Deal coalition', and the advent of the New Right, the ideology of exceptionalism gained new ground and was upheld by organizations like the Christian Coalition and think-tanks like the Heritage Foundation. Conservative America showed pride in its distinctive values of private enterprise, religiosity, patriotism, and law and order. This ideological stance was a major element in the confrontation with a declining USSR during the 1980s. The victory in the cold war and the collapse of the Soviet Union boosted this American sentiment of being different and proud of it.

The 2001 terrorist attack fostered the new unipolarism in global politics and the propensity of using preventive force abroad and harsh punishment at home. At present, the huge federal government budget required by the US imperial role and hegemonic ambitions breeds acute tensions with demands for better welfare policies and for restrictions in the growth of government bureaucracy. The thesis of American exceptionalism has been given new life by the New Right in its ideological response to the challenges stemming from the end of the cold war and the rise of international terrorism.

Although hardly exceptional, since it is deeply inscribed in the experience of Western modernity, the US model of society is certainly distinctive in many ways, first of all in the ways in which cohesion is maintained and conflict managed; it is characterized by a dynamic economy and an ethnically heterogeneous, conflict-ridden, and violent society, on the one hand, and by stable political institutions and widespread consensus on a few key underlying values, on the other. The two sides of the picture are closely integrated: in the American open society, continuous innovation, fierce competition, high expectations and opportunities to get ahead combine with a constant precariousness and a risk of 'losing' which produce constant conflict and widespread violence. Social crises periodically erupt, but they never become systemic, owing to the presence of stable and enduring political institutions, patriotism, and a well-entrenched liberal political culture; and contradictions are temporarily 'solved' through continuous growth and further segmentation (Martinelli 1974).

The challenges of class and ethnic differences have been met by occupational segmentation as a new model of social mobility, by the individual quest for material success, and by the universal right to consumption (which is what freedom amounts to for many Americans). As Verhoeven (2001) argues, consumption became the most powerful cement of American society in the 1950s. It was no longer a privilege, but a right—to some extent even a civic duty. Americans began to regard the meaning of work as the power to spend, and increasingly began to predicate their identity and social position on their power to consume. Consumption became the ultimate equalizer.

The threat of class conflict was contained not only by opposing labor organizations and socialist ideology, but also by offering abundant jobs and opportunities for social mobility within a segmented occupational structure where class identities found it difficult to emerge. The expansion of credit and the availability of easy money also played a role in turning the worker or professional into a consumer, and the consumer into a citizen. Class loyalties, still important in European politics, have been eclipsed in the United States where the vast majority lump themselves together as 'middle class' and the 'consumer' is more important than the 'worker' in defining social status.

Race and ethnic conflicts are managed in a similar way: 'the economic elite offered to members of minorities and new immigrants as well as all other Americans a passport to consumerism and a place somewhere in the great interdependency of the system of segmented wholeness' (Verhoeven 2001). As remarked in Chapter 5, however, ethnic identities seem more significant than class identities as a mobilizing factor in American politics, despite the similar strategies used to cope with them.

The American case seems to provide an answer to the classic sociological question: 'What are the foundations of solidarity in a highly individualistic society?' It does so by highlighting the role of stable political institutions, entrenched liberal culture, occupational segmentation, and widespread consumerism. The American model of society seems rather resilient. But it is a model under stress. Scholars and citizens in general have raised widespread concern about the fact that American citizens are losing confidence in their institutions, and are increasingly dissatisfied with market failures and diminishing consumer confidence, interest group pressures and divided government, nationality and multiculturalism, the cultural crisis of American values, the spread of violence and the decline of morals, and last, but not least, terrorism and growing hostility against Americans in the world.

We will discuss how and to what extent American values and institutions are changing with regard to two basic questions: first, whether the pressures produced by the imperial hegemonic role of the United States in the global world will endanger the distinctive organizing principles of the American model of society; second, whether the changing ethnic mix of American society—which is also a product of an increasingly global world—will change the hegemonic liberal culture and institutions of the compound republic.

10.2.3. AMERICAN HEGEMONY AND CIVIL LIBERTIES

In Chapter 5 we point out that American neo-imperial foreign policy and the war on terror raise potential risks for democracy. It is true that in the United States, political and religious leaders and citizens in general have not transformed their response to the 2001 terrorist attack into ethnic and/or religious warfare. But, on the other hand, the post-September 11 syndrome has led to the enactment of rules that restrict individual freedoms at home, and to the pursuit of aggressive policies against foreign countries in the name of the defense of freedom and democracy. Basic freedoms could also be in jeopardy, because US neoimperial foreign policy goes together with the growing weight of conservative moral and religious beliefs. The Republican Party's strategy of focusing on God and the family threatens individual rights (women's rights above all), personal moral preferences, and the freedom of scientific research.

American hegemony is a mixed blessing: on the one hand, American society can continue to develop while maintaining its distinctive cultural code and reproducing its specific institutional fabric also by virtue of its hegemonic position in the world. American hegemony has solid foundations: the United States enjoys a remarkable advantage in basic resources—above all primacy in scientific research and technological innovation, military might, control over international media, and the influence of US-based transnational corporations on international organizations like the IMF, the World Bank, and the World Trade Organization (WTO). On the other hand, American society does run the risk of imperial overstretching, and the costs of hegemony may be higher than the benefits in both economic and political terms. In the upswing phases of the economic cycle, the American economy is able to attract enough investment to finance a huge federal debt, and it is also able to preserve the central role of the dollar in international transactions. But in downswing phases, US economic and financial power loses ground to the euro in the international monetary system, and to China's booming economy and those of other aggressive exporting countries.

Even more serious than the economic and financial limits of American power are its political and cultural limits: whenever the American superpower displays unilateral arrogance in global politics, it provokes outright hostility and radical opposition among many peoples and countries in the world, and worries and suspicions among its allies. Unilateral arrogance and the predominance of hard power over soft power contradict a basic tenet of the American democratic tradition, namely the control of power through power, through a system of checks and balances. The fight against international terrorism risks restricting civil liberties and dividing the country into two opposite political camps.

A leitmotiv of the political discourse of the present administration—which echoes previous statements—is that American liberty is linked to the liberation of the rest of the world, that Americans fight to defend the freedom of others. It is added that September 11 raised a new challenge in a new form of evil and chaos. The question is whether the fight against chaos in the name of a rational and pragmatic civilization can be waged without renouncing basic freedoms and democratic guarantees. The passing of the Patriot Act under the justification of the 'war on terror' has raised widespread criticism for curtailing basic civil liberties of US citizens; abuses of prisoners in Iraq and in Guantanamo have raised protest in the world against American policies.

Moreover, American politics since September 11 tends to divide the country into two opposing ideological camps, each of which proclaims its own genuine interpretation of core American values. The 2004 presidential elections highlighted this split in the American electorate. The Republican-voting 'born again Christians' and other conservatives were determined to revitalize the basic values of individual freedom, the heterosexual family, Christian faith, hard work, free enterprise, and self-restraint—that are specific to the American creed—providing both a shield in an increasingly immoral society and a foundation for continuing US power in the world. On the other side stood the Democratic-voting liberals and ethnic minorities (most blacks and many Mexican Americans) who affirmed the core values of individual freedom, civil rights, and cultural pluralism, these also being specific to the American creed. The former accused their opponents of being against God and family: indeed, in his book, *Winning the Future*, Gingrich warns that America may be undermined and even destroyed if 'God be removed from American public life and we are reduced to the civilization of boredom that now characterizes a declining Europe' (2005). The liberals accuse their opponents of challenging another core element of the American creed: civil liberties, equality of opportunity, and respect for all. Abortion is the issue that best embodies the war between liberal and conservative America, between the America of individual rights and liberal-minded judges and the America of traditional values and evangelical churches. A well-organized and growing minority of antiabortionists try to reverse the consequences of the famous 1973 *Roe* v. *Wade* Supreme Court decision that made abortion a constitutional right.

The complex equilibrium of the open, plural society with its WASP hegemony is subject to growing strain. It faces the two opposite risks of a retreat into Christian fundamentalism on the one hand, and an incapacity to govern a society with a changing ethnic mix on the other. According to some scholars: 'the futures of the United States and the West depend on Americans reaffirming their commitment to Western civilization' (Huntington 1997: 307). According to other scholars, continuing US hegemony will depend on the ability of American society to be a model of the global society of the future—which cannot but be plural, interethnic, and multicultural. A possible compromise may stem from a manifold effort to strengthen the political and economic institutions of Western modernity (rule of law, representative democracy, and market economy) and to reaffirm the core values and beliefs that lie behind them (freedom of choice in personal preferences,

equal rights, and scientific rationality) in public life, while simultaneously granting recognition and effective means of emancipation to historically marginalized
minorities.

10.2.4. MULTICULTURALISM AND AMERICAN IDENTITY

These latter considerations introduce the second question: whether the changing
ethnic mix and the growing multiculturalism of American society may cause its
disintegration. In his most recent book *Who Are We?* (2004), Huntington fears
that the growing influence of Hispanic America, and the related identity politics,
may destroy the institutional fabric of American democracy and its Anglo-Saxon
cultural foundations. Huntington's concern is further exacerbated by the 'border'
studies which focus primarily on the Chicano population in the southwest and
argue that the ideal of national culture is a device with which to dominate the
Mexican-American population. Huntington criticizes these and other advocates
of multiculturalism on the grounds that they challenge a central element of the
American creed, by substituting the rights of individuals with the rights of groups
(defined largely in terms of race, ethnicity, gender, and sexual preference).

Other scholars expressed similar views before Huntington: Schlesinger (1991),
for instance, is concerned that multiculturalism may disunite American society,
and he recommends that Americans should try 'to vindicate cherished cultures
and traditions without breaking the bonds of cohesion—common ideas, common
political institutions, common language, common culture, common fate—that
hold the republic together'. Gitlin (1995) maintains that identity politics may
endanger the commitment to common egalitarian ideals which marked the civil
rights movement because they emphasize differences over commonality and they
target group-specific political goals.

Michael Lind (1995), the advocate of American liberal nationalism, is another
strong critic of multiculturalism. He provides a reading of American history as a
sequence of three different republics, each with its own conception of the national
community, civic religion, and political creed. The 'first republic' was Anglo-
America from the War for Independence to the Civil War, in which the national
community identified with the Anglo-Saxon and Anglo-Germanic element of the
population, the civic religion was Protestant Christianity, and the political creed
federal republicanism. The Civil War and Reconstruction created the 'second
republic' (Euro-American), that lasted until the mid twentieth century, in which
the national community was enlarged to the point of including all immigrants of
European descent and Christian religion, and with federal democracy as the main
political creed. The 'third republic' (multicultural America) is the present one;
it was born in the turmoil of the civil rights revolution between the 1950s and
the 1970s, but resulted from the 'intersection of black power conservatism and
white-backlash conservatism' and 'saw the triumph of group-consciousness and
racial preference programs'(quotas, affirmative action, etc.); in the third republic
there is no coherent national community, but rather five national communities

defined by race (white, black, Hispanic, Asian and Pacific Islander, and Native American), the civic religion is 'an ideal of authenticity, that stresses conformity to a particular racial or sexual or religious subcultures', and the political creed has been 'centralized multicultural democracy—the replacement of territorial federalism by a kind of Washington-centered racial federalism'. Lind fears that 'if multicultural America endures for another generation or two, the future of the United States is a bleak one of sinking incomes for the trans-racial American majority and growing resentment against the affluent and politically dominant white oligarchy', and argues for a fourth republic, capable of renewing the American nation-state in the direction of 'a color-blind, gender-neutral regime of individual rights . . . combined with government activism promoting a high degree of substantive social and economic equality.'

All these works, however different they may be, share the concern that a multiculturalism and identity politics combined with continuing inequality and oligarchic rule can cause the breaking apart of the American nation. But they overestimate such a risk, as I will argue by discussing at some length Huntington's thesis—since it is the most recent and radical.

For Huntington, American identity has had two primary components: culture and creed, which are closely related in that the creed has been a product of the culture. The former component consists in the values and institutions of America's original settlers—who were primarily Anglo-Saxon and Protestant—and it includes the English language and a political tradition centered on individual freedom. Immigrants from Western, Southern, and Eastern Europe between the mid-nineteenth and mid-twentieth century modified and enriched the original culture, but they did not fundamentally alter it. So too did blacks, although they were more slowly and only partially assimilated. The second component of American identity is the 'American creed', that is a set of universal principles and ideas articulated by the founding fathers: liberty, equality, democracy, constitutionalism, liberalism, limited government, private entrepreneurship, and market economy.

Huntington maintains that 'the end of the Cold War and social, intellectual and demographic changes in American society have brought into question the validity and relevance of both traditional components of American identity', with the consequence that 'without a sure sense of national identity, Americans have become unable to define their national interests, and as a result sub-national commercial interests and transnational and non-national ethnic interests have come to dominate foreign policy' (1997: 1).

American national identity is further threatened by Hispanic immigration, the extent and nature of which differ fundamentally from those of previous inflows; the assimilation successes of the past are unlikely to be duplicated with the contemporary flood of immigrants from Latin America. In the past, immigrants came from overseas and many of them had to overcome severe hardships to reach the United States. The pre-World War I immigration originated legally from different countries and was linguistically highly differentiated among Italian, Russian, Polish, Yiddish, English, German, Swedish, and Chinese. The flow fluctuated over time, with significant reductions due to the Civil War, World War

I, and the restrictive legislation of 1924. The immigrants dispersed among many enclaves, mostly in large metropolitan areas, but also in rural areas throughout the Northeast, the Midwest, and California.

Mexican immigration is fundamentally different on all counts, with the further feature that Mexicans settle predominantly in a region that was once part of their homeland, and assert special rights and claims over it. As a result, the assimilation of Mexicans into US culture and society is much more difficult than it was in the case of previous immigrants—as evidenced by differences between third- and fourth-generation Americans of Mexican origin in education, socioeconomic status, and intermarriage rates. In 2000, 86.6 percent of native-born Americans had graduated from high school. The rates for the foreign-born population in the United States were 83.8 percent for Asians, but only 49.6 percent for Latin Americans as a whole and 33.8 percent for Mexicans. Mexican immigrants and native Mexican-Americans lag behind the rest of the nation and other immigrant groups on a variety of socioeconomic indicators, including professional and managerial occupation, household income, and home ownership. The percentage of US marriages involving Hispanics marrying outside their ethnic group has declined in the past twenty-five years and is lower than among other minorities like Asians.

This situation prompts Huntington (2004) to ask a fundamental question: Will the United States remain a country with a single national language and a core Anglo-Protestant culture? And to give a shocking answer that 'by ignoring this question, Americans acquiesce to their eventual transformation into two peoples with two cultures (Anglo and Hispanic) and two languages (English and Spanish)'. Huntington's argument is that massive Hispanic immigration affects the United States in two significant ways: important portions of the country become predominantly Hispanic in language and culture, generalizing the Miami model, and the nation as a whole becomes bilingual and bicultural.

The argument is rather unconvincing. First of all, because American patriotism runs deep. The percentage of Americans who declare they are proud of their country (80%) is well above the figures for most EU states, as is the percentage of those who think that American culture is superior to other cultures (Micklethwait and Wooldridge 2004: 300). American citizens and institutions display the flag and sing the national anthem much more often than their European counterparts.

Besides, American society has proved to be rather successful in assimilating immigrants of all kinds. Hispanics are in fact different because of a stronger linguistic identity, but not more culturally different than immigrants from Asia. In the 1960s, when downtown American cities were inflamed by black riots and the most militant black groups declared that they wanted to form a separate nation, there were similar fears of American society breaking apart, but these fears proved completely wrong.

Moreover, Huntington's argument is weakened by the fact that he sometimes focuses on all Hispanics and sometimes on Mexicans alone, whereas the difference between Mexican and other Hispanic children in identifying themselves primarily as 'American', 'Hispanic' or 'Mexican', 'Cuban', and 'Dominican' is striking. Huntington argues that a sizable percentage of Mexican foreign-born residents speak Spanish at home and that there are greater pressures for children to maintain their native language alongside English. But he is also forced to acknowledge that 'English language use and fluency for first- and second-generation Mexicans seem to follow the pattern common to past immigrants.'

The less convincing aspect of Huntington's thesis is its contention that Anglo-Saxon and Mexican Americans embrace greatly different values, the evidence for which seemingly amounts to a list of stereotypes ranging from laziness to familism. Even if one accepts that most Mexicans fit the portrait of the 'Mexican character' described in the book, Huntington nevertheless forgets, first, that the very decision to migrate differentiates migrants from those who stay behind and, second, that the cultural and institutional context of the country of immigration usually changes the original values to a large extent. Moreover, some of the original 'ethnic' values may help assimilation rather than run counter it: for instance, the persisting strength of communal bonds among Spanish-speaking residents.

Illegal immigration is a serious problem for the United States, as it is in the EU, but American society does not seem seriously threatened by growing multiculturalism and the changing ethnic mix of its population. Huntington and similar critics overestimate such a risk. Historically constructed institutional patterns and cultural commonalities still hold the country together; the American nation is not breaking apart (Hall and Lindholm 1999).

10.2.5. THE EUROPEAN MODEL OF SOCIETY

According to the notion of society outlined at the beginning of this chapter, the conceptualization of the EU as a society is much more complex and controversial than for the United States. From our analysis, we can conclude that: (a) most European societies appear to share a significant number of common traits which make them specific even with regard to their closest societal model and single biggest comparator—American society; (b) shared values and common supranational institutions foster the slow construction of a European society, in spite of continuing great structural, cultural, and institutional diversity at the national level; and (c) a European society is in the making and a distinctive model of society is put forward by EU political representatives and scholars supporting the project of European integration. But is this enough to identify a specific European model of society?

The official documents of the European Commission—not only in the crucial years of the Delors Commission between 1985 and 1995 but also before and after it—frequently affirmed that there exists a specifically European model of society which reflects the values of the social market economy and seeks to combine an economic organization based on market forces, entrepreneurship, and freedom of opportunity with a commitment to the values of solidarity, social justice, mutual support and social cohesion, and to the institutions of civilized industrial relations and the welfare state (Delors 1988; Ross 1995; European Commission 1996, 2001).

There is no doubt that the political integration of Europe played a key role in economic growth and vice versa. The emergence of a borderless, traffic-free supranational state with uncontrolled movement of goods, services, capitals, and workers has given European companies a home market that is bigger and richer than the United States. The uniform regulatory apparatus across twenty-seven national markets has permitted development of uniform sizes, packaging, and technical standards that mean a product designed for one corner of the EU will work for the entire union and its half-billion consumers. The single currency makes formerly complicated sales transactions more efficient.

This societal model is thus driven by the single market and economic growth, which in turn act as catalysts for institutional and social development. Delors— himself a Socialist and a Catholic—has been a key intellectual figure in the development of this vision that combines elements of liberalism, socialism, and Christian social doctrine. Before Delors became the influential president of the European Commission, he had been Mitterrand's finance minister in 1983, at the time of the shift from socialist economic planning to a neoliberal policy of strong curbs on public spending and reduced taxes on commerce. He forcefully propounded the view that creation of the single market was a necessary but insufficient means to achieve stable economic growth, and that it had to be supported by three other factors: a monetary union, a policy of cohesion aimed at improving the infrastructure of the poorest member countries, and laws of social protection designed to prevent production transfers to countries with lower labor standards (Delors 1988).

The European model of society is coherent with the core values forming the common heritage of the peoples of Europe (social justice in a free society, democratic institutions, and human rights), and tries to combine the principles of the liberal tradition with those of the social democratic tradition. The special character of the European society stems from a combination of complementary/opposite values and institutions: on the one hand, the liberal democratic culture of individual freedom, constitutional rights, limits to power, and the competitive market; on the other, the social democratic culture of containing the inequalities that might threaten social cohesion, protecting the most vulnerable through active policies, and providing social and economic citizenship rights. On the one hand, the competitive market and the free circulation of people, capitalism, goods, and services; on the other, the welfare state and the ESM.

Much emphasis is also placed on organizing civil society at the European level, promoting the emergence of genuinely pan-European bodies representing Europe-wide constituencies, investing in education, and taking advantage of the new technologies of the information society. The economic and social actors of civil society are described by Commission documents as 'partners in governance', in the sense that they are increasingly part of a multilevel policymaking system more coherent with the reality of globalization than traditional nation-state government. The Lisbon strategy and the OMC (Zeitlin and Pochet 2005) are the most recent expressions of this set of policies and institutions.

The key question is whether competitiveness and welfare are really complementary or at least compatible goals. As Ferrera (2005) argues, economic integration and welfare imply two different logics: economic integration implies the breaking of barriers, the opening of national systems, freedom of circulation, and rules of nondiscrimination on the basis of specific identities. Welfare policies, on the contrary, have developed within the nation-state framework, and even 'universalistic' models of welfare imply a logic of social closure, insofar as people are mostly entitled to social protection and welfare provisions on the basis of their national citizenship (or of an even narrower professional status).

In the early decades of European integration, a competitive economy was made compatible with the ESM through the isolation of national welfare systems from the supranational mechanisms of the common market. The development of the free market fostered competitiveness that in its turn fostered high rates of economic growth and low unemployment. High rates of economic growth generated resources which could be spent on social protection, although the quality and the extent of welfare policies, provisions, and services varied much across Europe, giving rise to the different welfare models outlined above.

Some speak of the 1960s and 1970s as the 'golden age' of the welfare state, which has been ended by the 'external' forces of the global market. Giddens (2006) correctly criticizes this view, pointing out that welfare provisions were often inadequate, many workers had to respond to the bureaucratic hierarchies of mass production, few women were able to work if they wanted to, few young people entered further or higher education, old people were put out by a rigid retirement age, and the state generally treated its clients as passive subjects rather than as active citizens. And yet, it was a 'golden age' in the sense that it seemed possible to pursue at the same time market liberalization at the supranational, European level, and welfare policies at the national level. According to Gilpin's famous saying: 'Smith abroad and Keynes at home' (1987), economic integration and welfare state could and should remain loosely coupled.

The world situation changed deeply in the past two decades of the twentieth century. Intensifying globalization, the information and communication technology revolution, and the shrinking of manufacturing and its transfer to less developed countries made world competition more acute, and worsened the performance of Europe's social market capitalism with regard to America's market-driven capitalism. As shown in Chapter 2, since the 1980s average growth in the EU has declined in relative terms, per capita GDP has remained at 70 percent of the US level, while unemployment rates are much higher; these lower rates, together with shorter working hours, are responsible for lower per capita GDP, and completely outset increases in average productivity (European Commission 2003*a*).

These 'external' structural factors were one major source of tensions for European welfare policies, the other being represented by 'internal' demographic and social factors (the aging population, sharp decline in fertility, increase of single-parent families, and rigid employment structures). Free-market thinking and the ideology of liberalization and privatization increasingly challenged welfare policies and welfare ideology, first in the UK but then in other EU member-states as well. Moreover, the very process of European economic integration, and in particular the Monetary Union, introduced direct and indirect constraints on the implementation of national welfare policies. The Maastricht parameters that member countries have to respect in order to join and remain in the Monetary Union (maximum ceilings for the public debt, state budgets deficit, and inflation rate) have made the constraints on national state budget and public spending explicit, so that it is no longer possible to conceive a Union policy focused on liberalizing the markets and member-states policies designed at implementing welfare.

Some European scholars and political leaders think that the old division of labor between the EU and the member-states can be continued and suggest that national governments should take care of the social costs of the necessary increasing liberalization. But they neglect the fact that EU budgetary rules and EU monetary policy strongly reduce the range of options for traditional welfare policies and that every new step in the direction of liberalization—such as the recent Bolkestein directive on the liberalization of services—is perceived as a threat by many European citizens and fuels nationalist protest which can jeopardize the continuation of the integration process. The refusal of the majority of the French and Dutch voters to approve the constitutional treaty expressed similar fears of social dumping and declining social protection.

Opposite to this is the view upheld by other European scholars and political leaders, who think that the European Commission has wholly abandoned the ESM and the underlying values of social solidarity in favor of neoliberal capitalism, blame economic liberalization for worsened social conditions, and urge the Commission to stop the process. Both critics, in spite of their opposite ideologies, would like to go back to a situation which is no longer possible. A reform of the European social model is necessary.

Contrary to what the latter critics argue, the social market economy model has not been abandoned with the growth of globalization; what has instead taken place (or has been attempted) is a reorientation of policies. Rumford (2002), following Hooghe's account of European cohesion policy (1998), somewhat exaggerates the clash in the EU between the advocates of neoliberal capitalism and those of regulated capitalism, but gives an account of the shift in the social model upheld by the European Commission.

The postwar European social model gave way to a transnational social model, a move which is indicative of a broader shift from government to governance. The shift can be tracked through the transition from the Delors Commission to the Santer Commission. While the Delors Commission defended the idea of a 'European social model of society,' which already contained within itself the seeds of neoliberal governance, the Santer's Commission wholeheartedly embraced the idea of governance. Santer's motto for the post-Delors Commission 'do less, but do it better' reads like a pledge of good governance.

(Rumford 2002: 93)

Actually, what the Delors administration did was to reorient EU policy in light of globalization. Structural funds which were initially used mainly to ease conflicts among member-states are now increasingly aimed at enhancing the competitiveness of the EU economy in the global market, according to the view that the EU is now positioned as an intermediary between the conflicting demands of the nation-state and the global economy. This attitude also entails reevaluating civil society with regard to the state, and emphasizing governance rather than government. Since social and economic actors and organizations of civil society have their finger on the pulse of society and enable greater political representativeness, they increasingly assume responsibility for solving their own problems, and they work within multiple levels of governance to formulate European solutions to a range of European issues. On this basis, the OMC has been introduced as key instrument for the implementation of the Lisbon strategy.

Social protection and welfare remain common values and goals across Europe (sizable majorities of EU citizens consider social security, equality of opportunities, and the spirit of cooperation as a precious inheritance of the twentieth century). The ESM continues to be a fundamental part of what Europe stands for. Underlying it is a general set of core values: sharing risks widely across society, containing the inequalities that might threaten social solidarity, protecting the most vulnerable through active social intervention, cultivating consultation rather than confrontation in industry, providing a rich framework of social and economic citizenship rights for the population as a whole (Giddens 2006: 2).

Competitiveness and social cohesion continue to be propounded as joint goals by official EU documents, such as those outlining the Lisbon strategy in 2000. Globalization has not led to the abandonment of Keynesian economic policy at the EU level, for the simple reason that the EU has never been a planning state; rather, it has been a regulatory state which has steered a 'third way' between Keynesian welfarism and public ownership on the one hand, and neoliberal deregulation on the other (as argued in Chapter 5). The list of policies aimed at increasing competitiveness, such as making the single market more dynamic, raising investment in knowledge, improving EU macroeconomic policy, reforming policies for convergence and restructuring, achieving more efficient regulation, and reforming the EU budget (cutting back on agricultural spending in favor of research and infrastructures) are widely agreed on (European Commission 2003b, Sapir 2003).

These policies, however, must be consistent with bold innovations in welfare. The creation of European Monetary Union has actually encouraged a modernization of national welfare systems and a deep reassessment of their financial bases (Hemerijck 2005). But this is not enough. The risk that greater market deregulation—induced and required by globalization—threatens established welfare standards and produces a political anti-EU backlash that can be contained by two sets of changes which are already at work in the ESM and should be further pursued. First, a set of norms for cross-border regulation of welfare provisions should be further developed: for European citizens who are granted health care in any hospital of the EU; for social security contributions and provisions that are transferable within the EU; for pension funds that can look for clients and sponsors in every member-state.

Second, greater harmonization of welfare policies should be achieved, with the purpose of guaranteeing basic welfare standards in all EU member-states. This harmonization should be pursued with explicit reference to the fundamental rights listed in the Nice Charter (section on solidarity) and in the constitutional treaty, and to the OMC as a new instrument of multilevel governance; the OMC was introduced first in labor policies in the 1997 European strategy for employment and, more recently, in pensions, policies for social inclusion and health policies, in line with the 2000 Lisbon strategy. The harmonization of national welfare systems on the basis of a set of principles of social citizenship is a more viable solution than the direct transfer of regulatory competence to the EU level. This harmonization can use as an incentive for its adoption by member-states the condition that aid will be granted on compliance with a few basic welfare policy principles (health and work safety, equal opportunities for men and women, contractual labor relations, etc.), monitored through a rigorous set of social indicators.

The problem is not an easy one since, as scholars like Scharpf (Marks et al. 1996) have pointed out, European negative integration (i.e. the removal of impediments against the free circulation of people, capital, and goods) proceeds faster than positive integration (i.e. the creation of new institutions). But it seems the only way to keep a developed welfare system at a time when growing global competition in the cost of labor, demographic transitions in European countries and the strict Maastricht criteria for joining the European single currency—strict budgetary and anti-inflation controls—have made it difficult for several EU states to continue implementing generous and costly welfare policies.

10.2.6. THE EUROPEAN PROJECT OF A SOCIETY IN THE MAKING: ACHIEVING UNITY THROUGH DIVERSITY

The social market economy, that is the combination of a competitive market and welfare, is a first basic distinctive feature of the European model of society. A second basic distinctive feature is the attempt to build a political union which does not follow any previous historical pattern, in particular that of the nation-state. The EU is a new type of society that cannot be conceptualized on the model of a national society, or as a projection at the supranational level of the modern national societies in which we still live. Nor is the creation of the single market enough for the emergence of a European society; for this to come about, the fact that the European nations and peoples are becoming more closely linked and integrated by common forces and practices in a common economic space is a necessary but not sufficient condition. A normative consensus and an institutional cement are also required. As I argue in my analysis of the EU political system (Chapter 5), the process of EU institution building has moved far from the original Coal and Steel Community, but it is still a work in progress. The French and Dutch vote against the EU constitutional treaty has slowed down, but not interrupted the process. A cohesive and unitary European society does not exist yet, but it is in the making. There is no need to repeat this analysis. Here I discuss the question of a European common culture as the basis of normative consensus.

European unification was grounded on the decision to put an end to the European civil wars and on the perception of common economic interests; and it is made possible by the legacy of a shared cultural heritage. In his famous Zurich speech on September 19, 1946 Churchill argued for the making of the United States of Europe as the cure that would transform as if by a miracle the tragic state of postwar Europe. If Americans from places as distant and diverse as Texas and Massachusetts, Alabama, and Oregon could feel a shared sense of citizenship within their national framework, then surely Europeans could form their own 'national grouping'. 'Why should there not be a European group which could give a sense of enlarged patriotism and common citizenship to the distracted people of this turbulent and mighty continent? And why should it not take its right place with other great groupings in shaping the destinies of mankind?' And America must be the friend and sponsor of the new Europe.

In order to make that vision real, a new social and political project must develop that could foster a new European identity. The foundations of a sentiment of European belonging—alongside national and local identities—can be traced to common European historical heritage; but a distinctive European identity is developing within the European project in forming a political union where unity will be achieved through diversity (Martinelli 2004).

The European project can be defined as the achievement of unity through diversity. It rejects the belief that what is different is potentially hostile, and it forgoes the construction of a specific identity based on the 'us versus them' opposition. A European identity of this kind is not exclusive and may be weaker than traditional national identities; yet it seems better suited to a democratic form of global governance in terms of mutual understanding, peaceful relations, and multilayered cooperation.

The peoples of the EU countries have common cultural roots. They have values and institutions with ancient origins but which coalesced in the process of European modernization and then spread to other parts of the world. This common cultural heritage contributes to European political integration, but it cannot (and it does not need to) produce a distinctive, idiosyncratic identity which legitimizes the specificity of Europe as a single political entity in the way that national cultures legitimized the formation of European nation-states. This is because the political building of the EU cannot follow the path of nation building and cannot be grounded on the 'us versus them' opposition.

Identity and otherness are closely interrelated, of course. At least to some extent, I identify with somebody because we both feel different from somebody else. As Fontana (1994) argues, in the course of their history Europeans—more precisely those groups which were culturally hegemonic in European society—have defined a 'distorted identity' through the deforming lenses with which they have looked at the 'other' (the barbarian, the heretic, and the savage).

However, the lessons of history—religious fundamentalism and bigotry, ideological dogmatism, nationalistic aggressiveness—counsel against this negative and arrogant way of defining a common identity—an identity against somebody else—and its use building a political entity. For that matter, in the 'Europe of nations' it would hardly be feasible. European identity must gainsay the old belief that what is different is potentially hostile. For this reason, European political identity cannot become a rigid and closed set of beliefs and attitudes. It must instead be built around a project; it cannot be deduced from its origin, but rather from its future. The notion of the absence of limits—which I discuss in Chapter 1 as a typical feature of the modern European identity—provides the basis for the conception of Europe's present political identity as a project in the making, and in terms of its consequences.

The legitimacy of the process of European integration cannot be deduced from a separate cultural identity, for it is linked to the existence of a shared political plan and to the possibility that the foreseeable results on a planetary scale of such a plan are morally and politically defensible as viable responses to global problems.

Accomplishment of this project requires a political subject on a regional scale, a set of communitarian institutions which guarantee democratic accountability, a certain degree of homogeneity in people's living conditions, a common cultural heritage and shared values, and the multicultural interplay of complementary cultures.

The model of the EU is a specific and novel one, both institutionally and culturally. It cannot reproduce the model of European nation-building because it lacks the fundamental characteristics of a strong centralized power and a standardized culture articulated through a common language. For the first time in European history, the state now relies not on military structures for the integration of such a huge and economically potent body, but rather on a legal and economic community, and it does not seek to deprive its members of their cultural specificities. The EU is a multicultural entity with a core of shared values (representative democracy, free-market competition, basic human rights, social cohesion and civic solidarity, respect for different cultural heritages, and peaceful coexistence with all people on earth) at the foundations of common institutions. And it is a supranational union where legislative and executive powers are shared by a plurality of political bodies: the European Council of heads of states and governments (representing the governments of the member-states), the EP (representing the peoples of the member countries and regions), the European Commission, the Parliament, and the ECJ.

According to this model, unity should be achieved through diversity. Already in ancient Greek philosophy we find the notion of harmony stemming from contradictory elements. If one postulates unity at the beginning, there ensues a tendency to return constantly to the lost original model; if, on the contrary, one postulates diversity, unity is seen as a continuous effort driven by conflict and competition, and as never predetermined. As Eliot (1948) argued, European culture must be differentiated and plural, united in its diversity.

Unity should induce the redefinition of identities, both those of the European peoples and those of immigrants from other parts of the world, rather than their abolition. And citizens should share multiple identities—urban, regional, national, and supranational. The formation of a united Europe should be built around the notions of unity stemming from diversity and multiple citizenships.

This is a highly ambitious project. How much cultural diversity can a society tolerate without breaking apart? When conflicts erupt, multiple identities are brought under stress and many individuals choose to adhere to a single idiosyncratic identity. Moreover, the historical formation of fully integrated states out of a preexisting diversity of smaller societies—as in the cases of France, Germany, Russia, India, or China—was accompanied by violence and threats of violence to force recalcitrant minorities to join, and/or by hostility and open war against neighboring states. But the lessons of history (the many European civil wars) rule out the use of force in the process of EU building, and they advocate an attitude of peaceful coexistence and the rejection of war as the means to pursue national interests and settle international disputes. The attitudes of young Europeans toward war and peace are strikingly different both from those of their peers in the first half of past century and their contemporaries in other parts of the world. These attitudes have given way to the opposing images of the children of Venus and the children of Mars.

10.2.7. THE ACCEPTANCE OF PLURALISM AND THE STRENGTHENING OF *ETHOS* AND *EPOS*

We have argued several times that shared values are part of what is needed to make up a society, insofar as they made collective institutions and norms legitimate. But does a set of shared core values exist in the EU countries which can legitimize the thesis of the society in the making? Chapter 7 provides interesting evidence: it points out that there are two ways of agreeing on values. There may be a strong consensus on conceptions of the good. But major disagreements may subsist, as it happens in any modern society. Here, what counts is for actors to accept a pluralism of reasonable conceptions of the good rather than for them to all hold exactly the same values, and to agree on a reasonable framework within which differing and even conflicting values may flourish. The investigation of value surveys in Chapter 7 showed that Europeans not only widely agree on certain values but, more importantly, share a common reasonable viewpoint that goes beyond all the subsisting differences and serves as a framework for both personal judgment and acceptance of pluralism about the good life.

The development of attitudes of pluralism and tolerance avoid the risk that the recognition of multiple cultural identities within a single union becomes a destabilizing factor. In the historical experience of the European nation-states, multiethnicity and multiculturalism were seen as potential threats for national unity in that they altered the delicate balance between *ethnos* and *demos*. In the post-national model of the EU different ethnic and national identities are accommodated within a single citizenship. The scrupulous care with which the different languages of all member countries are protected in the EU institutions, the endless list of rights granted to EU citizens in the Nice Treaty, the refusal to formally mention Christianity within the text of the constitutional treaty, as well as some key sentences of the ECJ are all instances of the determination with which the EU tries to escape the traps of nationalism.

In order to continue the unfinished business of building the EU, however, two complementary goals should be pursued: first, the formation of the European *demos*, that is the fostering of a full-fledged European citizenship, added to—and not substituting—national and local identities; second, the fostering of those elements of traditional nationhood that are compatible with a multicultural supranational model.

Let us consider with regard to the latter the basic components of nationhood as defined by scholars of ethnicity and nationhood (Smith 1991; Tullio-Altan 1995): *ethnos, logos, topos, ethos,* and *epos.* The EU cannot rely on *ethnos* (i.e. on ancestral ethnic origins), since it fosters closure, exclusion, and discrimination, and runs counter to its core values. Ethnic specificities should be respected, but no single *ethnos* must dominate the others. The EU cannot rely too much on *logos* either; if language is taken as the basis of *logos*, European citizens cannot be forced to speak a single language, since multilingualism is considered a basic requisite for the respect of different cultural identities. In the EU 25, there are more than sixty languages spoken, 56 percent of the population is capable of speaking in one language other than its native one (and 28% in two), English is the best-known language besides the native one in nineteen countries and is spoken by 38 percent of the population. *Logos* has a larger meaning too, insofar as it refers to a specific way of thinking and in this respect scientific and philosophical education can play a major role in fostering a common European approach to reality. *Topos*, the symbolic transfiguration of the space in which Europeans live, may help to some extent. There are, in fact, distinctive common features of European cities, buildings, squares, and public and private spaces (in this respect the specific features of the European cities outlined in Chapter 8 are particularly relevant). However, the great variety of natural and human landscapes within Europe implies that *topos* can hardly be considered a strong identifying element.

We are then left with *ethos* and *epos*. Europe can certainly invest more in *ethos* (the basic core values, vision of the world, and practical knowledge that define the new European identity and encapsulate the basic rights and responsibilities of democratic citizenship—which include the acceptance of several reasonable conceptions of the good), and in *epos* (the great figures and events that testify to the common European heritage in arts, science, and culture). Both *ethos* and *epos* should be, alongside logos, basic components of educational programs for the next generations, and they should orient the activities of the media and various manifestations of public discourse; the purpose being to create a real European public space grounded on a shared political culture which orients people's choices on matters of common concern. The shared values of *ethos* can be strengthened by European *Lieux de mémoire*: monuments, celebrations, myths, heroes, holidays, hymns, flags, museums, and pilgrimages (Nora 1984). A EU flag and hymn already successfully exist. There is no reason why, as Kohli (2000) suggests, it should not be possible to repeat this success in other domains, primarily that of European founding myths and holidays. Cultural traditions have often been discovered and strategically implemented in nation-building. There are certainly difficulties in repeating this process at the supranational level—as the conflicts over the planned Museum of Europe and the complicated activity of the commissions for historians to draw up European history school texts show—but they can be overcome. Many streets and squares in EU cities are now dedicated to military victories and war heroes who have died fighting against other Europeans; hopefully, in the foreseeable future, alongside the names of those heroes who died fighting for liberty and democracy, they will also carry the names of great artists, scientists, cultural heroes, and builders of a united Europe.

With regard to the need to form a real European demos, institutional changes are necessary, such as true Europeanwide elections, greater harmonization of national laws, greater freedom in the circulation of people, services, goods, and money and the growth of a European public space (Mercier 2003). These processes of union building will be helped by an increasingly interconnected economy (favored by the euro), by a more and more homogeneous European social fabric, and by the strengthening of a common culture which should not be seen as a means to exclude others, but rather as a necessary basis for dialogue among civilizations.

If this project fails, it will provide support for the theory that nation-states can be built only on the basis of a homogeneous culture. If the project succeeds, the EU can become a model for other regions of the world to form large supranational and multicultural unions, and it can thus contribute significantly to democratic global governance. Our pride as Europeans can be based not only on the memory of a great past, but even more on the commitment to a project in the making which aims at universal peace, individual freedom, and social justice.

10.2.8. IS THE EUROPEAN PROJECT AGREED ON?

Are there ways to test the actual progress of the European project? In Chapter 7, we have seen how and to what extent the peoples of the EU agree on key common values. Here we briefly consider how much they feel themselves Europeans. The question of a European identity cannot be reduced to the percentage of EU citizens who feel themselves Europeans first and more than Germans or Spaniards, Lombards or Normands. It is actually much more complex. Yet the data of Eurobarometer and the European Value Study can be of some interest. How many EU citizens share a sense of belonging and agree with this project of a society in the making is, however, open to question. The continuing capacity of EU nation-states to attract the loyalty and identity of their citizens is well known. But is a European identity growing alongside strong national identities?

A society needs a feeling of belonging, a collective identity as experienced and expressed by individual citizens. Eurobarometer and the European Value Study data enable the operationalization of this dimension (Kohli 2000: 123). As originally formulated in 1975, the identity question was framed as an exclusive choice between different types of belonging: 'To which one of the following geographical units would you say you belong first of all: locality, region, country, Europe, or the world?' The pattern of responses was very similar across countries: 'country' was the first preference in all countries (except Great Britain and with higher percentages in Germany), 'town' the second, 'region' the third, whereas the 'European' and 'world' identities were consistently marginal. Duchesne and Frognier (1995) examined the correlation between the first and second choices on the assumption that the relations between different types of belonging need not be ones of mutual exclusion, and found that the development of a European identity is accompanied by the weakening of local attachments, not by the weakening of national identities. Hence, the polarization seems to be not between Europeanists and nationalists but rather between cosmopolitans and locals.

European identity does not need to be an exclusive identity. It should instead be part of a multiple identity, which is a condition that is growing with globalization (Martinelli 2004). And, as argued earlier, it is the result of a project in the making. In line with these considerations, since 1992, the Eurobarometer has reframed the question thus: 'In the near future, do you see yourself as nationality only, nationality and European, European and nationality, European only?' The latest available results show that an exclusionary attachment to European identity is still much in the minority; but if being European is conceived as part of a multiple identity it is now shared by a majority of citizens. Hopefully, in a not too distant future, we will call ourselves French Europeans and German Europeans, or Europeans of Spanish or Italian origin.

Two important conditions for building a common identity are the growth of similar lifestyles and daily attitudes, and the construction of a European public space. As for the growth of similar lifestyles, Europeans belonging to the same generation and/or the same professional group have more in common than others. For instance, for the age group ranging from about 16 to 40 (that is the young adults of Europe, who grew up in a continent that has been essentially without borders since they finished high school), it is easier to share a common identity. They are creating a unified European society of their own in offices and bars, soccer stadiums, health clubs, and Internet cafés, and tend to consider the entire continent—not just one country or city—their home (Reid 2004).

The construction of a European public space is slowly in the making. Authors like Habermas have insisted on the present weakness of and the urgent need for a EU wide public space, that is defined both as the physical space where citizenship is exercised and as the symbolic framework where a common world and a social bond are constructed. The research group coordinated by Arnaud Mercier (2003) shows that in the absence of a true European public space there are, however, micropublic spaces which prefigure what a future European public space will be, such as: the large number of European associations (about 17,000 of them belong to the network of the European Forum of Civil Society) which try to influence EU policymaking, connect European institutions and citizens, and represent experiences of transcultural communication; the wide array of programs of cultural and scientific cooperation within the EU; the activities of national and transnational mass communication networks; and the experience of electronic democracy at the local level.

10.2.9. A NEW STYLE IN INTERNATIONAL RELATIONS

A third major distinctive feature of the European model of society is a new style in international relations and a multilateral view of global governance (Martinelli 2002).

The essential forces driving the building of an EU—the deep yearning for peace on a continent that has known too much war, and the intense desire to again be a driving force in global economic and political affairs—have not subsided since those goals were first upheld by the founding fathers of the new Europe. But the EU needs to redefine its own mission in the new globalizing world.

According to those we can call 'the writers of the European success', the EU represents the new political model of international relations, the anticipation of the new global order, the most relevant political innovation of the past half-century. For Cooper, for instance, 'the EU is an advanced system of reciprocal interference in internal affairs' (2003: 30). Reid credits the EU with the 'invention of peace', both for putting an end to its long history of internal wars and for its peacekeeping role in world affairs (2004). For Leonard, the EU represents a new system of governance and a new modus operandi in international relations, based not on secrecy but on transparency, not on exclusion but on inclusion, not on threat but on persuasion. The method of the EU is the law and European law is also its foreign policy instrument. The EU employs passive aggression, that is 'instead of threatening the recourse to force in order to pursue its interests, Europe threatens of not using force, of drawing back its friendship and the perspective to join the Union' (2005: 51). Comparing the 2003 EU Security Strategy of 'preventive engagement' with the post-September 11 Bush doctrine of 'preventive war', Leonard argues that the latter doctrine attempts to justify action to remove a threat before it has the chance of being employed against the United States, and is therefore short term in conception and entirely military in kind. The European doctrine, in contrast, is aimed at building the political and institutional bases of stability rather than simply removing the immediate source of threat and it is therefore predicated on a long-term involvement, with hard power as just one of the means used (2005: 63). Whereas the US administration prefers using hard power, the EU aims at bringing together its aid, trade, and development assistance to prevent hotspots from collapsing into war.

In terms of military power there is no match: while the United States can send about 400,000 ground troops around the world out of a total of 650,000, the EU can deploy barely 85,000 out of a total of 1.2 million ground soldiers; and when it comes to satellite intelligence, transport aircraft, battle carriers, and guided missiles, the gap is staggering. Moreover, there is no European counterpart to the huge network of 737 US overseas military bases. However the EU is well equipped for peacemaking and humanitarian interventions, with thousands of aid workers for disaster relief, policemen, diplomats, pools of magistrates and election monitors moving around the world. The EU strategy for countries like Bosnia, Iraq, Afghanistan, and many African countries, focuses more and first on state building rather than nation-building. It is more patient and prefers 'engagement' strategies to 'exit' strategies. The focus is on establishing the rule of law, building institutions, and enacting economic reform. For instance, just after the fighting subsided in Bosnia, the EU negotiated a series of unilateral trade concessions with the Balkan countries which led on to 'Stabilization and Association Agreements'. The EU strategy of pre-emptive engagement is not an easy strategy; it has a better chance when dealing with countries which are potential new EU members than with others, but it represents a real alternative to the foreign policy of the present American administration.

The EU role in global politics is not limited to peacekeeping activities, or to its transformative power stemming from its ability to reward reformers and withhold benefits for laggards; it concerns the regulation of the world economy as well. Reid, among others, highlights the EU's fundamental role in the governance of the global market. 'Because of the sheer size of its market, and because the Eurocrats are more philosophically inclined to regulate than their counterparts in Washington or Tokyo, the EU has become a de facto global policeman for a whole panoply of agricultural, industrial and financial products. In the twenty-first century, the rules that run the global economy are largely Brussels' rules' (2004: 232). EU rules on manufacture, content, design, labeling, safety, and personal privacy about customers, employees, and suppliers have become the rules that manufacturers must follow all around the world. Corporate giants in different industries, including General Electric, Microsoft, Coca-Cola, Boeing, and Monsanto, have had to bow to EU regulators. The euro is challenging the dollar's rule in the world monetary system. Barely three years after its arrival on the world financial scene, in fact, the euro had virtually achieved equity with the dollar as a vehicle for international investments. According to Reid, 'the emergence and growth of the European Union as a countervailing power does not have to be a nightmare for Americans', first, because the world's largest trading market is a market wide open to American business, provided they comply with the rules and requirements imposed by the EU (which, however, are becoming international standards). Second, because an ambitious united Europe begins to take on some of the burdens concerning key problems of the global agenda that necessarily fall to a superpower.

Also authors who take a more realistic view of the problems facing the unfinished business of European unification, as Padoa Schioppa (2005), stress the fundamental role which the EU can play in guaranteeing global peace. He argues that, as in the twentieth century the United States has been the external power capable of putting an end to the wars stemming from the breaking of the European regional equilibrium, so the EU could be the 'external' power capable of effectively working for peaceful coexistence in the twenty-first century; external not in a spatial sense like the United States, but insofar as it represents a different, post-Westphalian model in international relations.

In this sense, benign hegemony seems an expression more applicable to the EU—provided that the EU is really capable of developing a single foreign policy, that does not yet exist—than to the United States. Benign hegemony is the term used by some American scholars of international politics, who stress the absence of the notion of empire in American history and argue for a better balance between soft and hard power in US foreign policy. Here I use the term in a different sense: the EU has the potentiality (that is the knowledge, the credibility, the principles—solidarity and multilateralism—and the economic resources) for exerting a cultural leadership, for leading the world toward peaceful coexistence. And it also has the duty of working for peace in order to compensate for the costs and tragedies of the European-initiated world wars and colonial exploitation. Member countries within the EU can develop a foreign policy which does not take the usual form of power politics and is characterized by a 'culture of cooperation' (Rhodes 1998; Bonanate 2002).

This view is open to two lines of criticism: first, the critique that the EU seems incapable of defining a single strategy in foreign policy and international security. It is widely recognized among European leaders and citizens alike that no single European nation-state will be able to successfully compete with the US super-power and with the rising powers of China, India, Russia, and Brazil in the next decades and to cope with the problems of the global agenda (energy, environment, migration, terrorism, etc.). But nationalism is a major obstacle against drawing the logical implication of this awareness, that is the adoption of a single European foreign policy. Second, the critique that the EU (or, for the moment, most EU member-states) can take a peaceful stance in global politics, only because the United States is willing to use force in this defense (a willingness that is weaker now than in the past). With the end of the cold war, in fact, Europe is strategically less important in US foreign policy, the role of NATO has to be redefined, the agenda of global issues has different priorities. The charge that the EU is a free rider on American military is a serious argument. It can be counterargued only with facts by European leaders who show a determination to strengthen European political integration in foreign policy and to accept the cost of an increase of EU hard power alongside its soft power. This in turn would allow a more equal partnership to develop with the United States in global governance. Leaders of both the European Left and Right agree on the need to maintain and develop the special relationship between the EU and the United States. Scholars of different cultural and political outlooks share the same view, without having to frame this view in the clash of civilization framework (Huntington 1997), according to which America and the EU should strengthen their cultural and political ties in order to compete successfully with the other world civilizations. I think it more appropriate to say that the United States and Europe as variants of the same civilization should cooperate in maintaining world peace and fostering democratic global governance.

This is not, however, the position of American neoconservatives, which is well expressed by Kagan (2002) who strongly challenges the thesis of the EU as the new model in global governance and the possibility of cooperation between the United States and the EU in international affairs. Europe and the United States do not have the same *Weltanschauung* and are following different and incompatible routes in international relations. The EU seeks to apply its experience of multilateral governance to global politics, and to submit interstate relations to an international rule of law, whereas the United States understands the true anarchic nature of world relations and is prepared to use force. Europe is no longer at the center of world politics. It is a regional power, while the United States is the only global power, the benign hegemony which uses force to uphold freedom and democracy. The opponents of this view—who can be found both in the European political Left and Right, and in the American Democratic Party—counterargue that a strong, responsible, and forward-looking united Europe can become a peaceful global player.

10.3. **A few conclusions**

From the various chapters of this book and, specifically, from this final chapter, we can draw a few conclusions that try to answer to the main questions we raised at the start of the volume.

First, despite the persistent diversity of its constituent states and regions, is now a European society with a specific cultural identity and distinctive institutions in the making is, that is rooted in a common past but is also inscribed in the political project of the present union. Specific institutions (like the 'social market economy' or the welfare state) and shared values (a distinctive blend of individualism and solidarity) are specific features of the European version of a common Western identity, and they can provide specific European responses to the challenges of globalization, which are not limited to meeting the functional demands of global competition but take into account such key questions as environmentally sustainable development, social cohesion, and universal human rights. The project of a united Europe is far from accomplished and now at a delicate crossroad, but is still a viable project.

Second, the EU and the United States are variants of the same civilization—Western modernity—and are growing more similar in many respects as a consequence of globalization and as a result of the political building of the EU (increasing market deregulation, growing intercultural and interethnic mix, similarity between the two polities as variants of the compound republic). The United States is less exceptional and the EU is less unique than some scholars used to think. The United States can still be seen to a large extent as a successful historical case of 'Europe outside Europe', in light of the theory of multiple modernities, since it has creatively adapted and developed values and institutions which are rooted in the European (Western) heritage. The EU, in its turn, is also less unique than commonly thought since it is going through a path of political integration which does not imitate the process of nation-building of modern European states, and resembles—at least to some extent—the long and painful making of the American union. These analogies should not, however, be pushed too far. Significant differences between the United States and the EU persist, and indeed are growing in several domains, such as demographic trends, urban patterns, forms of representative governments, attitudes toward religion and secularism, patriotism, law and order, war and peace.

Third, one gains the impression that America and Europe are exchanging roles and trading places and that a reversal (or crossover) of trends is taking place between them. Some of the features which have long been distinctive of the United States—primarily the continuous enlargement of the frontier and the strength of civil society associations—are now typical of the EU; whereas characteristics that were typical of the European nations at the beginning of the twentieth century—primarily imperial ambitions and belligerent attitudes in foreign policy—seem more applicable to the United States. As argued at the end of Chapter 5, the American political system seems to become more polarized in terms of moral cleavages and political cultures, while the EU is becoming less so; the traditional American liberal ethos is under attack, while the EU upholds civil liberties as a basic requirement for membership (although attitudes of xenophobic closure are growing); the traditional Tocquevillian portrait of American society as a web of associations is countered by the image of Americans 'bowling alone', while European civil society is gaining strength.

Fourth, globalization has an ambivalent impact on both the United States and the EU. It challenges both the more consolidated American model and the European model *in statu nascenti*. Globalization has contributed to make the United States the hegemonic power in the world; but it also creates the conditions for the growth of new powerful challengers of this hegemony, first of all China and India, and it puts an 'external' pressure on the American model of a free society. The United States has achieved unity amid diversity, but is faced by growing contradictions between the American creed and its hegemonic role. Globalization is responsible for what Micklethwait and Wooldridge call the paradox of the United States, that of being at once both the most admired country in the world and one of the most reviled; 'outside its borders, "America" has somehow become a code word for technological sophistication, meritocracy and opportunity as well as for primitive justice, imperialism and inequality' (2004: 24).

Hegemony is a mixed blessing for Americans: on the one hand, American society can continue to develop while maintaining its distinctive cultural code and reproducing its specific institutional fabric, and also by virtue of its hegemonic position in the world. Until a geopolitical rival is capable of posing a real challenge, Americans can continue to enjoy the privileges of hegemony although somehow reluctantly (in opinion polls nearly half of American citizens constantly favor isolationism). On the other hand, American society does run the risk of imperial overstretching, and the costs of hegemony may be higher than the benefits, in economic, political, and cultural terms. Internationally, the United States runs the risk of provoking widespread hostility and radical opposition whenever the American superpower displays unilateral arrogance in global politics and prefers the use of hard power over soft power; domestically, there is risk that the fight against international terrorism restricts civil liberties and divides the country into two opposite political camps.

Globalization has ambivalent effects on the future of the EU as well. On the one hand, it provides the best argument and strongest impulse for European political unity, in the sense that no single European nation-state can be a global player today. It certainly fostered the creation of the euro—the first multinational conversion on a Continental scale—specifically designed to challenge the global hegemony of the US dollar, and of the EU central bank—which is a powerful global actor capable of protecting the EMS from currency speculation much more effectively than national central banks of member-states could do in the past. On the other hand, it stirs nationalistic reactions to globalization and fosters social conflict between the potential 'winners' and the potential 'losers' of global market competition within European society. Both nationalistic feelings and fears of the global market risk slowing down—or even stopping altogether—the process of EU building, as the French and Dutch referenda on the constitutional treaty have shown.

The EU pursues the demanding goal of achieving unity through diversity, but it still has to prove that it can realize the project despite nationalist resistance and xenophobic reactions. Negative nationalism, which denies rights to other peoples in the name of a distorted national identity, has been an old European 'disease', responsible for bloody twentieth-century European 'civil wars'. Ethnic hatred, nationalistic chauvinism, unbound regionalisms, and the resurgent anti-Semitism are what Steiner defines the 'nightmare of European history' (2005). It is still alive and can provide the staunchest obstacle to European political integration, mostly when coupled with xenophobic fears. The negative impact of globalization does not only concern aggressive nationalism, but also the threat that cultural homologation represents for the rich cultural and linguistic diversity of the continent, for the image of Europe as a café crowded with people and words, conversation and dialogue.

It is not easy to evaluate which model of society is more effective in responding to the challenges of globalization. Rifkin (2004) strongly argues that the 'European dream' of an open multicultural society has now taken the place of the 'American dream'. Europe is 'the new city on a hill'. The American dream is exhausting its historical cycle; it was an amalgam of the forces that shook Europe from its medieval moorings—the Protestant Reformation and the Enlightenment—and propelled it into the modern age. The new European dream has dared to create a new synthesis: one that combines a postmodern sensitivity to multiple perspectives and multiculturalism with a new universal vision. The new European dream takes us into a global age. In order to prove his case, Rifkin discusses a multitude of social processes on both sides of the Atlantic, with an over-pessimistic view of the American future (from the withering of American work ethics and the decline in American civic-mindedness to the increase of social pathologies like drugs and gambling) and an over-optimistic view of the European future (from the 'European dream of perpetual peace' and the 'second Enlightenment' in European science and technology to the better quality of life in Europe). When stripped of its pamphlet overtones, however, Rifkin's argument that the EU is taking the place of the United States as the model of society better suited to the global world is partially convincing. But where Rifkin is wrong is in considering the 'European dream' as already achieved. The project of a united Europe is, in fact, far from accomplished and it is a dangerous intellectual attitude to consider it already achieved.

Fifth, the EU and the United States will continue to play different roles in global governance, ones that are partially complementary and partially competitive. America will continue to wield hegemony, although its costs may become greater than the benefits in both economic and political terms. The predominant foreign policy vision within the EU will be the pursuit of a polyarchic, multilateral, and mixed-actor model of global governance where the anarchy of sovereign states is mitigated and controlled by a plurality of nonstate actors: international governmental organizations centered on a reformed UN system; the actors of a transnational civil society (nongovernmental organizations, collective movements, transnational communities, and ethnic diasporas); and supranational unions like the EU itself (Martinelli 2002, 2004). The United States will keep its military might and rely on hard power as much as on soft power; Americans will continue to be 'children of Mars'. The EU will strive for appeasement, negotiation, and the nonviolent resolution of conflicts; Europeans will continue to be 'children of Venus'. And it is possible that as Leonard (2005) argues, US foreign policy will show the 'weakness of power', whereas the EU could profit from the 'power of weakness'. EU and US foreign policies will continue to be different also because of the prevailing attitude toward violence and its public legitimacy on the sides of the Atlantic; the American fascination with weapons and the individual right to their possession has no European counterpart—which suggests a grassroots tolerance of potential violence not accepted anywhere in the EU. These different views of the United States and the EU on their respective roles as world actors will compete and even conflict in dealing with global issues like energy, trade, international security, poverty, the environment, and in discussions about the future of NATO, the reform of the UN system, and the role of international organizations such as the WTO and the World Bank.

In spite of different foreign policy perspectives and different 'national' priorities, however, the United States and the EU are bound not only to compete, but also to work together. In the 1963 Frankfurt Paulskirche speech John Kennedy, stressing the growing cooperation in defense, trade, development, and monetary policies between the United State and the European Community, came to the point of saying that 'in the far future, there may be a great new union for us all'

(Kennedy 1963). It is a vision that is not less utopian now than forty-five years ago. And yet, although the relationship will be more or less turbulent, more or less friendly, according to the events of global politics and to the characters of governments and leaders of the two unions, it will remain a special relationship for a long time. *As any sea, the Atlantic Ocean not only divides, but also unites, the peoples on its shores.*

☐ APPENDIX WITH A SYNTHETIC PICTURE OF THE MOST RELEVANT TRENDS

Laurence Duboys Fresney

All the following maps were generated by using 'Philcarto' (software available on the Internet at: http://perso.club-internet.fr/philgeo). They show the European situation (twenty-five countries) and recall the corresponding US data on these ten topics:

— Fertility
— Women's employment
— Education expenditure
— Health expenditure
— Union membership
— Tax revenue
— Public debt
— Military expenditure
— R&D expenditures
— Patents delivered

Total fertility rate (2005)

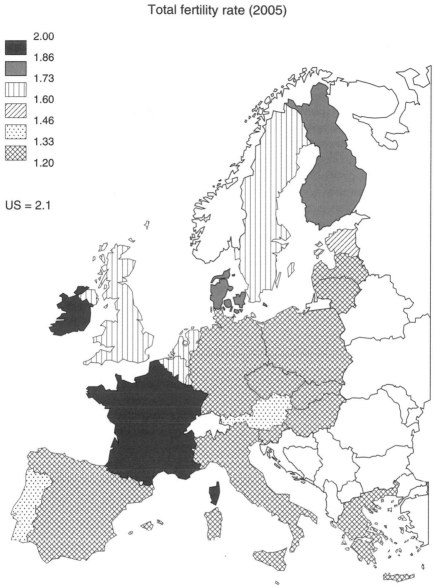

2.00
1.86
1.73
1.60
1.46
1.33
1.20

US = 2.1

Source: Eurostat

Total women employment rate
(% 15–64 years) 2004

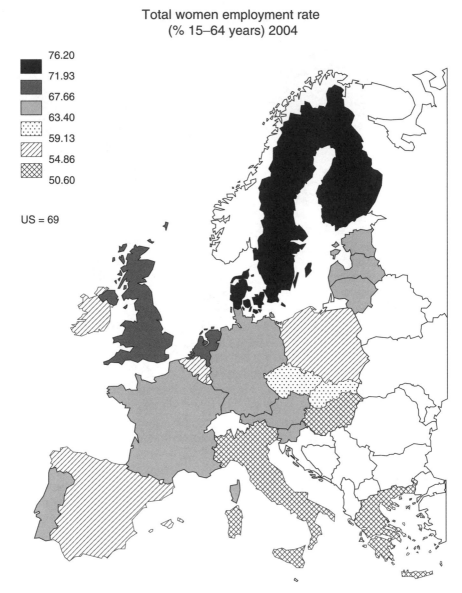

76.20
71.93
67.66
63.40
59.13
54.86
50.60

US = 69

Source: Eurostat

Total expenditure (public and private) on education (% GDP) 2004

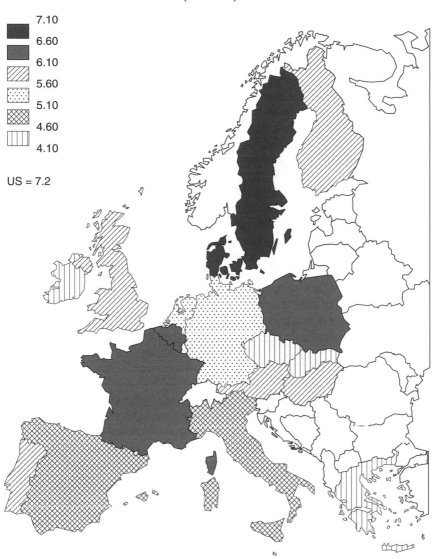

7.10
6.60
6.10
5.60
5.10
4.60
4.10

US = 7.2

Source: OECD, Education at glance (2005)

Total health expenditure (public and private) 2004 (% GDP)

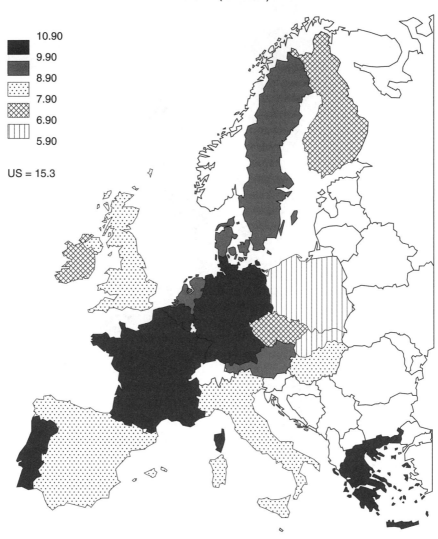

Legend:
- 10.90
- 9.90
- 8.90
- 7.90
- 6.90
- 5.90

US = 15.3

Source: OECD, Health data (2006)

Union membership rate (%)
2001–2

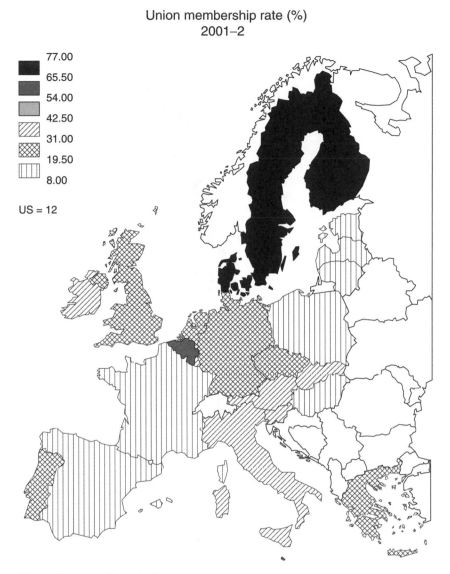

Source: European Commission

Total tax revenue 2003 (% GDP)

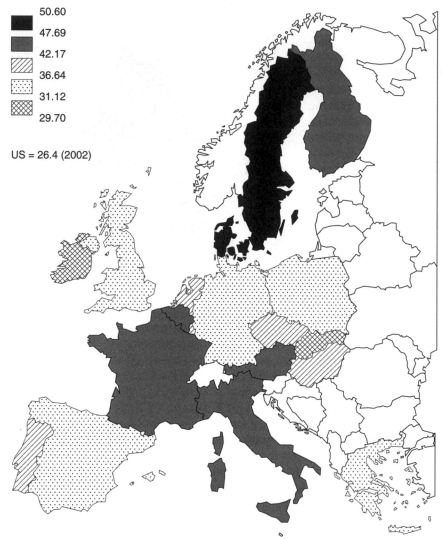

50.60
47.69
42.17
36.64
31.12
29.70

US = 26.4 (2002)

Source: OECD

Public debt 2004 (% GDP)

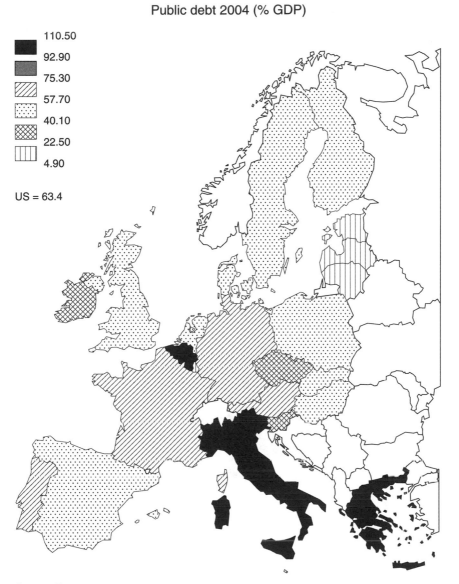

110.50
92.90
75.30
57.70
40.10
22.50
4.90

US = 63.4

Source: Eurostat

Military expenditure 2004 (% GDP)

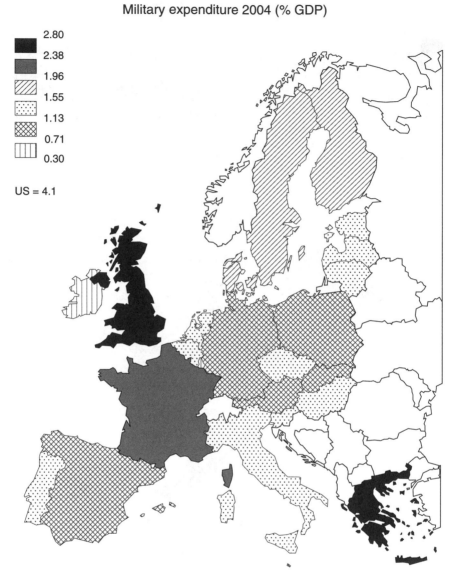

2.80
2.38
1.96
1.55
1.13
0.71
0.30

US = 4.1

Source: Eurostat

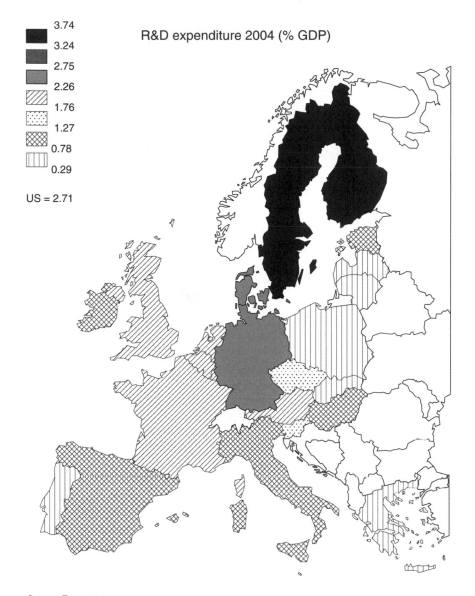

R&D expenditure 2004 (% GDP)

3.74
3.24
2.75
2.26
1.76
1.27
0.78
0.29

US = 2.71

Source: Eurostat

Number of patents delivered by USPTO
per million of inhabitants (2002)

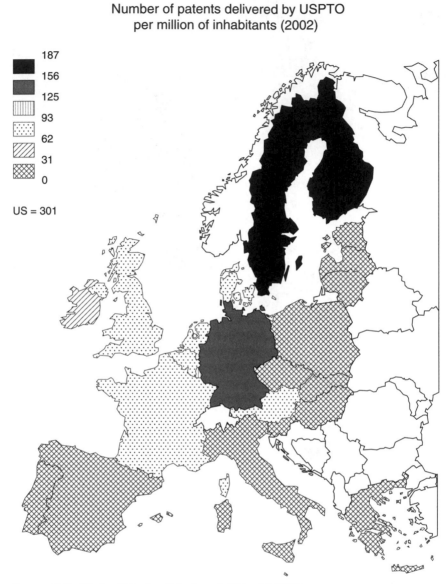

187
156
125
93
62
31
0

US = 301

Source: United States Patent and Trademark Office (USPTO)

☐ BIBLIOGRAPHY

Abromeit, H. (1998). *Democracy in Europe. Legitimising Politics in Non-State Polity.* New York: Berghahn Books.

Abu, L. and Janet, L. (1999). *New York, Chicago, Los Angeles: America's Global Cities.* Minneapolis, MN: University of Minnesota Press.

Adams, G. D. (1997). 'Abortion: Evidence of an Issue Evolution', *American Journal of Political Science*, 412(3): 718–37.

Adriaanse, J. H. (2001). 'Europe and Religion', in F. Cerutti and E. Rudolph (eds.), *A Soul for Europe. On the Political and Cultural Identity of Europe*, 2 vols. Leuven, Sterling, VA: Peeters.

Agier, M. (1999). *L'invention de La ville: banlieues, townships, invasions et favelas.* Amsterdam: Editions des archives contemporaines

Albert, M. (1991). *Capitalisme Contre Capitalisme.* Paris: Editions du Seuil.

Aldrich, J. (1995). *Why Parties?* Chicago, IL: University of Chicago Press.

American Civil Liberties Union (2004). Letter from ACLU Executive Director Anthony Romero Seeking More Information Regarding the Scope and Implementation of a Nationwide FBI Investigation Program to Question Thousands of Muslims in the United States. June 21, <http://www.aclu.org/safefree/general/18458leg20040621.html>

Andersen, S. and Eliassen, K. A. (eds.) (1996). *The European Union: How Democratic Is It?* London: Sage.

—— —— (eds.) (2000). *Making Policy in Europe.* London: Sage.

Anderson, B. C. (2004). 'Secular Europe, Religious America', *Public Interest* (Spring): 143–58.

Anderson, G. (2002). 'Dissolution of Unions in Europe: A Comparative Overview', Paper presented at the conference on 'Divorce in a Cross-National Perspective'. Florence, November 14–15.

Anderson, P. (1991). *Imagined Communities.* London: Verso.

Aparicio, S. (2004). 'Masacre en Madrid', *El Mundo.es*, March. <http://www.elmundo.es/ documentos/2004/03/espana/atentados11m>

Apel, K.-O. (1988). *Diskurs und Verantwortung.* Frankfurt am Main, Germany: Suhrkamp Verlag.

Armingeon, K., Beyeler, M., and Denegale, S. (2000). *Comparative Political Data Set 1960–1998.* Berne, Germany: Institute of Political Science, University of Berne.

—— —— —— (2002). *Comparative Political Data Set. 1960–2001.* Berne, Germany: Institute of Political Science, University of Berne.

Ashcroft, S. and Timms, N. (1992). *What Europe Thinks: A Study of Western European Values.* Aldershot: Dartmouth.

Attinà, F. (1986). *Il Parlamento Europeo e gli interessi comunitari.* Milan, Italy: Angeli.

Augé, M. (1992). *Non-lieux: introduction à une anthropologie de la sur modernité.* Paris: Editions du Seuil.

Badie, B. (1995) *Le fin des territoires: essai sur le désordre international et sur l'utlité sociale du respect.* Paris: Fayard.

Bagnasco, A. and Le Galès, P. (2000). *Cities in Contemporary Europe.* Cambridge: Cambridge University Press.

Bardi, L. and Ignazi, P. (2004). *Il parlamento Europeo*. Bologna, Italy: Il Mulino.

Barret, D. B., Kurian, G. T., and Johnson, T. M. (2001). *World Christian Encyclopedia: A Comparative Survey of Churches and Religions in the Modern World*. Oxford: Oxford University Press.

Bartolini, S. and Mair, P. (1990). *Identity, Competition and Electoral Availability: The Stabilisation of European Electorates, 1985–1995*. Cambridge: Cambridge University Press.

Baudrillard, J. (1988). *America*. London: Verso.

Baumgartner, F. and Leech, B. (1998). *Basic Interests*. Princeton, NJ: Princeton University Press.

——and Walker, J. (1988). 'Survey Research and Membership in Voluntary Associations', *American Journal of Political Science*, 32: 908–28.

Beaverstock, J., Smith, R., and Taylor, P. (2000). 'World City Network: A New Metageography?', *Annals of the Association of American Geographers*, 90(1): 123–34.

Beck, U. (2000). *What Is Globalization?* Cambridge: Polity Press.

Becker, J. M., et al. (2006). 'Die Proteste in Frankreich 2005. Interdisziplinäre Perspektiven der Konfliktforschung.' CCS Working Paper No. 1. Philipps-Universität Marburg: Center for Conflict Studies.

Becu, A. (1999). 'Trends in Premarital Childbearing', *Current Population Reports*. October: 23–197.

Bell, D. (December 1988). 'The Hegelian Secret: Civil Society and American Exceptionalism', Conference at Princeton University.

Bellah, R. et al. (1986). *Habits of the Heart*. New York: Harper & Row.

Bellah, R. N. (1967). 'Civil Religion in America', *Daedalus*, 96: 1–21.

Berger, P. L. (2004). 'Religion und Europäische Integration', *Transit: Europäische Revue*, 107–17.

——(2005). 'Religion and the West', *The National Interest*, 80 (Summer): 112–19.

Berger, S. (ed.) (1981). *Organizing Interests in Western Europe: Pluralism, Corporatism and the Transformation of Politics*. Cambridge: Cambridge University Press.

——and Dore, R. (eds.) (1996). *National Diversity and Global Capitalism*. Ithaca, NY: Cornell University Press.

Berman, M. (1982). *All That Is Solid Melts into Air: The Experience of Modernity*. New York: Simon & Schuster.

Berube, A. and Forman, B. (October 2002). *Living on the Edge: Decentralization Within Cities in the 1990s*. Washington, DC: Brookings Institution.

——and Frey, W. H. (February 2002). *City Families and Suburban Singles: An Emerging Household Story from Census 2000*. Washington, DC: Brookings Institution.

————(August 2002). *A Decade of Mixed Blessings: Urban and Suburban Poverty in Census 2000*. Washington, DC: Brookings Institution.

——and Thatcher, T. (August 2004). *The Shape of the Curve: Household Income Distributions in US Cities, 1979–99*. Washington, DC: Brookings Institution.

Bibby, J. F. (1999). *Politics, Parties and Elections in America*. Belmont, CA: Wadsworth.

Blondel, J., Sinnott, R., and Svensson, P. (1998). *People and Parliament in the European Union*. Oxford: Clarendon Press.

Blumenthal, S. (1982). *The Permanent Campaign*. New York: Simon & Schuster.

Bogdanor, V. (1989). 'The June 1989 European Elections and the Institutions of the Community', *Government and Opposition*, 24(2): 199–214.

Bonanate, L. (2002). *Rapporto dal futuro. 2004: lo stato dell'Europa e l'Europa come stato*. Gaeta, Italy: Artistic.

Bonazzi, T. (2004). ' "Not like us": il controcanto americano all'americanismo Europeo', unpublished paper.

Boorstin, D. (1960). *America and the Image of Europe. Reflections on American Thought*. New York: Peter Smith.

Booza, J., Fasenfest, D., and Metzger, K. (April 2004). *Living Together: A New Look at Racial and Ethnic Integration in Metropolitan Neighbourhoods, 1990–2000*. Washington, DC: Brookings Institution.

Bornschier, V. (ed.) (2000). *State-Building in Europe. The Revitalization of Western European Integration*. Cambridge: Cambridge University Press.

Bös, M. (2004). 'Ethnicity and Religion: Structural and Cultural Aspects of Global Phenomena', *Protosoziologie*, 20: 143–64.

Boudon, R. (1990). *L'art de se persuader des idées fausses, fragiles ou douteuses*. Paris: Fayard.

Boudreau, J. A. and Keil, R. (2001). 'Seceding from Responsibility? Secession Movements in Los Angeles', *Urban Studies*, 38(10): 1709–39.

Bourdieu, P. (1984). *Distinction: A Social Critique of the Judgment of Taste*. Cambridge, MA: Harvard University Press.

Braudel, F. (1993). *Grammaire des civilisations*. Paris: Flammarion.

Bréchon, P. (ed.) (2000). *Les valeurs des Français. Évolutions de 1980 à 2000*. Paris: Armand Colin.

—— (2002). 'Les grandes enquêtes internationales (Eurobaromètres, Valeurs, ISSP). Apports et limites', *L'Année Sociologique*, 52(1): 105–30.

Breen, R. (ed.) (2004). *Social Mobility in Europe*. Oxford: Oxford University Press.

—— and Luijkx, R. (2001). 'National Patterns of Social Mobility, 1970–1995: Divergence or Convergence? Some Preliminary Findings.' ISA Research Committee 28 on Social Stratification and Mobility, Mannheim Meeting. <http://www.mzes.uni-mannheim.de/rc28/>

Briggs, A. (1962). *Victorian Cities*. London: Penguin.

Brookings Institution Center on Urban and Metropolitan Policy. (April 2001). *Racial Change in the Nation's Largest Cities: Evidence from the 2000 Census*. Washington, DC: Brookings Institution.

Bruno, M. and Sachs, J. (1985). *Economics of Worldwide Stagflation*. Cambridge, MA: Harvard University Press.

Buck, N., Gordon, I., Hall, P., Harloe, M., and Kleinman, M. (2002). *Working Capital. Life and Labor in Contemporary London*. Oxford: Routledge.

Burgess, E. W. and Park, R. E. (1967). *The City*. Chicago, IL: University of Chicago Press.

Bush, G. W. (2002). 'President's Remarks to the Nation'. Speech at Ellis Island, New York, September 11. <http://www.whitehouse.gov/news/releases/2002/09/20020911-3.html>

'Bushspeak' (2001). *Newsweek*, September 19.

Butler, T. and Robson, G. (2004). *London Calling: The Middle Classes and the Remaking of Inner London*. London: Berg.

Cacciari, M. (1994). *Geo-filosofia dell'Europa*. Milan, Italy: Adelphi.

—— (1997). *L'arcipelago*. Milan, Italy: Adelphi.

Cameron, D. R. (1984). 'Social Democracy, Corporatism, Labor Quiescence and the Representation of Economic Interests in Advanced Capitalist Societes', in J. H. Goldthorpe (ed.), *Order and Conflict in Contemporary Capitalism: Studies in the Political Economy of Western European Nations*. Oxford: Clarendon Press.

Caplow, T. (1982). 'Christmas Gifts and Kin Networks', *American Sociological Review*, 47(3): 383–82.

—— (1994). 'The Reduction of Personal Authority', in S. Langlois (ed.), *Convergence or Divergence? Comparing Recent Social Trends in Industrial Societies*. Frankfurt, Montreal: Campus Verlag and McGill-Queen's University Press, pp. 215–23.

—— (1998). 'The Case of the Phantom Episcopalians', *American Sociological Review*, 63: 112–13.

—— (ed.) (2001). *Leviathan Transformed*. Montreal: McGill-Queen's University Press.

—— Bahr, H. M., Modell, J., and Chadwick, B. A. (1992). *Recent Social Trends in the United States: 1960–1990*. Frankfurt, Montreal: Campus Verlag and McGill-Queen's University Press.

—— Hicks, L., and Wattenberg, J. (2001). *The First Measured Century*. Washington: AEI Press.

Casanova, J. (1994). *Public Religions in the Modern World*. Chicago, IL: University of Chicago Press.

Castells, M. (1996). *The Information Age: Economy, Society and Culture—The Rise of the Network Society*. Oxford: Blackwell.

Cattan, N., Pumain, D., and Rozenblat, C. (1999). *Le système des villes européennes*, 2nd edn. Paris: Anthropos.

Cerutti, F. and Rudolph, E. (eds.) (2001*a*). *A Soul for Europe: On the Political and Cultural Identity of Europe*, vol. 1. Leuven, Sterling, VA: Peeters.

—— —— (eds.) (2001*b*). *A Soul for Europe: An Essay Collection*, vol. 2. Leuven, Sterling, VA: Peeters.

Chandler, A. D. (1990). *Scale and Scope. Dynamics and Industrial Capitalism*. Cambridge, Mass.: Harvard University Press.

Charalambis, D., Maratou-Alipranti, L., and Hadjiyanni, A. (2004). *Social Trends in Greece, 1960–2000*. Frankfurt, Montreal: Campus Verlag and McGill-Queen's University Press.

Chiesi, A. M. and Podestà, F. (2003). 'Economic Trends in the EU and the USA'. Paper presented at the biannual workshop of the CCSC International Group, Trento, 5–8 June.

Clarke, H., Dutt, N., and Rapkin, J. (1997). 'Conversations in Context: The (Mis)measurement of Value Change in Advanced Industrial Societies', *Political Behavior*, 19(1): 19–39.

Collins, R. (1999). *Macrohistory. Essays in Sociology of the Long Run*. Stanford, CA: Stanford University Press.

Colombani, J.-M. (2001). 'Nous sommes tous Américains', *Le Monde*, September 13.

Congressional Weekly Report, Washington, DC.

Cooper, R. (2003). *The Breaking of Nations*. London: Atlantic Books.

Coultrap, J. (1999). 'From Parliamentarism to Pluralism. Models of Democracy and the European Union's Democratic Deficit', *Journal of Theoretical Politics*, 11(1): 107–35.

CREDOC (2003). 'La diffusion des technologies de l'information dans la société française', *Collections des Rapports*, 231, by Régis Bigot.

Crouch, C. (1999). *Social Change in Western Europe*. New York: Oxford University Press.

—— (2001). *Storia dell'Europa occidentale*. Bologna, Italy: Il Mulino.

—— and Streeck, W. (1997). 'The Future of Capitalist Diversity', in C. Crouch and W. Streeck (eds.), *Political Economy of Modern Capitalism*. London: Sage.

Crozier, M., Huntington, S. P., and Watanuki, J. (1975). *The Crisis of Democracy. Report on the Governability of Democracies to the Trilateral Commission*. New York: New York University Press.

Dahl, R. (1956). *A Preface to Democratic Theory*. Chicago, IL: Chicago University Press.

—— (1976). *Pluralist Democracy in the United States: Conflict and Consent.* Chicago, IL: Rand McNally.

D'Andrea, D. (2001). 'Europe and the West. The Identity Beyond the Origin', in F. Cerutti and E. Rudolph (eds.), *A Soul for Europe: An Essay Collection*, vol. 2. Leuven, Sterling, VA: Peeters.

Darleen, E. and Liefbroer, A. C. (2002). 'Unmarried Cohabitation and Union Stability: A Test of the Selection Hypothesis Using Data on 16 European Countries'. Paper presented at the conference on 'Divorce in a Cross-National Perspective', Florence, Italy, November 14–15.

Davie, G. and Hervieu-Léger, D. (eds.) (1994). *Identités religieuses en Europe.* Paris: La Découverte.

Davies, N. (1998). *Europe. A History.* New York: Oxford University Press.

Davis, D. and Davenport, C. (1999). 'Assessing the Validity of the Postmaterialism Index', *The American Political Science Review*, 93(3): 649–64.

Davis, M. (1990). *City of Quartz: Excavating the Future in Los Angeles.* New York: Verso.

—— (2004).'Planet of Slums, Urban Involution and the Informal Proletariat', *New Left Review*, March/April: 5–34.

Dear, M. (2000). *The Postmodern Urban Condition.* Oxford: Blackwell.

De Graaf, N., Niewbeerta, P., and Heath, A. (1995). 'Class Mobility and Political Preferences', *American Sociological Review*, 47: 569–86.

De Joung, H. (1995). 'European Capitalism: Between Freedom and Social Justice', *Review of International Organization*, 10: 399–419.

Delanty, G. (1995). *Inventing Europe. Idea, Identity, Reality.* New York: St Martin's Press.

—— (2000). 'The Resurgence of the City in Europe? The Spaces of European Citizenship', in E. F. Isin (ed.), *Democracy, Citizenship and the Global City.* London: Routledge.

De la Porte, C. and Pochet, P. (eds.) (2002). *Building Social Europe Through the Open Method of Co-ordination.* Brussels, Belgium: PIE-Peter Lang.

Del Campo, S. (ed.) (1993). *Tendencias Sociales en Espana, 1960–1990.* Madrid: Fundacion BBV.

Delgado, M. and Lutz-Bachmann, M. (eds.) (1995). *Herausforderung Europa. Wege zu einer politischen Identitat.* München, Germany: Beck.

Delors, J. (1988). *La France par l'Europe.* Paris: Grasset.

Delwit, P. and Kulahci, E. (2004). *The Europarties. Organisation and Influence.* Brussels, Belgium: Editions de l'Université libre de Bruxelles.

Dirn, L. ([1990] 1998). *La société française en tendances 1975–1995.* Paris: Presses Universitaires de France.

Douglass, M. and Friedmann, J. (eds.) (1998). *Cities for Citizen: Planning and the Rise of Civil Society in a Global Age.* London: John Wiley & Sons.

Dreier, P., Mollenkopf, J., and Swanstrom, T. (2005). *Place Matters: Metropolitics for the Twenty First Century.* Lawrence, KS: University of Kansas Press.

Dubach, A. and Campiche, R. J. (1993). *Jeder ein Sonderfall? Religion in der Schweiz.* Zurich, Switzerland: NZN Buchverlag.

Duchesne, S. and Frognier, A. P. (1995). 'Is There a European Identity?', in O. Niedermayer and R. Sinnott (eds.), *Public Opinion and Internationalized Governance.* New York: Oxford University Press.

Durkheim, E. (1898). 'L'individualisme et les intellectuels', *Revue Bleue*, 4e série, X: 7–13.

—— ([1912] 1994). *Die elementaren Formen religiösen Lebens.* Frankfurt am Main, Germany: Suhrkamp.

Eade, J. and Mele, C. (eds.) (2002). *Understanding the City: Contemporary and Future Perspectives.* Oxford and Malden, MA: Blackwell.

Ebbinghaus, B. and Visser, J. (2000). *Trade Unions in Western Europe since 1945.* London: Macmillan.

Eder, K. and Giesen, B. (eds.) (2001). *European Citizenship between National Legacies and Post-national Projects.* Oxford: Oxford University Press.

Eisenstadt, S. N. (1987). *European Civilization in Comparative Perspective.* Oslo: Norwegian University Press.

—— (September 2001). 'The Civilizational Dimension of Modernity. Modernity as a Distinct Civilization', *International Sociology*, 16(3): 320–40.

Eliot, T. S. (1948). *Notes Toward the Definition of Culture.* London: Faber and Faber.

Emerson, M. O. and Hartman, D. (2006). 'The Rise of Religious Fundamentalism', *Annual Review of Sociology*, 32: 127–44.

Epstein, L. (1986). *Political Parties in the American Mold.* Madison, WI: University of Wisconsin Press.

Erikson, R. and Goldthorpe, J. (1993). *The Constant Flux.* New York: Oxford University Press.

Esping-Andersen, G. (1990). *The Three Worlds of Welfare Capitalism.* Princeton, NJ: Princeton University Press.

—— (1999). *The Social Foundations of Postindustrial Economies.* Oxford: Oxford University Press.

European Commission (1996). *First Cohesion Report.* Luxemburg: Office for the Official Publications of the European Communities.

—— (2001). *Unity, Solidarity, Diversity for Europe, Its People and Its Territory: Second Report on Economic and Social Cohesion.* Luxembourg: Office for the Official Publications of the European Communities.

—— (2003*a*). *European Economy 2003.* Luxembourg: Office for Official Publications of the European Communities.

—— (2003*b*). *An Agenda for a Growing Europe. Making the EU Economic System Deliver.* Luxembourg: Office for the Official Publications of the European Communities.

—— (2005). *Communication on the Social Agenda.* Luxembourg: Office for the Official Publications of the European Communities.

European Industrial Relations Observatory. Luxembourg: Office for the Official Publications of the European Union.

Eurostat Yearbook (various years).

Evans, G. (1991). 'Class and Voting: Disrupting the Orthodoxy', in G. Evans (ed.), *The End of Class Politics? Class Voting in Comparative Perspective.* New York: Oxford University Press.

Fabbrini, S. (ed.) (2002). *L'Unione Europea. Le istituzioni e gli attori di un sistema sopranazionale.* Bari, Italy: Laterza.

—— (2005). *L'America e i suoi critici. Virtù e vizi dell'iperpotenza democratica.* Bologna, Italy: Il Mulino.

—— and Morat, F. (eds.) (2002). *L'Unione Europea. Le politiche pubbliche.* Bari, Italy: Laterza.

Fainstein, S., Gordon, I., and Harloe, M. (eds.) (1992). *Divided Cities: New York and London in the Contemporary World.* Oxford: Blackwell.

Fallik, A. (1994). *The European Public Affairs Directory.* Luxembourg: Landmark Publications.

Farrell, C. and Lee, B. (October 2004). *Metropolitan Neighbourhoods with Sheltered Homeless Populations: Evidence from the 1990 and 2000 Censuses.* Washington, DC: Brookings Institution.

Feathermore, D. L., Jones, F. L., and Hauser, R. M. (1975). 'Assumptions of Social Mobility Research in the United States: The Case of Occupational Status', in S. M. Lipset and R. Bendix (eds.), *Social Mobility in Industrial Society.* Berkeley: University of California Press.

Ferrera, M. (2005). *The Boundaries of Welfare: European Integration and the New Spatial Politics of Social Protection.* Oxford: Oxford University Press.

Fincher, R. and Jacobs, J. M. (eds.) (1998). *Cities of Difference.* New York: Guilford Press.

Fiorina, M. P., Peterson, P. E., and Johnson, B. (2002). *The New American Democracy,* 3rd edn. New York: Longman.

Fligstein, N. (2001). *The Architecture of Markets.* Princeton, NJ: Princeton University Press.

Flora, P. (1999). *State Formation, Nation-Building, and Mass Politics in Europe: The Theory of Stein Rokkan.* New York: Oxford University Press.

—— (2000). 'Unity and Diversity of Europe', in B. Ebbinghouse and J. Visser (eds.), *Trade Unions in Western Europe since 1945.* Oxford: Macmillan.

Fontana, J. (1994). *Europa ante el espejo.* Barcelona, Spain: Editorial Critica.

Ford, P. (2001). 'Europe Cringes at Bush "Crusade" against Terrorists', *Christian Science Monitor,* September 19.

Forsé, M. and Parodi, M. (2004) (Engl. tr. 2005). *The Priority of Justice. Elements for a Sociology of Moral Choices.* Berne, Germany: Peter Lang.

Fowler, R. B. (1985). *Religion and Politics in America.* Metuchen, NJ: American Theological Library Association.

Frey, W. H. (June 2001). *Melting Pot Suburbs: A Census 2000 Study of Suburban Diversity.* Washington, DC: Brookings Institution.

—— (January 2003). *Boomers and Seniors in the Suburbs: Aging Patterns in Census 2000.* Washington, DC: Brookings Institution.

—— (October 2003). *Metropolitan Magnets for International and Domestic Migrants.* Washington, DC: Brookings Institution.

—— (May 2004). *The New Great Migration: Black Americans' Return to the South, 1965–2000.* Washington, DC: Brookings Institution.

Friedmann, J. and Wolff, G. (1986). 'The World City Hypothesis', *Development and Change,* 17: 69–84.

Fulbrook, M. (ed.) (1993). *National Histories and European History.* London: UCL Press.

Futuribles (2002). 'Les valeurs des Européens', special issue, n°277, juillet-août.

Galland, O. and Roudet, B. (eds.) (2005). *Les valeurs des jeunes Européens.* Paris: La Découverte.

Gaonkar, D. P. (ed.) (2001). *Alternative Modernities.* Durham, NC: Duke University Press.

Gellner, F. (1983). *Nations and Nationalism.* Oxford: Blackwell.

Genov, N. and Krasteva, A. (eds.). (1999). *Bulgaria 1960–1995.* Sofia: National and Global Development.

George, S. (1991). *Politics and Policy in the European Community.* Oxford: Oxford University Press.

Gibson, C. (1998). 'Population of the Largest 100 Cities and Other Urban Places in the United States, 1790–1990', working paper, 27. Washington, DC: US Bureau of Census.

Giddens, A. (1973). *The Class Structure of Advanced Societies.* New York: Harper & Row.

Giddens, A. (2006). 'The World Does Not Owe Us a Living. Reforming the European Social Model', paper presented at the workshop, *The Future of the European Social Models*. Venice, Italy: Policy Network and Glocus.

Gilbert, M. F. (2003). *Surpassing Realism: The Politics of European Unification since 1945*. Lanham, MD: Rowman & Littlefield.

Gilpin, R. (1987). *The Political Economy of International Relations*. Princeton, NJ: Princeton University Press.

Giner, S. (1994). 'The Advent of a European Society', *European Journal of Sociology*, 24(1).

Gingrich, N. (2005). *Winning the Future*. Washington, DC: Regency Publishing.

Gitlin, T. (1995). *The Twilight of Common Dreams: Why America Is Wracked by Culture Wars*. New York: Metropolitan Books.

Giuliani, M. (2006). *La politica Europea*. Bologna, Italy: Il Mulino.

Glaeser, E. and Shapiro, J. (May 2001). *City Growth and the 2000 Census: Which Places Grew, and Why*. Washington, DC: Brookings Institution.

Glatzer, W., et al. (1992). *Recent Social Trends in Germany: 1960–1990*. Frankfurt, Montreal: Campus Verlag and McGill-Queen's University Press.

Goetschy, J. (2003). 'The European Employment Strategy, Multilevel Governance and Policy Coordination: Past, Present and Future', in J. Zeitlin and D. M. Trubek (eds.), *Governing Work and Welfare in a New Economy: European and American Experiments*. Oxford: Oxford University Press.

Gorges, M. (1996). *Euro-corporatism? Interest Intermediation in the European Community*. Lanham, MD: University Press of America.

Gottdiener, M. and Hutchinson, R. (2006). *The New Urban Sociology*, 3rd edn. Boulder, CO: Westview Press.

Gottlieb, P. (January 2004). *Labor Supply Pressures and the 'Brain Drain': Signs from the Census 2000*. Washington, DC: Brookings Institution.

Gough, I. et al. (1997). 'Social Assistance in OECD Countries', *Journal of European Social Policy*, 7(1): 17–43.

Greeley, A. M. (1972). *The Denominational Society*. Glenview, IL: Scott and Foresman.

Greenberg, S. B. (2004). *The Two Americas. Our Current Political Deadlock and How to Break It*. New York: Thomas Dunne Books.

Greenwood, J. (1997). *Representing Interests in the European Union*. London: Macmillan.

——— Grote, J. and Ronit, K. (eds.) (1992). *Organized Interests and the European Union*. London: Sage.

Grundmann, R. (1999). 'The European Public Sphere and the Deficit of Democracy', in D. Smith and S. Wright (eds.), *Whose Europe? The Turn Toward Democracy*. Oxford: Blackwell.

Guardian, The (2006). 'The Attack on London. Special Reports' (2006). *The Guardian Digital Edition*. <http://www.guardian.co.uk/attackonlondon/0,,1524135,00.html>

Gundara, J. and Jacobs, S. (eds.) (1998). *Interculturalism in Europe: Cultural Diversity and Social Policy in the European Union*. Aldershot, UK: Avebury.

Habermas, J. (1985). *Der philosophische Diskurs der Moderne*. Frankfurt: Suhrkamp.

——— (1991). *Erläuterungen zur Diskursethik*. Frankfurt am Main, Germany: Suhrkamp Verlag.

——— (1998). *Die postnationale Konstellation*. Frankfurt am Main, Germany: Suhrkamp Verlag.

Hall, J. A. and Lindholm, C. (1999). *Is America Breaking Apart?* Princeton, NJ: Princeton University Press.

Hall, P. (1966). *The World Cities*. London: Weidenfield and Nicholson.

Hall, P. and Soskice, D. (eds.) (2001). *Varieties of Capitalism. The Institutional Foundations of Competitive Advantage*. Oxford: Oxford University Press.

Halle, D. (ed.) (2003). *New York and Los Angeles*. Chicago, IL: Chicago University Press.

Haller, M. (1994). *Toward a European Nation? Political Trends in Europe, East and West, Center and Periphery*. Armonk, NY: Sharpe.

—— (2002). 'Theory and Method in the Comparative Study of Values. Critique and Alternative to Inglehart', *European Sociological Review*, 18(2): 139–58.

Hallman, L. and Patterson, T. (1994). 'Individualizaton and Value Fragmentation'. Paper presented at XIIIth World Congress of Sociology, Bielefeld.

Hannigan, J. (1998). *Fantasy City: Pleasure and Profit in the Postmodern Metropolis*. London, New York: Routledge.

Hartz, L. (1955). *The Liberal Tradition in America*. New York: Harcourt, Brace.

—— (1964). *The Founding of New Societies*. New York: Harcourt Brace.

Harvey, D. (1985). *The Urbanization of Capital: Studies in the History and Theory of Capital Urbanization*. Baltimore, MD: Johns Hopkins University Press.

—— (1989). *The Condition of Postmodernity*. Oxford: Blackwell.

Haywood, J. (1997). *Völker, Staaten und Kulturen—Ein universalhistorischer Atlas*. Braunschweig, Germany: Westermann.

Hebel, K. (2005). 'Die USA als Konfliktherd? Europäische Konzeptionen amerikanischer Hegemonie'. Paper presented as part of the lecture series *Zwischen Vernunft und Barbarei—Perspektiven der Krisenprävention*, January 9. Marburg/Germany: Philipps-Universität Marburg.

—— (2006). 'American "Hyperpower" *vs*. Postmodern Europe? Transatlantic Relations and the UK–US "Special Relationship" after September 11'. Paper presented at St Antony's College Research Seminar, February 22. Oxford: St. Antony's College.

Heinelt, H. and Kübler, D. (eds.) (2005). *Metropolitan Governance. Capacity, Democracy and the Dynamics of Place*. London: Routledge.

Heinz, J., et al. (1993). *The Hollow Core: Private Interests in National Policy Making*. Cambridge: Harvard University Press.

Hemerijck, A. (2005). *Recalibrating Europe's Semi-Sovereign Welfare States*. London: Polity Press.

Henshaw, S. K., Singh, S., and Haas, T. (1999). 'Recent Trends in Abortion Rates Worldwide', *Family Planning Perspectives*, March, 25(1).

Hix, S. (1999). *The Political System of the European Union*. New York: St. Martin's Press.

—— and Lord, C. (1997). *Political Parties in the European Union*. London: Macmillan.

Hochshild, J. (1995). *Facing Up to the American Dream: Race, Class and the Soul of the Nation*. Princeton, NJ: Princeton University Press.

Hofstadter, R. (1948). *The American Political Tradition and the Men Who Made It*. New York: Knopf.

—— ([1964] 1996). *The Paranoid Style in American Politics and Other Essays*. Cambridge: Harvard University Press.

Hohenberg, P. and Lees, L. H. (1992). La *formation de l'Europe urbaine, 1000–1950*. Paris: Presses Universitaires de France.

Hooghe, L. (1998). 'EU Cohesion Policy and Competing Models of European Capitalism', *Journal of Common Market Studies*, 36(4).

Hooghe, L. and Marks, G. (2001). *Multi-level Governance and European Integration*. Lanham, MD: Rowman & Littlefield.

Hradil, S. and Immerfall, S. (eds.) (1997). *Die Westeeuropaischen Gesellschaften im Vergleich*. Opladen, Germany: Leske und Budrich.

Huber, E., Ragin, C., and Stephens, J. D. (1997). *The Comparative Welfare States Data Set*. Chicago, IL: Northwestern University and University of North Carolina.

Hughes, R. (1993). *The Culture of Complaint: The Fraying of America*. New York: Warner Books.

Hunter, J. D. (1994). *Before the Shooting Starts: Searching for Democracy in America's Culture Wars*. New York: Free Press.

Huntington, S. P. (1993). 'The Clash of Civilizations?', *Foreign Affairs*, 72(3) (Summer): 22–8.

—— (1997). *The Clash of Civilizations and the Remaking of World Order*. New York: Touchstone Books.

—— (September–October 1997). 'The Erosion of American National Interest', *Foreign Affairs*, 76(5).

—— (2004) *Who Are We?* New York: Simon & Schuster.

Inglehart, R. (1977). *The Silent Revolution. Changing Values and Political Styles Among Western Publics*. Princeton, NJ: Princeton University Press.

—— (1990). *Culture Shift in Advanced Industrial Societies*. Princeton, NJ: Princeton University Press.

—— (1999). 'Postmodernization Erodes Respect for Authority, But Increases Support for Democracy', in P. Norris (ed.), *Critical Citizens: Global Support for Democratic Governance*. Oxford: Oxford University Press, pp. 236–56.

—— and Baker, W. (2000). 'Modernization, Cultural Change, and the Persistence of Traditional Values', *American Sociological Review*, 65(1): 19–51.

International Monetary Fund (2003). World Economic Outlook. <http://www.imf.org/external/pubs/ft/weo/2003/01/>

Iversen, T. and Soskice, D. (2005). 'Distribution and Redistribution: The Shadow of the Nineteenth Century'. Paper presented at the International Seminars of the Graduate School in Social, Economic and Political Studies, University of Milano, May 27.

Jacobs, F. and Corbett, R. (2004). *The European Parliament*. London: John Harper.

Jan-Peter, P. (ed.) (1996). *Europe and Its Citizens*. Helsinki: Edita.

Jargowsky, P. A. (May 2003). *Stunning Progress, Hidden Problems: The Dramatic Decline of Concentrated Poverty in the 1990s*. Washington, DC: Brookings Institution.

Jaspers, K. (1947). 'Vom europaischen Geist', in J. Benda et al. (eds.), *L'esprit européen*. Neuchatel, Switzerland: Editions de la Boconnière.

Johnstone, R. L. (2001). *Religion in Society*. Englewood Cliffs, NJ: Prentice-Hall.

Jones-Corea, M. (ed.) (2001). *Governing American Cities, Interethnic Coalitions, Competition, Conflict*. New York: Russell Sage Foundation.

Kaelble, H. (1987). *Auf dem Weg zu einer europaischen Gesellschaft*. Munich, Germany: Beck.

Kagan, R. (June–July 2002). 'Power and Weakness', *Policy Review*, 113.

Kant, E. [1785] (Engl. tr. 1964). *Groundwork of the Metaphysics of Morals*. New York: Harper & Row.

—— [1797] (Engl. tr. 1996). *The Metaphysics of Morals, II, The Doctrine of Virtue*. New York: Cambridge University Press.

Kantor, P. and Savitch, H. V. (2002). *Cities in the International Marketplace: The Political Economy of Urban Development in North America and Western Europe.* Princeton, NJ: Princeton University Press.

Katz, B. (February 2005). *State of the World's Cities: The American Experience.* Washington, DC: Brookings Institution.

Katz, R. S. and Kolodny, R. (1994). 'Party Organization as an Empty Vessel: Parties in American Politics', in R. S. Katz and P. Mair (eds.), *How Parties Organize.* London: Sage.

—— and Wessels, B. (eds.) (1999). *The European Parliament, the National Parliaments, and European Integration.* Oxford: Oxford University Press.

Kennedy, J. F. (1963). Public Papers of the Presidents, J. F. Kennedy, Paulskirche speech, 25 June, Frankfurt.

Kennedy, P. M. (1986). *The Rise and Fall of the Great Powers.* New York: Vintage.

Kenworthy, L. (1999). 'Economic Integration and Convergence: A Look at the U.S. States', in *Social Science Quarterly*, 80(4): 858–69.

Keohane, R. and Hoffmann, S. (eds.) (1991). *The New European Community.* Boulder, CO: Westview.

Kim, S. and Smith, T. W. (2006). 'National Pride in Cross-National and Temporal Perspective', *International Journal of Public Opinion Research*, 18 (Spring): 127–36.

King, A. D. (ed.) (1996). *Re-presenting the City: Ethnicity, Capital, and Culture in the 21st Century Metropolis.* New York: New York University Press.

Kingston, P. (2000). *The Classless Society.* Stanford, CA: Stanford University Press.

—— Langlois, S., Lemel, Y., and Noll, H. H. (2002). 'Inequality: The Structuring Effect of Class in Four Societies', in Y. Lemel and H. H. Noll (eds.), *Changing Structures of Inequality: A Comparative Perspective.* Montreal: McGill-Queen's University Press.

Kitting, E. (2000). *Abortion in Europe: The East West Divided.* IPPF European Network, 28(2).

Knox, P. and Taylor, P. (eds.) (1995). *World Cities in a World System.* Cambridge: Cambridge University Press.

Kohler-Koch, B. (2000). *Network Governance Within and Beyond an Enlarged European Union.* Quebec City: Canadian European Studies Association.

Kohli, M. (2000). 'The Battleground of European Identity', *European Societies*, 2(2): 113–37.

Kreppel, A. (2002). *The European Parliament and Supranational Party System.* Cambridge: Cambridge University Press.

Kriesi, H., et al. (eds.) (1999). *Nation and National Identity: The European Experience in Perspective.* Zurich, Switzerland: Ruegger.

Kumar, K. (1988). *The Rise of Modern Society. Aspects of the Social and Political Development of the West.* Oxford, New York: Blackwell.

Ladd, E. C. (1994). *The American Ideology.* Storrs, CT: Roper Center.

Laffan, B. (1999). 'Democracy and the European Union', in L. Cram, D. Dinan, and N. Nugent (eds.), *Developments in the European Union.* Basingstoke: Palgrave.

Lamberti, J.-C. (1986–7). 'La liberté et les illusions individualistes selon Tocqueville', *The Tocqueville Review/La Revue Tocqueville*, VIII: 153–63; reprinted in: L. Guellec (ed.) (2005). *Tocqueville et l'esprit de la démocratie.* Paris: Presses de Sciences Po, 149–66.

Lane, J. E. and Ersson, S. O. (1999). *Politics and Society in Western Europe.* London: Sage.

Langlois, S., et al. (eds.) (1994). *Convergence or Divergence? Comparing Recent Social Trends in Industrial Societies.* Frankfurt, Montreal: Campus Verlag and McGill-Queen's University Press.

Lawrence, B. (1989). *Defenders of God: The Fundamentalist Revolt against the Modern Age*. San Francisco, CA: Harper & Row.

Le Galès, P. (2002). *European Cities: Social Conflicts and Urban Governance*. Oxford: Oxford University Press.

Lee, J.-H. and Przeworski, A. (1992). 'Cui bono? Una stima del benessere nei sistemi coporativisti e in quelli di mercato', *Stato e Mercato*, 36: 345–76.

Leggewie, C. (2005). 'Amerika und Europa: Zwei Wege zu Gott', in H. Strasser and G. Nollmann (eds.), *Endstation Amerika?* Wiesbaden, Germany: Westdeutscher Verlag.

Lehmbruch, G. and Schmitter, P. C. (1979). *Trends Toward Corporative Intermediation*. Beverly Hills, London: Sage.

Leonard, M. (2005). *Europe Will Lead the 21st Century*. London: Fourth Estate.

Levy, D., Pensky, M., and Torpey, J. (eds.) (2005). *Old Europe, New Europe, Core Europe*. London: Verso.

Light, I. and Rosenstein, C. (1995). *Race, Ethnicity, and Entrepreneurship in Urban America*. New York: Aldine de Gruyter.

Lijphart, A. (1999) *Patterns of Democracy: Government Forms and Performance in Thirty-Six Countries*. New Haven, CT: Yale University Press.

Lind, M. (1995). *The Next American Nation. The New Nationalism and the Fourth American Revolution*. New York: Free Press.

Lindert, P. H. and Williamson, J. G. (2003). 'Does Globalization Make the World More Unequal?', in M. D. Bordo and J. G. Williamson (eds.), *Globalization in Historical Perspective*. Chicago, IL: University of Chicago Press.

Lipset, S. M. (1979a). *The First New Nation: The United States in Historical and Comparative Perspective* (expanded edition). New York: W. W. Norton.

—— (1979b). 'American Exceptionalism', in M. Novak (ed.), *Capitalism and Socialism*. Washington, DC: American Enterprise Institute.

—— (1990). *Continental Divide. The Values and Institutions of the United States and Canada*. New York: Routledge.

—— (1996). *American Exceptionalism. A Double-Edged Sword*. New York: W. W. Norton.

—— and Bendix, R. (1959). *Social Mobility in Industrial Society*. Berkeley, CA: University of California Press.

—— and Marks, G. (2000). *It Didn't Happen Here. Why Socialism Failed in the United States*. New York: W. W. Norton.

—— and Rokkan, S. (1967). *Party Systems and Voter Alignments: Cross National Perspectives*. New York: Free Press.

—— and Zetterberg, H. (1959). 'Social Mobility in Industrial Societies', in S. M. Lipset and R. Bendix (eds.), *Social Mobility in Industrial Society*. Berkeley, CA: University of California Press.

—— —— (1966). 'A Theory of Social Mobility', in S. M. Lipset and R. Bendix (eds.), *Class, Status and Power: Social Stratification in Comparative Perspective*, New York: Free Press.

Lo, F. C. and Yeung, Y. M. (eds.) (1998). *Globalization and the World of Large Cities*. Tokyo: United Nation University.

Lodge, J. (1991). 'The Democratic Deficit and the European Parliament', Fabian Society Discussion Paper No. 4. London: Fabian Society.

Logan, J. and Molotch, H. (1987). *Urban Fortunes: The Political Economy of Place*. Berkeley, CA: University of California Press.

Logan, J. R. (ed.) (2002). *The New Chinese City: Globalization and Market Reform*. Oxford: Blackwell.

Lowery, D. and Brasher, H. (2004). *Organized Interests amd American Government*. New York, McGraw-Hill.

Lowi, T. J. (1979). *The End of Liberalism: The Second Republic of the United States*. New York: W. W. Norton.

Lucy, W. H. and Phillips, D. L. (December 2001). '*Suburbs and the Census: Patterns of Growth and Decline*'. Washington, DC: Brookings Institution.

Lynd, R. S. and Lynd, H. M. (1929). *Middletown: A Study in American Culture*. New York: Harcourt Brace.

Maddison, A. (1995). *Monitoring the World Economy*. Paris: OECD.

Mahoney, J. and Rueschemeyer, D. (eds) (2002). *Comparative Historical Analysis in the Social Sciences*. Cambridge: Cambridge University Press.

Mahood, H. R. (1990). *Interest Group Politics in America: A New Intensity*. Englewood, CA: Prentice Hall.

Mair, P. (1997). *Party System Change: Approaches and Interpretations*. Oxford: Clarendon Press.

Majone, G. (1996). *Regulating Europe*. London: Routledge.

Mancini, F. (2000). *Democracy and Constitutionalism in the European Union*. London: Hart.

Mann, M. (1998). 'Is There a Society Called Euro?', in R. Axtman (ed.), *Globalization and Europe. Theoretical and Empirical Investigations*. London: Pinter.

Manthorpe, R. (2006). 'Spirit of the Brits', *The Guardian*, July 1.

Manville, M. and Storper, M. (2005). 'Behavior, Preferences and Cities: Urban Theory and Urban Resurgence', *in Les Cahiers du Pôle Ville*, n. 13.

Marcuse, H. (1964). *One Dimensional Man: Studies in the Ideology of Advanced Industrial Society*. Boston: Beacon Press.

Marcuse, P. and Van Kempen, R. (eds.) (2000). *Globalizing Cities: A New Spatial Order?* Oxford: Blackwell.

Marks, G. and Steenbergen, M. (eds.) (2004). *European Integration and Political Conflict*. Cambridge: Cambridge University Press.

—— Scharpf, F., Schmitter, P. and Streeck, W. (eds.) (1996). *Governance in the European Union*. London: Sage.

Marsden, G. M. (1980). *Fundamentalism and American Culture. The Shaping of Twentieth-Century Evangelicalism 1870–1925*. New York: Oxford University Press.

Martinelli, A. (1974). *Structural Contradictions and Organizational Response in American Higher Education*, Ph.D. Thesis, University of California, Berkeley, CA. Italian edition (1978), *L'università americana*. Turin: Einaudi.

—— (2002). 'Globalization, Democratic Global Governance and the European Union', *The Tocqueville Review/La Revue Tocqueville*, XXIII(1): 49–71.

—— (2003). 'Proposal for the Volume: Social Trends in the European Union and in the United States', paper prepared for the biannual CCSC meeting in Madrid, November.

—— ([2002] 2004). *La democrazia globale*. Bari, Rome: Laterza.

—— (2005a). *Global Modernization. Rethinking the Project of Modernity*. London: Sage.

—— (2005b). 'The European Identity', in E. Ben-Rafael (ed.), *Comparing Modern Civilizations: Pluralism Versus Homogeneity*. Amsterdam: Brill Academic Publishers.

Martinelli, A., Chiesi, A., and Stefanizzi, S. (1999). *Recent Social Trends in Italy: 1960–1995*. Frankfurt, Montreal: Campus Verlag and McGill-Queen's University Press.

Massey, D. S. and Denton, N. (1993). *American Apartheid: Segregation and the Making of the Underclass*. Cambridge, MA: Harvard University Press.

Mayhew, D. R. (1986). *Placing Parties in American Politics*. Princeton, NJ: Princeton University Press.

—— (1991). *Divided We Govern: Party Control, Law-Making and Investigations 1946–1990*. New Haven, CT: Yale University Press.

Mazey, S. and Richardson, J. (eds.) (1993). *Lobbying in the European Community*. Oxford: Oxford University Press.

McCarney, P. L. and Stren, R. E. (2003). *Governance on the Ground: Innovations and Discontinuities in Cities of the Developing World*. Washington, DC, and Baltimore, MD: Woodrow Wilson Center Press/Johns Hopkins University Press.

McKinnon, A. M. (2002). 'Sociological Definitions, Language Games, and the "Essence" of Religion', *Method & Theory in the Study of Religion*, 14: 61–83.

Mendras, H. (1997). *L'Europe des Européens. Sociologie de l'Europe occidentale*. Paris: Gallimard.

—— (2002). *La France que je vois*. Paris: Editions Autrement.

Mercier, A. (ed.) (2003). *Vers un espace public européen*. Paris: L'Harmattan.

Michalowitz, I. (2002). 'Beyond Corporatism and Pluralism: Toward a New Theoretical Framework', in A. Warleigh and J. Fairbrass (eds.), *Influence and Interests in the European Union: The New Politics of Persuasion and Advocacy*. London: Europa Publications.

Micklethwait, J. and Wooldridge, A. (2004). *The Right Nation. Why America Is Different*. London: Penguin Books.

Mikkeli, H. (1998). *Europe as an Idea and as an Identity*. Basingstoke: Palgrave.

Mingione, E. (ed.) (1996). *Urban Poverty and the Underclass*. Oxford and Cambridge, MA: Blackwell.

Molnar, T. (1978). *Le modèle défiguré. L'Amérique de Tocqueville a Carter*. Paris: Presses Universitaires de France.

Molotch, H. (1996). 'LA as Design Product: How Art works in a Regional Economy', in A. J. Scott and E. Soja (eds.), *The City: Los Angeles and Urban Theory at the End of the Twentieth Century*. Berkeley, CA: University of California Press.

Mongardini, C. (ed.) (2001). *La nascita di una coscienza Europea*. Rome: Bulzoni.

Monkkonen, E. (1988). *America Becomes Urban*. Berkeley, CA: University of California Press.

Moravcsik, A. (2001). 'Federalism in the European Union: Rhetoric and Reality', in K. Nikolaidis and R. Hose (eds.), *The Federal Vision. Legitimacy and Levels of Government in the United States and the European Union*. Oxford: Oxford University Press.

Moriconi-Ebrard, F. (1993). *L'urbanisation du monde depuis 1950*. Paris: Anthropos.

—— (2000). *De Babylone à Tokyo: les grandes agglomerations du monde*. Paris-Gap: Ophrys.

Morin, E. (1987). *Penser l'Europe*. Paris: Gallimard.

Moulaert, F., Rodriguez, A., and Swyngedouw, E. (eds.) (2003). *The Globalized City: Economic Restructing and Social Polarization in European Cities*. Oxford: Oxford University Press.

Mumford, L. (1961). *The City in History: Its Origin, Its Transformations, and Its Prospects*. New York: Harcourt, Brace and World.

Myrdal, G. (1944). *An American Dilemma*. New York: Harper & Row.

Nagel, T. (1991). *Equality and Partiality*. New York: Oxford University Press.

Nelson, B., Roberts, D., and Veit, W. (eds.) (1994). *The Idea of Europe. Problems of National and Transnational Identity*. Oxford: Berg.

Nickell, S. J. and Nunziata, L. (2001). *Labor Market Institutions Database*. London: CEP, LSE.

Nieuwbeerta, P. (2001). 'The Democratic Class Struggle in Postwar Societies: Traditional Class Voting in Twenty Countries, 1945–1990', in T. Clark and S. M. Lipset (eds.), *The Breakdown of Class Politics*. Baltimore, MD: Johns Hopkins University Press.

Nora, P. (ed.) (1984). *Les lieux de mémoire*. Paris: Gallimard.

Norris, P. and Inglehart, R. (2004). *Sacred and Secular*. Cambridge: Cambridge University Press.

North, D. (1990). *Institutions, Institutional Change and Economic Performance*. Cambridge: Cambridge University Press.

Nugent, N. (1994). *The Government and Politics of the European Union*. Durham, NC: Duke University Press.

Nye, J. S., Zelikow, P. D., and King, D. C. (eds.) (1997). *Why People Don't Trust Government*. Cambridge: Harvard University Press.

OECD (various years). *National Accounts: Volume 1 Main Aggregates*. Paris: OECD.

—— (various years). *Historical Statistics*. Paris: OECD.

—— (2000). *Employment Outlook*. Paris: OECD.

—— (2002). *Economic Outlook Statistics and Projections*. Paris: OECD.

—— (2003). *Statistical Compendium, 1997–2002*. Paris: OECD.

—— (2004). *Labor Force Statistics*. Paris: OECD.

Offe, C. (2002). 'Is There, or Can There Be, a European Society?', in I. Katenhusen and W. Lamping (eds.), *Demokratien in Europa. Europaische Integration, Institutionenwandel und die Zukunft des demokratischen Verfassungsstaates*. Opladen, Germany: Leske & Budrich.

Olson, M. (1965). *The Logic of Collective Action*. Cambridge: Harvard University Press.

Olstrom, V. (1987). *The Political Theory of a Compound Republic, Designing the American Experiment*. Lincoln, NE: University of Nebraska Press.

Padoa Schioppa, T. (2005). *L'Europa della malinconia*. Milan: Bocconi University Press.

Pagden, A. (ed.) (2001). *The Idea of Europe, from Antiquity to the European Union*. Cambridge: Cambridge University Press.

Parkes, H. B. (1947). *The American Experience. An Interpretation of the History and Civilization of the American People*. New York: Knopf.

Parrington, V. ([1927] 1958). *Main Currents in American Thought*. New York: Harcourt Brace.

Paterson, W. (1991). 'Regulatory Change and Environmental Protection in the British and German Chemical Industries', *European Journal of Political Research*, XIX, 2–3: 307–26.

Pells, R. (1997). *Not Like Us. How Europeans Have Loved, Hated and Transformed American Culture since World War II*. New York: Basic Books.

Pennings, P. and Lane, J. E. (1998). *Comparing Party System Change*. London: Routledge.

Perin, C. (1988). *Belonging in America: Reading between the Lines*. Madison, WI: University of Wisconsin Press.

Perrot, M. (1999). 'The Family Triumphant', in *A History of Private Life*, vol. IV. Cambridge, MA: Harvard University Press.

Pfeifer, G. (1995). *Eurolobbysmus: organisierte Interessen in der Europaischen Union*. Europaische Hochschulschriften 31, Politikwissenschaft 271. Frankfurt am Main, Germany: Peter Lang.

Phillips, K. P. (1983). *Post-Conservative America*. New York: Vintage Books.

Piore, M. and Sabel, C. (1984). *The Second Industrial Divide: Possibilities for Prosperity*. New York: Basic Books.

Pomian, K. (1990). *L'Europe et ses nations*. Paris: Gallimard.

Popkin, S. L. (1994). *The Reasoning Voter: Communication and Persuasion in Presidential Campaigns*. Chicago, IL: University of Chicago Press.

Preteceille, E. (2000). 'Segregation, Class and Politics in Large Cities', in A. Baguasco and P. Le Gàles (eds.), *Cities in Contemporary Europe*. Cambridge: Cambridge University Press.

Putnam, R. D. (2000). *Bowling Alone: The Collapse and Revival of American Community*. New York: Simon & Schuster.

Pyle, R. E. and Davidson, J. D. (2003). 'The Origins of Religious Stratification in Colonial America', *Journal for the Scientific Study of Religion*, 42: 57–75.

Radaelli, C. (2003). *The Open Method of Coordination: A New Governance Architecture for the European Union?* Stockholm: Swedish Institute for European Policy Studies.

Rahir, K. (2006). 'Karikaturen-Streit: Frankreich fürchtet neue Unruhen in den Banlieues', *Spiegel Online*. February 2. <http://service.spiegel.de/digas/servlet/find/ON=spiegel-398725>

Raunio, T. (1996). Party Group Behaviour in the European Parliament. Tampere: University of Tampere Academic Dissertation.

Rawls, J. (1971) (rev. ed. 1999). *A Theory of Justice*. Cambridge, MA: Harvard University Press.

Reid, T. R. (2004). *The United States of Europe. The New Superpower and the End of American Supremacy*. New York: Penguin Press.

Reimers, D. M. (2005). *Other Immigrants. The Global Origins of the American People*. New York: New York University Press.

Rennie, D. (2003). 'God Put Bush in Charge, Says the General Hunting Bin Laden', *Telegraph*, October 17.

Resnick, P. (2005). *The European Roots of Canadian Identity*. Peterborough: Broadview Press.

Rhodes, C. (ed.) (1998). *The European Union in the World Community*. Boulder, CO: Lynne Rienner.

Riesebrodt, M. (1990). *Fundamentalismus als patriarchalische Protestbewegung: amerikanische Protestanten (1910–28) und iranische Schiiten (1961–79) im Vergleich*. Tübingen, Germany: Mohr.

Riffault, H. (ed.) (1994). *Les valeurs des Français*. Paris: PUF.

Rifkin, J. (2004). *The European Dream: How Europe's Vision of the Future Is Quietly Eclipsing the American Dream*. London: Penguin.

Rodrigues, M. J. (ed.) (2002). *The New Knowledge Economy in Europe: A Strategy for International Competitiveness and Social Cohesion*. Cheltenham: Edward Elgar.

Rokkan, S. (1970). *Citizens, Elections, Parties*. Oslo: Universitetsforlaget.

—— (1975). 'Dimensions of State Formation and Nation-Building: A Possible Paradigm for Research on Variations Within Europe', in C. Tilly (ed.), *The Formation of National States in Western Europe*. Princeton, NJ: Princeton University Press.

—— (1999). *State Formation, Nation-Building, and Mass Politics in Europe* (edited and with an introduction by Peter Flora). New York: Oxford University Press.

Rose, R. (1996). *What Is Europe?* New York: HarperCollins.

Ross, G. (1995). *Jacques Delors and European Integration*. Cambridge: Polity Press.

Rousseau, J.-J. (1762). *Du contrat social*. Paris: Aubier-Montaigne.

Rubery, J., Smith, M., and Fagan, C. (1999). *Women's Employment in Europe: Trends and Prospects*. London: Routledge.

Rumford, C. (2002). *The European Union. A Political Sociology*. Oxford: Blackwell.

Rushdie, S. et al. (2006). 'Manifesto: Together Facing the New Totalitarianism', *Internetavisen Jyllands Posten*, February 28.

Russell Mead, W. (2001). *Special Providence: American Foreign Policy and How It Changed the World*. New York: Knopf.

Salvadori, M. (2005). *L'Europa degli americani, dai padri fondatori a Roosevelt*. Bari, Rome, Italy: Laterza.

Sapir, A. et al. (2003). *An Agenda for a Growing Europe*. Brussels: European Commission.

Sassen, S. (1991 and 2001). *The Global City: New York, London, Tokyo*. Princeton, NJ: Princeton University Press.

Savage, T. M. (2004). 'Europe and Islam: Crescent Waxing, Cultures Clashing,' *The Washington Quarterly*, 27(3): 25–50.

Savitch, H. V. and Kantor, P. (2002). *Cities in the International Marketplace*. Princeton, NJ: Princeton University Press.

Sbragia, A. (1996). *Debt Wish: Entrepreneurial Cities, U.S. Federalism, and Economic Development*. Pittsburgh, PA: Pittsburgh University Press.

Scharpf, F. W. (1996). 'Negative and Positive Integration in the Political Economy of European Welfare States', in G. Marks, F. W. Scharpf, P. Schmitter and W. Streeck (eds.), *Governance in the European Union*. London: Sage.

Schilling, H. (2001). 'Reformation', in N. J. Smelser and P. B. Baltes (eds.), *International Encyclopedia of the Social & Behavioral Sciences*. London: Elsevier, pp. 12891–5.

Schlesinger, A. M. Jr. (1991). *The Disuniting of America: Reflections on a Multicultural Society*. New York: W. W. Norton.

Schlozman, K. and Tierney, J. (1981). *Organized Interests and American Democracy*. New York: Harper & Row.

Schmidt, A. V. (2002). *The Futures of European Capitalism*. Oxford: Oxford University Press.

Schmitter, P. (2000). *How to Democratize the European Union: And Why Bother?* Lanham, MD: Rowman & Littlefield.

—— and Streeck, W. (1991). 'From National Corporatism to Transnational Pluralism: Organized Interests in the Single European Market', *Politics and Society*, 19(2): 133–64.

Schröder, G. (2001). 'Regierungserklärung vor dem Deutschen Bundestag am 12. September 2001 zu den Anschlägen in den USA'. Deutscher Bundestag, Plenarprotokoll, 14(1): 86. <http://archiv.bundesregierung.de/bpaexport/regierungserklaerung/57/55757/multi.htm>

Schümer, D. (2004). 'Theo van Gogh: Die Niederlande nach dem Mord', *Frankfurter Allgemeine Zeitung* (*FAZ.net*), November 3.

Scott, A. J. and Soja, E. W. (eds.) (1996). *The City: Los Angeles and Urban Theory at the End of the Twentieth Century*. Berkeley, CA: University of California Press.

Segal, D. E. (2000). 'Western Civilization and the Staging of History in American Higher Education', *American Historical Review*, June: 770–805.

Sen, A. (1999). 'Democracy as a Universal Value', *Journal of Democracy*, 10(3): 3–17.

Sennett, R. (1990). *The Conscience of the Eye: The Design and Social Life of Cities*. New York: Knopf.

Shafer, B. (ed.) (1991). *Is America Different? A New Look at American Exceptionalism*. Oxford: Oxford University Press.

Simmel, G. (1910). *Soziologie der Geselligkeit*, Engl. tr. in D. N. Levine (ed.) (1971), *Georg Simmel, On Individuality and Social Forms*. Chicago, IL: University of Chicago Press, 127–40.

Singer, A. (February 2004). *The Rise of New Immigrant Gateways*. Washington, DC: Brookings Institution.

—— and Suro, R. (July 2002). *Latino Growth in Metropolitan America: Changing Patterns, New Locations*. Washington, DC: Brookings Institution.

Smith, A. D. (1991). *National Identity*. London: Penguin.

—— (1992). 'National Identity and the Idea of European Unity', *International Affairs*, 68(1): 55–76.

Smith, C. S. (2005). 'Ten Officers Shot as Riots Worsen in French Cities', *New York Times*, November 7.

Smith, M. P. (2001). *Transnational Urbanism: Locating Globalization*. Oxford: Blackwell.

Smith, R. J. and White, J. (2004). 'General's Speeches Broke Rules. Report Says Boykin Failed to Obtain Clearance', *Washington Post*, August 19.

Smith, T. (1990). 'Trends in Voluntary Group Membership: Comments on Baumgartner and Walker', *American Journal of Political Science*, 34: 646–61.

Sombart, W. (1906, Engl. tr. 1976). *Why is There No Socialism in the United States?* White Plains, NY: International Arts and Sciences Press.

Soskice, D. (1989). 'Perchè variano i tassi di disoccupazione: economia e istituzioni nei paesi industriali avanzati', *Stato e mercato*, 27: 333–78.

—— (1993). *Product, Market and Innovation Strategies of Companies and Their Implications for Enterprise Tenure. A Comparative Institutional Approach to Cross-Country Differences*. Berlin: Wissenschaftszentrum.

Stark, R. and Bainbridge, W. S. ([1987] 1996). *A Theory of Religion*. New Brunswick, NJ: Rutgers University Press.

Statistical Abstract of the United States (various years).

Steiner, G. (2005). *Une certaine idée de l'Europe*. Arles, France: Actes Sud.

Stoetzel, J. (1983). *Les valeurs du temps présent: une enquête européenne*. Paris: PUF.

Stone, S. A. and Sandholz, W. (eds.) (1998). *European Integration and Supranational Governance*. Oxford: Oxford University Press.

Storper, M. (1997). *The Regional World: Territorial Development in a Global Economy*. New York: Guilford Press.

Streeck, W. and Schmitter, P. (1991). 'From National Corporatism to Transnational Pluralism: Organized Interests in the Single European Market', *Politics and Society*, 19(2): 133–64.

Swatos, W. H. Jr. and Wimberley, R. C. (1998). 'Civil Religion', in W. H. Swatos, Jr. (ed.), *Encyclopedia of Religion and Society*. London: AltaMira Press, pp. 94–6.

Symeonidou, H. (undated). 'Marital Dissolution in Greece'. Working paper. Athens: National Center for Social Research.

Taylor, C. (2002). *Varieties of Religion Today: William James Revisited*. Cambridge: Harvard University Press.

Teaford, J. (1993). *The Twentieth Century American City*. Baltimore, MD: Johns Hopkins University Press.

Tesauro, G. (2001). *Diritto comunitario*. Padova, Italy: Cedam.

Therborn, G. (1985). *What Does the Ruling Class Do When It Rules? State Apparatuses and State Power Under Feudalism, Capitalism and Socialism*. London: Rodtledge.

—— (1995). *European Modernity and Beyond: The Trajectory of European Societies 1945–2000*. London: Sage.

Tilly, C. (1990). *Coercion, Capital and European States, AD 990–1990*. Oxford: Blackwell.

—— (1993). *European Revolution, 1492–1992*. Oxford: Basil Blackwell.

Tocqueville, A. (ed.) (1835–40) (Engl. tr. 2004 by A. Goldhammer). *Democracy in America*. New York: Library of America.

Todd, E. (1996). *L'invention de l'Europe*. Paris: Seuil.

Treiman, D. (1970). 'Industrialization and Social Stratification', in E. Laumann (ed.), *Social Stratification: Research and Theory for the 1970s*. Indianapolis, IN: Bobbs Merrill.

Trubek, D. M. and Trubek, L. G. (May 2005). 'Hard and Soft Law in the Construction of Social Europe: The Role of the Open Method of Coordination', *European Law Journal*, 11: 343–64.

Tsebelis, G. (1994). 'The Power of the European Parliament as a Conditional Agenda Setter', *American Political Science Review*, 88(1): 128–42.

Tullio-Altan, C. (1995). *Ethnos e civiltà*. Milan, Italy: Feltrinelli.

Tuveson, E. L. (1968). *Redeemer Nation: The Idea of America's Millennial Role*. Chicago, IL: University of Chicago Press.

Urban Audit Yearbook (2000). <http://ec.europa.eu/regional_policy/urban2/urban/audit/src/yearbook.htm>

Urry, J. (2000). *Sociology Beyond Societies: Mobilities for the Twenty First Century*. London, New York: Routledge.

Valli, V. (1999). *Politica economica Europea*. Rome, Italy: Carocci.

Van Schendelen, M. (ed.) (1998). *EU Committees as Influential Policymakers*. Aldershot: Ashgate.

Vanhove, T. and Matthijs, K. (2002). 'Recent Developments in the Socio-Demographic Evolution of Divorce and Remarriage in Belgium'. <www.iue.iit/Personal/Donkers/Divorce/Vanhove.htm>

Veltz, P. (1996). *Mondialisation, villes et territoires l'economie d' archipel*. Paris: Presses Universitaires de France.

Verhoeven, W. M. (2001). 'American Studies: Society', *International Encyclopedia of the Social and Behavioral Sciences*, vol. 1. Amsterdam, Elsevier, pp. 454–61

Von Beyme, K. (1982). *Parteien in westlichen Demokratien-uberarbeitete Neuausgabe*. Munchen, Germany: Piper Verlag.

Vorländer, H. (2004). 'Politische Kultur', in P. Lösche and H. Dietrich von Loeffelholz (eds.), *Länderbericht USA. Geschichte, Politik, Wirtschaft, Gesellschaft, Kultur*. Bonn: Bundeszentrale für politische Bildung: 288–318.

Wade, R. (2001). 'Winners and Losers', *The Economist*, April 28: 79–82.

Walker, M. (2000). 'Variable Geography: America's Mental Maps of a Greater Europe', *International Affairs*, 76(3): 459–74.

Wallace, H. and Young, A. (eds.) (1998). *Participation and Policy-Making in the European Union*. Oxford: Oxford University Press.

Wallis, J. (2003). 'Dangerous Religion. George W. Bush's Theology of Empire', *Sojourner Magazine* (September/October).

Walton, J. and Seldon, D. (1994). *Free Markets and Food Riots: The Politics of Global Adjustment*. Oxford: Blackwell.

Walzer, M. (1990). 'What Does It Mean to Be an American?', *Social Research*, 57: 591–614.

Ware, A. (1996). *Parties and Party Systems*. Oxford: Oxford University Press.

Warner, S. B. (1995). *The Urban Wilderness: A History of the American City*. Berkeley, CA: University of California Press.

Weber, M. (1920). *Gesammelte Aufsatze zur Religionssoziologie*. Tübingen, Germany: Mohr.

—— ([1925] 1978). *Economy and Society: An Outline of Interpretive Sociology*. Edited by G. Roth and Cl. Wittich. Berkeley, CA: University of California Press. Original edition: *Wirtschaft und gesellschaft*. Tübingen, Germany: Mohr.

Weiler, J. (1994). 'A Quiet Revolution. The European Court of Justice and its Interlocutors', *Comparative Political Studies*, 26: 510–34.

Wells, H. G. (1906). *The Future of America*. London: Chapman and Hall.

Wessels, W. (1997). 'The Growth and Differentiation of Multilevel Networks: A Corporatist Mega-Bureaucracy or Open City?', in H. Wallace and E. R. Young (eds.), *Participation and Policy-Making in the European Union*. Oxford: Clarendon.

Wilson, K. and Van der Dussen, J. (eds.) (1995). *The History of the Idea of Europe*. London: Routledge.

Wilterdink, N. (1993). 'The European Ideal. An Examination of European and National Identity', *Archives européennes de sociologie*, 34: 119–36.

Wimberley, R. C. (1980). 'Civil Religion and the Choice for President', *Social Forces*, 59: 44–61.

—— and Christenson, J. A. (1982). 'Civil Religion, Social Indicators, and Public Policy', *Social Indicators Research*, 10: 211–13.

Wittrock, B. (2000). 'Modernity: One, None or Many? European Origins of Modernity as a Global Condition', *Daedalus*, Winter.

Wolfe, A. (1998). *One Nation, After All*. New York: Viking.

World Bank (2003). *World Development Indicators*. Washington, DC: World Bank.

Wroe, A. (2002). 'Trust in Government: A Crisis of Democracy', in D. H. McKay, D. P. Houghton and A. Wroe (eds.), *Controversies in American Politics and Society*. Oxford: Blackwell Publishers, pp. 20–30.

Zaborowski, M. (ed.) (2006). *Friends Again? EU–US Relations After the Crisis*. Paris: Institute for Security Studies, European Union.

Zeff, E. and Pirro, E. (eds.) (2001). *European Union and the Member States. Cooperation, Coordination and Compromise*. Boulder, CO: Lynne Rienner.

Zeitlin, J. and Pochet, P. (eds.) (2005). *The Open Method of Coordination in Action*. Brussels, Belgium: Peter Lang.

Zijderveld, A. (1997). *A Theory of Urbanity: The Economic and Civic Culture of Cities*. New Brunswick, NJ: Transaction Publishers.

Zukin, S. (1995). *The Cultures of Cities*. Oxford: Blackwell.

Zunz, O. (1998). *Why the American Century?* Chicago, IL and London: University of Chicago Press.

☐ NOTES ON CONTRIBUTORS

Alberto Martinelli is Professor of Political Science and Sociology and former Dean of the Faculty of Political and Social Sciences at the University of Milan. He is former President of the International Sociological Association. He recently published *Global Modernization* (London: Sage, 2005) and *La democrazia globale* (Milano: UBE, 2004).

Mathias Bös (*1962) is Professor for Applied Sociology at the Department of Sociology and the Center for Conflict Studies at Philipps University, Marburg. His areas of interest include social change in Europe and North America, race and ethnic relations, and the sociology of migration.

Theodore Caplow, Commonwealth Professor Emeritus at the University of Virginia, was co-founder (with Henri Mendras) of the International Research Group for the Comparative Charting of Social Change.

Antonio M. Chiesi is Professor of Compared Social Systems and Methodology of the Social Sciences at the Department of Social and Political Studies, University of Milano, where he is also a coordinator of the Ph.D. course in Sociology.

Gérard Cornilleau is Senior Economist at the Economic Research Centre of Sciences Po, Paris (OFCE). He works on macroeconomic models, labor economics, and social policies.

Salustiano Del Campo is Emeritus Professor of Sociology at Complutense University in Madrid, member of the Spanish Academy of Moral and Political Sciences, and since 2003 President of the Institute of Spain.

Michel Forsé is a Senior Research Fellow at the French Centre for Scientific Research (CNRS). He has published several books on social change and social networks. He is now working on social justice and has recently published with Maxime Parodi *The Priority of Justice* (Bern: Peter Lang, 2005).

Kai Hebel (*1977) is a member of St. Antony's College, Oxford. He studied political science and American studies in Marburg, Berkeley, and Paris. His areas of interest include the Anglo-American 'special relationship', transatlantic relations, and ethnic conflicts.

Laura M. Holian is a Ph.D. candidate at the University of Virginia and Predoctoral Fellow at the Institute of Education Sciences. Her current research interests include social capital, academic achievement, and the links between families, schools, and communities.

Paul W. Kingston is Professor and Chair of Sociology at the University of Virginia. He has recently written about the social and economic consequences of education and the US stratification system, including *The Classless Society* (Stanford University Press, 2000) and 'How Meritocratic is the United States?' (*Research in Social Stratification and Mobility*, forthcoming).

Patrick Le Galès is Directeur de Recherche CNRS at CEVIPOF, and Professor of Politics and Sociology at Sciences Po Paris. He has published several books on cities and regions in Europe, comparative public policy, and local economic development. Recent publications include *European Cities* (OUP, 2002), *Changing Governance of Local Economies in Europe* (OUP, 2004), *Gouverner par les instruments* (Presses de Sciences Po, 2004).

Maxime Parodi is a sociologist and an Associate Research Fellow at the French National Foundation for Political Sciences (OFCE). He has recently published *La modernité manquée du structuralisme* (Paris: PUF, 2004).

Mathieu Zagrodzki is Ph.D. candidate in political science at CEVIPOF/Sciences Po Paris. He works on crime, police reform, and urban policing in Los Angeles and Paris. He recently published '12 ans de community policing à Los Angeles', *Politique et Management Public*, n1, 2007.

⬚ INDEX